# MEN and SUPERMEN

# MEN
# and
# SUPERMEN

THE SHAVIAN PORTRAIT GALLERY

*Second edition, corrected.*

By ARTHUR H. NETHERCOT

BENJAMIN BLOM  New York / London

*Printed in U.S.A. by*
NOBLE OFFSET PRINTERS, INC.
NEW YORK 3, N. Y.

*Acknowledgment is made to The Public Trustee and The Society of Authors for permission to quote from the works of Shaw. I also wish to express my gratitude to Northwestern University for its generosity in granting me time and money to help write this book, and to Moody E. Prior for his valuable criticism and advice.*

*A. H. N.*

# CONTENTS

# PREFACE ON VENTRILOQUISM

NO BOOK ON BERNARD SHAW would be quite valid without a preface. The present preface, however, is too brief to be properly Shavian — unless the foreword to *Fanny's First Play* be considered as a criterion. With this as a standard, then, it may be sufficient to say that the ensuing study offers itself primarily as an interpretative, analytical, and sometimes critical guide to the portrait gallery of the most distinguished playwright of his long generation.

From the beginning of Shavian criticism it has been a favorite technique of one school of critics to shout derisively that Shaw is no real dramatist because he cannot create characters apart from himself: that they are puppets and that he speaks and pulls the strings from behind the curtain; that he is the ventriloquist and they are his dummies; that he has invented nothing but perambulating phonographs. The other school furiously jams these figures back into the mouths of those who uttered them, and maintains that, although Mr. Shaw's personality breathes through everything he ever wrote, he has actually, like all great comic dramatists, merely stripped and laid bare the realities of character so that they are simplified and exposed for everyone's observation. Augustin Hamon, the French translator, psychologist, sociologist, and Socialist whom Shaw himself chose as his official French translator early resented the marionette comparison and defended his hero by writing a whole book on Shaw as *The Twentieth Century Molière*. Only two years previously Archibald Henderson, in the first of his Boswellian labors, *George Bernard Shaw/His Life and Works,* had nevertheless tacitly accepted the second comparison when he wrote: "Another trait, vexing to lovers of dramatic objectivity, is playing ventriloquist: endowing his characters, out of character, with his own individual ideas, notions and locutions." On the other hand, James Bridie, in an essay recently contributed to S. Winsten's Shavian birthday sheaf, *G.B.S. 90,* announced, after citing a considerable list of Shaw's "varied and living characters," that he had "no patience with people who say that Shaw can create only walking gramophones."

As for Shaw himself he naturally resented the "gramophone" school of criticism; in fact, he pickled it eternally for posterity in the immortal wrangle of London's dramatic critics about the authorship of Fanny's first play, centering in Vaughan's pronouncement: "Well, at all events, you cant* deny that the characters in this play are quite distinguishable from one another. That proves it's* not by Shaw, because all Shaw's* characters are himself:* mere puppets stuck up to spout Shaw. It's* only the actors that make them seem different." And Bannal agrees: "There can be no doubt of that:* everybody knows it." And yet, obviously, Shaw did create the characters of *Fanny's First Play,* who "are quite distinguishable from one another."

So what *is* the truth about Shaw's characters? What are his theories about characterization, and what were his sources and models for fictional writing — narrative and dramatic? Using his dramatis personae as he does, in what he almost immediately began to call his novels and plays "of ideas," that is, as the natural and only possible means of expressing those ideas, has he actually done no more than offer his audiences a series of somewhat differently decorated mouthpieces or megaphones? Are there easily recognizable and constantly repeated types, classifications, and categories of people in his fictional works? And if there are, are these works any the less valid and permanent for that reason?

* This is the first, last, and only time that I shall follow Shaw's absurd, eccentric, and self-contradictory system of using or not using apostrophes. But I shall leave him his colons, since he is so deeply in love with them.

# MEN and SUPERMEN

# I

## THE QUINTESSENCE OF IBSENO-SHAVIANISM

IT WAS IN 1891 THAT BERNARD SHAW first discovered — or at least first recognized and plainly stated — his basic divisions of human beings, divisions which, later expanded and elaborated upon, were to mark his dramatis personae to the end of his career. Whether or not he always consciously realized his continued and consistent applications of his early theories to his own works is of little consequence, since he reiterated many times in *The Quintessence of Ibsenism* and later works that many great artists, especially poets, have died without rationally understanding their own meanings. Creative artists, in fact, should not be expected to be able to interpret their own obscurities. As he put it in 1891: "I have also shewn that the existence of a discoverable and perfectly definite thesis in a poet's work by no means depends on the completeness of his own intellectual consciousness of it." This doctrine of inspiration, or what used to be called "the divine afflatus," is of course in thorough accord with Shaw's own mysticism, which increased as he grew older.

### 1. *The Quintessence of Ibsenism*

It was in 1891, then, that Shaw published *The Quintessence of Ibsenism,* the first of his works to have a direct and evident influence on his later career as a playwright. Soon it became a commonplace of modern dramatic criticism to say that this book should really have been entitled *The Quintessence of Shavianism* and to warn readers that it was an invaluable aid to the understanding of its author but that it should be used very cautiously and judiciously as an aid to the understanding of its subject. But, whatever one may feel about the soundness of its treatment of Henrik Ibsen (and it certainly says plenty of wise and true things about him), its central position as a key to the ideas of Bernard Shaw is inescapable. Its pivotal place in the development of his thought, in fact, he fully admitted in 1949 when he reprinted in his *Sixteen Self Sketches* the autobiographical sketch which he had written for Frank Harris thirty years earlier. Speaking of the "Anti-

Shakespear* Campaign" which he and Harris were conducting together (though they both loved Shakespeare and knew more about him than any other journalists in London), he stated that between 1889, when "Ibsen's first broadside on England caught the London theatre between wind and water," and 1894, when "Shaw's first shot at Shakespear was fired," Shaw had written his book on Ibsen "and was judging everything by the standard set up by the terrible Norwegian."

The story of how he came to write the book is sketched in the preface to its first edition. In the spring of 1890 the Fabian Society planned a series of papers for its summer meetings to be presented under the general title of "Socialism in Contemporary Literature." Most of the papers as finally read had little or nothing to do with Socialism, but, at any rate, Shaw's on Ibsen was read on July 18, 1890, with Mrs. Annie Besant in the president's chair.[1] His acquaintance with Ibsen's works was then relatively new. In fact, in his later preface to *The Irrational Knot,* which he wrote about 1880, though it was not published until 1885–87, in serial form, he insists that he wrote this youthful novel, with its final chapter "so remote from Scott and Dickens and so close to Ibsen," years before Ibsen came to his knowledge. Similarly, in the preface to *Widowers' Houses* he states that he wrote the first two acts of that play (originally intended to be a collaboration with William Archer) in 1885 before he knew anything about Ibsen. Nevertheless, he goes on to say in the preface to *The Irrational Knot,* he and some of his Socialist friends became so much excited over the translation of *A Doll's House* by Miss H. F. Lord that in the latter eighties they got up a private reading of the play, in which Shaw was cast for the role of none other than Krogstad. By 1890, however, as Archibald Henderson tells us in *Bernard Shaw/Playboy and Prophet,* he had gone even further, and when his friend Sir Walter Besant had written a short story entitled "The Doll's House and After," Shaw, even then insisting on having the last word, had added a prose sequel to it, "Still after the Doll's House," which was published in the magazine *Time.* In these chief ways the stage had been set for the emergence of *The Quintessence* in the following year. As suggested by R. F. Rattray in *Bernard Shaw: A Chronicle,* Shaw probably got his title from Schäffle's *The Quintessence of Socialism,* which he had reviewed for *To-day* in 1889.

In the first chapter of his book, entitled "The Two Pioneers," Shaw initiated his categorizing by distinguishing two antithetical types of reformer: one "who declares that it is right to do something hitherto regarded as infamous," and the other "who declares that it is wrong to do something that no one has hitherto seen any harm in." The first, whom he dubbed "the indulgence preacher," is publicly stoned and cursed, but secretly adored as a savior. The second, "the abstinence preacher," is publicly treated with

* Shaw always insists on depriving Shakespeare of the final *e* in his name.

tremendous respect, but privately hated like the devil. Sometimes, however, as Shaw pointed out, the same individual may be an indulgence preacher in some respects and an abstinence preacher in others, as was Shelley.

But this classification, however striking, is really only a subsidiary one, since (happily) all men are not reformers. It is in his second chapter, entitled "Ideals and Idealists," that Shaw lays the whole groundwork for his system. For here he makes his partition of mankind into three types: the idealists, the realists, and the Philistines. And the determination of the proper assignment of each individual to his type depends on his use or rejection of masks to hide the face of the truth, which many fear to confront. These masks are our so-called "ideals," and those who refuse to look at anything but them are "idealists." The person who insists on tearing off these masks, in order to expose the reality underneath, is the realist. And the satisfied persons, who neither erect masks nor bother themselves about realities, but vegetate contentedly as they are, are the Philistines. Out of every thousand persons, Shaw guesses, there are 700 Philistines, 299 idealists, and only one lone realist. The last, obviously, is going to have a difficult time in life.

Since these three types play such a significant role in Shaw's dramatic characterization, it will be well to see more fully how from time to time he defined them and what identifying traits he attributed to each. In his five juvenile novels, *Immaturity, The Irrational Knot, An Unsocial Socialist, Cashel Byron's Profession,* and *Love among the Artists* (all written between 1879 and 1884, and all first published in Socialist magazines in the latter eighties, with the exception of *Immaturity,* which the reading public did not see until 1930), the Philistine, the idealist, and the realist are all present, but they are not yet clearly labeled or analyzed as such. The novels were merely germinal in helping Shaw sprout his ideas.

Of the trilogy, the Philistine is the lowest in the scale. He is, in general, comfortable, easy-going, satisfied with things as they are. He is astonished and somewhat disturbed by the eccentric, the reformer, the firebrand who refuses to be placid and complacent about the status quo; but he undertakes no active opposition. The Philistine, moreover, has no real understanding or appreciation of art and beauty. As Shaw put it in 1895 in his review of *The Triumph of the Philistines* by Henry Arthur Jones (who it is now obvious was always pretending to attack Mrs. Grundy and her fellow-Philistines, but who always ended by supporting the Philistine position himself): "A Philistine is a prosaic person whose artistic consciousness is unawakened and who has no ideals." Thus in *The Sanity of Art* Shaw comments on how "the British Philistines" were utterly unable to understand the purposes or methods of Whistler's impressionism. Nor can the Philistine understand science any better. In the preface to his translation of *Three Plays by Brieux,* for instance, in a discussion of Zola, Shaw remarked: "The scientific spirit was unintelligible to the Philistines and repulsive to the dilettanti." To sum it up in a word, as Shaw does in *The Quintessence,* the Philistines are "Society."

The idealists are a much more interesting lot, but at the same time much more dangerous, for they are active while the Philistines are passive. Shaw has turned his dissecting scalpel loose on the idealists with unrelenting thoroughness and greater precision than on any other type, for to him they are the main Enemy. They are the ones who construct "fancy pictures" and expect everyone to act as if these illusions were real. Because of thir[2] own fear of admitting many truths about life, they try to force everyone, including themselves, to conform to their static policy of idealism, without examining its foundations and its past. They are the main factor interfering with Progress — or at least with the little progress that mankind can make before the appearance of the Superman.

Shaw's use of these terms "idealist" and "idealism" has worried some of his critics. For instance, H. S. Duffin[3] in *The Quintessence of Bernard Shaw* announces somewhat grudgingly that he will use Shaw's terminology "without altogether assenting to its propriety." In fact, he continues, "Neither 'idealism' nor 'morality' in the senses given them by Shaw is recognized by the New English Dictionary." Though the protest is somewhat schoolmasterish, Shaw himself had already admitted the original turn he had given the words, and had defended it both in the book and in the preface to the 1913 edition, which brought his first study of Ibsen up to date after Ibsen's death. Even in 1891 he had explained patiently, "For we unfortunately use this word ideal indifferently to denote both the institution which the ideal masks and the mask itself," and had added that the trouble comes when some identify the mask of their "ideal" conceptions of institutions with the fact of the actuality, and refuse to admit that these are two separate matters. Realists have ideals too, in the sense of goals to be attained, but they do not confuse these goals with the existent truths. As possible synonyms for ideals and idealism he had originally offered "conventions" and "conventionalists," but had rejected them as unsatisfactory. In 1913, however, because confusion still obtained among the readers of dictionaries, he suggested that "idols" and "idolatry" might be substitute terms, but desisted because "If you call a man a rascally idealist, he is not only shocked and indignant but puzzled: in which condition you can rely on his attention. If you call him a rascally idolater, he concludes calmly that you do not know that he is a member of the Church of England." Still, if Shaw had made the change, it might have emphasized more vigorously his own function as an iconoclast, a breaker of idols and images.

By the time he had come to write plays himself and in the late nineties to publish them with their luxuriant prefaces, because he was having difficulty at first in getting the plays themselves produced, he had found another pair of useful synonyms: "romance" and "romanticists." In the preface to his *Unpleasant Plays* he had referred contemptuously, more or less in passing, to the way in which some people regard the marriage laws as "a romantic ideal," but in the preface to the volume of *Pleasant Plays,* in which he continued his own onslaught on the debased and trivial modern taste in stories and plays, he developed his thesis at length, summing it up in the declaration, "for idealism, which is only a flattering name for romance in politics and morals, is as obnoxious to me as romance in ethics or religion," and concluding confidently, "At all events, I do not see moral chaos and anarchy as the alternative to romantic convention . . ." Romance is "the great heresy to be rooted out from art and life — as the root of modern pessimism and the bane of modern self-respect."

Idealism, conventionalism, idolatry, romance, illusion, traditionalism, prejudice — they are all the same; they are all the Enemy. And how does this Enemy behave? How is the idealist to be recognized? For it is essential that he be recognized, since he is "higher in the ascent of evolution than the Philistine" and more dangerous. Since he "has taken refuge with the ideals because he hates himself and is ashamed of himself," the idealist pulls up his mask between himself and his unconscious opinion of himself, and hates the highest in the scale — that is, the realist — even more. He brings his hatred out into the open "and strikes at him with a dread and rancor of which the easygoing Philistine is guiltless." He will proclaim his ideals by every means available to him — "in fiction, poetry, pulpit and platform oratory, and serious private conversation." In his rage and fear of disillusionment, he will accuse the Enemy of immorality and filthiness, he will ostracize him, take his children away from him (thus violating his own ideals of family affection), burn him, even crucify him.

So spoke Shaw in his chapter on "Ideals and Idealists." In his critiques of the individual Ibsen plays he went on to brand his antagonist so conspicuously that recognition would be unmistakable. *The Lady from the Sea,* he wrote, traces the origin of many ideals to unhappiness, to dissatisfaction with the reality, for Ellida has nothing to do but dream and be idolized by her husband. In *Pillars of Society* the idealist will recognize "only those facts or idealistic masks of facts which have a respectable air," and persists in mentioning these "on all occasions and at all hazards," overlooking the fact that a "truthteller who cannot hold his tongue on occasions may do as much mischief as a whole community of trained liars." In his discussion of *Little Eyolf* (added in 1913), on the other hand, Shaw admits that it is only fair to point out that "ideals are sometimes beneficent, and their repudiation sometimes cruel." In "The Lesson of the Plays" he agrees with Ibsen that the quintessence of Ibsenism is that there is no Golden Rule, no formula, to be applied on all occasions: "conduct must justify itself by its effect on happiness and not by its conformity to any rule or ideal." (In 1913, however, in response to a criticism by Henderson, and in harmony with his own prevalent position as a follower of the utilitarian philosophy of Bentham and Mill, he significantly changed "happiness" to "life.") He reminds us that the idealist often demands our deep sympathy, since idealism springs only from "the weaknesses of the higher types of character," and points out that Ibsen's most tragic specimens of "vanity, selfishness, folly, and failure are not vulgar villains, but men who in an ordinary novel or melodrama would be heroes." Immorality, as Shaw uses the term, does not necessarily indicate improper, indecent, or mischievous behavior; it simply implies conduct which does not conform to current ideals in religion, social institutions, etc. But, he asserts in connection with *Little Eyolf,* though the most mischievous ideals are social ideals which have hardened into institutions, laws, and creeds, it is not until they have become assimilated into an individual that they can strike that individual down. As he says in "The Technical Novelty," in the new plays the conflict is not the old one between clear right and wrong, for in them the villain is at least "as conscientious as the hero, if not more so . . ." Indeed, the problem is often to decide which is the hero and which the villain. As a matter of fact, there are no longer any villains or heroes.

As for the one man in a thousand, the lonesome realist, Shaw also perceived an ambiguousness of terminology, because of the contemporary fictional associations of the word, but he attempted to take care of the problem by suggesting to his readers that if they were not satisfied with "my own description of its meaning (I do not deal in definitions)" they should associate it "not with Zola and Maupassant, but with Plato." However much or little this may help, since Plato also dealt in his own fashion with ideals, there is no question about Shaw's continually referring to his realist as "the highest." He is the man who has "risen above the danger and the fear that his acquisitiveness will lead him to theft, his temper to murder, and his affections to debauchery." He is the "true prophet," and yet he is denounced and persecuted, not by "the ignorant and stupid," but by "the literate and the cultured." So at length the realist altogether loses patience with ideals, and founds his life on his respect for himself and on "faith in the validity of his own will." It is his individualism that triumphs, not his egotism. The idealist who equates realism with egotism and who pronounces that egotism means depravity is wrong. For the realist demands that a man live to be "himself" and not merely "a good man" according to the "ideals" of others. Yet the realist himself recognizes that life is always a case of "The ideal is dead: long live the ideal!" New ideals replace the old after the old are exposed, but each new one is "less of an illusion than the one it has supplanted; so that the destroyer of ideals, though denounced as an enemy of society, is in fact sweeping the world clear of lies." This is the only kind of progress that humanity as we know it can make.

From this point of view Ibsen himself illustrates Shaw's favorite dramatic situation of an idealist becoming aware of his errors and turning into a realist; for most idealists have the intelligence to understand the truth if they will allow themselves to do so. In a comparison of Ford Madox Brown, G. F. Watts, and Ibsen in 1897, in which he discussed Brown as a realist and Watts as an idealist in painting, with the natural and expected contrast in the reception of the two by the public, Shaw asked his readers, "Have you forgotten that Ibsen was once an idealist like Mr. Watts . . . ? . . . Or have you not noticed how the idealists who are full of loathing for Ibsen's realistic plays will declare these idealistic ones are beautiful, and that the man who drew Solveig the Sweet could never have descended to Hedda Gabler unless his mind had given way?" There is always the chance that the idealist may reform. In 1898 Shaw himself was sardonically attacked by Robert Buchanan, the critic-poet-novelist whose only claim to fame today derives from his puritanic impugning of the Pre-Raphaelites in his notorious essay, "The Fleshly School of Poetry." Buchanan waxed sarcastic about Shaw (Shaw said Buchanan "idealised" him) as "The Naked Man posing as a Realist," and ridiculed him for "the daring shamelessness of a powerful and fearless nudity." Buchanan's own preference was for a man "clothed and in his right mind." But the true realist is never the slave of any such inhibitions. If mental clothing is in his way, he will strip it off without hesitation and with no anxiety about modesty. If "right mind" means the idealist's mind, he will be glad to be out of it. There is always hope that good may come of the process.

## 2. *The Truth about* Candida

The neatest and most concrete specimens of the three types to be found in a single play occur in *Candida*. Indeed, it seems as if this favorite Shavian comedy, written in 1894, must almost have been composed with *The Quintessence* open at the author's elbow, so closely do its chief characters fit into the previously worked out formula.*

When Archibald Henderson wrote in both his books on Shaw that a fitting sub-title for *Candida* would be "A Mystery," he was not thinking so much of the famous but ambiguous "secret in the poet's heart" as he was of the motivation and interpretation of the characters as a whole. For of course the tantalizing "secret" is embedded only in the final stage direction and would therefore not challenge the spectator for solution; but the problem of the meaning of the characters and their relationships forms the backbone of the whole play, whether read or seen. Perhaps the fact that for years critic after critic, reader after reader, spectator after spectator have interpreted Candida, Morell, and Marchbanks according to their own tem-

* The following discussion is a revision and expansion of my article, "The Truth about Candida," in the *Publications of the Modern Language Association* (*PMLA*) for September 1949. [4]

peraments and predilections may help to explain why the play, like the similarly enigmatic *Hamlet* of Shaw's self-selected arch-rival, has proved to be one of the most popular in the repertoire. To judge from most of the printed comments on Shaw's play, and particularly on its heroine, it still remains a mystery. At least, there is little agreement as to its interpretation.

To Duffin Candida is "a Shavian intellectual woman, full-fledged, not an Ibsenite womanly woman on the point of being reborn"; and she has a mind "almost as free from conventionality as Marchbanks' own." As for Marchbanks, "Every one of the screens that commonly stand between man's eyes and naked reality is down . . . : orthodoxy, morality, convention, respectability, good form, duty . . . He has achieved that acme of immorality — abhorred of the Philistine — irresponsibility." And to Duffin the Philistine is Candida's "great baby" of a husband, the Rev. James Mavor Morell, so unlike his wife in almost every respect. So, he says, a "far more natural and powerful reciprocal attraction draws Candida and Marchbanks together," for "their reaction to life is alike vital, joyous, real." For Duffin it is hard to understand how any real sympathy, "except of an unsubstantial emotional sort," can exist between Candida and her husband.

On the other hand, Hamon announces dogmatically: "Candida is commonplace from the intellectual point of view, but has a great soul, is eminently intuitive, reading others' minds, and seeing things naked, just as they are in their pure reality." To Hamon, Morell "symbolizes Christian Socialist idealism, and is clear-sighted, bold, sure of himself, sensible," but "a man who takes short views." Marchbanks "symbolizes poetic idealism," but is "vague and confused in his mind." His love for Candida is "ideal, romantic, and ethereal," and both he and Morell suffer in their loves. But in Candida herself "there is no internal struggle." Although "she is a realist . . . , freed from all conventions," she "stays with her husband because she loves him, and not Eugene." For she is also "the mother-woman . . . , the creature of her own natural physiological function, motherhood."

To Henderson, although, as he says, Shaw's "maternal heroine is compact of candor and sympathy," she is scarcely capable of divining what is really going on in Marchbanks' heart. In fact, commonsensical and unscrupulous as she is, she is really lying — or at least deceiving herself — when she tricks the two men into believing that she chooses Morell because he is the weaker of the two. Love alone "dictates her course," although she sees the chance to educate Marchbanks a bit in the process.

Frank Harris goes even beyond Duffin, Hamon, and Henderson in his admiration for the play, which to him is Shaw's greatest and maturest work — "a vital, powerful, humane, and perfectly charming play." Yet Harris (or perhaps his ghost-writer, Frank Scully, who claims to have really written most of the Shaw biography) sums up the meaning of the play by asserting that Morell "hasn't the least inkling that Candida possesses a soul, that she yearns for understanding, for someone to share her idealist dreams and longings. So little conception, indeed, has her husband of his wife's mind and heart, that he closes his offer by saying, self-confident in his manly philistinism: 'That is all it becomes a man to offer a woman.'"

To William Irvine (whose *The Universe of G.B.S.* is the best all-around critical biography of Shaw), Candida is "a realist placed between two romantics, whom she regards with maternal indulgence"; she is, "we might almost say, Benthamite rationalism and detachment" on the "domestic plane." And he quotes with approval G. K. Chesterton's conclusion, as "more accurate than the author's own." For G. K. C. found in the play "the reality of the normal wife's attitude toward the normal husband, an attitude which is . . . insanely unselfish and yet quite cynically clear-sighted . . . She regards him in some strange fashion at once as a warrior who must make his way and as an infant who is sure to lose his way."

Preening himself on his unorthodoxy, Edmund Fuller, in his rather elementary and generally imperceptive *George Bernard Shaw: Critic of Western Morale,* proposes "a great heresy about *Candida*—namely, that it is first-rate theatrical balderdash, as hopelessly romantic as anything against which Shaw ever inveighed for the same sin," and summarizes the theme of the play as symbolizing in Marchbanks "the inarticulate and consequently ineffective groping of genius toward perceptions transcending the advanced idealism then current." If the poet really perceives anything, he concludes, it "is lost in the waves of sentiment that engulf him."

As two final specimens of how the critics fall out when considering *Candida,* there are James Huneker and Eric Bentley, among the earliest and the latest of Shaw's enthusiastic missionaries in America. To Huneker in his essay on *Candida* Candida is "a womanly woman," standing "on her solid, sensible underpinnings," and Marchbanks is a "thin-skinned idealist." But Bentley (as anyone knowing Bentley might expect) takes quite a different line in his *Bernard Shaw.* To him Morell represents the person who becomes "utterly disillusioned," Marchbanks represents the one who becomes " 'educated' in the sense of being enabled to see that his true nature is not what he thought it was," and Candida represents the one who "operates as a catalyst . . . , effecting change without being changed . . ."

Out of all this contradictory welter of intuitive women, intellectual women, womanly women, and mother-women, realists, idealists, and Philistines, disillusioned people, educated people, romanticists, Benthamites, and catalysts, can any truth be distilled or extracted? When one critic labels as a realist a character whom another critic has labeled an idealist, and still another critic labels as an idealist another character whom another critic has labeled a Philistine, who is crazy — the critics, the author, or the audience? What *is* the truth about *Candida* the play and Candida the woman?

I myself have seen and enjoyed such professional actresses as Katharine Cornell and Cornelia Otis Skinner, as well as various amateurs, in the role of Shaw's most admired comedic heroine. I have watched the women in the audience wipe their eyes unashamedly and heard the men sigh secretively over their idol of womanly perfection. And yet I am confident that if the actresses had acted the part as Shaw wrote it and that if the audiences had known Shaw's real opinion of Candida there would have been hisses and boos instead. For there is no doubt that Shaw himself intended his three leading characters to represent, primarily, Marchbanks as the developing realist, Morell as the wavering idealist, and Candida — how disillusioning this will be to the romanticists! — as the static Philistine.

In the chapter on "Ideals and Idealists" in *The Quintessence,* Shaw had analyzed his cross-section of a thousand persons on the basis of their attitude toward marriage and the family, which of course is the prime theme of *Candida.* The Philistines are those who "find the British family arrangement quite good enough for them"; they "comfortably accept marriage as a matter of course," never dreaming of calling it an "institution," either "holy" or otherwise, and thrive happily within it. The idealists realize that marriage, for plenty of those involved in it, is a failure, but do not have the courage to face that fact, and therefore go to all sorts of excessive extremes to defend the "ideal" which for them masks the face of the truth. The isolated realist is the individual "strong enough to face the truth the idealists are shirking" — the man who insists on tearing off the masks and revealing the illusions beneath. And in each case, as already shown, Shaw discusses in detail the characteristic behavior of each type.

Candida, Morell, and Marchbanks all behave in almost perfect conformity with the Shavian formula for their types. Candida is one of the "satisfied ones." As Henderson has acutely observed, there is some doubt of the validity of her advanced principles when judged in the light of her conduct. When she announces to her husband that she would give her "goodness and purity" to poor Marchbanks as willingly as she would give her shawl to a beggar dying of cold, if there were nothing else to restrain her, she knows perfectly well that she is risking nothing, since she will always be restrained by her love of her home and family. As to the way in which the Philistines, according to *The Quintessence,* coerce the idealists "into conformity with the marriage law," recall the way in which Candida's father, Burgess, another Philistine, though of a much coarser brand, a vulgar, materialistic, sharp but naively sincere "old scoundrel," as Morell calls him, brutally reminds the infatuated Prossy, Morell's secretary, that her recent predecessor was "young-er," — a characteristic which Shaw himself later remarked was sufficient reason for Candida's cannily getting rid of her. Candida has her father's shrewdness, but has refined it in her womanly way. Most of Candida's critics, moreover, promptly admit that she has no ideals, in the Shavian sense. As for her attitude toward art, everyone will recall how she practically hypnotizes herself by gazing at the poker while Marchbanks is absorbed in reading his poetry to her, and how, when awakened to herself, she confesses candidly, "Those sonnets of yours have perfectly addled me." Likewise, when Shaw gives his first affectionate description of his heroine in his stage directions, he emphasizes that when Marchbanks gave the family a large reproduction of Titian's Virgin of the Assumption he "did so because he fancied some spiritual resemblance between" the picture and Candida, and yet, says Shaw, the "wisehearted observer . . . would not suspect either her husband or herself of any such idea, or indeed of any concern with the art of Titian." Nor is this basic inartisticality in any fundamental contradiction to Burgess's early remark: "I allus had a turn for a bit of potery. Candy takes arter me that-a-way: huse ter make me tell her fairy stories when she was on'y a little kiddy not that 'igh!" For if Candida's taste in poetry and fairy stories takes after her father's she obviously has no taste at all. It is merely a case of like father, like daughter. No, Candida's concern is with her husband, her two children (who never appear on the stage), her cook, her scrub-brush, her lamp chimneys and paraffin oil, and her red onions. When Morell returns ebulliently from his speech before the Guild of St. Matthew, her main question is, "How much was the collection?"

As for the conflict between the idealist and the realist, so graphically described by Shaw in *The Quintessence*, when the realist insists on shouting from the housetops that marriage is a failure for many people and that its compulsory character ought therefore to be abolished, here, with a slight allowance for the habit of Shavian exaggeration, is a neat picture of the relations among the three main characters in *Candida* — even to Morell the idealist's appealing against Marchbanks the realist to Candida the Philistine, and in his fear actually grasping Marchbanks threateningly by his coat lapel preparatory to making a bodily attack on him. Another of Shaw's tips as to the identifying traits of a Philistine is that when the realist cries out the truth about a great deal of family life the idealist will react against him in the violent fashion previously described, but "The Philistine will simply think him mad." One of the surest laughgetters in *Candida* is the series of passages in which Prossy, shocked by the startling things Marchbanks has said to her about love, informs Burgess that the poet is mad, and Burgess agrees with her. Burgess has already informed Marchbanks sotto voce that Morell is "mad as a 'atter," for Morell has told his father-in-law some realistic home truths about the latter's methods as an employer of labor. When Lexy Mill, the curate, succumbs to the epidemic and announces his fear that Prossy "is a little out of her mind sometimes," Burgess is "overwhelmed," as well he might be. But the remarks draw attention to Burgess, Prossy, and Lexy as minor Philistines in the play.

And how does Morell finally react after the poet has jeered at his illusions that his marriage is a happy one and that such an unearthy angel as Candida (for through much of the play Eugene too has his idealistic illusions so far as she is concerned) could love such a fool and windbag as her husband even if he is wellmeaning? First, Morell exclaims pathetically, "Marchbanks: some devil is putting these words into your mouth. It is easy — terribly easy — to shake a man's faith in himself. To take advantage of that to break a man's spirit is devil's work. Take care of what you are doing. Take care." But when the poet persists in his revelations, the preacher pleads, with a new display of his forensic powers, "In the future — when you are as happy as I am — I will be your true brother in the faith . . . I will help you to believe that every stroke of your work is sowing happiness for the great harvest that all — even the humblest — shall one day reap. And last, but trust me, not least, I will help you to believe that your wife loves you and is happy in her home. We need such help, Marchbanks: we need it greatly and always. There are so many things to make us doubt, if once we let our understanding be troubled. Even at home, we sit as if in a camp, encompassed by a hostile army of doubts. Will you play the traitor and let them in on me?" This sounds suspiciously as if Morell were a member of those "prostitute classes" whom Shaw pillories in the preface to his *Unpleasant Plays* as professional people "who are daily using their highest faculties to belie their real sentiments." Yet Shaw also had a qualified good word to say for the Rev. James some years later in the preface to *Getting Married:* "What an honorable and sensible man does when his household is invaded is what the Rev. James Mavor Morell does in my play . . . He is so far shrewdly unconventional as to recognize that if she chooses the other man, he must give way, legal tie or no legal tie; but he knows that either one or the other must go. And a sensible wife would act in the same way." In a real marriage of sentiment there should be no false shame of seeming conventional in facing the situation.

On the other hand, to revert to the play itself, Candida's innocently cruel and piercing remarks about her husband as her "boy . . . spoiled from his cradle," her ruthless analysis of the reasons the women flock to his services and meetings, her disconcerting appraisal of the actual ineffectiveness of his Sunday sermons — all of which make even Eugene cry out against her insensitiveness to Morell's suffering — have obviously cut deep into the clergyman's self-esteem and confidence in his marriage. But in spite of all sympathy, pleas, and confessions, Marchbanks will have none of Morell's "metaphors, sermons, stale perorations" and pushes forcibly through to a showdown between his ideas and his opponent's. As he says over and over again to Morell, Candida, and Prossy, he wants to get at their "real" selves, he wants "real" answers, but nobody will give him the truth. It is not for nothing that in this chapter in *The Quintessence* Shaw continues to cite Shelley as a specimen of what he calls a realist and the world generally calls an idealist, and that in the early productions of *Candida* in the late nineties Marchbanks was made up to look like Shelley, "femininely hectic and timid and fierce," as Oliver Elton, quoted by Henderson, put it in a review of 1898.

The famous scene in which Candida makes her choice between her two men bears a strong resemblance to a similar scene in Ibsen's *The Lady from the Sea,* which Shaw had interpreted at some length in *The Quintessence.* Here Ellida corresponds to Candida; the sailor who mystically claims her as his wife and wants to draw her away to the sea with him corresponds to Eugene; and the respectable doctor who has married her corresponds to Morell. When the seaman assures her of her own free will and freedom to choose, and her husband "drops his prate about his heavy responsibility for her actions," she decides without any hesitation to stick with her house-keeping. Candida, like Ellida, wishes to "belong to herself," first of all, but she never really appreciates her husband's mental sufferings or his moral courage in going through with the showdown with Eugene. Her "wise-hearted maternal humor" helps her to carry off her domestic crisis with skill and a little pathos, but she has remained essentially impervious to the tremendous tensions which have encircled her. She is the one who at the end announces Shaw's favorite lesson that Eugene has "learnt to live without happiness," but when she and her husband turn to embrace one another after Eugene's flight into the night, Shaw ends his play by reminding his readers what his audiences could only guess: "But they do not know the secret in the poet's heart." The secret, as we shall see, is that Eugene has lost his illusions about Candida — that is, he has lost his ideals. He has be-come a realist.

So the evidence in *The Quintessence* and in the play itself as to the classification of the main character types matches very accurately. But there is further and even more definite evidence to confirm these conclusions in the later comments of Shaw and his friends on his play. He himself em-phasized the "mother incarnate" quality in Candida in his stage directions, and in a letter to Ellen Terry once confided, "Candida, between you and me, is the Virgin Mother and nobody else." In fact, he wrote a whole series of letters to Miss Terry between 1896 and 1899, in which he made it quite clear that he had had her definitely in mind in creating Candida, and suggested that she could therefore scarcely be so ungenerous as to refuse to play the role. He even went so far in pointing the parallel as to assert that she and Janet Achurch were the only two women he had ever met "whose ideal of voluptuous delight was that life should be one long con-finement from the cradle to the grave." Candida's instinctive and unscru-pulous method of managing people by "engaging their affections" was al-ways his affectionate diagnosis of Terry's character. And when he finally really sent her the manuscript and she read it, she wrote by return mail on October 19, 1896: "I've cried my poor eyes out over your horrid play, your *heavenly* play . . . It has touched me more than I could tell of." When Terry was touched (and it was not a hard thing to do), she really melted. Yet Shaw's equally close but less romantic friend Beatrice Webb, as Shaw promptly informed Terry, had called Candida bluntly "a sentimental prostitute" — probably thinking of the way in which she draws Eugene on to make love to her, knowing all the time that she is arousing his passion only to tantalize him. Terry was left almost speechless. All she could get her pen to trace was an underscored *"Well!"* In spite of her disapproval, however, in another letter to her in 1899, Shaw repeated that even in this mother play, as in most of his plays, he had "prostituted the actress more or less by making the interest in her partly a sexual interest." He left Candida tottering on her pedestal by referring to her wryly as "Candida, with her boy and her parson, and her suspicion of trading a little on the softness of her contours . . ."

More significant, however, is the way in which Shaw describes his comedy's dramatic conflict in the preface which he wrote for his volume of *Pleasant Plays.* "Here, then," he writes, "was the higher, but vaguer, timider vision, and the incoherent, mischievous, and even ridiculous, unpracticalness, which offered me a dramatic antagonist for the clear, bold, sure, sensible, benevolent, salutarily shortsighted Christian Socialist idealism." The "higher vision," with all its weaknesses, must go to the realist, Marchbanks, in spite of his earlier false ideals about Candida; the "benevolent . . . shortsighted Christian Socialist idealism" must obviously go to Morell, who, the commentators inform us, was modeled on the ex-clergyman Socialist litterateur, Stopford Brooke (whom Shaw had known in the Bedford debating society), seasoned, thinks Rattray, with dashes of Fleming Williams and Canon Shuttleworth.[5] It was apparently a characteristic of Christian Socialist clergymen of the Guild of St. Matthew to indulge in emotional humanitarianism and sentimental sermons, if one can judge by Shaw's review of Wilkie Collins's *The New Magdalen* in 1895.

With Marchbanks as the realist and Morell as the idealist, what is there left for Candida to be but the Philistine? If it be asked why we have to have a Philistine in the play at all, here is how Shaw himself dissected his heroine in a letter he wrote to Huneker in 1904 in explanation of his play, which Arnold Daly's production had at last made the hit of the New York season:

*Don't ask me conundrums about that very immoral female, Candida. Observe the entry of W. Burgess: "You're the lady as hused to typewrite for him." "No." "Naaaow: she was young-er." And therefore Candida sacked her. Prossy is a very highly selected young person indeed, devoted to Morell to the extent of helping in the kitchen but to him the merest pet rabbit, unable to get the slightest hold on him. Candida is as un-*

*scrupulous as Siegfried: Morell himself sees that "no law will bind her." She seduces Eugene just exactly as far as it is worth her while to seduce him. She is a woman without "character" in the conventional sense. Without brains and strength of mind she would be a wretched slattern and voluptuary. She is straight for natural reasons, not for conventional ethical ones. Nothing can be more coldbloodedly reasonable than her farewell to Eugene: "All very well, my lad: but I don't quite see myself at fifty with a husband of thirty-five." It is just this freedom from emotional slop, that makes her so completely mistress of the situation.*

*Then consider the poet. She makes a man of him finally by showing him his own strength — that David must do without poor Uriah's wife. And then she pitches in her picture of the home, the onions, and the tradesmen, and the cossetting of the big baby Morell. The New York hausfrau thinks it a little paradise, but the poet rises up and says, "Out then, into the night with me" — Tristan's holy night. If this greasy fool's paradise is happiness, then I give it to you with both hands, "life is nobler than that." That is the "poet's secret." The young things out in front weep to see the poor boy going out lonely and broken-hearted in the cold night to save the proprieties of New England Puritanism; but he is really a god going back to his heaven, proud, unspeakably contemptuous of the "happiness" he envied in the days of his blindness, clearly seeing that he has higher business on hand than Candida. She has a little quaint intuition of the completeness of his cure; she says, "he has learnt to do without happiness."*

*As I should certainly be lynched by the infuriated Candidamaniacs if this view of the case were made known, I confide it to your discretion . . . I tell it to you because it is an interesting sample of the way in which a scene, which should be conceived and written only by transcending the ordinary notion of the relations between the persons, nevertheless stirs the ordinary emotions to a very high degree, all the more because the language of the poet, to those who have not the clue to it, is mysterious and bewildering and therefore worshipful. I divined it myself before I found out the whole truth about it.*

Shaw's implication that when he first wrote his play he was not fully conscious of all its overtones and inner meanings is not a confession of weakness on his part but is in complete harmony with his theory of artistic inspiration. In fact, in his own somewhat unorthodox interpretation of Wagner's Ring cycle in *The Perfect Wagnerite,* he quoted Wagner himself on the subject: "How can an artist expect that what he has felt intuitively should be perfectly realized by others, seeing that he himself feels in the presence of his work, if it is true Art, that he is confronted by a riddle about which he, too, might have illusions, just as another might?" And Shaw explained further that by "true Art" Wagner meant "the operation of the artist's instinct, which is just as blind as any other instinct." He had said much the same thing several years before in defending his elucidation of Ibsen. Nevertheless, even though admitting that the artist himself might not always realize the full meaning of his work, Shaw insisted in his articles on stage production for *The Saturday Review* that the first obligation of both the manager and the actor is to fulfill the intentions of the playwright, as shown in his explanations and directions.

In his *Sixteen Self Sketches,* in setting Duffin right on certain interpretative guesses about Eugene's "secret," Shaw corroborates his letter to Huneker when he reiterates that his meaning is that "the domestic life is not a poet's destiny: 'life is nobler than that.' The starry night, and not the cosy room with the paraffin lamp, is the place for him." Duffin's alternative explanation, that Marchbanks is confident that sooner or later Candida will come to him, is, cries Shaw, "wildly silly." Irvine, seeing *Love among the Artists* as "an early attempt at a 'Candida,'" draws the "secret" from both of them "that artists do not need love."

This realistic and disillusioning approach to the character of Mrs. Candida Burgess Morell by her creator has remained almost unknown, though Huneker, after printing it in an article in *The Metropolitan Magazine* in 1904, preserved it in his *Iconoclasts* in 1905. Moreover, most of those who remember it wish that Shaw had never written it. Its sardonic analysis has proved much too astringent for them. That clever sentimental sham and perverse liar, Frank Harris, in his biography not only suppresses the most important part of the letter but has the effrontery to claim that the bit he quotes was part of an argument *he* once had with Shaw in which he defended Candida against her author as being "as vital in conception and as powerful and moving in execution as the best of the English classics." Even the generally straight-visioned Henderson turns sentimentalist in the presence of this "maternal heroine" who is so "compact of candor and sympathy," as he puts it in the second version of his biography, where he reduces the letter to one sentence. Yet in the first version he had printed the letter whole, but had cried out pathetically to his readers: "with Shaw's own dissection of his greatest play, I find it quite impossible to sympathize or agree." Searching desperately for some way of salvaging his heroine-worship, he comes up with this lame explanation: "Shaw seems merely to be taking a fling at the 'Candidamaniacs,' as he called the play's admirers; his 'analysis' strikes me as a batch of Shavian half-truths, rather than a fair estimate of the play's true significance." Still sore and sensitive when he wrote his second version, Henderson referred to "the credulous Huneker," apparently forgetting that Shaw himself had chosen Huneker to edit the two volumes of Shavian theatrical criticism, *Dramatic Opinions and Essays,* in 1907, in spite of the fact that in the preface to *The Irrational Knot* he had referred to his American friend as "a man of gorgeous imagination and incorrigible romanticism." Only Eric Bentley in *The Playwright as Thinker* is bold enough to reprint the letter entire and to remark, "This analysis is at many points in accord with mine, at some points not." At the latter points, in fact, he would go even beyond Shaw, and even suggests that the play might have been named *The She-Devil's Disciple.* At this juncture, however, Bentley's temerity and iconoclasm prove too much even for himself, and he also yields to Candida's essential charm. "The sweetness which she pours over the whole play," he concedes, "is not the suspect and poisonous sweetness of a she-devil. It is genuine," even though "it is combined with other, less amiable qualities . . . *Candida* is the sweeter for not being all sugar."

When the Shavian dramatis personae are considered as a whole, it will become apparent that Candida does not stand alone, but that she is actually only one of the most conspicuous and successful representatives of certain of Shaw's chief character classifications. Primarily she is both the mother-woman and the Philistine. Perhaps, too, there is a dash in her of the womanly woman. My guess is also that in her younger days she would have qualified as a specimen of woman as the pursuer. She might almost be described as an Ann Whitefield at a later stage in Ann's career. Many of Shaw's most lovable and "vital" heroines (a favorite epithet of his) fall into these categories. In fact, he implies over and over again that, from this point of view, the perfect wife and mother is practically always a Philistine, plus. Once or twice, as in the case of Jennifer Dubedat from *The Doctor's Dilemma,* she may be an idealist. But never, never can she be a realist.[6]

Finally, let me admit freely that Shaw too has clearly fallen in love with Candida* — which only goes to show that it is possible for a man who prides himself on being a realist and even a cynic to fall in love with a Philistine and admire her for the good qualities she has while forgetting those she has not. Shaw was obviously using Prossy as his interpreter when he had her remark, at the very outset of the play, before the audience has yet met its heroine: "It's enough to drive anyone out of their senses to hear a perfectly commonplace woman raved about in that absurd manner merely because she's got good hair, and a tolerable figure . . . She's very nice, very good-hearted: I'm very fond of her and can appreciate her real qualities far better than any man can." The critics have all blindly overlooked the fact that the rest of the characters in the cast, on whose reactions they have based their opinions, are all men.

That is the whole truth about the chief characters in *Candida.* But offering it has anticipated, only for purposes of preliminary illustration, the presentation of the full and varied series of Philistines, idealists, and realists in the Shavian portrait gallery.

---

* Irvine even suggests that the menage à trois in the play may reflect the situation in which Shaw fell temporarily in love with May Morris, the daughter of one fellow Socialist, William Morris, and the wife of another, Henry Halliday Sparling.

# I I

## THE PHILISTINE

ALTHOUGH SHAW WAS obviously indebted to Matthew Arnold for the label "Philistine" which he attached to the lowest class in his human phyla, and although the characteristics which he attributed to this class were very similar to those that Arnold had detected and isolated, he never seems to have been so much worried by its members and its numerical superiority as Arnold was. To Arnold the Philistines were the main Enemy to culture and enlightenment; to Shaw they were secondary to the idealists, who constituted the real threat to his realists — these realists who might also be described as his "chosen people," even his "remnant." In fact, as in the case of Candida, some of his Philistines are likable, often lovable, and in their limited ways even admirable persons. There are many specimens and varieties of Philistines in Shaw's novels and plays, but their number tends to diminish as he grows older, as is only natural since they are not in most cases intimately involved in the central conflict between the other two classes. In fact, as a nonagenarian, he admitted to Stephen Winsten in one of the latter's *Days with Bernard Shaw* that he himself was "all out for a healthy Philistinism which will laugh, though not urgently, at the mystic pretensions" of the "diseased languor" of modern aestheticism in painting, sculpture, and writing. Inasmuch as the female Philistine has already been richly illustrated in the charming Candida, and other similar examples will appear later among the genus *mother woman,* further immediate discussion of the type might well be primarily focused on the male sex.

In Shaw's pre-dramatic, or novelistic, period, perhaps the best example of the male Philistine is the bourgeois John Hoskyn, who, in spite of his limitations, is permitted to marry the admirable Mary Sutherland — Shaw's early favorite type of unbeautiful but distinguished, intelligent, unemotional, sensible heroine — about three-fourths of the way through the story, *Love among the Artists.* Hoskyn has not yet reached middle-age, stoutness, or floridity, but is obviously close to all of them. He is good-natured, easily impressed, and a little gullible, but has still made a considerable success in business. As part of his courtship he takes Mary to the Crystal Palace, the circus, the music halls, and even to athletic events and Madame Tussaud's. To her surprise, since she had once started out to be an artist and something of an intellectual, she finds that she enjoys the experience and his company, for he gives her a comfortable, homy feeling. In fact, she has turned into a bit of a Philistine herself. And when she discovers that Hoskyn genuinely admires her person, holds "her acquirements in awe, without being himself in the least humbled," and, on a visit to the Academy, is "quite delighted" to find that she despises all the pictures he prefers, her defenses are broken down, and she turns into just the kind of housewife and hostess that a man like Hoskyn is proud of.

There is, indeed, a strong family resemblance between Hoskyn and Bompas, the husband in *How He Lied to Her Husband,* though Bompas is treated as a purely farcical figure. This little playlet, a sort of distorted echo from *Candida,* was so misinterpreted by audiences that Shaw was impelled to cable agonizedly to Henderson: "Need I say that anyone who imagines that How He Lied to Her Husband retracts Candida, or satirizes it, or travesties it, or belittles it in any way, understands neither the one nor the other?" Nevertheless, there is a striking similarity between the central triangular situations of the two; and in the farce Shaw is certainly having some fun at his own expense, as is his frequent fashion. Bompas, married to the superficially attractive, pretentious, affected South Kensington female, Aurora, who is indulging timidly in a strictly respectable flirtation, is himself "a robust, thicknecked, well groomed city man, with a strong chin but a blithering eye and credulous mouth." He believes that he appreciates the beautiful poet-athlete Henry's poetic powers, but actually he is only flattered by their application to his wife; and when Henry calls him "a sordid commercial chump, utterly unworthy of her," he is so delighted that he insists that he print the poet's book at his own expense, as a tribute to the charms of Aurora, and in spite of the fact that she, Philistine-like, admits that she hasn't had time to read most of the manuscript herself — and besides, she never could remember verses.

Any hint of unusual physical prowess is, to Shaw, another immediate cause for suspecting the Philistine nature of its possessor. Take Alastair Fitzfassenden of *The Millionairess,* amateur tennis champion and heavy-weight boxer, with a famous solar plexus punch which he does not hesitate to use on his wife, Epifania Ognisanti di Parerga, when she needs disciplin-ing. "He is," says Shaw, "a splendid athlete, with most of his brains in his muscles." In fact, "if his uncle had not pushed him into an insurance office, where he was perfectly useless," he would have become a professional in one or the other of his sports. Moreover, "Nature, in one of her most unaccountable caprices, has endowed Alastair with a startlingly loud singing voice of almost supernatural range," but unluckily has neglected to give him anything like a musical ear. So, after losing money in an attempt to become an operatic tenor, he has met an American, who showed him how to kite checks. Still, although he made a fortune with unbelievable rapidity, he lost it almost as fast, and now cannot afford to let Eppy divorce him. When she discovers that he has spent part of the previous night perfectly innocently in the arms of Polly Seedystockings, she denounces him as "an even more sexless fish" than she had taken him for. We shall meet Polly and Alastair again, as a well-matched Philistine couple.

Reginald Bridgenorth, of *Getting Married,* has all the instincts of a gentleman and a manly man when he knocks his wife down in front of the gardener in order to give her grounds for the divorce she has demanded. He has even gone to the nauseating length of taking a woman to Brighton for the same reason: "Do you know what that feels like to a decent man?" He is, says Shaw, "hardened and toughened physically, and hasty and boyish in his manner and speech." He has lived like a gentleman on the income of his property, "solicitor-managed," but although he is muddled, rebellious, untidy, and forgetful, and obviously "needs the care of a capable woman," he is nevertheless "a likeable man, from whom nobody apprehends any malice nor expects any achievement."

But business and the professions, as well as the leisured aristocracy, also produce their Philistines. Johnny Tarleton, in *Misalliance,* "an ordinary young business man," is, as his friend Bentley Summerhays puts it, "all body and no brains." (Bentley himself, as we shall see later, is all brains and no body.) Johnny, says Bentley, doesn't really understand his own business, or rather his father's business, although he has been at it for ten years. He is a complete materialist, with no altruism in him. Even writing, to him, is a business. He admits that he reads a good deal, but he wants "a book with a plot in it," not an idea that "the chap that writes it keeps worrying." He pays his authors to amuse him and make him forget, not think. But he has many pronounced opinions of his own, such as that independence for women is all wrong. The Polish acrobat Lina Szczepanowska is more disgusted by his proposal of marriage than by that of any of the others, but he takes her rejection well and she finally admits that he's "not a bad sort of chump." Poor complacent Johnny stamps himself when he remarks that he's sick of having the real rulers of the country like himself — "Sane, healthy, unpretending men like me" — told that they're Philistines.

The army, the church, and politics are also prone to produce their Philistines. The army is an especially rich forcing ground, and Shaw starts out early to exploit it. In *The Philanderer,* for instance, the audience is introduced to Colonel Daniel Craven, a retired officer, who, because of a fine figure and a "goodnaturedly impulsive, credulous" personality, carries off successfully and pleasantly his affectation of being the "bluff, simple veteran." He is now, after never having had to think as an officer and a gentleman, "being startled into some sort of self-education by the surprising proceedings of his children," who have joined the new Ibsen Club. In the past, his actions have been more or less automatic, in response to what he has considered his "duty." After giving up his first sweetheart to his friend Cuthbertson because he "knew his duty" (she preferred Cuthbertson anyhow), he finally married for money, and even got to be very fond of his wife. He regards himself as a "manly man"; in fact, when he learns that he is not going to die of "Paramore's Disease" after all, one of his main regrets is that he has lost his "old manly taste" for beefsteak (certainly here speaks Shaw the vegetarian-ventriloquist). Manly men were of course not supposed to be at home in Ibsen Clubs in the nineties, since weekly periodicals like *Truth*, in excoriating the London performance of *Ghosts*, had howled that only "The sexless," only "Effeminate men and male women," were at all interested in "the Scandinavian humbug" and his works. Craven also complains to Dr. Paramore that as a result of his being guaranteed that he had not long to live he had "done a lot of serious thinking and reading and extra church going" which now turn out to have been a waste of time. Shaw once told Henderson that some of Craven's mannerisms, especially his habit of exclaiming, "Now really!" were taken directly from his rival Socialist, Henry M. Hyndman. Moreover, in a letter to the American actor Mansfield in 1895, quoted by Henderson, Shaw advised: "The man who plays Craven must be a handsome, genial old boy of whom the public are thoroughly fond."

Major Petkoff, of *Arms and the Man*, is likewise a sort of Philistine in his general good-natured obtuseness. In *Press Cuttings* Lady Corinthia sneers at General Mitchener as a Philistine. But of military Philistines there is no end, as will be abundantly apparent when we see Shaw paying his disrespects to the army among the rest of the professions.

Nor is the church by any means exempt from the same charge. Chaplain de Stogumber, the true-born Englishman in *Saint Joan*, narrow-minded and bloodthirsty in his pursuit of heresy, mouths all the shibboleths when with false humility he disagrees with Warwick and Cauchon: "you are too learned and subtle for a poor clerk like myself. But I know as a matter of plain commonsense that the woman is a rebel; and that is enough for me. She rebels against Nature by wearing man's clothes and fighting. She rebels against The Church by usurping the divine authority of the Pope. She rebels against God by her damnable league with Satan and his evil spirits against our army. And all these rebellions are only excuses for her great rebellion against England." Yet, detestable as the fanatical Stogumber appears before Joan's burning, he is so overwhelmed by the actual execution that in the epilogue he turns into a doddering old parish priest, "with a silly but benevolent smile," but loved by his small country parish. Shaw has many other churchmen similar to him, from the duty-obsessed Reverend George Lind in *The Irrational Knot* to the "gaitered English bishop" in *Geneva*, who, after a series of shocks and swoons, finally drops dead when he is assured that "There are no poor in Russia."

*Geneva* also gives us, among the politicians, Sir Orpheus Midlander, the well-meaning muddler of a British foreign secretary, whose genial manner and generally "pleasant and popular personality" disarm almost everybody he meets. He confesses modestly, "Upon my honor I don't know how I got landed where I am. I am quite an ordinary chap really," and he accuses the Judge apologetically of being "a bit of an idealist," whereas he himself, being forced to deal with Power, can't afford such a fine ideal as justice. Charles, now become "the Victorious" in the epilogue to *Saint Joan,* knows the shoddy secret when he defends himself to Cauchon: "Yes: it is always you good men that do the big mischief. Look at me! . . . I have done less harm than any of you. You people with your heads in the sky spend all your time trying to turn the world upside down; but I take the world as it is, and say that top-side-up is right-side-up; and I keep my nose pretty close to the ground."

Even the remarkable and lovable Waiter in *You Never Can Tell* is essentially the Philistine in his general outlook on life and particularly in his views on marriage. "Balmy Walters," as he is known among his intimates, is apparently, we are told by Henderson and Harris, modeled on Shaw's friend, later the Lord Chancellor, R. B. Haldane, who was acting as a sort of catalyzing agent between the Fabians and Liberals on one side and the Conservatives on the other. William the Waiter is "a silky old man . . . , but so cheerful and contented that in his encouraging presence ambition stands rebuked as vulgarity, and imagination as treason to the abounding sufficiency and interest of the actual." William's commonsense, down-to-earth philosophy is typified in his encouraging remarks to Valentine on marriage: "every man is frightened of marriage when it comes to the point; but it often turns out very comfortable, very enjoyable and happy indeed, sir — from time to time. *I* was never master in my own house, sir: my wife was like your young lady . . . But if I had my life to live twice over, I'd do it again, I'd do it again, I assure you. You never can tell, sir: you never can tell." This passage, it might be pointed out, was apparently written while its author was trying to make up his mind about Charlotte Payne-Townshend.

Lady Ariadne Utterword, Captain Shotover's second daughter in Shaw's symbolistic drama of the First World War, *Heartbreak House,* represents the class in England which he calls "Horseback Hall." As he argues in his preface, it is hard to say whether Horseback Hall or Heartbreak House is more responsible for the plight of the country. For the inhabitants of Horseback Hall are the upper-class Philistines, rich, stupid, complacent, governing millions, riding to hounds and the steeple-chase, and calling upon one another socially without perceiving the cataclysm which is almost upon them. Those who live in Heartbreak House are the aesthetic intellectuals, the Sunday revolutionists, and the idealists who talk and discuss and speculate and theorize, but never get around to the intelligent action and leadership that the times demand.

Ariadne married a man with an expression like that on the figurehead of her father's ship ("wooden yet enterprising," as the Captain puts it). As a child, she confesses, she longed "to be respectable, to be a lady," and so she married at nineteen to escape the disorder and confusion of her home. As the wife of Sir Hastings Utterword, "governor of all the crown colonies in succession," she has found order, discipline, and happiness. And now that she has come home again and seen the state of things there, she regrets that she has returned — and her father agrees with her. Nurse Guinness reminds her, "You were always one for respectability, Miss Addie." Her regard for "what is right" is shown even in her demand that her sister Hesione kiss her because "I do want you to behave properly and decently." Although the first impression created by the precipitateness of her speech and action is "one of comic silliness," this is erroneous, and her blonde handsomeness and elegant dress at once draw men like the philanderer Hector Hushabye, her sister's husband, and Randall Utterword, her husband's brother, after her. But she warns them that she is "a rigidly conventional woman," not at all Bohemian just because she is a Shotover. In fact, she loathes Bohemianism. "No child," she cries, "brought up in a strict Puritan household ever suffered from Puritanism as I suffered from our Bohemianism." When Hector tries to convince her that she is neither Puritan nor Bohemian, but alive and powerfully attractive, she informs him that she is, rather, a woman of the world, who has found that "if you will only take the trouble always to do the perfectly correct thing, and to say the perfectly correct thing, you can do just what you like." Ariadne's obsession for appearances even leads her to plead that they let the burglar Dunn off so that they all won't be dragged into the police court, but when he tries to blackmail them in a travesty of Shaw's views on punishment (which Shaw in his later essay on "Imprisonment" insisted should be taken seriously), she discovers that she has a conscience after all and that he should be punished.

Ariadne finally fully exposes her true self when she quotes her husband's diagnosis that the only thing wrong with the Captain's house (like England) is that it has "no proper stables." The "people who hunt," she concludes, "are the right people and the people who don't are the wrong ones." She knows that her husband could run the country properly, and advises them: "Get rid of your ridiculous sham democracy; and give Hastings the necessary powers, and a good supply of bamboo to bring the British native to his senses." Failing the country's following of this sensible counsel, she prepares, Philistine-like, to go back to her "numskull" (as the Captain politely calls her husband) "with the greatest satisfaction when I am tired of you all, clever as you are." Clearly, there is no help for England in her kind.

It might perhaps be expected that Shaw would sardonically make Adam, the father of all mankind ("old everybody's father," as Cain insultingly calls him), a Philistine. And that is what he essentially has done in *Back to Methuselah.* In the first play in this serial drama, *In the Beginning,* there is for a time some hope for Adam. He is a dreamer rather than a thinker, but he knows some things by intuition — such as that human life must not be allowed to disappear from the earth. But he wants to change, to improve. He is, unfortunately, a procrastinator, and yields easily to the Serpent's suggestion that he put off weeding the Garden until tomorrow. Eve knows that he is lazy, that he will not take trouble with his body and cannot bear pain, and the Serpent tells her that he will be in her power because of his desire. He quickly becomes bored, and is even in a hurry to die. What he wants, he says, is certainty. "Fear is stronger in me than hope." But the wise Serpent wants no certainty, for if she binds the future thus she binds her own will, and thus limits the possibility of progress. Adam, however, is afraid to listen to her, and so the Serpent has to whisper the secret of the creation of new life to Eve.

A few centuries later Adam has deteriorated even more. He has an unkempt beard and looks "worried, like a farmer." In fact, about all he can think about is his digging, and is taunted about the monotony of his existence by Eve and Cain. Adam has now completely forgotten his dreams, but Cain has inherited the quality of dreaming, though in a twisted, dangerous fashion. For a moment Adam is tempted by some of Cain's ideas — his military way of life, his proposal to make slaves of other people and let them do the work; but after he considers the matter he decides that instead of following Cain he "will dig, and live." He is content with things as they are. Although he realizes that most of his grandchildren "die before they have sense enough to know how to live," he still thinks it is "No matter. Life is still long enough to learn to know how to dig . . ." Even after eons have elapsed, in the vision epilogue at the end of the play, after Eve, Cain, and the Serpent have all made their more or less intelligent comments on the course of humanity, Adam is capable only of remarking: "I can make nothing of it, neither head nor tail. What is it all for? Why? Whither? We were well enough in the Garden . . . Foolishness, I call it."

That is always the opinion of the Philistine when he looks about him in the world and observes others laboriously and excitedly trying to change the conditions which suit him so well and in which he is contentedly drowsing. It is no wonder that there are so many Philistines in the world, Shaw implies, when Adam himself was one.

# III

## THE IDEALIST

WHEN SHAW DECIDED to make idealism rather than Philistinism the focal point of his attack on British society, he was striking at a hidden but angrily inflamed nerve, the condition of which was capable of causing not only an accelerated automatic reflex reaction but also excruciating pain to the patient. For the idealists, with their erection of romantic masks and their idolization of duty, self-sacrifice, and altruism, though often at the expense of ruining the individual's own life and happiness, had dominated Victorian life for decades. But even Frederic, W. S. Gilbert's Pirate Apprentice in *The Pirates of Penzance,* as far back as 1879 had been unconsciously restive under "the repeated acts of theft and pillage" which he had committed "at a sense of duty's stern dictation," and was delighted when he thought he saw a chance to escape from the tyranny of the Stern Daughter of the Voice of God. Frederic had been taken in by the ideals of the pirates; he had become "the Slave of Duty."

### 1. *The Repudiation of Duty*

Twelve years later Shaw came to the rescue of Frederic's suppressed desire: he repudiated duty altogether. One's duty, he informed the public, is a thing one should never do. It is the "primal curse." If there is to be social progress, some established duty must be rejected at every step. Otherwise, freedom to advance is impossible. The repudiation of Man's duty to God, he insisted, has already been accomplished, and Man is now in the stage of exalting his duty to his neighbor. Only, however, when Man realizes that an equally cogent duty is owed to himself will the reign of duty be overthrown, for only then will Man's God become "his own humanity; and he, self-satisfied at last, ceases to be selfish." In the process, Man will have discarded the policy of idealism; and "Nature," the instinct, the "Will," will shape Man's progress to his eventual and higher goal.

The battle which Ibsen and Shaw were primarily responsible for precipitating in England was then, in a sense, one between the dutiful and the undutiful, and it was fought out with special vigor and clarity on the platform which Shaw, soon after *The Quintessence,* was to choose as particularly his own — the stage. Though the first place where Shaw fully expressed these iconoclastic but also seminal views was his book on Ibsenism, the very title of this basic work confesses that he did not claim complete originality for them. Of course, for several preceding years, in *Thus Spake Zarathustra* and *Beyond Good and Evil,* Friedrich Nietzsche had also been assaulting the old conceptions of duty and virtue, proclaiming the magnificence of the ego, glorifying the instincts and the Will as the emancipators, deriding self-sacrifice, scorning the idealists, and prophesying the Superman. But since Shaw has stated dogmatically in a footnote to the expanded edition of *The Quintessence* as well as in a review of Nietzsche's works in 1896 that he never heard of Nietzsche until a German lady accused him of plagiarism after the publication of the 1891 volume, we must accept his explanation that he was simply part of a world movement, in which Schopenhauer, Wagner, Strindberg, and Ibsen also played leading roles. Certainly on two vital matters Shaw and Nietzsche disagreed: Woman and Socialism. For Nietzsche would have enslaved the first and eradicated the second. Ibsen was much more congenial to Shaw, for, although the Norwegian was only incidentally interested in Socialism, his other views were highly sympathetic to the Irish expatriate.

In the British theater of the nineties the forces soon began to line up in sharply defined sides. It is a surprising but almost unnoted fact that in the twenty-five or so years before the outbreak of the First World War the conception of duty and ideals becomes the real focus of the action and dominates the climactic scene in almost every important play. On the conservative side, striving vainly to uphold the old "standards," were ranged Henry Arthur Jones, Sir Arthur Wing Pinero, and Sir James M. Barrie. Lined up on the side of the rebels, demanding the destruction of the old hypocrisies, were Oscar Wilde (most of the time), John Galsworthy, and three notable revolutionaries of their day — now unfortunately almost forgotten — Sydney Grundy, St. John Hankin, and Stanley Houghton. Of course Shaw was in the vanguard of this rebel group.*

## 2. *The Slaves of Duty*

Shaw's onslaught on the idealists began early, and progressed from utter contempt to a sort of half-hearted pity, which he did his best to conceal under a forced ruthlessness. Even in *Immaturity* he had told the story of Jim Vesey, a sixty-year-old landscape painter, easy-going but sharp-sighted about his past — a man whose early life had been ruined by an incautious marriage to a woman who "could tell lies by the dozen in the way of duty and self-sacrifice." Similarly, Robert Smith, the realistic Shavian hero, angrily recalls

---

* The previous section of this chapter is a condensation of my article, "The Quintessence of Idealism; or, The Slaves of Duty," in *PMLA,* September 1947. Examples of specific plays of the quarter-century before the First World War which are governed by this theme will be found discussed in this article.

his own case and explodes: "I remember how I secretly hated the solemn humbug my parents used to pour forth on me, when they were seized with an attack of duty."

In the same fashion, Adrian Herbert, the pathetically second-rate but utterly devoted painter in *Love among the Artists,* has been securely fastened to his mother's apron strings, but has been unable to revolt successfully against his sense of duty except in private confessions to his friends. So imbued is Adrian himself with the conception, however, that even after he has broken his engagement to Mary Sutherland in order to wed the Polish pianist Aurelie Szczympliça, he admits that, in being the "most infatuated lover in the world" to his wife, he falls "short in his duty to himself."

Shaw's prime specimen of the idealist in his novels, however, is the pathetically appealing Marian Lind in *The Irrational Knot,* who has the misfortune to fall in love with the ruthlessly Shavian Edward Conolly, transplanted American inventor. Shortly after they have met at an amateur concert, she begins calling him a cynic and lecturing him on what she considers his duties, though manifestly at the same time being reluctantly fascinated by his unconventionality. As soon as she gets Conolly's remarkable letter of proposal, she begins wishing that she "could make some real sacrifice for his sake," since they belong to absolutely different social spheres. She confesses to her other lover, Sholto Douglas, that what has happened realizes "a romantic dream" of hers. Like Mrs. Vesey, when Marian perceives that her husband is dissatisfied with her, she tells her confidante, Nelly McQuinch, "I am clinging to him with all my heart and soul, and you must help me." Her devout clerical brother, the Rev. George Lind, tries to explain to Conolly that his sister "has been educated to feel only in accordance with her duty," but the other scornfully responds that so far as he can see "what you call her education . . . appears to have consisted of stuffing her with lies, and making it a point of honor with her to believe them in spite of sense and reason." Marian's rigidity, of course, is no surprise to the reader, who has discovered that her father, Reginald Lind, is not only an idealist too, but also a hypocrite. Although, on the news of Marian's marriage, he at first indulges in all the old clichés of "a parent asserting his proprietary rights in his child," he bitterly disappoints his idealist-son, the Rev. George, by finally accepting the marriage blithely and even praising it. After all, he says, he is a Liberal. Poor George, although his ideals of his father have been uprooted, still refuses to give up those ideals. The Linds are truly an exemplary family.

Nevertheless, because of the heartlessly analytic way Conolly treats Marian and practically forces her into her lover Douglas's arms, she regains the reader's sympathy in spite of her limitations. Even after the elopement, all Conolly can say is: "she made the mistake of avoiding all realities." When she realizes her error and wishes herself back with her purely rational hus-

band, she still feels that she can't honorably desert Douglas. Her scruples go
so far that, when she learns what a bounder Douglas really is, she refuses to
consider marriage with him, exclaiming, "I am suffering for my folly and
egoism: and I deserve to suffer." Nevertheless, she seems to be constantly
maturing, and when she makes the magnificent admission concerning her
husband (magnificent, at least, from the Shavian point of view), "I should
like to be amongst women what he is amongst men, supported by my own
strength," she seems to be on the point of graduating into realism. But Shaw
resolutely refuses to let her make the grade, and at the end, in spite of the
coming child, she is not allowed to become quite strong enough to repudiate
all duties, ties, and conventions, and accept Conolly's offer to return to him
"FREE."

Shaw's final comment on Marian when he came to write a preface to his
novel a couple of decades later, was merely: "And the heroine, nice, amiable, benevolent, and anxious to please and behave well, but hopelessly sec-
ondhand in her morals and nicenesses, and consequently without any real
moral force now that the threat of hell has lost its terrors for her, is left
destitute among the failures which are so puzzling to thoughtless people."

Among the fifty-three plays, long and short, which Shaw composed and
published during his ninety-four years, the critic looking for specimens of
the idealist finds that here is surely Shaw's — if not God's — plenty. They
are in nearly every case marked by their worship of duty and honor, their
talk about self-sacrifice, their devotion to romantic illusions, their search for
plausible excuses to extenuate their conduct, the ease with which they are
shocked by unconventional or merely perfectly frank ideas and behavior, and
the extremes to which they go in their attacks on the nonconformist. It will
be profitable to examine a few representative samples of the type in order
to discover some of the chief viewpoints and institutions which Shaw thinks
humanity is prone to idealize. These are, then, some of the masks which he
believes must be destroyed if man is to progress.

The first of these faulty fabrications that he selected for his assault was
material success, symbolized by the gaining of money and the maintenance
of a smug respectability. In his very first play, *Widowers' Houses,* which he
started as a collaboration with William Archer, but finished alone in 1892,
with Archer's thankful blessing, he presented as depressing and despicable a
lot of materialistic idealists as could well be got within the scope of three
acts. In his preface he described his play as a "bluebook" play, or dramatized
Fabian essay, a relatively new type which, he believed, would "hold the stage
far better than conventionally idealist dramas."

The situation in *Widowers' Houses* turns on the conversion of young
Dr. Henry Trench from his scruples about owning slum property to his
agreement to improve the property in order to get a higher price when the
city buys it so that a new street can be cut through. Sartorius, the gentle-

manly but self-made capitalist (based, as Shaw told Henderson, on "an Irish stationer to whom I never spoke; his imposing manner suggested his character"), sheds crocodile tears over the sufferings of the poor, but insists that they are too ignorant and shiftless to know how to adjust themselves to better conditions anyhow. Nevertheless, he falls in with the callous suggestion of his daughter Blanche (based in some respects on Shaw's actress-friend, Florence Farr) that he turn them out, improve the property, and get in a better class of tenant — knowing perfectly well that the city will expropriate the property as soon as the repairs have been completed. Previously he had carefully kept Blanche in ignorance of the source of his income, and he is full of sententious utterances about his duty as "the father of a motherless girl," his duty to the "vestry," his duty to society, etc., and is shocked by the suggestion of Lickcheese, the vulgar slum rent collector, that Blanche might be made part of a money bargain with Trench. Lickcheese, with his early Uriah Heep humility, proves as harsh toward the poor as anyone else, and after his sudden and unexpected rise in the world informs Sartorius democratically, "You and me is too much of a pair for me to take anything you say in bad part, Sartorius." Young Trench, suffering feebly from compunctions when he learns the true source of his own and Sartorius's incomes, is always snatching at excuses, but eventually reveals the basic weakness of his character. He becomes "a living picture of disillusion," and later is "coarsened and sullen," but still shows little sense of his own responsibility, particularly since he wants to marry Blanche.

In the last scene it is "duty" which swings the scales for all of them. Trench's mentor, the elderly social climber, William de Burgh Cokane, who, according to Henderson, had been suggested to Shaw by his mother's stories and her father's solicitor's imitations of a man he himself had never seen,* opens the attack by maintaining: "No: this is a matter of principle with me. I say it is your duty, Harry — your *duty* — to put those abominable buildings into proper and habitable repair . . . In questions of duty there is no room for persuasion, even from the oldest friend." This oblique approach is ably seconded by Sartorius: "I certainly feel, as Mr. Cokane puts it, that it is our duty: one which I have perhaps too long neglected out of regard for the poorest class of tenants." Lickcheese, the most miserable hypocrite of them all, chimes in: "Not a doubt of it, gents, a dooty. I can be as sharp as any man when it's a question of business; but dooty's another thing." Trench still has enough self-respect to reply: "Well, I don't see that it is any more my duty now than it was four months ago. I look at it simply as a question of so much money." But this cynical and "realistic" viewpoint leads him to the same decision as the idealists had already reached, when he realizes that Blanche will go along with the bargain.

* Rattray records, however, that Sydney Olivier was afraid that Shaw had modeled Cokane on *him*.

In commenting on his own play in his later preface Shaw waxes sarcastic at the expense of Trench's "stage Socialism" and its thoughtless upholders. He points out that one speech from "a practical business man" like Sartorius, whose exceptional business ability he admires because of its very perfection, punctures Trench's idealism. The young man is undergoing the "reality of the everyday process known as disillusion." Yet he never becomes a true realist since he quickly shuts his eyes again, at least part way, after they have been opened for him. Shaw also twitted the critics for having dismissed Sartorius simply "as a sophistical villain," and so having "got hopelessly astray as to the characterization in the piece," whereas what he wanted to imply was that society itself was guilty of having made the agent and the landlord what they are. Contemptuously he added that his portrait of Lickcheese, "an effective but quite common piece of work, pleased better than any of the rest." His essential contentment with the overall results of his play as a challenge to the world was expressed in a single sentence in the letter which he wrote to *The Star* immediately after the reviews started coming out: "The very success with which I have brought all the Philistines and sentimental idealists down on me proves the velocity and penetration with which my realism got across the footlights."

Alick West, in his *George Bernard Shaw: "A Good Man Fallen among Fabians,"* while showing a grudging admiration for *Widowers' Houses* when he denies that it can be called a great play, but adds that "only by comparison with great plays can it be judged," concludes that the central weakness in Shaw's conception lies in its un-Marxist failure to inspire the audience — that is, the proletariat — with a vision of their own unity and potential concerted creative strength; it preaches cynicism and the objective point of view of the spectator rather than active opposition and revolution in the form of class conflict.

Shaw took his real revenge on his reviewers through Cuthbertson, in his next play, *The Philanderer.* For, after describing him as "a man of fervent idealistic sentiment" and "the leading representative of manly sentiment in London," a man whose face is marked with "the lines of sedentary London brain work, with its chronic fatigue and longing for rest and recreative emotion, and its disillusioned indifference to adventure and enjoyment, except as a means of recuperation," Shaw divulges after several minutes that the old fellow is really a dramatic critic. Cuthbertson is a "manly man," who holds that smoking is not natural to the female sex, who once had a "true English wife and a happy, wholesome fireside" — until the pair found they couldn't get along together, and who announces that he is "now going to speak as a man of the world: that is, without moral responsibility." He is happy that he and his old friend Colonel Craven don't make jests of "sacred things" as Charteris does. "Thank Heaven," he exclaims, "we belong to the Old Order." In a letter to Richard Mansfield in 1895, quoted by Henderson,

Shaw confessed: "Cuthbertson is a caricature of Clement Scott, whose double you must have somewhere in the New York press." Scott was of course Shaw's favorite antagonist, the horrified, Roman Catholic, anti-Ibsenite dramatic critic of *The Daily Telegraph,* to whom Shaw once devoted a whole article in *The Saturday Review* in 1896, developing his earlier tribute in *The Quintessence.* Henderson even remarks that Cuthbertson's avowal that the whole modern movement is abhorrent to him is in virtually the same words as were used by Scott in his attack on Ibsen.

Cuthbertson's idealism, of course, is confined to manly sentiment and has nothing to do with business. John Tarleton, of Tarleton's Underwear, in *Misalliance,* is both a self-made business success and an avid purveyor of sentiments. On his counters the customer finds piles of "The Romance of Business, or The Story of Tarleton's Underwear. Please Take One!" Tarleton, who calls himself "Plain John," is "mad on reading" and is always opening free libraries. He is "a perfect whirlwind," a "vital man," "an immense and genial veteran of trade," "indefatigable at public work." His trouble is lack of discrimination and discipline. As a man with a "super-abundance of vitality" he is immensely attracted to the Polish acrobat, Lina Szczepanowska, and "propositions" her, though loyally pointing out that he still puts his wife first. He has great respect for parenthood, especially motherhood, and is hurt to the quick by his pert daughter Hypatia's callous candidness about his character. In fact, at one point he is sufficiently jarred to exclaim violently: "Hold your tongue, you young devil. The young are all alike: hard, coarse, shallow, cruel, selfish, dirty-minded. You can clear out of my house . . ." But although he is driven almost to hysterics by the discovery of family incompatibilities, he repents, and decides to read *King Lear.* As Shaw comments in his preface, "A very distinguished man once assured a mother of my acquaintance that she would never know what it meant to be hurt until she was hurt through her children." But of course poor sensitive Tarleton always had his underwear to fall back on.

When Shaw came to portray Boss Mangan in *Heartbreak House,* he had apparently forgotten that he had admired the munitions king, Andrew Undershaft in *Major Barbara,* for his success in making money and in his Swiftian preface had argued eloquently that any methods are to be condoned for avoiding poverty, the greatest of crimes against society. As Mazzini Dunn diagnoses his benefactor-exploiter, Mangan "thinks of nothing else" but money because he "is so dreadfully afraid of being poor." Mrs. Hushabye had already labeled him as "a perfect hog of a millionaire," and yet when he appears he turns out to be "carefully frockcoated . . . , with a careworn, mistrustful expression, standing a little on an entirely imaginary dignity . . . , and features so entirely commonplace that it is impossible to describe them." But it is soon clear that despite his "movie" speeches about never making up his mind to do something that he doesn't bring it off he is only "playing the strong man." In spite of Ellie Dunn's defending him as her fiancé, he later tries to get out of the engagement by saying that he is in love with Mrs. Hushabye and admitting that he ruined Mazzini on purpose: "You've been wasting your gratitude: my kind heart is all rot. I'm sick of it." But there have been more masks than his reputation for a kind heart: his whole business reputation is a mask and a fraud. For he really has no money of his own, and never did. Everything belongs to the syndicates and the shareholders. Perhaps here is the real difference between him and Undershaft, for Undershaft has never concealed anything. But the poor, pathetic Boss is so shocked and disillusioned by everybody's performing a moral and spiritual strip tease just before the air raid that he starts to tear off his own clothes: "We've stripped ourselves morally naked: well, let us strip ourselves physically naked as well." But despite his flash of vision, he remains enough of a captive of idealism to pontificate, "How are we to have any self-respect if we don't keep it up that we're better than we really are?" When Shaw has had all of Mangan that he can stand, he lets the Boss's constant "presentiment that he is going to die" come true. He and the Burglar, who take refuge in the gravel pit during the air raid, are killed by a bomb, which explodes Captain Shotover's cache of dynamite. As Shaw ironically puts it, the "two burglars, . . . the two practical men of affairs," are the only ones to die in the raid.

The characteristic lines of the business man and the financier converge in Mendoza, of Mendoza, Ltd., in *Man and Superman*. Mendoza is plausible enough to persuade even the great American millionaire, Hector Malone, to invest in his corporation without investigating its nature. When Mendoza turns up as the leader of the band of Socialistic brigands in the Spanish Sierra Nevada, he is described as a "tall strong man," with a general "Mephistophelean affectation," a swagger, and "a certain sentimentality." His mouth and eyes are "by no means rascally; he has a fine voice and a ready wit; and whether he is really the strongest man in the party or not, he looks it." And he talks it too, for he soon announces that, as a Jew, he is "not a slave to any superstition," and that common sense is good enough for him. He has swallowed up "all the formulas, even that of Socialism," but proudly boasts that his purpose is to "secure a more equitable distribution of wealth" by holding up motor cars. Shaw admits in his preface that he got the idea of Mendoza's incorporating himself from the suggestion of "a certain West Indian colonial secretary" to Sidney Webb, "the encyclopedic and inexhaustible," that he should "form himself into a company for the benefit of the shareholders," but in the play Mendoza himself explains that after he had learned his cosmopolitanism as a waiter at the Savoy he had gone to America, where he had met a train robber who gave him the idea of forming a syndicate, to be financed by "capitalists of the right sort" — such as Malone. Mendoza's romantic account of his unhappy love for

Louisa Straker, the cook (a tribute, according to Shaw's bibliographer, F. E. Loewenstein, to Mary Farmer, the Shaw cook and housekeeper at Pickards Cottage), together with his proud confession of his addiction to verse-making (Shaw admits in his preface, "The theft of the brigand-poetaster from Sir Arthur Conan Doyle is deliberate"), early arouses suspicion that he is not really so tough-minded as he seems — a suspicion which is thoroughly confirmed when he is transformed into the Devil in the hell scene.

Here he has considerably deteriorated in both character and appearance, though he is still very plausible in speech and manner. But, "in spite of an effusion of goodnature and friendliness," he "is peevish and sensitive when his advances are not reciprocated." He does not look as if he could work very hard or endure very much; in fact, his whole aura is one of disagreeable self-indulgence. His smooth defense of himself and his activities simply nauseates Tanner-Don Juan, who turns the Satanic idealism inside out. Hell, states Don Juan, is merely "the home of the unreal and of the seekers for happiness. It is the only refuge from heaven, which is . . . the home of the masters of reality, and from earth, which is the home of the slaves of reality." In hell a man is simply "an appearance, an illusion, a convention," without a body. He has no social, political, religious, or sanitary questions to bother him there. In fact, just as on earth, everything is idealized, and a man calls his own appearance beauty, his own emotions love, his own sentiments heroism, and his own aspirations virtue; and since there are no hard facts to contradict him, his life becomes "nothing but a perpetual romance, a universal melodrama." So eloquent is Juan on the topic that the Devil is himself enthralled — as all idealists are by words. He later returns to the attack, but of course is beaten down by Juan. For some inexplicable reason Hamon sees Mendoza as "the New Man under a different visual angle," in the completely incompatible company of Straker, Nicola, and William the waiter. At least they all are, or have been, servants.

Roebuck Ramsden in the same play must also have had a considerable success as a business man, for he is "the man of means," living in ease and solid comfort. Through his active civic life he has got his "broad air of importance" and power. But, says Shaw, "He is more than a highly respectable man: he is marked out as a president of highly respectable men, a chairman among directors, an alderman among councillors, a mayor among aldermen." His trousers have been tailored from a cloth of mixed colors to "harmonize with the religions of respectable men." And yet this paragon of the proper, this dignitary of the decent, has been an advanced thinker, a liberal, even a radical in his time, and still plumes himself on his progressive position. When Tanner knocks him between the eyes by publicly calling him "an old man with obsolete ideas," he violently asserts that he has always hated the narrowness and prejudices of the British public, and still demands the right to think for himself: "You pose as an advanced man. Let me tell you that I was an advanced man before you were born . . . I am *more* advanced than I ever was. I grow more advanced every day." Tanner presses his point home inexorably and impishly: "More advanced in years, Polonius." Although Ramsden denies indignantly that the ideas in Tanner's book are too advanced for him, he is quickly put to the test in the case of Violet Robinson, who is about to have a child — as everybody erroneously concludes, without the benefit of a registry or a church service. Although Ramsden, like almost everyone else, is shocked at the news, Tanner hounds him into forgoing his "duty" and abnegating his "principles" about the "purity" of the English home, if only, in Ramsden's words, to save Violet from being driven to run to Tanner for protection.

As the Statue in the dream scene in hell, however, Ramsden is finally tempted to some candidness about himself. Although he has first gone to heaven, he finds the life there very boring, and often visits hell, where he experiences a sensation of "holiday joyousness." Indeed, the hellish life in which "you have nothing to do but amuse yourself" proves so tempting that he announces that he has left heaven forever. His moral disintegration is so rapid that, as he says, "since Juan has stripped every rag of decency from the discussion I may as well tell the frozen truth." So he breaks down and admits that Juan's picture of the role of the pursuing woman in courtship and marriage is the truth, that he is impressed by the other's views on the impersonality of the sex relation and on aristocratic marriages, and that even he was once accustomed to tell idealistic lies when courting women and believed them himself.

It is the idealists like Mendoza and Ramsden, then, that find the atmosphere of hell most invigorating. We might even conclude that all the satisfied denizens of hell are idealists, from the slick robber baron of business to the superannuated reformer whose youthful radicalism has hardened to a middle-aged petrifaction.

As implied in the case of the Statue, a common propensity of idealists is to prettify everything connected with the establishment and continuation of family life so that it has little relation to reality. The romanticizing and exaggerating of the importance of love and sex are perhaps at the root of it all. Mrs. Hesione Hushabye in *Heartbreak House* furnishes a neat example.

As in all of Shaw's "vital" women, there is an aura about Hesione that draws everyone, especially the men, to her. As he confessed in a letter to Mrs. Pat Campbell in 1929, he had "sucked her blood" for the character. Hesione's very appearance is symbolical, with her "magnificent black hair, eyes like the fishpools of Heshbon, and a nobly modelled neck." Unlike her sister, Lady Ariadne Utterword, she does not wear corsets, and is dressed "anyhow" in a rich black robe that shows off her white skin and Junoesque contours. She is no housekeeper, and forgets that she has invited people to visit her. "What a lark!" is her favorite expression, as new situations develop.

She has the faculty of being able to fall in with everybody's mood, of understanding the sexual cross-currents that are swaying others, and of trying to
help with advice and plans in others' love affairs. It is even a lark when
she discovers that the "Marcus Darnley" who has been philandering glori-
ously with young Ellie Dunn is really her own husband Hector, whose
amorous exploits and tall stories she is thoroughly used to and quite proud
of. Now that the edge of their own youthfully violent love has worn off,
she has even played a kind of magnanimous pander and "invited all sorts
of pretty women to the house on the chance" of giving him another opportunity to repeat the one real love affair he had had with her. She is usually,
as she herself says, either coaxing or kissing or laughing. On one of her
exits, she herself announces, "Now *I* am going off to fascinate somebody"
— the occupation of most of the dwellers in *Heartbreak House*. Hector classes
her with "vampire women, demon women," and agrees with the Captain
that she has used him up and left him with nothing but dreams; and Ellie
confirms the diagnosis by labeling her with skeptical admiration "a siren
. . . born to lead men by the nose." But Ellie warns her, too, not to "slop
and gush and be sentimental."

   Like all idealists, then, Hesione has her sensitive spots, which the realist,
intentionally or unintentionally, is likely to probe. So when Ellie tells her
frankly her materialistic reasons for planning to marry Mangan, Hesione
rises "superbly" to her feet and upbraids her: "Ellie: you are a wicked sordid
little beast. And to think that I actually condescended to fascinate that creature there to save you from him!" In reply to Ellie's scathing comment that
if she had married Hector she would have made a man of him, not a household pet, Hesione flames out: "You dare!" But in a moment she has
smoothed down again and has admitted that maybe Ellie is right. As the
curtain goes down on act I, Shaw has her and the Captain rhapsodize on
the relationship between men and women as follows: "What do men want?
They have their food, their firesides, their clothes mended, and our love at
the end of the day. Why are they not satisfied? Why do they envy us the
pain with which we bring them into the world, and make strange dangers
and torments for themselves to be even with us?" Yet to Mangan she remarks that it matters little which men govern the country so long as "we,"
the "devil's granddaughters," the "lovely women," govern them. During the
air raid she is delighted by the explosions and "the sound in the sky," which
reminds her of Beethoven; and as the final curtain descends, she exclaims,
responding only to the thrill of the raid and missing its meaning, "But
what a glorious experience! I hope they come again tomorrow night." She
is an incorrigible romanticist throughout. But she seems to be childless too,
and therefore can scarcely symbolize, as Irvine asserts, "England at home, or
woman's love and domesticity," to contrast with her sister Ariadne's symbolizing of "empire, or England abroad."

The motivation of idealistic Orinthia, King Magnus's official but platonic mistress in *The Apple Cart* (intended, according to Shaw's letters in 1929, to be another tribute to Stella Campbell, but, according to her replies, an unappreciated one), of Lady Corinthia, Prime Minister Balsquith's "Egeria" in *Press Cuttings,* and of Lady Magnesia in *Passion, Poison, and Petrifaction,* perhaps the worst farce that Shaw ever wrote, all illustrate the romanticization of love.

Love forces itself into all sorts of idealizations — especially after marriage, as both the philandering husbands in *Overruled* (originally entitled *Trespassers Will Be Prosecuted*) prove. Gregory Lunn, in the midst of his desperate struggle between his conscience and the Life Force, interrupts his protestations of love to Mrs. Juno by crying, "No: I recall you to your duty." His unjealous wife calmly describes him as her "sentimental husband . . . one of those terribly uxorious men who ought to have ten wives." As for Mrs. Juno's husband Sibthorpe, who anticipates Philip Barry in his theory of marriage holidays, he is stuffed full of talk about romance. He also has a conscience and insists on being treated as a sinner even if he has sinned only in intention. He talks of "a married woman's duty" to speak only to men who dislike her, and justifies his conduct by philosophizing: "We're not perfect; but as long as we keep the ideal before us" by admitting we're wrong, we can go ahead and sin with a clear conscience. Lady Britomart, the terrific dowager of *Major Barbara,* would agree with Juno, but is annoyed by her husband Undershaft's "preaching immorality while he practiced morality."

Incidentally, Duffin regards all four characters in *Overruled* as "good Philistines." Henderson describes Lunn as "an honest fellow" and Juno as "a conventional Philistine would-be he-man." In the light of our definitions, both critics seem to be wrong. Shaw, in fact, in his *Self Sketches,* reprimands Duffin for failing to see anything more than triviality in some of Gregory's remarks, and informs him: "The subject of the play is the overruling by the Life Force of bourgeois morality and the conscience formed on it." There is here at least a suspicion of a reflection of Shaw's early Fabian associate, the journalist Hubert Bland, who, as H. G. Wells phrased it in his autobiography, was "a sort of Tom-cat man," but who on the outside preserved the most formal Victorian conventionalities and "thought it made a love affair more exciting and important if one might be damned for it." Mrs. Bland, an electrifying Bohemian in spite of the fact that she was popularly best known as the author of the novels for juveniles written under the name of "E. Nesbit," in partial retaliation for her husband's philandering fell in love with Shaw, who then faced the problem of dealing with another pursuing woman, but handled it with his usual finesse.

Parenthood as well as love and marriage also has its ideal masks. A too exalted conception of marriage and fatherhood, for example, is responsible for many of poor Crampton's troubles in *You Never Can Tell*. Crampton is a "tall, hard and stringy" man, with "an atrociously obstinate, ill tempered, grasping mouth, and a querulously dogmatic voice." He is "highly nervous and sensitive," with "wistful, wounded eyes" and "a plaintive note in his voice." Yet he is also, in his way, a shrewd man, as well as a "perfect egomaniac." The trouble with him is that early in life "I found that most of the things that were good for me were nasty." He is involuntarily disappointed, in spite of his boasted harshness, when his newly discovered children do not treat him like a long-lost father, and he begins to act, Shaw says, like "a father robbed of his children," although previously he would have nothing to do with them. In fact, many years ago he had deserted them and his domineering wife, Mrs. Clandon. Now he soon starts to talk about "home," along with "duty, affection, respect, obedience," as a means of winning them over. So, after being subjected to the terrible twins and Gloria for a time, he tries to placate and be kind to them, and by the end of the play some of his illusions about himself commence to disappear. Nevertheless, Shaw is completely justified in rapping Duffin's knuckles for writing, "Crampton is a thoroughly likeable old fellow." Shaw comments acidly in his *Self Sketches:* "Anyone who could like Crampton could like anybody."

Exaggerated conceptions of the proper relationships between mothers and children often produce even worse situations than those involving fathers. Captain Brassbound, in the melodrama, *Captain Brassbound's Conversion,* has for years been suffering from one of the most dreadful Oedipus complexes on record — though he would never recognize it under that name.[7] He has become morbid and introverted, and a smoldering craving for revenge has motivated his whole life. He is handsome but joyless; his mouth is set grimly; his face is composed "to one tragic purpose." He speaks briefly but pointedly. He is, on the whole, "interesting, and even attractive, but not friendly." For he is convinced that his uncle, now Sir Howard Hallam, the famous judge, once cheated his widowed mother, an uneducated Brazilian woman, out of her husband's estate, and drove her to drink and madness. He is therefore pursuing "justice on a thief and a murderer"; and Shaw's sermonizings on justice and vengeance, and the futility of the latter, as well as on "the vengeance of society, disguised as justice by its passions," constitute the main theme of the play. In consequence of his misanthropy, Brassbound has become "Black Paquito," a notorious Moroccan smuggler. When accident places Sir Howard, accompanied by his irresistibly feminine sister-in-law, Lady Cicely Wayneflete, in Brassbound's power, the Captain's lifelong ambition seems about to be satisfied. But he has not reckoned with the tender-hearted but sure persuasiveness of Lady Cicely. In spite of all his talk about the proper duties of sons and brothers, and his insistence that he never changes his mind, she soon winds him around her little finger, and convinces him that he has been "one of the Idealists — the Impossibilists," and that his idealization of his mother and his hatred of his uncle are thoroughly unjustified. There are no duties, she tells him: "Do whatever you like. That's what I always do." Though his initial reaction after his conversion is to exclaim, "Damn you! you have belittled my whole life to me," he soon kisses her hand, and her eyes grow wet. Not long afterwards he is proposing to her, but she manages to wriggle out of that dilemma with her usual skill. As he "turns and flies," Marchbanks-wise, from the woman who will have none of him, he thanks her for what she has done for him in teaching him the "secret of command at last," for, as she has said, no one who is in love with any real person can truly manage other people.

One of the last places where one might expect to scratch an apparent realist and find an idealist underneath would be in the proprietress of a string of high-class international brothels, disguised as hotels. Yet Mrs. Warren, of *Mrs. Warren's Profession,* displays all the symptoms. She is, says Shaw, "a genial and fairly presentable old blackguard of a woman," who has carefully kept her college-bred daughter Vivie in ignorance of the source of her income.[8] When Vivie returns from Cambridge ready to become a full-fledged actuary, one of Mrs. Warren's friends, the well-meaning architect Praed, warns the practical Vivie that she has turned out to be very different from her mother's "ideal," for "people who are dissatisfied with their own bringing up generally think that the world would be all right if everybody were to be brought up quite differently." Mrs. Warren is clear-sighted enough on most matters. Because she knows the brutalized sporting gentleman, Crofts, so well through her own past relationship with him, she quickly perceives the real nature of his attentions to her daughter. She makes a shrewd, persuasive, realistic defense of the way in which she and her sister Liz, both brought up in respectable poverty, turned to prostitution in order to save themselves from the horrors of labor in a white lead factory. Her decision is of course in perfect harmony with Shaw's creed that the worst social evil is poverty, with its accompaniments of malnutrition, crime, and political imbecility. Her plea (which Shaw told Henderson was "only a paraphrase of a scene" in his novel, *Cashel Byron's Profession* — hence the echo in the title) reconciles even Vivie to her temporarily, but Shaw makes her give herself away as the second act curtain goes down: *"Mrs. Warren (with unction).* Blessings on my own dearie darling — a mother's blessing! *(She embraces her daughter protectingly, instinctively looking upward as if to call down a blessing.)"* She has already, however, revealed herself as the "conventional woman at heart" that Vivie calls her at the end. She pretends to worry about Vivie's safety, "and night coming on, too!" She appeals to the "conventional authority" of a mother, and she falls back on Vivie's "duty as a daughter." Like Wilde's Mrs. Erlynne, she makes Crofts a sentimental speech about how her "girl's little finger" is more to her than his "whole body," and when he receives this display "with a sneering grin" she flushes "at her failure to impose on him in the character of a theatrically devoted mother." When she makes her final bid to keep Vivie's allegiance and argues, "If I didn't do it, somebody else would; so I don't do any real harm," Vivie indicates that her mother's real crime has been in remaining in "business" after she no longer had any need to do so; in fact, if her statements mean anything, she has lived one kind of life and believed in another. She is a thorough hypocrite; that is, a thorough idealist.

Nevertheless, as Shaw points out in his preface, "Mrs. Warren is not a whit the worse than the reputable daughter who cannot endure her." His aim has been to throw the blame of Mrs. Warren's profession on society and not on the woman herself, as his guilty-conscienced critics would prefer. "Mrs. Warren's defence of herself is not only bold and specious, but valid and unanswerable. But it is no defence at all of the vice which she organizes" and "it is none the less infamous of society to offer such alternatives." It is strange that in the preface to *Back to Methuselah,* devoted largely to an attack on Darwinism, Shaw is compelled to admit that the Darwinian theory made a great appeal to Socialists because it confirmed Robert Owen's theories about the importance of environment, and "implied that street arabs are produced by slums and not by original sin: that prostitutes are produced by starvation wages and not by female concupiscence." *Mrs. Warren's Profession,* however, is practically the only one of Shaw's plays which seems to be based on the sort of deterministic philosophy which Hamon too carelessly assumed to be characteristic of all his works, simply because he was a Socialist.

Mrs. Dudgeon in *The Devil's Disciple,* based, as Shaw tells us in his preface, chiefly on Dickens's Mrs. Clennam in *Little Dorrit* and slightly on Mrs. Gargery in *Great Expectations,* represents the reverse side of the picture. Her capacity to love, if she ever really had any, has soured to universal hate, for she symbolizes "dead Puritanism." She is an elderly matron with a grimly trenched face. Detested at home, she has "an unquestioned reputation for piety and respectability among her neighbors, to whom drink and debauchery are still so much more tempting than religion and rectitude, that they conceive goodness simply as self-denial. This conception is easily extended to others-denial, and finally generalized as covering anything disagreeable." In other words, it is obvious that Mrs. Dudgeon is an exemplification of the "abstinence preacher" of *The Quintessence of Ibsenism,* just as her son Dick, whom she hates more than anyone else, illustrates the "indulgence preacher." Her only guide-word is "duty"; indeed, the concept of duty runs heavily through the whole play like a dissonant chord. Her recently dead husband's "duty," she says, was to stay at home with his family. She weeps at her own "duty as a widow." She is confident that she knows God's choice: "Why should we do our duty and keep God's law if there is to be no difference made between us and those who follow their own likings and dislikings, and make a jest of us and of their Maker's word?" She even shuts the door as if it "had to be made to do its duty with a ruthless hand." Just once does Shaw waver in his pitiless portrayal of her hardness, when he allows her to explain her own past by charging that the preceding minister had persuaded her to marry "the Godfearing" one of two brothers "against her heart" when she was in love with the other — the father of the bastard orphan, Essie. Consequently the present minister, Anthony Anderson, lost his influence with her when he "married for love." Love, sex, and beauty are to be feared. As Shaw put it when differentiating between Puritans and Philistines in his review of Henry Arthur Jones's *The Triumph of the Philistines:* "But his identification of Puritanism with Philistinism seems to me to be a fundamental confusion . . . A Puritan is no doubt often at the same disadvantage as the Philistine in respect of his insensibility to Art; but he is a fanatical idealist, to whom all stimulations of the sense of beauty are abhorrent, because he is only conscious of them in so far as they appeal to his sex instinct, which he regards as his great enemy." Mrs. Dudgeon dies cursing her son Dick, the Devil's Disciple, after he has put her out of the house which his father has willed to him rather than to his wife.

But beauty, too, can become a false ideal. Praed, Mrs. Warren's friend, the artist-architect, with his "eager, susceptible face and very amiable and considerate manners," really has no strength of character, because he is dedicated to looking for the romance in life.

It is the beautiful past which Count O'Dowda worships in *Fanny's First Play*. He even dresses "with studied elegance a hundred years out of date," and regards himself as not "a modern man in any sense of the word." He is a sort of Miniver Cheevy who wants to shut out the nineteenth century with its ugly industrialism and Philistinism, and who believes that "Love beautifies every romance and justifies every audacity." Since he thinks he has brought his daughter up to avoid all possible uglinesses, he is shocked to hear the things about the relations between parents and children that she has put into her play. After all, "there are reticences which everybody should respect"; there are "veils" which "no human creature" should tear down.

The two fathers in the play within a play are also minor idealists. The excitable Mr. Gilbey is always terribly shocked at what he hears about his son's goings-on from Monsignor Grenfell, Darling Dora Delaney, and the rest. Nevertheless, later on he "swanks about what a dog" his son is. Mr. Knox, on the other hand, "comes in almost furtively, a troubled man of fifty, thinner, harder, and uglier than his partner, Gilbey." Knox is always worried by what people will think about the scandal, and yet he has treated his own employees very harshly. Knox never really had "that happiness within himself" that his wife was looking for, although he made her think so when he was in love with her.

Like Praed and O'Dowda, the suave, courtly, elderly Lord Summerhays, K. C. B., in *Misalliance,* is a man of delicate feelings. But, unlike them, he is also a doer. Johnny Tarleton calls him "perhaps the strongest man England has produced in our time," and praises his colonial administration; and the elder Tarleton echoes his son with flatteries of the other's "genius for government," learned at Jinghiskahn, where, as Summerhays admits, "you have to govern the right way . . . , or go under and come home." Summerhays is an exemplar of the iron fist in the velvet glove, and can't understand "these democratic games" played in England; what is needed to be successful is either an aristocratic democracy or a democratic aristocracy. The shrewd, motherly Mrs. Tarleton, sees through him early, and teases him: "Let you alone for giving a thing a pretty turn. You're a humbug, you know, Lord Summerhays . . . you and I know it, don't we?" His relationship with the young Hypatia Tarleton — and here is a turn in his character that Duffin misinterprets — furnishes the real touchstone. Although Hypatia tells him that he's the only one she can talk frankly to because he's made a fool of himself by proposing to her, he still can't bear her brutally frank remarks about himself and her. He tries to dress his own feelings about her up prettily, and demands pathetically, "Can no woman understand a man's delicacy?" When, at the end of the play, young Percival joins her in her foray against the older generation, including Summerhays and her father, Summerhays is so frequently shocked and revolted and dazed at the succession of body blows that the reader almost weeps in pity at the plight of the poor fellow and his ideals. Shaw's younger generation, however, seldom shows any mercy to the older one. Nevertheless, Shaw in his admonishments of Duffin in his *Self Sketches* insists that he does "not want to abolish the family," and regards it as "the natural social unit," even though by itself it is "narrowing and unsocial."

One of the most frequent characteristics of the idealist is to manufacture heroes for himself and worship them, or even to set himself up in the hero's role. The charming Mrs. Jennifer Dubedat in *The Doctor's Dilemma* is a confirmed and unshakable hero-worshiper.[9] Her hero is of course her husband, the able but rascally artist, Louis Dubedat. Jennifer has a feminine fascination that nobody can resist. Sir Colenso Ridgeon's housekeeper Emmy is taken by her at first sight and announces to the doctor that "she'll put you in a good temper for the day, because it's a good deed to see her, and she's the sort that gets round you." Ridgeon himself is soon smitten, and allows himself to be interested in her husband's case, although she is "shocked by" a little white lie that he tells. Jennifer is so confident of Louis's essential goodness and greatness that, she says, none of those who have turned against him (apparently many) have been able to accuse him of any faults when face to face with her. She realizes that he has slight weaknesses involving money and women, but nevertheless insists that if he ever "really dishonored himself by a really bad action" she would kill herself. She reveals her own secret, however, when she describes her girlhood and her dreams of some day sacrificing herself for some man of genius who needs her. Thus she tacitly confesses herself to be both the pursuer and the mother woman as well as the determined idealist. The infatuated but sympathetic Ridgeon thereupon decides to let Louis die by turning him over to another doctor, in order to preserve Jennifer's ideals of her hero. Even immediately after Louis's death she behaves beautifully, dresses herself radiantly, and announces to the assembled and amazed doctors: "We have had a wonderful experience; and that gives us a common faith, a common ideal, that nobody else can quite have. Life will always be beautiful to us: death will always be beautiful to us." Only the epilogue shows her in her true colors as a rather silly, romantic, shallow woman, incapable of understanding what Ridgeon has done and on the verge of marrying again (Louis has told her to, to prove how happy she had been with him). She has written her husband's biography: *The Story of a King of Men. By His Wife.* She is insulted when Ridgeon tells her of his feelings for her, and calls him cruel and inhuman when he tries to disillusion her about Louis. She is a blind idolizer to the end. Shaw himself wrote to Lillah McCarthy, who was to create the role of Jennifer: "I am sorry to have to tell you that the artist's wife is the sort of woman I hate, and you will have your work cut out for you in making her fascinating." So far as the average theater spectator was concerned, Lillah's job could not have been very hard for the first four acts — it is the fifth that upsets the apple cart, if it is properly understood. If Jennifer had turned out to be a pure Philistine like Candida, it wouldn't have been so bad.

Dubedat himself, incidentally, is also something of an idealist as well as an artist. In spite of the fact that he claims to be a disciple of Bernard Shaw, he betrays a basic ignorance of Shaw's ideas when he shocks and puzzles Sir Patrick Cullen by announcing that he strives toward his "ideal" of the Superman "just as any other man strives towards his ideal." Even on his tragically effective death bed he reflects: "I know that in an accidental sort of way, struggling through the unreal part of life, I havn't always been able to live up to my ideal." But in his "own real world," he maintains, he has never been untrue to himself. The number of times he has been untrue to others apparently does not matter. Still, in his *Self Sketches,* Shaw defends Dubedat to the extent of remarking that the artist illustrates one of his "pet theses, which is that no man is scrupulous all round. He has, according to his faculties and interests, certain points of honor, whilst in matters that do not interest him he is careless and unscrupulous . . . He had his faith, and upheld it."

Judith Anderson, the young wife of the middle-aged parson in *The Devil's Disciple,* is, however, an unequivocal case, though she finds, to her own stunned surprise, that she has contradictions in her character that she had never suspected. Lacking in "vitality," she is "pretty, proper, and lady-like." She has been "petted into an opinion of herself sufficiently favorable to give her a self-assurance which serves her instead of strength." In her face are the "pretty lines of a sentimental character formed by dreams." Henderson styles her a "New England Lydia Languish." She is, then, a rather "pathetic creature" who needs manly protection in return for the adulation she can give; and from this point of view, Shaw states, her husband might have done worse, and she could scarcely have done better. Naturally, at first meeting, a fragile female of this type could hardly do less than be genteelly repelled by a bold, impudent rogue with such a reputation as Dick Dudgeon's. She is "ostentatiously shocked" when orphan Essie, whom she has condescended to without sympathy or understanding, simply mentions Dick's name; and when, on being introduced to her, Dick promptly acknowledges the introduction by commenting, "I'm sorry to see by your expression that you're a good woman," she is so shocked that she can find no reply. In fact, being shocked is her commonest experience. To her own unsuspicious incredulousness she falls head over heels in love with the spawn of Satan. The usual spell of the lovable reprobate over the pure and conventional woman exerts itself. Though she swears to her husband, "I do hate him," she unconsciously confesses the true state of her feelings in her next sentence, "I can't get him out of my mind." From then on, her conflicting feelings make her behave like a real womanly woman to Dick, "raging at him like an angry child," courting him instinctively to stay with her, and bursting into tears when he rebuffs her. Finally, when the British soldiers start to lead him off to jail in mistake for her husband, she is so overwhelmed by his unexpected sacrifice that she "almost falls" into his arms, and when he, to make the masquerade complete, asks for a farewell kiss, she, "with a sudden effort, throws her arms round him; kisses him; and swoons away, dropping from his arms to the ground as if the kiss had killed her." On her husband's return she is torn between duty and instinct in telling the truth about the arrest, and she completely misunderstands his behavior in his plans for saving Dick. As Duffin remarks, her "romantic folly" would never have come to light if her husband had only taken five seconds to explain the purpose of his flight. Later, all her pride and coldness gone, she helps Dick to divine her new feelings for him, and, even after he has repulsed her at the gallows, there is no longer any restraint on her part, and she clings to his hand and "throws herself on his breast in agony." Her shame and revulsion are of course great when Anderson brings back the American troops in the nick of time, and saves Dick. To Dick's comment that he has behaved like a fool in the whole affair, her reply is, "Like a hero"—to which he ironically responds, "Much the same thing, perhaps." And as the curtain goes down, she makes him promise never to tell her husband what has actually gone on. After all, Henderson suggests, since Anderson has really turned out to be a hero too, it is natural that her love should flood back to him. Here is romantic hero-worship quintessentialized in the form of the new satiric melodrama that Shaw was then writing.

Male specimens of the genus are also not hard to find. There is, for example, Hector Hushabye, alias Marcus Darnley, in *Heartbreak House*. Marcus Darnley is the pseudonym Hector takes when he goes out philandering, and enchants young Ellie Dunn so that she wonders whether she ought to marry Boss Mangan after all. Hector, a "very handsome man of fifty, with mousquetaire moustaches, wearing a rather dandified curly brimmed hat," has had a life, as he tells Ellie, which "has been one long romance . . . He is a Socialist and despises rank, and has been in three revolutions fighting on the barricades." After he has received the revelation of his real identity "with a mixture of confusion and effrontery," and Ellie has called him a liar, a braggart, and a coward, Hesione Hushabye assures her privately that if anyone presumes to doubt Hector's courage "he will go straight off and do the most horribly dangerous things to convince himself that he isn't a coward." His peculiarity is that he never boasts of anything he has actually done, and all the tall tales he tells are made up. Nevertheless, he does vindicate his claim to his own peculiar brand of heroism when, in the last act, after his wife hears the "splendid drumming" of the planes in the sky, he calls it "Heaven's threatening growl of disgust at us useless futile creatures," and becomes Shaw's prophetical mouthpiece when he goes on to explain: "I tell you, one of two things must happen. Either out of the darkness some new creation will come to supplant us as we have supplanted the animals, or the heavens will fall in thunder and destroy us." When Mangan asks whether he will "save England" with "his moustache and fine talk," he says yes, if England will let him, but England, he is afraid, prefers Mangan. Nevertheless, during the raid he turns on all the lights in the house again after the others have turned them off, and is disgusted when the raid is over and they are all safe—except for the two "burglars." His bravery, however, seems to stem from the same emotion as his wife's: "And how damnably dull the world has become again suddenly!" Here is one of the troubles with Heartbreak House, the symbol of England itself. This sort of heroic idealism, this thrill-seeking, can scarcely save the world—if the world deserves saving.

The idealism of Mazzini Dunn, in the same play (a regular rabbit warren of idealists), is more quietly appealing, even if not much more useful. Mazzini is, as Mrs. Hushabye says, a man who improves on acquaintance. In the middle of the play she tells him frankly: "I'm beginning to like you a little. I perfectly loathed you at first. I thought you the most odious, self-satisfied, boresome, elderly prig I ever met." With his usual meekness Mazzini rejoins: "I daresay I am all that. I never have been a favorite with gorgeous women like you." He confesses that many women have fallen in love with him because they thought him quite safe, and quickly fallen out for the same reason. Mrs. Hushabye consequently informs Ellie that her father is "a very wonderful man . . . : the only one I ever met who could resist me when I made myself really agreeable." Ellie, of course, has always thought her father "the best man I have ever known," even if he has not been a success in the worldly sense.

The truth about him comes out little by little in the play. As Mrs. Hushabye somewhat fuzzily describes his antecedents, "Mazzini was a celebrity of some kind who knew Ellie's grandparents. They were both poets, like the Brownings; and when her father came into the world Mazzini said 'Another soldier born for freedom!' So they christened him Mazzini; and he has been fighting for freedom in his quiet way ever since. That's why he is so poor." Certainly Mazzini's "fight" has been quiet, and its result invisible. He is "a little elderly man with bulging credulous eyes and earnest manners." His parents gave him "the noblest ideas," but no profession. So he went into business. Mangan befriended him and gave him capital, and when the business failed (along with the capital of other investors) Mangan, who had planned things that way all along, bought it up and made Mazzini manager. And, strange to say, Mazzini proved to be an excellent manager (showing how Big Business needs both the operator and the organizer), though he has been very poorly paid. Mangan knows his man well enough to comment, "He'd think anything rather than the truth, which is that he's a blamed fool, and I am a man that knows how to take care of himself." And Mangan is right, since Mazzini refuses to believe the revelation of how he has been exploited. Perhaps Shaw intends to imply that the apparently extraneous Billy Dunn, the burglar,* is Mazzini Dunn's other self — the "thinking" Dunns versus the "drinking" Dunns. When Mazzini, to everybody's astonishment, captures the burglar and almost shoots him, the burglar complains: "You, that nigh blew my head off! Shooting *yourself,* in a manner of speaking!" But it is Hector who compares the success of Mazzini, "as an idealist," with that of Mangan, "as a practical business man" — to Mazzini's advantage. Nevertheless, Mazzini even idealizes all the misfits in the play by describing them as "very charming people, most advanced, unprejudiced, frank, humane, unconventional, democratic, free-thinking, and everything that is delightful to thoughtful people." After explaining how he once tried to reform the world by joining societies and writing pamphlets in

---

* In his essay on "Imprisonment," however, Shaw assures his readers that the Burglar here, with his carefully calculated blackmailing, "is not a joke; he is a comic dramatization of a process that is going on every day." Similarly, in a speech that he had made to the Executive Committee of the Fabian Society in 1885 he had humorously compared the profession of burglar to that of the speculative capitalist.

expectation of the revolution which never came, he states his final philosophy: "It's amazing how well we get along, all things considered . . . I often feel that there is a great deal to be said for the theory of an overruling Providence, after all."

According to Shaw's implications, even the first murderer in the Garden of Eden was an idealist and self-romanticizer. He was also a primitive Darwinian, with his fallacious deterministic ideas about the survival of the fittest and the winnowing out of the weak by the strong. Cain, in *Back to Methuselah,* contrasts himself conceitedly with his father Adam, who never does anything but dig: "No progress! No advanced ideas! No adventures! . . . To be the first murderer, one must be a man of spirit." He is portrayed as "insistently warlike . . . To his parents he has the self-assertive, not-quite-at-ease manner of a revolted son who knows that he is not forgiven or approved of." But he makes much more impression on Adam than he does on Eve. When he suggests taming other people to work for them as slaves, Adam alone is struck by the idea; Eve calls him a "monster," a "fool to his very marrow." Intoxicated by the terrible joy of killing, he wants his mother to create more so that he can destroy more, and goes on to describe how battle can intensify the beauty and pleasures of love. "Man," he tells his mother, "shall be the master of Woman, not her baby and her drudge." Eve, however, scathingly but ineffectually tries to expose to him his real bondage to his pampered wife, Lua. Although he thinks himself a hero, Eve calls him "Anti-Man," and scolds him violently for exalting the physical only. In a sort of parody on Ibsenian and Shavian individualism, Cain maintains that in not listening to the Voice in the Garden and in killing his brother he was merely asserting *himself,* as Abel should have done too. Then, he insists, afterward the Voice "gave me right . . . He who bears the brand of Cain shall rule the earth . . . I dare all truths . . . without danger I cannot be great." Echoing some of the arguments of Byron's Cain, he maintains that by quitting his digging he has set himself free to learn "nobler crafts" of which the others know nothing. Soon he evolves the theory that in the end a man like himself "dictates what the Voice shall say." More and more drunk with his own eloquence and new thoughts, he tells his father, "I revolt against the clay . . . Stay with the woman who gives you children: I will go to the woman who gives me dreams." He is afraid of nothing, will be bound by no conventions. But Eve reprimands him by pointing out that she has had such thoughts too, but had rejected them: "I thought for a moment that perhaps this strong brave son of mine, who could imagine something better, and could desire what he imagined, might also be able to will what he desired until he created it." When, however, he admits, "I do not know what I want, except that I want to be something higher and nobler than this stupid old digger," Shaw makes it clear that Cain's dreamy ideals actually lack all but the first of the four steps that the

Serpent has described to Eve in the first act as necessary to creative evolution: "To desire, to imagine, to will, to create." Finally, Eve sums up her denunciation of her son by voicing her dissatisfaction thus: "He steals and kills for his food; and makes up idle poems of life after death; and dresses up his terror-ridden life with fine words and his disease-ridden body with fine clothes, so that men may glorify and honor him instead of cursing him as murderer and thief." The echoes here of the opening of the second chapter of *The Quintessence,* on death, masks, and ideals, written thirty years earlier, may be unconscious on Shaw's part, but they are unmistakable.

Anyone knowing Shaw knows his belief that false concepts of patriotism are often at the bottom of evil actions, and especially of wars. Thus General Sir Pearce Madigan, in *O'Flaherty V.C.,* Shaw's anti-war "Recruiting pamphlet," is an impervious idealist in his attitude toward king, patriotism, war, duty, and all the rest of the shibboleths of a period of war hysteria. General Strammfest, in *Annajanska, the Bolshevik Empress,* another "Revolutionary Romancelet" of the war, is modeled on the same pattern, though he is of another nationality. In spite of the revolution, he still adheres, in his private thoughts at least, to the old regime. According to him, only the dogs yawned at court, for "they had no imagination, no ideals, no sense of honor and dignity to sustain them." The General had no such handicaps.

But the converse, suggests Shaw, can also be true. Non-resistance can be as much of a romantic ideal as belligerence and pugnacity. Androcles, in *Androcles and the Lion,* is a "humanitarian naturalist," who seems to be an utter coward except when animals are abused. Like Keegan in *John Bull's Other Island,* he is a follower of St. Francis, and is all for kindness and pacifism. Shaw himself, no pacifist or non-resister, of course does not agree, but, at the end of his farce-of-ideas, through his hilarious arm-in-arm waltz of Androcles with Tommy the lion he implies that the proper combination for the future is the strength and force of the lion plus the love and understanding of the Christian slave. "Whilst we stand together," says Androcles to the lion as the curtain goes down, "no cage for you: no slavery for me." From this point of view, which echoes the philosophy of the conclusion of *Major Barbara,* the lion and the giant armorer Ferrovius represent the same force. Yet in his postscript Shaw describes Ferrovius as "the Pauline Ferrovius, who is comparatively stupid and conscience ridden." (To Shaw, Pauline Christianity is equivalent to "Crosstianity," a term which he appropriated from his friend Captain Wilson[10] of the Dialectical Society to indicate the religion of the crucifixion, which he regards as completely different from the doctrines of true Christianity.) Nevertheless, Shaw approves the way in which Ferrovius finally gives way to his militant spirit, which — unlike his assumed pacifism — is "natural" to him. In fact, Shaw is reminded of the conversion of his own parson, Anthony Anderson, to militarism — and of the behavior of most Christian ministers, who promptly become idealists almost to a man as soon as war really comes and makes them abandon their former principles. Irvine would add Todger Fairmile, the Salvation Army wrestler in *Major Barbara,* to the comparison, since Todger also "makes converts by the sweet reasonableness of physical intimidation." It might be added that the "intelligent, cultivated, amiable emperor," as Henderson describes him, stands between the two extremes. Although he becomes "a cruel fool" because Roman institutions forced his tyranny upon him, he politicly inclines toward the side which can best strengthen his own position, since he is too sophisticated to have any religious convictions of his own. Historically this emperor is merely a generic character. He is certainly not Nero. Actually, he of course ought to be Tiberius, since the story of Androcles (which was told by Aulus Gellius and originally had nothing to do with Christianity) was first associated with his reign. But this emperor refers to the reign of Domitian as well in the past. On the other hand, there is nothing in him of Constantine, the first imperial convert to Christianity, many years in the future.

Aubrey, the preacher-burglar of *Too True To Be Good* (the "threat" in this title is commented on by Duffin), may well serve to complete this selected portrait gallery of Shaw's idealists. Aubrey, or Popsy, a "quite good-looking" young man with a "disarmingly pleasant" voice, first turns up with Nurse Sweetie as a beginning burglar in the suburban sickroom of the wealthy but discontented Patient. As he himself admits, he is a "born preacher" and "can preach anything, true or false." He delivers his first sermon to Mops, the Patient, at the end of Act I, on the theme: "The well brought up maiden revolts against her respectable life. The aspiring soul escapes from home, sweet home . . . henceforth my gates are open to real life, bring what it may." And the Patient comments, "Thank Heaven he's a fool, a lovely fool: I shall be able to do as I like with him." But it soon becomes apparent that he is essentially a conservative, who would be content without any change, so long as he can preach. He has a delicate mind, but when he tells Sweetie, now passing herself off as the Countess, that he can't endure a woman who has no self-respect, she, remembering his former love for her because of the "extraordinary sympathy" between their "lower centres," lectures him: "Don't you be a hypocrite, Popsy: at least not with me." But he is shocked (as well he might be!) by the Patient's figure of people as merely "inefficient fertilizers . . . walking factories of bad manure." He continues to be disgusted by her "mental pictures" and exclaims: "I really cannot stand intellectual coarseness. Sweetie's vulgarity I can forgive and even enjoy. But you say perfectly filthy things that stick in my mind, and break my spirit." But Aubrey still complains to Mops that she hasn't the "instincts of a lady," and he reproves Colonel Tallboys for whacking Mrs. Mopply with his umbrella, though he thanks him for doing so; after all, though, such an act is "unworthy of the name of Briton." In discussing his future with his father, the Elder, he defends his conduct: "If I become an honest man, I shall become a poor man; and thus nobody will respect me . . . If on the contrary I am bold, unscrupulous, acquisitive, successful and rich, everyone will respect me, admire me, court me, grovel before me." Thus, with a parody of the philosophy of Andrew Undershaft, he concludes: "I shall spend another six years on the make, and then I shall retire and be a saint." It is no wonder that Tallboys calls him "the most abandoned liar I have ever met."

Yet it is to Aubrey, rather than the more suitable Patient, that Shaw delegates the final task of trying to explain his play, which apparently is based on his favorite old theme of "men and women with their minds stripped naked." Unlike Sempronius's father, the Ritualist in *The Apple Cart* who got up Lord Mayor's shows, military tattoos, and big public ceremonies, and could never look at nature or people unless they had had their "nakedness dressed up artificially for him," and unlike Mrs. Baines, the head of the Salvation Army in *Major Barbara,* who never looked at anything she didn't want to see, Aubrey now lauds the mental and spiritual undressing that his colleagues have undergone in the preceding moments. However, turning characters upside down as Shaw has done is not quite the same thing as turning them inside out as he says he has done. He himself has to admit his inconsistency in having "given the rascal the last word," and in his preface, in remarking that some of the spectators "felt that they had had a divine revelation," he reminded them that they had "overlooked the fact that the eloquent gentleman through whose extremely active mouth they had received it was the most hopeless sort of scoundrel: that is, one whose scoundrelism consists in the absence of conscience rather than any positive vices, and is masked by good looks and agreeable manners." Nevertheless, Aubrey the preacher, "the new Ecclesiastes," who has previously announced that his gift of preaching is not confined to what he believes, delivers a sermon on the effects of the war on society and especially on the younger generation, prolonged until nobody remains on the stage to hear it and he himself is enveloped in the swirling fog. He talks about "idealisms," "realities," "duties," and "masks," in the Shavian fashion of forty years before, and shows that he himself remains primarily the idealist. He admits that he "shrank from the revelation" of the truth, and that he wants "affirmations to preach," but cannot find them.

As Irvine sums him up, "Aubrey is by no means, as severe critics have remarked, Shaw's last desperate view of Shaw, but he is inevitably an exaggeration of that part of Shaw which stood as spiritual forefather to the twenties. Seldom has an author had the opportunity, at such long range, to criticize a phase of his own tradition." Shaw himself admits in his final stage directions that "fine words butter no parsnips," and that action is all that counts. In fact, he writes, "The author, though himself a professional talk maker, does not believe that the world can be saved by talk alone. He has given the rascal the last word; but his own favorite is the woman of action, who begins by knocking the wind out of the rascal, and ends with a cheerful conviction that the lost dogs always find their way home. So they will, perhaps, if the women go out and look for them."

The conclusion is inescapable that idealizing is all-persuasive and often difficult to distinguish. As a frontispiece for Shaw's *Sixteen Self Sketches,* published when he was ninety-two, the author presented a new engraving of himself, in seventeenth-century style, accompanied by the following apology:

> On Shakespear's portrait Morris ruled
> Ben Jonson was by it befooled;
> For who of any judgment can
> Accept what is not like a man
> As like the superhuman bard
> Who in our calling runs me hard?
> Here is my portrait for your shelf,
> More like me than I'm like myself.
> Not from the life did Pikov draw me
> (To tell the truth he never saw me)
> Yet shewed what I would have you see
> Of my brief immortality.

This Shavian mask Shaw himself has described in his list of illustrations as "Myself Idealized."

# IV

## THE REALIST

SHAW ALWAYS INSISTED that he did not believe in either heroes or villains, and that he simply portrayed human beings with a mixture of motives and actions. But in the melodrama of the nineteenth century, which he was so familiar with and which he used with affectionate irony for the groundwork of several of his plays, there were definite and well-recognized heroes and villains, without whom the play would have collapsed invertebrately. There are few, if any, pure-bred villains in Bernard Shaw; but if any candidates for the function are to be found in him they occur among his rigid and unswerving idealists. Nor is there any doubt at all about where to look for his heroes — for he was too modestly apologetic in maintaining that he did not create any. His heroes, of course, display themselves unmistakably in his category of "the highest" — that is, the realist.

### 1. *Early Specimens*

Just as there are different gradations among his idealists, some being more reprehensible and some more lovable than others, so his realists approach perfection by degrees. Some are flawed and some are polished; some are static and some are dynamic, spinning out the plot from within themselves like the spider as they develop. In fact, even before Shaw had reduced his human fauna to categories and applied basic labels to them, he had been at work with some assiduousness on the realist in his novels. Not always, it is true, did he work his specimens out with complete clarity and lack of contradictions, but the main outlines were observable even from the time of *Immaturity*.

This first novel, like so many first novels, was in a way a piece of self-flattery, since Shaw was obviously projecting himself into the character of his unripe hero, Robert Smith. Smith, in spite of his callowness and provincialism, is critical, skeptical, and hard to please. He is youthful but independent, and hesitant to form relationships with others. In other words, although Shaw does not use the term directly, Smith is realistic. And he is matched with Harriett Russell, the kind of heroine to whom Shaw was early attracted. Harriett is Scotch. Shaw does not say whether this origin accounts for her being both rational and charming without being positively beautiful. It is hard to turn her into a racial type, since he relatively seldom draws on Scotland for his characters or for national characteristics. But Harriett's chief defect seems to be a certain lack of imagination. Perhaps her general domination by pure common sense prevents her from meeting Shaw's later complete standards for realism, but she is clearly a girl whom he admires. Another interesting specimen, although her outlines are somewhat blurred, is Lady Geraldine Porter, whom Shaw describes as "robustly minded." Lady Geraldine, a wealthy patroness of the arts, has the unconventional, dogmatic turn of mind which stamps most of Shaw's realists, in spite of the fact that she indulges in such self-consciously deprecatory remarks as to say of herself, "Philistine as I am, I enjoy aestheticism after a fashion." That qualification is enough to mark her as only a part-way realist.

Nevertheless, Shaw was enough impressed by his own creation to reintroduce Lady Geraldine into *Love among the Artists* as "a lady of strong common sense, resolutely intolerant of the eccentricities and affectations of artists." But she merely pops in and pops out again as one of the minor links that Shaw, like so many other novelists, was fond of forging to draw the social world of his dramatis personae together. Mary Sutherland, his new heroine, is a more complex case. Another example of his early favorite feminine type, Mary is distinguished-looking rather than beautiful; intelligent, naturally analytical, and sensible rather than emotional. After (to the reader's considerable surprise) she has deterred the terrible-tempered musician, Owen Jack, from going through with his proposal to her, in spite of her guilty feeling that it is her duty to "fill the empty place in Jack's heart," she gives in to the siege laid against her by the Philistine John Hoskyn, in whose presence she never felt humbled as she often did because of the exactingness of Jack or the "delicate taste and nervous solicitude for her dignity and comfort" that had marked the attentions of her previous lover, the artist Adrian Herbert. The scale is really turned in Hoskyn's favor by Lady Geraldine, who assures Mary that geniuses like Jack do not make good husbands or wives. Although Mary protests feebly that she will "never admit that a man is not the better for being a hero," she still acts on Lady Geraldine's common sense advice, and abdicates as the realist that she has started out to be.

Shaw's verdict on Mary is confirmed in *Cashel Byron's Profession,* where she turns up incidentally, along with most of the rest of the cast of *Love among the Artists,* as a London hostess, famous for her "Sunday evenings," where she brings together all the clever people she meets and makes them so comfortable that they are only too eager to come again. As one of her friends puts it, "But she has not, fortunately for her, allowed her craze for art to get the better of her common sense." There is probably not a happier couple in England than she and her unimaginative husband. But common sense is not sufficient to make a complete realist.

There are other realistic disappointments in *Cashel Byron's Profession*. Cashel himself, the famous pugilist, though he is at first so simple and direct as to seem almost stupid, and although he always wants to know the real truth about things and is apparently not impressed by mere appearances, turns out to be "a man of emotion who never thinks." In spite of the shocking lecture that he insists on delivering at Mary Hoskyn's party on "executive power," culture, art, and prize fighting, he is tremendously impressed by the discovery of his dead father's social standing, marries the aristocratic Lydia Carew, and, with one of Shaw's impish tricks of prestidigitation, ends by becoming a Radical M. P.

Lydia herself, however, is Shaw's most complete study of a realist so far discussed. She has been brought up as a bluestocking by a wealthy, disillusioned, intellectual father, who spent most of his time traveling and who had a considerable reputation as a cynical critic, philosopher, and student of sociology, science, and the fine arts. Left an orphan, she herself is a discriminating critic of art and literature, opinionated and independent enough to be feared by most men, but sometimes naive and ignorant of everyday life. Although she questions the sincerity of most people's conduct in such matters as mourning family deaths, she is still capable of being momentarily shocked by the discovery of Cashel's "profession" and by his natural and somewhat vulgar behavior. Nevertheless, fascinated against her will by the strangeness of this handsome, virile young man, and being, after all, "eminently reasonable," she eventually comes to typify aristocratic tolerance and broadmindedness, and marries him. Shaw thus balances his "man of emotion who never thinks" against his "woman of introspection, who never stops thinking." Lydia herself, after stipulating that Cashel give up boxing, describes her match as "a plain proposition in eugenics." But then, after all this realism and frank reasonableness, marriage claims its prey. Lydia now has little time left to think, even about herself, and eventually, after she has become a mother, she comes to regard Cashel himself as merely one of her children — as, in spite of his Radicalism, he probably deserved to be.

Contrasting with what might be considered as Lydia's deterioration is the ripening of her companion, Alice Goff. Alice starts out as the complete idealist. She idealizes her mother, who herself is stuffed with ideals about wifely duty, filial duty, and all the rest. Alice also idealizes the gentleman; and she cannot appreciate art. For most of the way through the novel she is the embodiment of middle-class snobbery and prudishness. But then, through the technique of a mere author's fiat, which mars so much of Shaw's characterization, she comes to recognize the truth about herself, and is reborn. With equal abruptness so is Lucian Webber, whom she marries. Whatever one may think of the plausibility of the affair, here at least is one of the earliest instances of the favorite Shavian pattern of an idealist being turned into a realist.

Leaving Stanley Trefusis, the unsocial Socialist, to be treated as a Socialist as well as a realist, there remain the two previously mentioned characters in *The Irrational Knot* — the ineffable Edward Conolly, who marries the idealist Marian Lind and treats her so brutally, and Marian's close friend, Elinor McQuinch. The remainder of what needs to be said about Conolly, being also one of Shaw's New Men and an American, as well as the most thorough-going and uncompromising realist in his novels, may also be profitably postponed until later. Shaw himself, when he came to write a preface to a new edition of his novel some years afterward, made a sort of recantation and apology for Conolly: "When I was tired of the sordid realism of Whatshisname (I have sent my only copy of *The Irrational Knot* to the printer, and cannot remember the name of my hero) I went to the piano" — and played *Carmen!* This music, "exquisite of its kind, . . . could enchant a man like me, romantic enough to have come to the end of romance before I began to create in art for myself." Nevertheless, Shaw brought Conolly back to the scene again in *Love among the Artists,* where he has mellowed slightly.

In *The Irrational Knot,* which rigidly poses the conflict between the realist and the idealist, with a resolute attempt to alienate from his realist the sympathy of the average reader (i.e., the Philistine and the idealist — though Shaw does not yet use these terms openly), Nelly McQuinch is a much more pleasant specimen. Nelly is "a small, lean, and very restless young woman with keen dark eyes staring defiantly from a worn face." She is a rebel, a great reader, and a would-be fiction writer — in fact, she finally publishes a novel which is highly praised by the intelligentsia. She is sharp-tongued, and has retained no illusions. She assures Marian that she doesn't ever mean to be married, and, as Shaw's raisonneur, she announces later: "Marriage is a mistake. There is something radically wrong in the institution." Her good instincts are shown by the fact that she is immediately irritated by Conolly on their first acquaintance. But although Shaw entrusts her later with the task of telling him some home truths that he needs to know, the engineer is only good-humored and superior about it all, and Shaw keeps the nose of his story reined tight toward its unhappy conclusion, in which Conolly calls in vain on his wife for a final repudiation of all womanly duties and principles.

## 2. *The Triumph of the Realists*

After Shaw had abandoned the privacy of the novel, which must always remain a closed circuit between the author and the individual reader, for the living theater, in which the playwright's conceptions become embodied in the actors' flesh for a massed audience, he brought his consuming concern in the clash between the idealist and the realist to an early climax in *Arms and the Man*. In this anti-militaristic comedy, which represents the triumph of realism over idealism, almost every character of any consequence eventually finds his place in the realistic category, whether he has been there by nature from the start or has discovered the truth about himself and life only after a more or less soulwrenching conversion. At long last, too, Shaw has decided to make peace with his public, and give it what it wants. He has learned that he can, paradoxically, create romantic situations and sympathetic characters in an ostensibly anti-romantic play. The audience can like the whole cast of *Arms and the Man* to its sentimental heart's content — an entirely new departure for Bernard Shaw.

The change is especially notable since in the three preceding plays, which Shaw mockingly confessed in his group title were "Unpleasant Plays," almost none of his characters — and none of his realists — had failed to find their unadmiring critics. The mysterious preface-writer who signs himself merely "M." in the American edition of *Plays Pleasant and Unpleasant* says disgustedly of young Dr. Trench and Blanche Sartorius, while trying also to remain scientifically objective, "*Harry* and *Blanche* are the natural products of their environment, and consummate their sordid, fleshly union without a vestige of illusion as to the baseness of their motives." Trench, it is true, does become a selfish, cynical, half-way realist, bribed by his desire for Blanche, but his impulses in admitting his disillusion are still mean, and he has none of the tolerance and broad understanding that marks the true member of the guild.

Charteris, in *The Philanderer,* is something of a problem. He is referred to frequently and apparently sincerely by his associates as a philosopher. He has no illusions, even about himself, and Julia charges, correctly though wrathfully, "There is not in his whole nature one unselfish spot." He loves to conjure sarcastically with terms like "duty." Ranging himself among the anti-idealists, he remarks that he loathes the "scientific conscience" as he does "all the snares of idealism." But even if he is to be taken at his own evaluation, he is an unsympathetic realist so far as most of the audience are concerned. The skeptic might almost maintain that Charteris is really an idealist because of the way he idolizes individualism. Nevertheless, Shaw himself once vehemently assured Archibald Henderson, who frankly confessed his distaste for Charteris: "Charteris is not passionless, not unscrupulous, and a sincere, not a pseudo, Ibsenist." Obviously the author felt hurt and insulted because, as everybody recognized, he had built much of himself into his Philanderer.

On the other hand, critics like Duffin feel that "Charteris somehow contrives to be a very likeable person." It is even easier, however, for most people to like Grace Tranfield, who, although drawn to Charteris, appraises him with a realistic eye, and concludes that it is safer to remain simply on terms of friendship with him. But through most of the play she is primarily an agreeable sample of the pursuing woman.

Vivie Warren in *Mrs. Warren's Profession* is another anomaly. Praed sums her up after meeting her once: "I'm not sure, from what I have seen of her, that she is not older than any of us." Yet Vivie is just out of college. She is ruthless for truth, and demands to have every mystery surrounding both her mother and her father revealed. She has lost all her illusions about "love's young dream" and "the romance and beauty of life." She never cries or faints; she wishes to be kept from sentimentality; she sees through "fashionable morality"; she rejects her "duty to her mother." She does not believe in "circumstances" shaping life; man makes his own character. But when, after she has at first taken the revelation of her mother's "Profession" with some philosophic equanimity, she learns that Mrs. Warren is still in "business," she reacts somewhat as Trench and Blanche did when they first learned the source of her father's and his incomes. Indeed, Vivie can never quite bring herself to use the proper term for her mother; she still has reticences. In addition, although Frank Gardner, her exquisite loafer of a lover, one day sees "a touch of poetry" about her which has previously been missing, she has some of the qualities of the Philistine in her negative attitude toward the fine arts. Her leading characteristic is that she is dominated by her ambition. She wants to amount to something. As the aesthetic Praed sadly puts it, she is primarily "a great devotee of the Gospel of Getting On." In other words, she is a pragmatic materialist — which falls somewhat short of being a true realist.

Vivie's creator also had a rueful and injured comment to make on the girl in his valedictory to play-reviewing in 1898. Wrote Shaw: "One of my female characters, who drinks whisky, and smokes cigars, and reads detective stories, and regards the fine arts, especially music, as an insufferable and unintelligible waste of time, has been declared by my friend Mr. William Archer to be an exact and authentic portrait of myself, on no other grounds in the world than that she is a woman of business and not a creation of romantic impulse." He goes on to brand Archer's identification as preposterous, as he would hardly do if he thoroughly approved of Vivie himself. In fact, in his *Self Sketches,* he returns to the charge in attacking Charles Shaw's[11] statement that Bernard modifies his "objections to smoking when, as in the case of a woman, it is a symbol of revolt." No, reiterates Shaw, "I hate to see a woman smoking; but I do not on that account represent women in my plays as non-smokers. Vivie Warren smokes cigars because her living original did so.* Louka smokes cigarettes because Bulgarian girls do." Nevertheless, more recent critics than Archer, such as Alick West,

* This original, thinks Rattray, was Susan Lawrence.[12]

still feel that Shaw identifies himself to a considerable extent with Vivie, just as he had done with her predecessors like Lydia Carew, Trefusis, and Conolly.

Certainly Louka, in *Arms and the Man,* although full of feminine schemes and wiles, is a more appealing character in her streaks of realism than is the mannish Vivie. In fact, to West she is the only real and convincing character in the play, because she sees the reality of capitalist society, as Bluntschli and the others do not. She is a "proud" and "defiant" girl who has no sympathy for the romantic raptures which her mistress Raina indulges in before her transformation. She appeals to Sergius's "common sense" to deter him when he tries to make love to her. She too is ambitious, and has a "soul" above that of a servant. She is not ashamed of the devices she has used when her love for Sergius is at stake, and she promptly avails herself of her first opportunity to call her former mistress democratically by her Christian name. Still she is repelled by the more self-adjusted realism of her fellow-servant Nicola, even though it is he who has "made a woman" of her; and she tells him disdainfully, "You take all the courage out of me with your cold-blooded wisdom." Shaw describes Nicola as a "middle-aged man of cool temperament and low but clear and keen intelligence," possessing "the imperturbability of the accurate calculator who has no illusions." Nicola, however, knows his place, and candidly admits that he has "the soul of a servant": "Yes: that's the secret of success in service." The opinion of the reformed Sergius, after Nicola has renounced his claims to Louka's hand, is that this renunciation is "either the finest heroism or the most crawling baseness," and he leaves the decision as to which is the proper description to the ultimate authority, the complete realist, Captain Bluntschli, the Swiss mercenary. Bluntschli minces no words: "Nicola's the ablest man I've met in Bulgaria."

Bluntschli himself, of course, is the ablest man in the play [13] the ablest that Shaw had yet put into any of his plays. Although he is, on the whole, of "undistinguished appearance" and has "a hopelessly prosaic nose," he also has "clear quick blue eyes, . . . a sense of humor," and "all his wits about him." After Sergius has admitted that he and his prospective father-in-law, Major Petkoff, had been completely outtraded by "that consummate soldier," Sergius spitefully but truly describes Bluntschli as "like a commercial traveller in uniform. Bourgeois to his boots." Yet Bluntschli's famous tales about the typical military mind are as contemptuous as Shaw's own. His hilarious description of the ridiculously suicidal but lucky cavalry charge was based, according to Henderson, not on "The Charge of the Light Brigade," but on Kinglake's more realistic account. Graham Wallas had also given Shaw an officer's story of a similar ironical episode in the Franco-Prussian War.

Bluntschli is so sure of himself and so unself-conscious that he is not only

perfectly willing to admit to Raina that he is nervous and scared to death
of being captured but even offers to cry if she scolds him. He has seen so
much of life and is so tolerant of it that he is not bothered by such human
weaknesses as other people's lying, and he knows how to puncture Raina's
vanity when she waxes melodramatic. He even belittles himself by talking
about his own "incurably romantic disposition," and Raina, vexed at the
unflattering response that she has got after practically proposing to him,
calls him "a romantic idiot." But when he discovers that she is really twenty-
three and not seventeen, he behaves very sensibly, asks Petkoff for his
daughter's hand in a practical fashion, and laughs "a boyish laugh of delight" when Raina happily calls him her "chocolate cream soldier." Although
the play in which Bluntschli appears no longer has the shocking novelty that
it once did, he himself is a captivating conception. But after all why should
he not be, since he was modeled on Shaw's non-pareil Socialist friend, Sidney
Webb? Irvine, however, remarks that in Bluntschli "with some exaggeration
one might maintain that Shaw discovered the dramatic potentialities of
the Benthamite robot." West is even more contemptuous when he damns
Bluntschli as representing "the prosaic practicality of Fabianism," a man
"with no principles and no aim in life, except to make money."

The romantic pair of Raina Petkoff and Sergius Saranoff, however, are
the prize exhibits, because of their transformations. Sergius is the kind of
handsome, dashing, moustached young officer that any susceptible young
lady would adore. Bluntschli derisively remarks that Sergius led the fool-
hardy but lucky Bulgarian cavalry charge "like an operatic tenor." (Raina's
own reference to *Ernani* in connection with Bluntschli suggests that part
of the idea for the play may have come to Shaw from that opera.) Sergius's
constant play-acting, his chivalrous kneeling and kissing of ladies' hands, and
his impressive idealization of the "higher love," all give Shaw a chance to
travesty popular romantic love scenes that he is not slow to seize. Perhaps
his happiest turn was an outright theft from his friend the "hidalgesque
and fantastic" Cunninghame Graham, as Henderson calls him. Graham —
once, like Shaw, also on the staff of *The Saturday Review* and also the
author of a book on Morocco that was to give Shaw some ideas for *Captain
Brassbound's Conversion* — had recently made a telling speech in the House
of Commons, in which he had introduced the haughty phrase, "I never
withdraw." Shaw sagaciously put the words into the mouth of Sergius,
and had him ring various changes on them, such as "I never apologize," "I
am *never* sorry," and "Nothing binds me." In fact, so fond did Shaw grow
of the idea that he used several variations of it for other later characters.

It is not remarkable that a sentimental girl like Raina, perhaps based
slightly on the actress Alma Murray (although Shaw once startled Pearson,
after remarking that Annie Besant "had absolutely no sex appeal," by
adding that she was Raina's original), should at the beginning worship

even Sergius's portrait as if it were an ikon. She is first shown to the audience on a balcony, "intensely conscious of the romantic beauty of the night, and of the fact that her own youth and beauty is a part of it." Byron and Pushkin are her favorite authors. She rhapsodizes about "heroic ideals," war, and patriotism. To her "the world is really a glorious world for women who can see its glory and men who can act its romance." She wants her relationship with Sergius to be "quite perfect" — "the only really beautiful and noble part of my life." She is prone to engage in day-dreaming, always picturesquely. She is inordinately proud of the Petkoffs' culture, which is based on an inside flight of stairs and the only library in Bulgaria (stocked with a few gift books and some paper-covered, broken-backed novels). She pretends to be shocked at the "coarseness" of one of Sergius's stories, and also pretends to feel remorse at her own lying.

Yet, as it turns out, both Raina and Sergius are only sham romanticists. In fact, Shaw has warned his readers about Sergius at the outset in a lengthy stage direction, which would of course be accessible to an audience only through the impersonation of a highly skilled actor. The contradictory idealism and realism in Sergius are due, Shaw says, to the advent of Byronism in Bulgaria. So this "clever, imaginative barbarian has an acute critical faculty." He broods on his own and others' perpetual failure "to live up to his imaginative ideals." His life is full of "petty disillusions" which his "infallibly quick observation" is continually drawing to his attention. Thus he is always seeing himself on his own stage, and he is not sure which is his real self, for he perceives at least six different characters within him. Though he finds in battle that, to his surprise, he really is a brave man (for a brave man will defy anything that "sets itself up against his own will and conscience"), he finally admits that war is "the dream of patriots and heroes! A fraud, Bluntschli, a hollow sham, like love." As he puts it fairly early in the play, "The glimpses I have had of the seamy side of life during the last few months have made me cynical." But he is not too cynical to succumb to the campaign of Louka and to give up Raina when he sees she too is a changed person, and is about to capture Bluntschli. In the last act Bluntschli as the author's spokesman comments on Sergius: "He's found himself out now." The play, as Shaw stated in his preface to Archer's *The Theatrical World of 1894,* was intended to be an "attempt at Hamlet in the comic spirit," but the obtuse audience dismissed his "introspective Bulgarian" merely as a "swaggering impostor of the species for which contemporary slang has invented the term 'bounder.'"

Nor should Raina's transformation come as an utter surprise to an alert audience, for Shaw hints just after the rise of the curtain that her mind is always questioning and commenting on her own actions. She remarks to her mother, for instance, "When I buckled on Sergius's sword he looked so noble: it was treason to think of disillusion or humiliation or failure."

But she obviously was thinking of them. Later she admits that she is always being tempted to "shock his propriety — to scandalize the five senses out of him!" And after she has been subjected to the sterilizing influence of Bluntschli for a time we find her manner changing abruptly "from the heroic to the familiar," as she demands of him: "How did you find me out?" Frankly she confesses her own previous play-acting, and is glad it is over. Her last illusions disappear when she hears about Sergius and Louka, and she can fall an easy victim to her own sense of humor. Even in learning the whole truth about Bluntschli she can look facts in the face. She, like the rest, is now a true realist.

### 3. *The Diabolonians*

Rebels always extract a special pleasure from shocking the conventional and the orthodox by siding with other rebels, and turning devils into gods — and vice versa. For it is almost axiomatic with them that the rebel who has to keep his eyes open and his brain sharp in order to survive will see the true facts more clearly than the conservative who sees only what it will profit him to see. Shaw's fondness for imps and devils goes back to his childhood when he was a patron of the pantomime, but it did not stop there. There is a dominant element of impishness in all his thinking and writing, and the Devil becomes incarnate over and over again in his favorite characters — that is, in his realists. Not all of these realists, it is true, embody what in his preface to *Three Plays for Puritans* he calls "Diabolonian ethics," but many people would only too eagerly admit that several of his most abominable characters, as well as the author himself, are the devil personified. Certainly such self-consciously infuriating heroes in the novels as Sidney Trefusis in *An Unsocial Socialist* and Owen Jack in *Love among the Artists* made this sort of diabolical impression on most of their associates.

The first self-confessed adherent of Mephistopheles in the plays is Dick Dudgeon in *The Devil's Disciple,* modeled upon Richard Mansfield, who, says Henderson, failed to be properly grateful. Dick taunts the assembled relatives and neighbors at the reading of his father's will by telling them the history of his discipleship — how he was brought up in "the other service," but how he perceived from the first that the Devil was his "natural master and captain and friend." For he realized that the Devil "was in the right, and that the world cringed to his conqueror only through fear." So Dick prayed secretly to him and promised him his soul. In this way he escaped having his spirit broken in his mother's Puritan "house of children's tears," and became a man as a result. In the preface Shaw broadens out the character by tracing the whole Diabolonian genealogy from Prometheus and Siegfried through Bunyan and William Blake to Nietzsche and even (playfully) Robert Buchanan. Nevertheless, Duffin complains that Shaw has not made sufficiently clear in the play itself what he means by Dick's "devil-

worship." Irvine, too, finds that "As a puritan Dick is impressive, but as a
diabolonian he is a little tame." However this may be, anyone remembering
the opening chapter of *The Quintessence* will soon begin to recognize that
one big reason for Dick's unpopularity is that he is one of Shaw's "indulgence preachers," just as his Puritan mother is an "abstinence preacher."
Or, as Irvine puts it, he is "a natural ascetic in revolt against an unnatural
ascetic." Dick's "good" consists of thinking and saying and doing things
that society has forbidden, but in the end, after his self-surprising deed in
risking his life to save the Rev. Anthony Anderson, he has convinced the
inhabitants of the little New Hampshire hamlet of Websterbridge that he
is a hero and not a devil. As he has told Judith to tell her husband, "I am
as steadfast in my religion[14] as he is in his." In fact, at the end of the play
the two men are preparing to reverse their professions, Anderson to exchange
the church militant for the Springtown militia, and Dudgeon to "start presently as the Reverend Richard Dudgeon" and "wag his pow" in the minister's old pulpit, where he can preach his personal doctrines even to Shaw's
heart's content. West sees this kind of conversion of a rebel, which Shaw
intended to be "a criticism of idealism in terms of realism," as actually a
surrender of the rebel and "his reconciliation to the society he had challenged," and interprets it as a revelation of Shaw's own abnegation of the
principles with which he had begun.

The mystery of why Dick behaved in a way so seemingly out of character is one if the Shavian cruxes, through no fault of the author's, but because of the sheer perversity and sentimentality of audiences, directors, and
actors. Why did Dick let himself be captured in mistake for Anderson?
Was his motive a hidden love for Judith, as she wants desperately to believe?
Was it respect for Anderson? Was it unconscious admiration for their
family life? Was it a desire to increase the colonists' determination to resist?
Was it the martyr complex? Was it mere diabolonian recklessness?

Of course, the average audience would like to believe that the deed was
one of self-sacrifice for love, not knowing, or forgetting, Shaw's usual contempt of self-sacrifice. Indeed, after one of the reviewers had insisted that
what Dick said was only a gentlemanly lie to hide the real state of his
feelings and preserve Judith's respectability, Murray Carson every night
thereafter "confirmed the critic by stealing behind Judith, and mutely attest-
ing his passion by surreptitiously imprinting a heartbroken kiss on a stray
lock of her hair whilst he uttered the barren denial." Unfortunately, as Shaw
says, he was in Constantinople at the time and had no knowledge of the
sacrilege until too late. Yet he makes it clear in both the dialogue and the
preface that Dick, to his own initial bewilderment, was simply acting according to the "law of his own nature." He acted for himself alone, and
not for Judith, or Anthony, or society at large. Self-sacrifice as a motive for
altruistic actions, Shaw implies, is permissible, even admirable, so long as it

is performed out of a genuine inner compulsion and desire and not because of a sense of "duty" or social pressure. Dick's character is so independent that he always does what he alone thinks right. In this case, although in his renunciation of the opportunity for love he reminds one somewhat of Marchbanks in his realization that this sort of bourgeois domesticity is not for him, he incidentally saves two other people while he preserves his own self-respect. His diabolonian realism is tinged with mysticism and his own brand of Puritanism, but he sees himself and the others realistically nevertheless.

The Devil's Disciple finds a strange, though very minor, echo in The Shewing-Up of Blanco Posnet, the second of Shaw's two plays with an American setting. Blanco is a disreputable blackguard, "with the fire of incipient delirium tremens" in his eye. But he "carries his head high, and has a fairly resolute mouth." He interlards his somewhat synthetic American frontier slang with scraps of moral verse, which show his respectable upbringing. But now he is a reckless rebel, conducting a one-man war against God himself (a circumstance which so shocked the Lord Chamberlain that he forbade the performance, and the play had to be given by the Abbey Theatre in Ireland). For, as Blanco sees him, God — or at least the God of his hypocritical rascal of a brother, Elder Daniels, and the God of the churches — is another abstinence preacher. But this jealous God, nevertheless, says Blanco, finally caught up with him to spite him because he had no use for Him. Then suddenly Blanco, to his own discomfited surprise, emulates Dick Dudgeon and performs a good deed. He runs off with his brother's horse in payment for a debt (an act which he says neither God nor the Devil tempted him to do; he did it on his own), he meets a woman with a sick child, he gives her the horse, and, thus demounted, he is overtaken and arrested as a horse-thief, while the child dies. So God, who to Blanco is equivalent to the Devil, has had his revenge by turning him into a "softie." When Feemy Evans also turns into a softie, however, and refuses to testify against him, Blanco experiences a conversion. He climbs onto a table as "Elder Blanco," and, grappling with Job's problem of the reason for good and evil, tells the assembled frontiersmen and -women in Shaw's name that it is all a question of playing the "great game" versus the "rotten game," and that God and the Life Force (though Blanco naturally does not know the term) sometimes overcome man's individualism and independence. What man must learn is to accommodate himself to the mysterious purposes of the Lord. When Duffin, unable to believe his eyes when they saw Shaw's text in this moral mood, remarked that Shaw was "wisely content to leave it [the problem of evil] at its irony," Shaw in his Self Sketches solemnly corrected him by reminding him of Blanco's question about the origin of the croup, and its answer. "There is," says Shaw, "a studied theory of Creative Evolution behind all my work; and its first complete statement is the third act of *Man and Superman*."

At this point it would certainly be appropriate to discuss John Tanner, whose addiction to *Revolutionist's Handbooks, Maxims for Revolutionists, Socialism, Don Juanism,* and shocking Roebuck Ramsden would qualify him as one of Shaw's diabolonians. As Shaw says in his preface, Tanner is "a true Don Juan, with a sense of reality that disables convention, defying to the last the fate which finally overtakes him." Ann wins him only after she "dares to throw away her customary exploitations of the conventional affectionate and dutiful poses and claim him by natural right for a purpose that far transcends their mortal personal purposes." But, since Tanner is also a tentative adumbration of the coming Superman, and since Supermen of course must be realists, he will fit even more appropriately into a later chapter.

But the prize specimen of Shaw's diabolist, the one who is the most soundly and philosophically based, is Andrew Undershaft — "Saint" Andrew Undershaft — from *Major Barbara,* which, as Shaw confided to Henderson, might well have been called *Andrew Undershaft's Profession.* So as to leave no possible doubt as to the impression that Shaw wishes his "hero" (as he specifically designates Undershaft in his preface) to create, he has Adolphus Cusins lavish all sorts of affectionately diabolical labels on him, running all the way from "a most infernal old rascal" to "Mephistopheles," "Machiavelli," "Dionysos," and "The Prince of Darkness." The motto which Undershaft has chosen for his munitions firm is "Unashamed." He is an ingratiating anti-Christ, however: "Always clever and unanswerable when he was defending nonsense and wickedness," says his wife; "always awkward and sullen when he had to behave sensibly and decently." "But," she confides further to her scandalized son Stephen, "your father didn't exactly *do* wrong things: he said them and thought them: that was what was so dreadful." On the surface, Shaw's stage direction attests, Andrew seems easy-going, kind, patient, and simple. But he has "a watchful, deliberate, waiting, listening face, and formidable reserves of power, both bodily and mental." He is the kind of strong man who is gentle because he has "learnt by experience that his natural grip hurts ordinary people unless he handles them carefully." But he is not afraid to hurt when it is necessary. Shaw once told Henderson that he got the germ of the idea for Undershaft from his author-neighbor Charles McEvoy, whose father, who had fought on the side of the Confederacy during the American Civil War, had, at the close of the war, set up a factory to manufacture torpedoes and various other explosives. Since the elder McEvoy was a "grey-haired gentleman, of peculiarly gentle nature and benignant appearance," Shaw was tickled by the ironic contrast, and decided to put him into a play.

Undershaft's terrifying discovery, which Shaw himself had first made when he read Henry George's *Progress and Poverty* in 1882 and followed it up with Marx's *Capital,* is that poverty is "the greatest of evils and the worst of crimes, and that our first duty — a duty to which every other consideration should be sacrificed — is not to be poor." This summary of his doctrine — another phase of his theory of one's duty to oneself — Shaw presented to his stunned and incredulous public in his magnanimous preface appropriately entitled "First Aid to Critics." Many years later in his *Self Sketches* he confessed that his hatred of the slum tenements that his nurse sometimes took him to when he was a child was really at the bottom of his philosophy and led him after fifty years to writing *Major Barbara.*

However understandable psychologically Shaw's conclusions may be, Undershaft's philosophy, which seemed to be a direct negation of the anti-militaristic views expressed in such works as *Arms and the Man,* has shocked and puzzled and stunned not only naïve motion picture audiences but also more sophisticated critics like Henderson and Duffin. Even Eric Bentley acknowledges that in *Major Barbara* we have some pretty "tough dialectic." Shaw's argument is not only that it was infinitely better for Undershaft to make his sensible choice between poverty and "a lucrative trade in death and destruction" from his own individual point of view, but also that society as a whole and on the whole profited by the trade in cannons and the establishment of a model town for the workers, even though it is utterly anti-democratic and the caste system prevails. Here perhaps one might raise the embarrassing question that Vivie Warren asked her mother and that Shaw then seemed to approve of. Granted that it was proper for Mrs. Warren to embark on her "profession" to escape poverty, why did she continue in it after she had become rich? Is the munitions industry so much more socially valuable than prostitution? If the answer is that at least it provides comfortable living and working conditions for its employees, Mrs. Warren could undoubtedly reply that she did the same thing for her girls.

Actually, of course, Shaw is, as often, making his main point, as his compatriot Jonathan Swift did in *A Modest Proposal,* by fantastic exaggeration. In a better organized society, preferably a Socialist society, the government would not leave it to each individual citizen to find his own means of avoiding poverty. The state would see that the citizen had his place in the whole. Thus Shaw, through Undershaft and Peter Shirley, attacks the whole structure of private charity through such organizations as the Salvation Army. Shirley represents the "honest poor man," whom society pretends to admire but really despises and rejects. The less scrupulous Bill Walkers really get along better in our world today. Undershaft is the "wicked rich man," who has been more lucky and successful than Bill Walker and whom all look up to and honor.

The choice "St." Andrew offers Dolly Cusins is whether or not he has the courage to accept the instruments offered him to "make war on war." Man is naturally destructive, he has reminded Lomax (echoing the Devil in *Man and Superman*). Even the Salvation Army has the motto, "Blood and Fire." Similarly, maintains Undershaft, "My sort of blood cleanses: my sort of fire purifies." He believes in power, he trusts in strength. Only after a man can stand solidly on his own feet can he afford to think about the "virtues." After people's bodies are fed, he echoes Marx, their souls can be fed too. "Your Christianity," he tells the family, "which enjoins you to resist not evil, would make me a bankrupt. My morality — my religion — must have a place for cannons and torpedoes in it . . . There is only one true morality for every man; but every man has not the same true morality." And he soars to greater mystic heights. He is, he insists, a "confirmed mystic." He feels always that he is after all "only the instrument of a Will or Life Force which uses him for purposes wider than his own." Even while he is announcing the "true faith of an Armorer," he also reminds his hearers that even an Armorer has no will of his own any more. He is driven by a will of which he is only a part. The Devil has become God's Advocate.

On a more prosaic but still plausible plane is Irvine's sagacious comment that Undershaft is really a Marxian rather than a Nietzschean figure, for he "preaches struggle because he believes in class struggle," and when he foresees his own downfall and superseding he does so in the belief that he will be followed not so much by the Superman as by a classless society. His manufacturing of munitions is simply his way of leveling an accusation against society. As Bentley says, Undershaft has simply remained in the capitalistic phase of the conflict. From either point of view, however, his mind and methods are diabolonian. Alick West, on the other hand, writing from the rigidly Communistic point of view, sees Undershaft only as a capitalist, and regards the play as the final step in Shaw's fall from the grace in which he began his career — a good man fallen not only among Fabians, but eventually among capitalists. But Paul Hummert, in an unpublished study of the Marxist elements in Shaw's works, interprets *Major Barbara* as the most complete statement so far of Shaw's Marxism and writes: "West completely ignores the significance of Undershaft's waging war on war, of Undershaft's proletarian origin, of Undershaft's strengthening the workers, of Undershaft's hatred for poverty caused by the factory system. Indeed, if Undershaft were to be simply the champion of capitalism, why didn't Shaw make him a wheat tycoon, or a wood magnate — why a munitions manufacturer?"

It may be somewhat startling to find a bishop of the Church of England classified among the diabolonians. But, after all, Bishop Alfred Bridgenorth of *Getting Married* admits himself, "I'm a very funny bishop." Bridgenorth, patterned on Mandell Creighton, the late Bishop of London, and somewhat cryptically nicknamed "the Barmecide" by the members of his family, perhaps because most of them regard the intellectual feasts that he spreads before them as illusory, is so open-minded that he is tolerant even of the Devil. As he says, "If we are going to discuss ethical questions we must begin by giving the devil fair play . . . England never does. We always assume that the devil is guilty: and we won't allow him to prove his innocence, because it would be against public morals if he succeeded . . . And the consequence is that we overreach ourselves; and the devil gets the better of us after all. Perhaps that's what most of us intend him to do." This sample of the Bishop of Chelsea's mischievous humor and latitudinarian thinking (James M. Bridie in *G.B.S.* 90 calls him "Laodicean") is borne out by his broad views on marriage, divorce, Mahomet, polygamy, duty, and the celibacy of clergymen. He is the raisonneur of this most discursive of discussion dramas, and voices Shaw's own opinion that the only solution to the problem of marriage is to "make divorce reasonable and decent."

In politics, perhaps, even more than in the church, one might expect to find the diabolonian, or at least the Machiavellian, realist. Warwick in *Saint Joan* is touched with this brush, but perhaps is really little more than a practical soldier-politician. Old Hipney in *On the Rocks* is the homely, shrewd, deceptively simple political analyst and strategist throughout, disillusioned with democracy and ready for any strong, intelligent dictator to lead the world out of the mess it is in. He voices unpopular ideas with great authority and conviction. But King Magnus in *The Apple Cart* is the best and most fully developed representative of the genre, disarming and appealing because of his suaveness, cleverness, and humor. Frankness on obvious points is part of his shrewdness, as when he admits to the Cabinet that he has not won his inherited position on his own merits. Orinthia tells him that he is less of a fool and less of a moral coward than any other man she has known; in fact, he has almost the makings of a first-rate woman in him. Lysistrata is even sharper. When Magnus points out that the people have unconsciously found out long ago that democracy is a humbug, and that not only do the people themselves not govern but that "the responsibility and the veto now belong neither to kings nor demagogues as such, but to whoever is clever enough to get them," she chimes in smartly, "Yourself, sir, for example?" Magnus modestly admits that he is still in the running. The whole Cabinet realizes that he has always been too clever for them in dealing with crises. He even goes so far as to admit to Orinthia that she is right, "in a way," when she resentfully charges that she believes he would sign her death warrant without turning a hair. Yet he knows how to use flattery too when the occasion calls for it, as in his dealing with Boanerges, the new President of the Board of Trade.

In his preface Shaw explains that his play exposes "the unreality of both democracy and royalty as our idealists conceive them," but adds that the real contest is between democracy and royalty on the one hand versus plutocracy, represented by the great trust, Breakages, Inc., on the other. In this contest royalty, being the cleverest, wins by threatening to use the methods of democracy. Says the King, echoing Sergius's rhetoric, "I never fight. But I sometimes win." He should have said, "But I always win."

In comparison with Magnus, Charles II in *In Good King Charles's Golden Days* is only a diluted diabolonian, but he would be highly appreciative of Magnus's creed and technique. Charles, under his favorite nom de plume of "Mr. Rowley," realizes that since his "father's business is abolished in England" he himself is "far less important now . . . than Jack the fish hawker," and that he must live by his wits. He analyzes the current political situation shrewdly. He expresses Shaw's own view on the inadequacies of governments and elections. He hates "blood and battles." At the age of fifty, he has learned too much about most women, and has come to love his wife Catherine truly and to appreciate her fine qualities. Bodies are all alike, he has concluded. "It is the souls and the brains that are different." Admitting to a "troublesome conscience," he declares that, nevertheless, no two consciences are the same any more than any two human beings are the same, and comes out for a relativistic philosophy: "What is right for one is wrong for the other." In his preface Shaw claims that he has rendered the Merry Monarch "an act of historical justice."

Finally, Shaw has even given us a specimen of an ex-diabolonian in Captain Shotover of *Heartbreak House,* whose stories of his own youth make his allegiance quite clear. In fact, Nurse Guinness goes still further when she remarks, "They say he sold himself to the devil in Zanzibar before he was a captain; and the older he grows the more I believe them."

### 4. *The Disillusioned*

The foregoing diabolonians and Machiavellians have always been sure of themselves, and so there has been little opportunity for character development in their cases. But the many Shavian characters who have achieved ultimate realism only through a series of disillusionments are perhaps more dramatically interesting.

Even in his potboilers, long and short, Shaw is so obsessed with the good moral lesson of learning by experience that he fills them up with characters who adjust themselves to life by jettisoning their false ideals and becoming realists. Sometimes this process has taken place in the antecedent action, but when it takes place actively on the stage it furnishes the backbone of the plot. In the former instance, it is because Annajanska, the Grand Duchess of the Panjandrums of Beotia, early saw through the illusions and shams at court and realized that she was "only a girl like other girls" that she was able to take advantage of the Revolution and transform herself into the Bolshevik Empress. Before the war O'Flaherty, V. C., was as romantic and visionary as any Irishman, but the war's disillusions built up his character so that he was able to stand up not only to General Sir Pearce Madigan but even to his own mother. In *The Glimpse of Reality* the rakish young fifteenth-century Italian noble Ferruccio, when he was young, "dreamed and romanced: imagining things as I wanted them," but when he is threatened with death, he comes "up against something hard: something real," and begins to discard his illusions. His religion is the first thing that falls away from him, and he is ready to look all truths in the face. He concludes, "When I believe in everything that is real as I believed for that moment in death, then I shall be a man at last." So impressed by his transformation are the hired murderers that they decide to let him go. And in *Village Wooing* the young woman who is simply and economically named "Z" is a romanticist who has always yearned to travel, but when she actually gets her chance is so disappointed by what she sees that she is glad to go back to the reality of her own village.

The most instructive case from the one-act potboilers, however, is that of Henry the poet in *How He Lied to Her Husband*. Henry first wanders onto the stage as "a very beautiful youth, moving as in a dream." He presses his "hands to his eyes to shut out reality and dream a little." His married inamorata, Aurora Bompas, emphasizes the point by telling him cautiously, "It's very nice of you to live with me in a dream, and to love me, and so on." When he tries to allay her presumed fears about her husband's reactions by telling her, "I have followed the Greek ideal and not neglected the culture of my body. Like all poets I have a penchant for pugilism," she becomes genuinely alarmed, and confesses, "I thought you were only a boy, a child, a dreamer. I thought you would be too much afraid to do anything." So Henry begins to awake to the truth about his ideal. At first he gropes through his past memories (or are they Shaw's memories?): "Once or twice in my life I have dreamed that I was exquisitely happy and blessed. But oh! the misgiving of the first stir of consciousness! the stab of reality! the prison walls of the bedroom! the bitter, bitter disappointment of waking!" He cannot at once relinquish his original character, however, and exclaims, "This is some terrible dream . . . Help me to find my way back to the heights." But finally he is forced to admit that he can see nothing but the ruins of their dream remaining. At last he grants the truth, and diagnoses his case and all such cases as "growing pains." He faces reality just before the topsy-turvy scene with the unexpectedly proud and definitely not insulted husband: "The process of growing from romantic boyhood into cynical maturity usually takes fifteen years. When it is compressed into fifteen minutes, the pace is too fast; and growing pains are the result."

These growing pains are by no means confined to Henry Apjohn. Epifania Fitzfassenden of *The Millionairess* comes through the period with perhaps the least inconvenience and suffering, but her transformation from her girlhood world which her imagination "had peopled with heroes and saints" to her mature one of callous pragmatism can be better treated under her basic type of the Manly Woman.

Gloria Clandon, Valentine's opponent in the Duel of Sex in *You Never Can Tell,* has been taught by her advanced thinker of a mother to reject all duties as such, to obey nothing but her sense of right, and to respect nothing that is not noble; and yet she speaks of all this as her duty. She wants to discuss all matters "coolly and rationally," and yet she "loves the name of mother" while hating that of father. She is emotionally unaffected by the unhappiness of her newly discovered father, Crampton, wants no "pretty speeches" from Valentine, and insists that she does not intend to get married. Her growing pains are therefore concentrated but severe, in their brittlely farcical fashion, before she learns what life has intended for her. Gloria reverses the usual process, perhaps, in that her disillusion has taken place in a purely abstract manner under her mother's tutelage before the girl really had any illusions of her own to get rid of.

It is the anemic runt of an intellectual, Bentley Summerhays, who first describes Joey Percival, the amateur aviator and famous "man with three fathers" in *Misalliance.* (The name may well have come from the aeronaut, Percival Spencer, who, according to the reminiscences of Blanche Patch, Shaw's faithful but un-Shavian secretary, in *Thirty Years with G.B.S.,* conducted Shaw's own first aerial flight in 1906 in a balloon.) Joey has Bentley's brains, combined "with a full-sized body," but the combination has not produced equilibrium or a liberal mind. Joey is afraid of doing anything incorrect. As the son of "three fathers," he distrusts all "wild impulses." He is simply too well brought up. He has a half-felt desire to be free, but says he can be so only if he can count on the behavior of other people. He demands the "protection of a good stiff conventionality among thoroughly well-brought up ladies and gentlemen." But when Hypatia gets to work on him his standard ideals begin to disintegrate. Under her direct and unabashed treatment he finally breaks down and tells the family how their roles in the garden were suddenly reversed and he, the pursued, became the pursuer. Spurred by his new radical frankness, he asserts boldly that it really doesn't matter "which particular young man some young woman will mate with." Holding out against premature capture, he argues that he hasn't enough money to marry, but when Hypatia demands of Tarleton, "Papa: buy the brute for me," he bargains successfully with the successful business man, while announcing brazenly that love is not necessary for a satisfactory marriage. His liberation from his former priggish idealism is clinched by his admission that he no longer has any veneration for the older generation or for paternal sentimentality as such. Another Shavian realist has been made.

The Elderly Gentleman in *Back to Methuselah* is a much more tragic case — in fact, the most tragic case of all, since his transfiguration results in his death. Starting as a pure-bred British idealist, with an adulation of the British past, with assorted inhibitions, with a high degree of shockability, and with apparently conventional conceptions of God, science, and human progress, under the rapid influence of the Long Livers he reveals the suppressed doubts that he has long had, tries to persuade his colleagues to tell the truth about the Oracle's ambiguous but derisive answer, refuses to go back home with "liars," and bursts out: "I cannot live among people to whom nothing is real. I have become incapable of it through my stay here. I implore to be allowed to stay." But the only way he can be granted his request is to die from the Oracle's "emanations." He has purchased his "glimpse of reality" with death. But he died happy.

Mrs. Mopply and her daughter, known interchangeably as the Patient and Mops, in *Too True To Be Good,* represent a similar process, with the daughter experiencing her growing pains and beginning to adjust her previously worthless life at least two acts before the mother. In her final self-summary, in which she discusses with the Sergeant and the Elder the inadequacies of poverty, wealth, and love, and the necessity of keeping the world going "by the people who want the right thing killing the people who want the wrong thing," she announces, "I have found myself out thoroughly — in my dream." As Shaw puts it in his preface, the main moral of the play is the cruelty of our society to the rich and the discovery that a so-called "good time" brings only unhappiness. The illusions about the life of the wealthy must be destroyed.

But Shaw's most elaborate and sympathetically treated case of disillusionment is that of Ellie Dunn in *Heartbreak House.* No one probes the heights and depths of romance and heartbreak and comes out with a more Shavian philosophy than she. Described as young, pretty, slender, fair, and intelligent-looking, "evidently not a smart idler," she nevertheless is dominated by all sorts of illusions when she first comes to Captain Shotover's. She intends to marry Boss Mangan purely out of "honor and gratitude" to him for what she thinks has been his goodness to her father. When the romantic Mrs. Hushabye demands why Ellie doesn't marry someone she loves, Ellie refuses to listen, although even then she is carrying on a clandestine flirtation with the gallant Marcus Darnley, who soon turns out to be Hector Hushabye. She is attracted to the story of the love of Desdemona for Othello, which she doesn't consider exactly a "romance" because "It might really happen"; but she finds Othello's jealousy "horrible." Yet she insists that she doesn't "fall in love with people."

When Darnley's true identity is revealed, Ellie is in "great distress," but outwardly appears to recover quickly, and "damns" herself bitterly for having been such a fool as to be taken in so easily. Yet the results of her disillusion begin to show themselves immediately. As Shaw says, "She begins prowling to and fro, her bloom gone, looking curiously older and harder."

She confides to Mrs. Hushabye, "I have a horrible fear that my heart is broken, but that heartbreak is not like what I thought it must be." Hesione assures her, "It's only life educating you, pettikins" — in other words, it is growing pains. Consequently, when Mangan frankly discloses how he really ruined her father "as a matter of business," she is not shocked and overwhelmed as she would have been that morning, and calmly assures him that she intends to marry him anyhow. Since marriage is a woman's business, she will marry him to make "a domestic convenience" of him — and also so that she can be near Hector. To her father she promises that she won't do anything she doesn't want to do and mean to do for her own sake. To the shocked and sentimental Hesione she asserts that if she can't have love that is no reason why she should have poverty.

This cynical and mercenary stage, however, is only a temporary one in her development. After Mangan in his trance has heard the others confess their true opinion of him, she comments philosophically on his outraged sufferings, "His heart is breaking: that is all . . . When your heart is broken, your boats are burned: nothing matters any more. It is the end of happiness and the beginning of peace" — a typically Shavian doctrine. It is the old Captain who ushers her into a new phase. When he tells her that she should look ahead and she insists that she is being very prudent in marrying Mangan, he reminds her that, although it may be prudent to gain the whole world and lose one's own soul, the world has a faculty of slipping away, whereas one's soul sticks to one if one sticks to it. Ellie responds with Shaw's own earlier doctrine that it's only the old-fashioned who think one can have a soul without money. "Young people nowadays know better." After she has expressed the further views of the "modern girl" on morality and income, and he has preached the old-fashioned view on selling oneself, she disagrees by upholding the indivisibility of the soul and the body. Nevertheless, as she listens to him explain his dreams and his hopes, she feels that she could be calmer and happier married to him than to anyone else — though he promptly informs her that he probably still has a black wife somewhere in Jamaica. Together they reach the climax of their conclusions about life. They agree that she is "one of those who are so sufficient to themselves that they are only happy when they are stripped of everything, even of hope." With this discovery, Ellie begins to feel "as if there were nothing I could not do, because I want nothing," and the Captain praises her discovery: "That's the only real strength. That's genius."

Just before the air raid starts, Ellie sums up what she has learned about life as the result of the day's disillusioning experiences: "There seems to be nothing real in the world except my father and Shakespear. Marcus's tigers are false; Mr. Mangan's millions are false; there is nothing really strong and true about Hesione but her beautiful black hair; and Lady Utterword's is too pretty to be real. The one thing that was left to me was the Captain's

seventh degree of concentration; and that turns out to be—" And the
Captain booms out: "Rum." Nevertheless, she does not retract her choice
of him as her "spiritual husband and second father," the "natural captain"
to whom she gives her broken heart and her "strong sound soul." Yet while
she proclaims, "I know my strength now," and waxes very mystical about
the possible blessings on everything except Mangan's money, simultaneously
admitting that she doesn't understand a word of what she has said, but
knows that it means something, the Captain remains sound asleep. Perhaps
Shaw's meaning is that in the purely spiritual union between Ellie's youth,
vigor, and new skepticism, and Shotover's experience and aspirations something of value to society might have been found. But, when the invading
air fleet attacks, Ellie, remembering the England which actually exists,
calmly and clear-sightedly, with none of the thrill-seeking emotionalism of
Mrs. Hushabye, calls on Hector to set fire to the house so that it will be
marked out for the bombs of the raiders. When their bombs miss the main
target, blow up the clergyman's house, and kill only the two "burglars," she
is acutely disappointed, and prays that the planes will return again the next
night.

A further clue to the meaning of Shaw's symbolism is to be found in his
preface, where he assaults one element in English society, Heartbreak House
as opposed to Horseback Hall, as aiming at being advanced and free-
thinking, and being familiar enough with revolutionary ideas—on paper
alone. Power and culture, he says, have been put into separate compartments; and since England had to admit that it had not learned how to live,
all it could do was to boast that it knew how to die. But when it did not
die, and the war had torn off many of the masks from education, art, science, and religion, all that resulted was that society was left "glorying grotesquely in the license suddenly accorded to our vilest passions and most
abject terrors." Few were like Ellie, he implies, in realizing that most of
society must be destroyed before a better society can start to be built.

Another class of idealists, a few of whom are capable of having their
illusions demolished and becoming realists, are the politicians and statesmen.
Sir Arthur Chavender, the "Bolshy premier" of *On the Rocks,* is a first-rate
specimen, but since he is even more interesting as one of Shaw's full-length
portraits of a political leader, he will be presented later as such. The Secretary of the League of Nations in *Geneva,* written some years after Shaw
had himself attended a meeting of the League and just before the outbreak
of the Second World War, is a sufficiently characteristic example to stand
for his type. The Dutch Senior Judge of the Court of International Justice
at the Hague is another example in the same play, but, although he is even
more of an idealist and optimist at first, he is not so far developed as the
Secretary. In general, the Judge's approach is more positive, the Secretary's
more negative.

Shaw describes the Secretary as "a disillusioned official with a habit of dogged patience" because of the necessity of dealing with ignorant and prejudiced "distinguished statesmen" of the nationalist stamp. "One pities him," says Shaw, "as he is of a refined type, and, one guesses, began as a Genevan idealist." Early in the play he tells the hopeful Judge that he was once on his side, until his experience taught him how hopeless it was to try to knock out "supernationalism" (which he carefully distinguishes from internationalism) in the League. What Geneva needs most, he is bitterly convinced, is something higher than nationalism, "a genuine political and social catholicism." At present, the League hangs over Europe "like a perpetual warcloud." He grants that the League is not quite futile, since in little ways that the public knows nothing about it is possible to sidetrack the nationalists; but as a real power in world politics it is useless. Finally, goaded by the dangerous inanities of Begonia Brown and the rest, he reviews his personal history. When he arrived at Geneva, he admits, he was himself "a patriot, a Nationalist," regarding his own appointment as a victory for his country in the game of diplomacy. But the atmosphere of Geneva soon changed him into an Internationalist. Now, he bursts out, "I am the ruthless enemy of every nation, my own included. Let me be frank. I hate the lot of you." He hates the Jew and the Widow because in each of them two or three nationalities mixed together are worse than one. He hates the Russian because "his government has declared for Socialism in a single country . . . Trotsky is nothing to me; but I hate all frontiers; and you have shut yourself into frontiers." He hates the Newcomer and even Sir Orpheus, because they are all "enemies of the human race." Yet he still has confidence that "Geneva will beat you yet," though probably not in his time. Better informed than the rest about such things as the quantum theory and astronomical orbits, he is skeptical to the last about the value of the trial of the dictators, and so Shaw is forced to give the last encouraging word to the more optimistic Judge, but through the disillusioned Secretary he has been enabled to utter some of his most caustic views about the League of Nations and the possibilities of international coöperation. He has demonstrated the unlikely possibility that even a politician can be a realist.

## 5. The Nature Worshipers

Disillusioned and consequently clear-sighted or iconoclastic and diabolonian as people like the Secretary and King Magnus may be, their realism is relatively narrow and limited because they lack a leavening quality which people like Dick Dudgeon and Andrew Undershaft have. These broader and completely adjusted characters are in harmony with themselves and come to be in harmony with their environments because they feel strongly within themselves a link with something better and greater than they. This is what Shaw in his earlier works called simply "Nature," to whose power and operations, under the conventional label of "the Lord," even Blanco Posnet was converted in the end. "Nature," "the Lord," "spirit," and "Life" are of course synonymous with the favored term of the Creative Evolutionists, the "Life Force." Many of Shaw's realists are marked characteristically by their realization and acknowledgment of the role played by Nature in their lives.

Mrs. Knox, in *Fanny's First Play*, according to her friend Mrs. Gilbey, "is very religious, but she's quite cheerful." Mrs. Gilbey herself, although described by Shaw as "placid," is not always quite so cheerful, since her conception of religion is indicated by her remark to her husband: "Now, Rob, you know we're all sinners. What else is religion?" But Mrs. Knox, "a plain woman, dressed without regard to fashion, with thoughtful eyes and thoughtful ways that make an atmosphere of peace and some solemnity," knows that if a girl like her daughter "hasn't happiness in herself, she won't be happy anywhere." To the men Mrs. Knox points out the difference between Margaret's impulses and those to which they have been tempted to give way: "But don't think, you two men, that *you'll* be protected if you make what she did an excuse to go and do as *you'd* like to do if it wasn't for the fear of losing your characters. The spirit won't guide *you*, because it isn't in you; and it never has been." Thus the staunch religionist turns out to be the tolerant and liberal one. Even though she can take Darling Dora's "measure without prejudice," she feels that Bobby Gilbey ought to marry her, simply because he feels that he ought to. It is Nature speaking, and Nature should be respected.

It would be hard to find two women more superficially different than Mrs. Knox and the good-looking, resolute, young Roman patrician, Lavinia, in *Androcles and the Lion*. Mrs. Knox is middle-aged and serious; Lavinia is young and always laughing, even with death just around the corner of the arena. Yet both are clear-sighted and fearless in speaking their minds, and both respond to their inner natures as the only trustworthy guides to their conducts. As a Shavian primitive Christian, who rejects the Beatitudes as spurious, Lavinia is unorthodox enough to argue cogently that it is only the weak who are meek, and her nature forces her to applaud Ferrovius's ill-suppressed instinct to fight his persecutors. Lavinia speaks eloquently to the young Roman Captain about the necessity of facing bravely "the great reality," which is God. "Nothing else is real enough to die for," she assures him, even though she isn't quite certain what God is. "When we know that, Captain, we shall be gods ourselves." Although in his notes Shaw describes her as "a clever and fearless freethinker," at the end of the play she is still refusing to be "prudent," and planning to continue to "strive for the coming of the God who is not yet." Her hearkening always to the voice of this inner spirit is so devoted and sincere that, under the influence of her beauty, fearlessness, and convictions, the aristocratic Captain, at the outset an apparently conventional and utterly humorless imperialist officer, begins to discard his false ideals and is well on the road to becoming a humane realist himself as the curtain goes down.

Margaret Knox was urged to a more free and open life by hearing the "good swinging" hymns at the "great Salvation Festival at the Albert Hall." Barbara Undershaft, "the Salvationist," who, Henderson suggests, may have been partially modeled on Eleanor Robson, achieves her ultimate spiritual peace by breaking with the Army and accepting in the place of its teachings the philosophy of her sainted father, the munitions millionaire. Like Lavinia, she is energetic, robust, and jolly — that is, vital. Her mother says that ever since she has been a major in the Army she has shown a propensity to have her own way and order people about which cows even Lady Britomart. Her dominant motif is shown at once when she asserts confidently, "My father has a soul to save like everyone else," and she sets out to save it according to Salvationist principles. To her, there are neither good people nor scoundrels: "there are just children of one Father." Religion, she believes, is not an unpleasant subject; in fact, it "is the only one that capable people really care for." Her true Christianity, however, Shaw says in his preface, vindicates itself quickly as opposed to the Crosstianity of the Army, with its emphasis on confession, forgiveness, atonement, the Gibbet, and all the rest of the Pauline errors. When Mrs. Baines idealistically accepts the huge donation of conscience-money from Bodger the distiller, whereas Barbara, in her skilled and ruthless operations on Bill Walker's soul, has turned down his bribe of a single pound when his sincere reformation does not accompany it, then her spiritual dilemma proves temporarily too much for her. But, as Shaw says, her "return to the colors," or rather her adoption of new colors, "will clearly lead to something hopefuller than distributing bread and treacle at the expense of Bodger."

The wily Undershaft realizes all along that it "is through religion alone that we can win Barbara." When the love-sick Cusins points out that "Barbara is quite original in her religion," Undershaft agrees triumphantly, exclaiming, "Her inspiration comes from within herself." It is part of her Undershaft inheritance, and the true Undershaft religion is to displace her temporarily misconceived one. She must even become disabused of her romantic love for the common people and their poverty before she can join her father in helping the children of the poor "to climb up beside us." As E. Strauss observes in *Bernard Shaw: Art & Socialism,* this attack on the "poor but honest" common man is pointed up by the picture of Snobby Price, who talks like a Socialist, but acts like a rascal. So in the depths of her despair and disillusionment she regains her faith through her father's reassurance and arguments for the good that she can still do by adopting his methods. When he tells her of his spiritual conviction that even he is in the grip of a higher power or will than his own, she surrenders to it. She has had a living illustration of how the old religion and morality have failed, and she perceives that a new belief is called for. She becomes "transfigured" as she realizes that her new mission is to let herself be used by God in "the work he had to create us to do because it cannot be done except by living men and women." Her growing pains are over, and the acceptance of the mystical creed of the Life Force accompanies her coming of age as a realist. All Shaw's adumbrations of the future Superman, as shown in great men of the past like Julius Caesar and the Shavian Don Juan, share this same worship of the Nature which is within them and all created things.

# V

## THE FEMALE OF THE SPECIES

WHEN SHAW WROTE *The Quintessence of Ibsenism,* he had entitled his first chapter "The Two Pioneers," and had devoted it to two of his favorite character types, the abstinence preacher and the indulgence preacher. He had entitled his second chapter "Ideals and Idealists," but in it, in addition to the idealist, he had offered his conception of the Philistine and the realist. In his third chapter, "The Womanly Woman," he had contrasted the new woman, like Marie Bashkirtseff, with the "ideal" woman of romantic convention, and, in the process of showing the obstacles that the female sex would have to clear away before it could gain its goal of independence and equality with man, had discussed, directly or indirectly, the three sometimes overlapping categories into which womanhood had previously fallen: the womanly woman, the pursuing woman, and the mother woman. In the following years he was to illustrate each of these types richly in his plays.

As his preliminary whipping boy Shaw chose the famous crusading and Radical editor of *The Pall Mall Gazette* and *The Review of Reviews,* William T. Stead, who in 1890 had published a horrified account of the emancipated Marie Bashkirtseff's diary, in which he confessed that he could scarcely bring himself to believe that such a person as Marie could be a woman at all. Obsessed with many ideals, although paradoxically enough he had assisted in tearing the masks away from many others (along with Shaw, William Morris, and Mrs. Besant he had been one of the leaders of the famous Socialist fiasco in 1887 which became known derisively as "Bloody Sunday in Trafalgar Square"), Stead was particularly tender about his ideal of womanliness, and concluded concerning this shocking specimen of the sex: "Marie was artist, musician, wit, philosopher, student, anything you like but a natural woman with a heart to love, and a soul to find its supreme satisfaction in sacrifice for lover or for child." Stead's opinion of the whole duty of woman, thus unabashedly stated, was representative of that of Victorian society.

One of the most prominent traits of the womanly woman, then, is self-sacrifice, in Shaw's opinion perhaps the most abominable of all the idealist abominations. For the ideal of self-sacrifice has been forced upon the "ideal"

woman by the "ideal" or "manly" man as one means of keeping her subordi-
nated to his desires and needs. So thorough and long-continued has been
the indoctrination that he has taken in woman herself, so that most women
have set up the same standards of womanhood as he, not realizing that "the
self-sacrificer is always a drag, a responsibility, a reproach, an everlasting
and unnatural trouble with whom no really strong soul can live." The extreme instance of this kind of self-surrender, says Shaw, is "the reckless
self-abandonment seen in the infatuation of passionate sexual desire," from
which everyone who becomes its object instinctively shrinks. Nevertheless,
as he was forced to admit later, even this extravagant and repulsive pursuit
is only the result of the tireless effort of the Life Force to express itself.
However this may be, woman is generally unconscious both of the larger
implications and of the fact that man is simply using her as a convenience.
Instead of rebelling or loathing herself, she constructs a lovely picture of her
sweetheart's "beautiful, disinterested, pure, sublime devotion to another by
which a man's life is exalted and purified and a woman's rendered blest."
But after the marriage is realized and its usual disappointments are discovered, the idealization is immediately continued under another mask, for
the self-respect that woman has lost as a wife she tries to regain as a
mother. So, though now experienced herself, she still countenances the illusion of ideal love as "a useful and harmless means of getting boys and girls
to settle down." Thus the idealists will listen to no other belief than that
"a vocation for domestic management and the care of children is natural to
woman," and conclude that women who lack these abilities are not women
at all but members of "the third, or Bashkirtseff sex." Woman, decided
Shaw, has become even more the slave of duty than the slave of man, and
unless she repudiates her womanliness and all her duties — to husband,
children, society, the law — all except her duty to herself — she cannot eman-
cipate herself.

Another leading characteristic of Everywoman, declares Shaw in the
"Epistle Dedicatory" of *Man and Superman,* is her unscrupulousness. This,
too, has been forced upon her by man, without his realizing its cause and
often with his violent objection. For woman pursues her purpose with "a
total disregard of masculine fastidiousness." Thus her seductiveness, her fits
of emotion and passion, her tricks, her lies and intrigues are part of the
pattern which has been built up in her by a society which has refused to
allow her to be a free individual in a state of free and equal citizens. In
"The Two Pioneers" Shaw, with his characteristic exaltation of intuition
and instinct over reason, had even warned that the moment woman "sets
about doing things for reasons instead of finding reasons for what she wants
to do, there is no saying what mischief she will be at next." Nevertheless,
although he understands and sympathizes with the dominant "womanly"
types of woman, Shaw's approval goes to the new woman, or Bashkirtseff

sex. Even this type, however, can go to such extremes at times that it earns the flick of his satire.

## 1. *The Womanly Woman*

As a matter of fact, Shaw had already been contemplating the genre of the womanly woman in his early novels, particularly in *An Unsocial Socialist*. Here the sweet Gertrude Lindsay, believing herself in love with the unsocial Sidney Trefusis, the incarnation of Shaw's just-discovered principles of Marxism, has to be persuaded by this cynical young man that she would do much more good by marrying her simple-hearted admirer, Chester Erskine. Sidney's clinching argument, in fact, is, "You will have sacrificed yourself, and will have the happiness which follows that when it is worthily done." His facile arguments about the beauty of renunciation finally wear her down, and Sidney hastily joins the father of his dead wife with the relieved exclamation: "There goes a true woman . . . I have been persuading her to take the very best step open to her. I began by talking sense, like a man of honor, and kept at it for half an hour, but she would not listen to me. Then I talked romantic nonsense of the cheapest sort for five minutes, and she consented with tears in her eyes . . . Yes; you sometimes have to answer a woman according to her womanishness, just as you have to answer a fool according to his folly."

So fresh in Shaw's mind was his thoroughgoing contemplation of the womanly woman in *The Quintessence* that he created Blanche Sartorius in *Widowers' Houses* to incarnate more of his findings. Trench himself calls Blanche's attention to the fact that she had helped him out in his proposal — not, of course, "on purpose," but only "instinctively." Blanche at different times pouts, speaks "with a petulant sigh," "looks round at him for a moment with a reproachful film on her eyes," "bristles," then speaks "desperately," and indulges in other assorted feminine wiles. She even pretends that she doesn't want to marry, but only wants to stay with her father. Yet Sartorius is acquainted with her inflexibility, and knows the truth of her feelings. Of course her feminine and purely instinctive behavior finally wins the prize she is after.

Julia Craven in *The Philanderer*, a reflection of Mrs. Jennie Patterson, Shaw's first mistress, whose persistence caused him infinite trouble, is cut off the same bolt according to the same pattern, but Shaw is even more careful to label her as to her type. "A beautiful, dark, tragic looking woman," Julia makes her first appearance "raging furiously," and, when she finds that Charteris will not let her get at her rival, Grace Tranfield, she strikes him in the face, and informs him immediately afterward: "You belong to me." She threatens scandal, screams and rages, and then turns pathetic and weeps. Sylvia contemptuously calls her "the family baby." Charteris charges her with being jealous of everybody. She wheedles, play-acts, and calls all

Charteris's other women old, ugly, and vicious. Remembering that only
women who are vouched for as unwomanly can be members of the Ibsen
Club, Grace demands that Julia be expelled because of her "thoroughly
womanly conduct." Everybody has discovered that when there is a quarrel
or scandal at the Club, a womanly woman is at the bottom of it. Yet Julia
has previously asked to be told why she is "more womanly than the rest of
them." Old Cuthbertson's eyes, however, light up as he calls her "A fine
creature — every inch a woman. No Ibsenism about *her!*" and adds, "A
woman of that sort likes a strong, manly, deep-throated, broad-chested
man." When Julia recognizes her defeat at the end and bursts once more
into tears, Sylvia scathingly sums her up: "Well, you *are* a womanly one."
Yet even Shaw softens a bit just as the curtain goes down, perhaps remembering that when there are womanly women man has made them so, for
his final stage direction reads: "The rest look at Julia with concern, and
even a little awe, feeling for the first time the presence of a keen sorrow."
Desirable men like Charteris, nevertheless, are repelled by "womanly"
conduct. When Grace herself, temporarily infatuated, like Shaw's actress
friend, Florence Farr, slips into some womanly wiles, Charteris promptly
shies off when he sees her give herself away.

Strangely enough, neither of the womanly women in Shaw's first two
plays showed any marked tendency to self-sacrifice, since they were pursuing
their ends by other means. Nor were they primarily idealists — since idealists
rather than Philistines indulge in self-sacrifice and the womanly woman can
be either. It is the outwardly hard but inwardly idealistic Mrs. Warren in
Shaw's third play who first displays this characteristic. For Mrs. Warren,
after rather self-consciously beginning to whimper and pretend to emotions
that Vivie assures her she does not feel, calls on the rights of a mother in
order to soften her daughter's imperturbability, and reminds her of the
sacrifices she has made in not being able to satisfy her mother love when
she decided it would be best to educate Vivie away from home. Vivie is
merely disgusted, and is never taken in or shaken by her mother's patent
cunning.

It is amusing to note in passing that the Strange Lady in *The Man of
Destiny* has all the tricks of a womanly woman, and yet Shaw adores her.
For the Strange Lady was of course his impersonation of Ellen Terry. She
pretends timidity before Napoleon, and counterfeits wiping away a tear.
She actually breaks down "in the childish rage of impotence" and weeps. She
tries cajolery in vain and racks her brains "for some device to outwit him."
She play-acts until her "heroic pose" becomes ridiculous; and "she leans her
cheek on her hand and laughs at him." She is not above trying her arts
on the stupid lieutenant, too. After she has temporarily bested Napoleon
in one exchange, he accuses her: "You have been guilty of indelicacy — of
unwomanliness." But she is not perturbed, since the device has succeeded.

Because of her hypocrisy — charming as it is — Napoleon tries to diagnose her conduct and methods as typically English, but she gets the last word by informing him that though her grandfather was an Englishman her grandmother was Irish. As the candle burns out, the playlet ends with the pair sitting with their elbows on the table and their cheeks in their hands, simultaneously turning their eyes and looking at one another.

This Strange Lady, indeed, might well be interpreted as a self-sacrificer, since she has embarked on her dangerous mission not for herself, but for her mysterious yet easily recognizable friend. In her explanation of the differing motives in men and women for performing heroic actions, she asserts that great men do great deeds for themselves alone, but that as for women, like herself, "It is only through love, through pity, through the instinct to save and protect someone else, that I can do the things that terrify me."

Womanly women adopt all sorts of disguises. Violet Robinson in *Man and Superman* at first appears to be a realist or a Shavian new woman, but she turns out to be only a shrewd and practical though attractive woman, a pursuer, and a Philistine — that is, a womanly woman. Ann understands and admires her friend, though she admits that "Violet's hard as nails." Octavius, Violet's innocent brother, huffily springs to her defense: "Oh no, I am sure Violet is thoroughly womanly at heart." Whereupon Ann retorts, "Is it unwomanly to be thoughtful and businesslike and sensible? Do you want Violet to be an idiot — or something worse, like me? I have a great respect for Violet. She gets her own way always." Best of all, Violet gets her way "without coaxing — without having to make people sentimental about her." Ann's analysis is the genuine tribute of one expert to another, who happens to use a different but still highly successful technique.

That sensuous, cruel, and charming minx, Cleopatra, in *Caesar and Cleopatra,* develops in the space of a few months from an uncertain, vacillating child to a fascinating, ruthless queen, but it is her womanliness that marks her more than her queenliness. The Persian guardsman in the opening scene reminds his Egyptian comrades: "Cleopatra is not yet a woman: neither is she wise. But she already troubles men's wisdom." Even at this age (Shaw prefers to make her sixteen, although she is generally supposed to have been twenty or twenty-one at the time of Caesar's arrival), she exhibits a love of cruelty toward her slaves, announces that her ambition is to do just what she likes when she is old enough, and admits that she likes "men, especially young men with round strong arms," though so far she is also afraid of them. The wise Caesar, perceiving that the way to control her is through her thirst for power, threatens her with a dire fate unless she makes the Romans "believe that she is a woman." She responds quickly and in a great surge of pleasure over her new role exclaims, "I am a real Queen at last — a real, real Queen!"

But this change is only superficial. After her ducking when she is thrown
from the lighthouse into the sea, which she claims has washed the conceit
out of her, she enters into another and more externally mature phase. Now
she thinks only of Caesar; as Charmian points out to her, she tries to
"imitate Caesar in everything . . . He makes you so terribly prosy and
serious and learned and philosophical." The faithful, savage old nurse,
Ftatateeta, reproaches Cleopatra in another way, for Shaw waggishly makes
her comment, "You are like the rest of them. You want to be what these
Romans call a New Woman." However much Cleopatra may want to be
a New Woman, she is incapable of being anything but a womanly woman.
She may plagiarize from her new hero and explain her new philosophy
by saying, "I do what must be done, and have no time for myself. That is
not happiness; but it is greatness." She may maintain to Pothinus that she
understands Caesar "by instinct," but when Pothinus treacherously betrays to Caesar her little plot to rule her conqueror, Caesar remarks tolerantly
that such behavior is "only natural." So are her lies when she dogmatically
denies Pothinus's charges and Caesar is not shocked, since he understands
women.

For Cleopatra has not changed underneath. Her goal in a lover is not
a "god" like Caesar, but a man like Antony — "one who can love and hate —
one whom I can hurt and who would hurt me." In this combination of
sadism and masochism there is perhaps even an element of self-sacrifice to
the perverted pleasure of the loved one. Her vengeful character has not
altered, either, as is evident in the way in which she passionately orders
Ftatateeta to murder Pothinus for his betrayal, and then immediately turns
all her blandishments on Caesar and Apollodorus, who innocently remarks,
"Cleopatra grows more womanly beautiful from week to week." At one
moment she "languishes" at Caesar, and the next she is unperturbed by the
discovery of the murder of Pothinus, except to kiss Ftatateeta "repeatedly
and savagely." Finally, as Caesar prepares to depart, she comes before him,
having carefully calculated all her effects as if he were an ordinary man:
"cold and tragic, cunningly dressed in black." Caesar, who has forgotten
all about her in the business of departure, summarizes: "What! As much
a child as ever, Cleopatra! Have I not made a woman of you after all?"
He should have said, "Have I not made an adult of you after all?" For
the wiles and natural instincts of the woman and the adolescent girl are the
same. As Shaw says in his notes, "The childishness I have ascribed to her,
as far as it is childishness of character and not lack of experience, is not a
matter of years." Thus she throws herself into Caesar's arms when he
promises to send her Mark Antony, and when he kisses her on the forehead, proclaiming, "Farewell: I do not think we shall meet again," she
"is much affected and begins to sniff." Of course, Shaw artfully suppresses
the fact that she actually followed Caesar to Rome, and there bore Caesarion

to him. But Shaw wrote Ellen Terry that he wouldn't want her to play the role of Cleopatra, because "She is an animal — a bad lot. Yours is a beneficent personality."

A much more crudely drawn woman of approximately the same period of Shaw's work is Lady Corinthia Fanshawe, from *Press Cuttings,* who is openly conceived as a travesty on the womanly woman, for she is farcically contrasted with her fellow-officer of the Anti-Suffraget League, Mrs. Banger, a manly woman. By the usual cajolery and trickery, the ultra-feminine Lady Corinthia tries to dominate General Mitchener, of the War Office, who is helping to direct operations in this civil war of Votes for Woman, but when she is convinced that the General is impervious to her blandishments, she consents to become Balsquith's "Egeria" in order to fulfil his "ideal of romantic happiness." Apparently, according to some of Shaw's letters to Mrs. Campbell in 1912, Lady Corinthia was a partial reflection of the wife of Sir Edward Strachey.

Shaw's theater is full of womanly women, most of whom, however, belong primarily to other classifications. But his uninterrupted interest in the type is proved by his introduction of Barbara Villiers, the Duchess of Cleveland, formerly Lady Castlemaine, and mistress of King Charles II, into one of his last plays, *In Good King Charles's Golden Days.* Barbara makes her entry "in a tearing rage," and accuses Charles of using Isaac Newton's house (the locale of this curious congeries of famous people, most of whom probably never met anywhere in reality) as a place of assignation. Famous for her tantrums, she storms, rants, and even suggests that Charles kill her so that he can be happy with "that low stage player," Nell Gwynn. Squeamish and excessively delicate in public, she provokes George Fox (who by a turn of Shavian fate happens also to be present) to remark soberly, "She prates over-much about unfaithfulness," although her affairs with Churchill and others are soon brought out. Prudishly, she is outraged by Kneller's aesthetic allusions to her "curves"; such talk, she feels, is indecent. Charles has to reprimand Nell for making poor Barbara blush. Strongly acquisitive, she is always demanding things from the King, who at one juncture remarks to his wife that so far as the two things the Duchess is most interested in, men and money, are concerned, "Barbara is insatiable. Grab, grab, grab." Shaw sums her up in his preface as "the voluptuous termagant Castlemaine." Thus Barbara is only a somewhat restricted specimen of the womanly woman, but she possesses enough of the distinguishing traits to afford a profitably entertaining study.

## 2. *The Pursuing Woman*

Most womanly women, of course, are pursuers of men, either openly or furtively. Some unwomanly women also are. The majority of Shaw's women are pursuers, in one form or another. In fact, although he vocifer-

ously and properly denies any originality at all in discerning and isolating
the type, he has specialized so much in it that by popular decision he has
been assigned special property rights therein, and his theory that in most
instances it is actually the woman who takes the initiative in the love chase
has become accepted almost without question. Critics like Irvine, however,
like to give at least a philosophical priority to Schopenhauer, who in such
essays as "On Women" and "On Genius," and such books as *The World as
Will and Idea,* anticipated many of Shaw's theories as to female motivation
and behavior.

His own pursuit of the pursuing woman began in the days when he
was trying to be a novelist. *An Unsocial Socialist* furnishes three prime examples, one of whom, Gertrude Lindsay, has already been discussed. The
second, Mrs. Henrietta Jansenius Trefusis, whom Shaw portrays as a particular kind of Jewess, is from the start both a womanly woman and a
pursuer. After she has caught her husband Sidney, she continues so to
smother him with her affectionate attentions that he is driven to escape
from her lovely and luxurious embraces. Henrietta is both neurotic and erotic.
When she discovers her husband in his hiding place, a passing boy over-
sees her passionately kissing him, and when Trefusis escapes again, she
actually brings on her illness and death by pursuing him to his house on a
cold winter night dressed in a light costume that she has been too precipitate
to change. The third woman who is attracted to the magnetic but cagey
Sidney is Agatha Wylie, a much more intelligent woman than Henrietta
or Gertrude, who falls in love with him while she is a schoolgirl, is not
taken seriously by him, thinks she has fallen out, but unconsciously pursues him still. After Sidney has finally proposed, and she has at first refused
him, he tells their mutual friend Lady Brandon what has happened, whereupon Lady Brandon promptly exclaims, "Says she does not love you! Don't
believe her; she has taken trouble enough to catch you." And the catch
makes a successful marriage — as marriages go, states Sidney in a postscript.

The catalogue of pursuers in the plays is almost unlimited. There is the
"vital" Blanche Sartorius, who is responsible for "instinctively" starting
the quarry, and, at the kill, follows the bewildered but not unwilling Trench
"remorselessly," as he realizes that, through her shrewishness, she is really
making love to him — "provocative, taunting, half defying, half inviting
him to advance, in a flush of undisguised animal excitement." Trench,
seeing what is in the wind and enjoying it all, pretends to be coy, whereupon, with an exertion of somewhat unfair pressure, she "suddenly kneels
down beside him with her breast against his right shoulder; taking his
face in her hands, and twisting it sharply towards her." That is the end
of the bachelorhood of young Harry Trench, as she, in conclusion, "flings
her arms round him, and crushes him in an ecstatic embrace."

Charteris, the great philanderer, also finds it advantageous to play coy, as Grace reminds him in the first scene. But he, reminding her in turn that it is not his fault if half the women he speaks to fall in love with him, tells her that he fled only that she might pursue. Later, he informs the indignant Cuthbertson that Grace wants to marry him, Charteris, in spite of his dubiousness; and that Julia wants the same thing. In fact, Julia's frank and passionate letter shocks her father. In the staid rooms of the Ibsen Club Shaw actually stages her pursuit physically: "A chase now begins between Julia and Charteris, all the more exciting to them because the huntress and her prey alike must conceal the real object of their movements from others." As Julia stalks him, Charteris dodges and doubles around the revolving bookcases, the alcove, and the fender until he is rescued by Cuthbertson, who invites all the gentlemen to go to lunch in "the Ibsen fashion — the unsexed fashion." Julia then, despondently anticipating her defeat, gives the balding Dr. Paramore enough encouragement "to keep any other woman from getting him," casts a "Parthian glance" at him "as she flies," and will stand no competition, no matter how unintentional, from Grace. When she perceives that she has clearly lost Charteris, she promptly asks for Paramore's address, and, "a most determined woman," starts off to his house after him, still a little uncertain of what she intends to do or how he regards her, but resolved to marry someone. When the doctor earnestly confides his supreme admiration for her, a "new hope" springs up within her. For a moment she struggles with her memories, and then, much like Hedda Gabler with Tesmer, unenthusiastically accepts him. Half a loaf, to her, is better than no bread, just as it is to the anemic and over-delicate Nora Reilly in *John Bull's Other Island,* who has silently and dismally pursued Larry Doyle *in absentia* while he was away for eighteen years in England, and then on his return to Ireland, when she is convinced that she will never get him, gives in to the entreaties of the robust English civil engineer, Tom Broadbent. Judith Anderson is also rebuffed in her pursuit of the Devil's Disciple, and has to be content with her old husband.

The canny Louka, in *Arms and the Man,* understands the ways of her sex as well as practises them. She early warns Sergius of Bluntschli as a rival: "And I tell you that if that gentleman ever comes here again, Miss Raina will marry him, whether he likes it or not." In the role of a prophet she is infallible, as the audience is fully convinced even before it learns that Raina has placed her portrait, suitably inscribed, in the pocket of her father's old coat before she gave it to her "chocolate cream soldier." Louka herself follows the same female techniques in displaying her charms to Sergius, tantalizing him by withholding her kisses, displaying her naked, bruised arm to him, trapping him into making his vow, and then holding him to it when he thoughtlessly kisses her hand, which she has "timidly" but calculatingly offered him.

Lawyer Bohun, Q. C., in *You Never Can Tell,* similarly interprets the true intentions of the two Clandon girls. He tells his colleague McComas that if Dolly doesn't marry McComas she will marry someone else. As for Gloria, she intends to get married at once. When she flushes and protests, he dogmatizes in his usual fashion, "Oh, yes, you do: you don't know it; but you do." And of course she does, playing with the fearful and fascinated Valentine much like Blanche with Trench, and finally, gripping his arms tightly, kissing him until he gasps, "breathless."

Jennifer Dubedat, devoted and idolizing wife as she is in *The Doctor's Dilemma,* confesses innocently to Dr. Ridgeon that her artist-husband "came to me like a child. Only fancy, doctor: he never even wanted to marry me: he never thought of the things other men think of! I had to propose it myself." Harmoniously with her romantic naiveté, she never suspects that her affirmative answer to Louis' question as to whether she had any money had something to do with his consent.

The pattern is carried out with many variations. Even Ellie in *Heartbreak House* finally admits that she never really intended to marry Mangan; she simply wanted to prove that he could not escape if she wanted him. Ermyntrude, the American millionaire's widow and the daughter of Archdeacon Daffodil Donkin of the Church of England in the egregious farce, *The Inca of Perusalem,* is a pursuing woman par excellence, and wraps the surprisingly willing Inca around her little finger. King Magnus's Orinthia is an excellent example of methodology, but is eventually defeated in her duel with Queen Jemina. Aloysia Brollikins determines to marry young David Chavender, the son of the Prime Minister in *On the Rocks,* and does. Epifania, the title character in *The Millionairess,* is a pursuing woman as well as a managing one, as her capture of the Egyptian doctor after she has tired of her husband, Alastair Fitzfassenden, shows. Slightly reversing the picture, Charles II in *In Good King Charles's Golden Days* remarks that it is unlike Louise de Kéroualle to have pursued him to Newton's house. She denies her pursuit, but by implication refutes her denial, since she explains that she merely came to get a love charm from "Mr. Newton the alchemist." Later she admits to the amused and admiring King, "When I was sent to England to captivate you with my baby face, it was you who captivated me with your seventy inches and your good looks." Charles bridles a little at this flattery.

In *Too True To Be Good* the Patient falls in love with Aubrey the burglar at first sight, and when she notices shortly afterward that he has forgotten the pearls, she exclaims, "Thank Heaven he's a fool, a lovely fool: I shall be able to do as I like with him." But the Patient, differing from Sweetie, is not of the permanently pursuing type. Sweetie is correct in pointing out to her that three-fourths of her feeling is "only unsatisfied curiosity," and at the end Mops announces that she is ashamed that she fell in love with "that thing . . . I got tired of him sooner than Sweetie did." Sweetie herself progresses through a whole series of affairs, from Aubrey to Colonel Tallboys to Sergeant Fielding, and always has her way—until she gets tired. As she elegantly puts it, "What I say is that a love affair should always be a honeymoon. And the only way to make sure of that is to keep changing the man." When she meets the manly Sergeant, however, she abandons her airs and manners, and unabashedly snuggles up to him, remarking, "Well, isn't it natural?" Disappointed in his somewhat tardy response, she "rises quickly to escape from him," but he seizes her "in a hearty embrace" and kisses her masterfully. Reasoning with himself to satisfy his instincts, he concludes, "But if I settle down with this girl she will keep the others off. I'm a bit tired of adventures." Sweetie discovers the same truth: "Well, if the truth must be told, so am I. We were made for one another, Sergeant." It is just a matter of time, it seems, before most Jills find their Jacks.

*Village Wooing* may be a minor work in the Shaw canon, but its heroine, "Z," is as flagrant an example of the ways of the pursuing woman in condensed form as he ever created. Though Blanche Patch thinks that the original of "Z" may have been Mrs. Jisbella Lyth, postmistress at Ayot St. Lawrence, there is, however, no good reason to assign this particular predatory characteristic to her. Finally, after she has, in her own phrase, "nailed" the penny-a-line author, "A," she confesses that she wonders at her own nerve. "I'm not a bit like that, you know, really." And then, having thus tried to calm her victim down for the long haul of domestic life, she comes out with a typical Shavian excuse: "Something above me and beyond me drove me on." Obviously, the Life Force has been at work again.

Shaw reveals more animus against Leo Bridgenorth, of *Getting Married,* than he does against almost any other of his pursuing women, with the exception of Blanche and Julia. Although to the casual observer Leo is "very pretty, very youthful, very restless, and consequently very charming to people who are touched by youth and beauty," when coldly studied her "restlessness is much less lovable than the kittenishness which comes from a rich and fresh vitality." Her restlessness has also taken the form of suing for a divorce from her bungling but chivalrous husband Rejjy because she has fallen in love with Sinjon Hotchkiss, whom she has provocatively pursued, in spite of the fact that he likes her husband better than her. Full of a sense of her own importance, she "affects a special intimacy with Lesbia, as of two thinkers among the Philistines." This butterfly Shaw pins firmly to the cardboard of his exhibit by stating that, because of her conviction of her own cleverness and superiority to common people, "she recklessly attaches herself to clever men on that understanding, with the result that they are at first delighted, then exasperated, and finally bored." This is what happens to Sinjon. Flighty enough himself, he veers toward Mrs. George Collins, and when he definitely throws Leo over she demands that Rejjy immediately have the divorce decree annulled. Strangely enough,

Leo, like Mrs. George, is naturally polyandrous, and confesses to the shocked General Boxer that since she loves both men she would like to be married to both; in fact, she would "like to marry a lot of men." Apparently Shaw feels that her essential lack of "vitality" disqualifies her from carrying out this ambition, though no pursuing woman could desire more. Duffin is certainly correct in concluding that her "incompatibility" with her husband will soon reassert itself.

As minor exhibits in the same show are Edith Bridgenorth and Cecil Sykes, her fearful but not too unwilling victim in *Getting Married*. He is a serious young gentleman, "somewhat careworn by an exacting conscience." After he has finished reading Belfort Bax's essays on *Men's Wrongs,* he protests mildly against the marriage, especially since he seems to suffer from a slight Oedipus complex and is always worrying about the welfare of his mother and sisters. But after the temporary doubts of both Edith and himself have been resolved, the dominating Edith sees to it that the necessary vows are taken, properly if hastily, though poor Cecil slinks in afterward "with an unnatural air, half foolish, half rakish, as if he had lost all his self-respect and were determined not to let it prey on his spirits."

*Pygmalion,* like *Candida,* has been one of Shaw's most popular but at the same time most misunderstood plays, at least when represented on the stage or in the moving pictures, where the author's anticlimactic prose postscript cannot appear; and the future of Liza Doolittle has been as generally misconstrued as the character of Candida. Nevertheless, it must be admitted that in the moving picture version Shaw himself deliberately allowed the audience to be misguided as to the relationship between Liza and Higgins. When Liza, "that rapscallionly flower girl" (whose ancestry, Rattray notes, has been traced to Kipling's Badalia Herodsfoot through Maugham's Liza of Lambeth), first takes refuge from the driving rain in the portico of St. Paul's Church, she is "not at all a romantic figure." Though she is fond of referring to herself righteously as "a good girl," she impresses Mrs. Pearce, Higgins's housekeeper, as "very common," with "a dreadful accent" — the very thing, of course, that attracted Henry Pygmalion Higgins, the phonetician, to her. Shrewd, materialistic, coy, and somewhat slow-witted as she seems at first, her "innocent vanity and consequential airs," coupled with her display of vulgar knowledge about how a real "gentleman" should behave, prepare the audience for the discovery that she is ambitious to improve. Higgins, in his resolve to teach her to "behave like a duchess," knows that he will have to overcome what he calls her "Lisson Grove prudery" and her antipathy toward talking "grammar" (incidentally, Shaw sometimes has Liza's latter trouble himself, especially when he is dealing with inverted or compound subjects and verbs), but Higgins is not daunted by the prospect.

The way in which this unpromising piece of material turns into a quick but appealing snob (West comments sourly on how Shaw in his plays of this period came close to accepting the "whole social order of ladies and gentlemen" whom he had previously ridiculed) and the story of her devastating and explosive loquacity at Mrs. Higgins's tea, culminating in her famous "Not bloody likely," are too well known to demand recounting.[15] But the manner in which her "new small talk" is delivered takes in all the Eynsford Hills, though the mother is shocked by the "new ways." The real crux of the play, however, lies in the relationship between Liza, who of course is ultimately transformed into a real Galatea, and the three men, Henry Higgins, Colonel Pickering, and Freddy Hill. Just before her first bath, Liza propounds the problem, "Who'd marry me?" And that is the question that is uppermost in her mind throughout, in spite of the difficulty she has in getting Higgins to be at all concerned with it.

For there seems little doubt that for a long time Liza hopes that she can interest him in her. If the many signs of her suppressed affection that Shaw has planted are not enough, the understanding Mrs. Higgins later points out the truth to the obtuse males: "The girl is naturally rather affectionate . . . She had become attached to you both." And yet, she continues reprovingly, they "didn't even thank her, let alone pet her." Eliza's father, the reformed dustman, puts the situation more crudely: "If it had been only one of them, you could have nailed him; . . . but one of them chaperoned the other, as you might say."

By the climactic scene, Liza has reluctantly made up her mind, though she has a final try. To Higgins's remark that he has treated her like everybody else, she snaps, "I can do without you: don't think I can't." On his admitting that, although he can do without anybody, he has learnt something from her and will miss her, she bursts out that he is a devil who can twist the heart of a girl. "And you don't care a bit for me." Higgins, the callous realist, almost recalling Conolly in *The Irrational Knot,* explains that he cares for humanity and she's a part of it. This information is no consolation to a girl who is dying for love, and who, as she says, doesn't notice the things he does, but only that he doesn't notice her; but she announces bravely, "I won't care for anybody that doesn't care for me." When Higgins suggests the alternative of his adopting her as a daughter or her marrying Pickering, she flashes fiercely at him: "I wouldn't marry you if you asked me; and you're nearer my age than what he is."

The showdown is over, but Liza has had an ace in the hole all along. Prefacing her revelation with the remark that she has always had chaps enough wanting her "that way," she informs the protesting Higgins that she has been getting sheets and sheets of letters from Freddy Hill two or three times a day; that he loves her, and she thinks she could make something of him; that every girl has a right to be loved, and she only wants to be "natural." Yes, she cries desperately at the "thunderstruck"

Higgins, "I'll marry Freddy, I will, as soon as I'm able to support him."
(In the first version of the play Shaw wrote, "as soon as he's able to
support me.") And she means it. It is this pragmatic and Philistine decision
that sentimental audiences refuse to accept, preferring to believe that, after
Liza has found her way of putting Higgins in his place and asserting her
independence by offering her services "as an assistant to Professor Nepean,"
Higgins's chief rival, she will come back to him and find that he's not
really the tough-minded ogre he has pretended to be, but has been in
love with her all along. In fact, even Shaw's postscriptural assurance that
Eliza's instinct has told her not to marry Higgins, since he obviously will not
make a good husband, has not shaken the public confidence. The only
sop that Shaw will throw to them, however, is that even after Freddy becomes a man, a florist, and a successful green-grocer, following a series of
business vicissitudes, "it is notable that though she never nags her husband,
and frankly loves the colonel as if she were his favorite daughter, she has
never got out of the habit of nagging Higgins that was established on the
fatal night when she won his bet for him." And, womanlike, she goes even
further: "She has even secret mischievous moments in which she wishes
she could get him alone, on a desert island, away from all ties and with
nobody else in the world to consider, and just drag him off his pedestal and
see him making love like any common man." Nevertheless, in her more
normal moods, "Galatea never does quite like Pygmalion: his relation to
her is too godlike to be altogether agreeable."

From Shaw's most famous unsuccessful pursuer to his most famous
successful one is a natural culminating step. And his most famous successful
one is, of course, Ann Whitefield in *Man and Superman,* a role written for
Lillah McCarthy. In his "Epistle Dedicatory" Shaw frankly warns the
reader what to expect from this prototype of predatory females. Generalizing
philosophically, he remarks that, as a result of woman's new power and
aggressiveness which have come through her recent emancipation, "Man
is no longer, like Don Juan, victor in the duel of sex. Whether he has
ever really been may be doubted: at all events the enormous superiority
of Woman's natural position in this matter is telling with greater and
greater force." And Shaw cites Shakespeare's plays as evidence that in the
past, too, woman has always taken the initiative, at least as Shakespeare
conceived her. He might also have cited Fletcher's *The Wild-Goose Chase*
and plenty of other earlier works. And where did the idea of Ann come
from? From nowhere else than "the fifteenth century Dutch morality
called Everyman." Shaw asked himself, "Why not Everywoman?" Ann was
the result. Rather cautiously for Mr. Shaw, he qualifies his implication a
bit: "every woman is not Ann; but Ann is Everywoman." What, then, are
the characteristics of the Shavian Everywoman?

In his preface he had already commented on her "unscrupulousness," brought about partly by male hypocrisy. Tanner warns that Ann will "commit every crime a respectable woman can," and is the more dangerous because she "has plenty of money and no conscience." Later he tells her to her face that she has "no conscience — only hypocrisy . . . yet there is a sort of fascination about you." He also calls her "an incorrigible liar" when she fibs about her sister Rhoda's illness in order to get into Jack's car herself. Shaw's stage directions sum up this phase of her character by saying that in some people Ann perhaps inspires a certain amount of fear, "as a woman who will probably do everything she means to do without taking more account of other people than may be necessary and what she calls right. In short, what the weaker of her own sex sometimes call a cat."

She is also, to people like the gullible Ramsden, "a wonderfully dutiful girl." In fact, Ramsden doesn't remember ever having heard her give her own wish as a reason for doing anything or not doing it. It has always been "Father wishes me to," or "Mother wouldn't like it." This she calls her "duty to her parents." Obviously, then, since it was her dead father's choice that she have Tanner as well as Ramsden for a guardian, she couldn't possibly interfere. Even back in her and Tanner's schooldays, when Jack was in the midst of a youthful experimental love affair with "a girl named Rachel Rosetree" (a tantalizingly realistic character, whom none of Shaw's biographers seem to have tried to identify)[16] Ann had felt it her "duty" to stop their misconduct.

Consequently she is, or makes people believe she is, an unselfish self-sacrificer. When Tanner bluntly avers to the credulous Octavius, "Vitality in a woman is a blind fury of creation. She sacrifices herself to it: do you think she will hesitate to sacrifice you?" Tavy heroically defends his idol: "Why, it is just because she is self-sacrificing that she will not sacrifice those she loves." Tanner assures him that he is making "the profoundest of mistakes," and that it "is the self-sacrificing women that sacrifice others most recklessly."

Thus Ann also represents Shaw's favorite "vitality"; in fact, in his stage directions he calls her "one of the vital geniuses," without — he assures the reader — her being "oversexed," which would be a "vital defect." Tanner, however, has already compared her to a boa constrictor. At school, she wouldn't let him call his soul his own. She "bullied all the other girls" with her "virtue." Yet she tempted all her male playmates, with the exception of Tavy, who was, she admits, "always a really good boy." Tanner tells her plainly, "You were insatiably curious as to what a boy might be capable of, and diabolically clever at getting through his guard and surprising his innermost secrets." Later, to Tavy, he cites Maeterlinck's "book about the bee" as an example in natural history which should be an "awful lesson to mankind."

Yet Ann has very delicate feelings and is easily shocked. She is "stricken to the soul" by her mother's crass reference to her father's death and "hastily leaves the room to conceal her emotion" — when she was looking for an excuse to get out anyway. She is hurt when Tanner makes his remark about her tempting the boys. "All timid women," she lectures him later, "are conventional: we *must* be conventional, Jack, or we are so cruelly, so vilely misunderstood."

There are also certain fields of knowledge or activity that Everywoman is not supposed to be interested in. Although, with a touch of idealism, Ann once confesses that she always hoped that what Tanner did as a boy "would be something really heroic at last," she is not at all interested in his revolutionary book or in his attempt to give her an account of his spiritual and moral history. She is merely "bored" when he tries to tell her of his mission to "shatter creeds and demolish idols," and deflates him with "I am afraid I am too feminine to see any sense in destruction." His renewed attempt to make her another fervid speech on politics is pricked by an "I don't mind your queer opinions one little bit."

Doña Ana de Ulloa in the dream scene in hell is of course merely an Ann Whitefield of an earlier period in history, before the modern era of female aggressiveness set in. She is a conventional Catholic, insulted at finding herself in hell, which, as Don Juan Tanner obligingly informs her, is "the home of the unreal and of the seekers for happiness," as well as the "home of honor, duty, justice, and the rest of the seven deadly virtues." Ana cannot understand why, when she screamed as a matter of duty at the killing of her father in the duel with her would-be lover, she has been sent to hell as a reward of duty — "I, who sacrificed all my inclinations to womanly virtue and propriety." Prudish as Ann, she continues to be shocked when she meets her father and the Devil in the same place with her, and resents Juan's "idea of a woman's mind" as "cynical and disgusting materialism." In defending marriage, she pontificates that "most marriages are perfectly comfortable." Nevertheless, after hearing Juan expound his views of the Life Force and his determination to spend the rest of his life in contemplation in Heaven, "the home of the masters of reality," she announces that she will go with him — though there is some reason for believing that she has made this decision because she still believes that it is the proper place to go. Though the Devil assures her that she will have an apotheosis and be at his palace before he and the Statue get there through the trap door, she nevertheless asks him earnestly where she can find this Superman they have been talking about. Told that he is not yet created, she cries dedicatedly in her role of Everywoman: "Then my work is not yet done. (*Crossing herself devoutly*) I believe in the Life to Come. (*Crying to the universe*) A father — a father for the Superman!" And with this prophetic demand, she "vanishes into the void."

The questions that immediately arise are: Is she "apotheosized" to the

Devil's palace in the abyss? Or does she pursue Juan to Heaven and get him as Ann does Tanner? At least, immediately afterward, as the dream evaporates, Tanner exclaims, as Ann and the rest overtake him, "The Life Force! I am lost!"

These are the alternatives that would immediately suggest themselves to the ordinary inquisitive reader. But Shaw himself has provided a much more metaphysical answer for the extraordinary but still inquisitive reader. For in a leaflet which he himself wrote to give a synopsis of his "Don Juan in Hell" scene for baffled audiences he stated of Ana: "Love is neither her pleasure nor her study: it is her business. So she, in the end, neither goes with Don Juan to heaven nor with the devil and her father to the palace of pleasure, but declares that her work is not yet finished. For though by her death she is done with the bearing of men to mortal fathers, she may yet, a Woman Immortal, bear the Superman to the Eternal Father." Some of the readers of this explanation undoubtedly thought it blasphemy.

Back on the earth again, "the home of the slaves of reality," Ann continues her unscrupulous career. She has, it is true, a "faint impulse of pity" when she breaks the news to Octavius that her mother and father want her to marry Jack, not him. She tells him romantically that he "must be a sentimental old bachelor" for her sake, and she does not "dread disillusionizing Jack" about her intentions because "he has no illusions" about her anyway — which shows how little she really understands Jack. Jack, still fighting, recapitulates her character to her acquiescent mother as a liar, a coquette, a bully, a hypocrite, and "almost something for which I know no polite name." That is, she is Everywoman; and she is fascinating. She is, then, all ready to turn into the Philistine mother woman. Tanner, realizing that he will be regarded as a renegade, but that he is in the toils of the Life Force, which Ann admits candidly that she can't understand (she says "it sounds like the Life Guards" to her), imagines how Ann will start dwindling into a wife as soon as she has snapped the trap shut. But Ann, Philistine-like, is not bothered by the picture: "After all, what difference would it make? Beauty is all very well at first sight; but who ever looks at it when it has been in the house three days? I thought our pictures very lovely when papa bought them; but I haven't looked at them in years." For of course Ann is a Philistine, or, if she has shown some slight traces of idealism, will become one soon, like Candida. She cannot be a realist, as some critics have called her. For Ann, remember, is Everywoman, and in Shaw's original classification there is only one realist in a thousand. Everywoman can scarcely be one woman in a thousand.

So Everywoman, even if she does swoon — more or less synthetically — under the strain of her pursuit, again captures another skilled duelist of sex. Yet Ann is sincere when, after her rapid recovery, she asserts, "But you very nearly killed me, Jack, for all that."

It would be unfair to Shaw to leave this discussion of woman as the pursuer without letting him state his final views on the type, in order to correct any possible one-sidedness or distortion. For in his *Self Sketches* he selected Duffin as representative of this incomplete understanding of his attitude toward women, and set him right thus: "Have I really conveyed to you that when it comes to the relations of the sexes there is no female but the spider female? Ann Whitefield in Man and Superman does not fill up my field of vision as completely as she has filled up yours. The tragedy of Mrs. Knox in Fanny's First Play, mistaking Knox's transfiguration by carnal love for what Mrs. George adored in the Bishop from whom she kept so carefully apart, is not a spider tragedy; and Major Barbara, Lesbia Grantham, Lina Szczepanowska you have noted in subsequent passages as getting quite as far from the bee and the spider as my least philoprogenitive men . . . I am not sure that I shall not deal dramatically with the anti-maternal woman some day. I am by no means unacquainted with the species."

A full-length Shavian portrayal of this type would have been well worth having.

### 3. *The Mother Woman*

The influence of Candida — or perhaps I should say Ellen Terry — upon Shaw was overwhelming and permanent, although he saw very little of her after 1906 and their correspondence slackened greatly after 1900. Their first actual and apparently somewhat disappointing meeting under the stage of the Strand Theatre on December 16, 1900, probably had nothing to do with this change, as Christopher St. John demonstrates in her edition of the letters; but the date nevertheless marked a significant point in their relationship. For Miss Terry had gone to the theater that Sunday on Shaw's invitation to see for herself the final transmutation her Romeo-by-mail had made of her in trying to move her from her theater to his.

In 1899 Shaw had written his comic melodrama, *Captain Brassbound's Conversion,* as his final effort in his seemingly hopeless struggle to get Terry to act in one of his plays. When she had become a grandmother for the first time, she had remarked that now nobody would ever write another play for her. Shaw — ever the chivalrous Irish knight when a charming woman was concerned — said that *he* would; and *Brassbound* was the result. But when Terry first read it in manuscript she gave the stubborn author one of his hardest shocks by emphatically pronouncing the role of Lady Cicely Wayneflete, which he had labored over with such zealous love, to be not at all like her, by predicting that the play would never make a penny, and by advising her friend (who was by now himself happily married to Charlotte Payne-Townshend)[17] to peddle his manuscript to her chief rival, Mrs. Pat Campbell (whom she called Mrs. "Pat Cat"). After reflecting on the matter, however, and discovering that her personal maid had noticed the great resemblance between her mistress and Lady Cicely in their habit and methods of getting their own ways, she reread the play and became highly enthusiastic about it. The fact that it was only several years afterward that she did act in it, with greater success in the United States than in England, is another story.

Lady Cicely, whom West strangely regards as the realist of the play, was perhaps Shaw's supreme effort to portray his favorite type of Philistine: the mother woman. It is true that in this case the mother woman is a young old maid, who will obviously never marry, and that perhaps he never consciously realized that he was drawing another example of the female Philistine, but he made it abundantly clear that he conceived his heroine as the mother woman par excellence. In the letter to Terry in which he had stressed the fact that he had made the interest in Candida "partly a sexual interest" he had also asserted: "In Lady Cicely I have done without this, and gained a greater fascination by it . . . I try to show you fearing nobody and managing them all as Daniel managed the lions, not by cunning — above all, not by even a momentary appeal to Cleopatra's stand-by, their passions — but by simple moral superiority." Whether Shaw exaggerated his achievements, or even overreached himself, can perhaps be seen by examining the character which he has actually created.

He describes Lady Cicely on her first appearance in the missionary's garden on the heights overlooking the harbor of Mogador in Morocco as "between thirty and forty, tall, very good-looking, sympathetic, intelligent, tender and humorous" — altogether a "woman of great vitality and humanity." It quickly becomes apparent that Lady Cicely likes everything and everybody — or thinks quite sincerely that she likes everything and everybody — but really sets out to make things over into her own image and reflection. The very fact that she does not realize the truth about her own motives and conduct indicates at once that she is no realist. Her behavior is instinctive and "natural," but she is incapable of viewing it objectively and analytically. She is a charming innocent and a sentimental humanitarian, and her chief weapon for getting her own way is flattery. She invariably finds excuses for everybody. She gets on best with people, she says, when they can see her face. She lies innocently to Rankin, the missionary, about Brassbound's conduct in order to save him, and persuades Rankin himself to suppress the truth of what has happened. She even keeps her brother-in-law, the great Judge Howard Hallam, under her thumb by making judicious references to the journalistic habits of English newspapers, reminding him of probable family reactions, and generally agreeing with everything he says but twisting it so that it takes on a slightly different meaning. A bit of stage business that Shaw assigns to her gives her away: "unconsciously making her right hand stalk about the table on the tips of its fingers in a tentative stealthy way which would put Sir Howard on his guard if he were in a suspicious frame of mind."

All this, however, merely arises from her all-enveloping maternal spirit. She immediately begins to mother Brassbound's brigands, for, to her, "all men are children in a nursery." "Ah," she exclaims to the Captain, "if I could only shew you my children from Wayneflete Sunday School!" She ties up Marzo's wound as if she were a hospital nurse, and turns Brass-bound out of his bedroom to put his man into it. But she plays no favorites, and mends Brassbound's coat without invitation. As Johnson, another of the bandits, puts it, "From what I can make out, she means to make herself matron of this institution." Shortly after her visit to the American cruiser *Santiago* it is discovered that she has completely altered the sleeping ar-rangements of the stokers, and she assures Kearney, the American captain, that "the one thing that one misses on a man-of-war is a woman." Marzo, the invalid, calls her "no lady . . . She saint. She get me into heaven — get us all into heaven." But the Captain and Sir Howard are not so sure, for the latter assures the astounded and curious Captain that "half a dozen such women would make an end of law in England in six months." But she talks Brassbound out of his vengeful mood, "all resistance beaten out of him." She is afraid of nothing — or, rather, is simply lacking in any sense of danger.

At one point Lady Cicely remarks apologetically of herself: "I'm afraid I'm a dreadful fool. But I can't help it. I was made so, I suppose." This is far from Shaw's opinion, of course, since Lady Cicely acts always by in-stinct and intuition, not by reason. Only at the very end does she show any sign of analytical and critical power, when she realizes that Brassbound has unconsciously almost mesmerized her into agreeing to marry him. She has diagnosed him to himself as "one of the Idealists — the Impossibilists!" and advised him to follow the course always taken in her world: that is, to get married "straight off to some girl with enough money . . . , and plenty of sentiment." When he promptly applies her suggestion to herself, she informs him with alarm: "I have never been in love with any real per-son; and I never shall. How could I manage people if I had that mad little bit of self left in me? That's my secret."

The final comment as to Shaw's success in his attempt to transform Ellen Terry into Lady Cicely Wayneflete may be left to the cast of the copyright-ing performance of the play given in Liverpool in 1899 and to her daughter Edith Craig. According to Ellen herself in her letter to Shaw, the cast "all loathe Lady Cicely. A 'tremendous humbug.' 'Arch' (!) 'Detestable woman,' etc., etc. I said 'It's because I read it wrong,' but Edy who was in front, absorbed, and loving the play, says I could not read the lines other than I did, but that it seemed to her you *thought* your Lady C. *one* sort of woman and have *written* another." Still, "Everyone loved the play"! Messrs. Duffin and Henderson would agree with the verdict of the cast about the play, but emphatically disagree with its verdict about Lady Cicely, whom they cite as a delightful example of the "eternal feminine," using her charms for "modern, progressive, Shavian ends."

From the preceding description it is obvious that one can be a mother woman without being a mother, but that if one is a Philistine one is a Philistine, regardless. Before proceeding to the more fruitful members of the genus, however, it might be well to mention some other Shavian specimens who are, in their various ways, mothers without having, or showing, any children. The most interesting of these is Lesbia Grantham in *Getting Married,* who can't bear having a man around the house, but would love to have children without the bother of a husband. She is sure that there are many women like herself who would like to be mothers but not wives, and Shaw supports her eloquently in his preface. She is at least a pseudo-realist about herself and about men — a sort of inverted John Tanner, for she escapes from the Life Force. But she assures poor, tortured, smoke-redolent General Boxer Bridgenorth, who has been pursuing her doglike for years, that his "calls of nature" and "natural appetites" mean nothing to her, since "an English lady is not the slave of her appetites." The subject of "reasonable marriage contracts" had been close to Shaw's heart ever since he wrote his preface to his *Unpleasant Plays,* and he gives it major development in the preface to *Getting Married.* Irvine suggests that in her independence and fastidiousness Lydia may be a reflection of Charlotte Payne-Townshend. At the end of the play, however, and in spite of other marriage provisos reminiscent of those of Millamant, Lesbia announces that her observations of the day's doings have convinced her that her original attitude toward marriage is the correct one, and she concludes, echoing other similar statements by Shaw, "I'm afraid I think this rage for happiness rather vulgar." In his *Self Sketches,* however, Shaw adds a sort of postscript when he reminds the reader that Lesbia has hinted "that her imagination provides her with a series of adventures which beggar reality."

Jennifer Dubedat, too, is essentially a mother woman in her almost morbid care of her rascally artist of a husband, who has given her no children, but since she is one of Shaw's prime examples of an idealist she should not be kept in the company of the Philistines. And in *The Millionairess* there is Polly Seedystockings — whose real name is Patricia Smith. Polly Seedystockings is of course only the pet name she uses with her lover, Alastair Fitzfassenden, the amateur tennis champion, heavyweight boxer, and husband of Epifania Ognisanti di Parerga. She is introduced by Shaw as "a pleasant quiet little woman of the self-supporting type." She has a "dear wise old father" too. Although unmarried she's the real weekday wife of Alastair, who looks after his clothes, diet, etc. She regards herself as more of a "mind mate" than a "soul mate" to Alastair — a woman with whom he can be thoroughly comfortable. Her genius, she says, is for making people happy. In the last act, at the Cardinal's Hat, which has become "home" to her even if it is a hotel, Alastair pays her the supreme compliment that one can pay a Philistine mother woman as he looks out of the window at the "blessed quiet": "I don't know which is more comforting, you or the river . . ."

But close to a dozen of Shaw's most memorable and in most cases most lovable women are physical, as well as spiritual, mothers, and in most cases also Philistines. Mrs. Bridgenorth, wife of the remarkable Bishop of Chelsea in *Getting Married,* is "a quiet happy-looking woman of fifty or thereabouts, placid, gentle, and humorous." Marriage, she quickly admits, "came natural" to her. "Of course people must get married," she is convinced. "The world must go on, mustn't it?" When a skeptic raises the question as to why people should be held together in families, her unruffled answer is, "Because of the children" (she has had six herself). The Bishop adores her, although tacitly admitting that they move on different planes of thought and experience. She unworriedly reads his anonymous love-letters to him at breakfast when they are worth hearing, and he demonstrates his affection for her by frequently kissing her hand.

Contrasting with Mrs. Bridgenorth in respect to social origin is Mrs. Tarleton, wife of the self-made, successful business man, John Tarleton, in *Misalliance.* Mrs. Tarleton, who is "a shrewd and motherly old lady who has been pretty in her time, and is still very pleasant and likeable and unaffected," has retained many of her bourgeois pruderies. Although she refuses to be intimidated by the aristocracy and insists that "they're only human creatures like ourselves after all," she is still shocked by their lack of any "notion of decency," especially in their selection of topics of conversation. And she continues to be shocked at "the things girls say nowadays" and by her husband's talk about Natural Selection. Naturally, she treats her grown daughter Hypatia and son Johnny, as well as their guest Bentley Summerhays, like children still. But Johnny, the complete bourgeois young business man, is her special pet. She has a great maternal pride in his appearance, admires his ideas, and is always "scenting a plot against her beloved Johnny." But, characteristically of her type, she many times seems to get at the truth of a situation or person by simple intuition. Mrs. Gilbey of *Fanny's First Play* is cut out of the same cloth, but according to a smaller pattern.

Shaw's own favorite from among his later plays is undoubtedly Lady Chavender from *On the Rocks.* This time, however, he has drawn an eminently sensible mother who is so misunderstood by her hoydenish children that they are in active revolt against her. She blames herself in discussing the matter with her husband, the prime minister: "It serves us right, dear, for letting them bring themselves up in the post-war fashion instead of teaching them to be ladies and gentlemen." Modestly, but not quite truthfully, she admits that her daughter Flavia is right: "I am a bad wife and a bad mother. I dislike my daughter and treat her badly . . . I was not born for wifing and mothering." Shaw's diagnosis of her is that "She is a nice woman, and goodlooking; but she is bored; and her habitual manner is one of apology for being not only unable to take an interest in people, but even to pretend that she does." Nevertheless, Sir Arthur refuses to take her at her own evaluation. He embraces her affectionately, and calls her "the best of wives . . . , the very best as well as the very dearest." And of course she regards him as "the best of husbands." Actually she has a grudge against her husband's career because it keeps him away from home so much. In her womanly, intuitive way she is very sharp. When she learns of the proposed match between her son David and Alderwoman Aloysia Brollikins, she astonishes Aloysia, who has expected the marriage to be regarded as a misalliance, by taking the situation with utter calm, and assuring her that there are two things she herself cannot take the slightest interest in, "parliamentary affairs and love affairs," both of which bore her to distraction. "Nobody ought to marry anybody . . . But they do." But she has previously confided to Sir Arthur that such a match might really be good for David, since his wife would have all the qualities that he lacks. When she tells Sir Arthur about her theories of cross-breeding of the classes and of her weariness of "well bred people, and party politics, and the London season, and all the rest of it," he comments sagely: "I sometimes think you are the only really revolutionary revolutionist I have ever met." Nevertheless, even though she has lost her illusions about good society, her reactions and views are mostly negative. Her husband stamps her with her essential label when he expresses his gratitude to her for having sacrificed herself to keeping his house and sewing on his buttons.

Even several of Shaw's queens — his later ones, not his earlier ones like Cleopatra and Catherine the Great — are essentially domesticated creatures. Queen Philippa in *The Six of Calais* has borne the uxorious Edward III eleven children, but finds that her hardest job is to look properly after "the greatest baby of them all," her husband. She intervenes for the welfare of the six hostage burgesses by petting and flattering him, and he gives in to her pleading and weeping. But when one of the burgesses, Peter Hardmouth, flings the epithet "Henpecked!" at the king she reverses herself. Still, in spite of her demand for punishment of the insult to her dignity and character, the king in great good humor decides to be lenient.

Queen Catherine of Braganza, in *In Good King Charles's Golden Days,* is no such farce figure, but she is another Philistine mother woman. The first thing the audience sees her do is tidy up her boudoir, in which her consort, Charles II, is negligently dozing. He remonstrates with her for doing a "chambermaid's work" for him, and adds gratefully, "There is nobody like a wife." She even absolves him of any real unfaithfulness to her in spite of his legion of mistresses; in fact, he has already sworn to George

Fox: "You do not know my wife. To her only can I never be unfaithful." And the last the audience sees of her after she has fetched Charles's boots and helped him into his coat and wig is when she throws herself on her knees at the prie-dieu as he goes out.

Jemima, queen to Magnus in *The Apple Cart,* is Shaw's epitome of domesticity. She is always knitting. Magnus calls her affectionately "my poor dear Jemima," and "my stupid wife," and confesses that he can't imagine what he would do without her. "If she dies, I shall have to carry on as best I can without her, though the prospect terrifies me." In fact, he assures his official but purely ornamental mistress, Orinthia, "The smallest derogation to Jemima's dignity would hit me like the lash of a whip across the face. About yours, somehow, I do not care a rap." It is because, he explains, Jemima is part of his "real workaday self," and he gives a vivid and heartfelt description of their married life, with all its unromantic inadequacies, their mutual limitations, and their necessary concessions. Orinthia unsuccessfully and mischievously tries to shame him by calling Jemima "your old Dutch" and referring ironically to "your common healthy jolly lumps of children and your common housekeeper wife"; but at the end of the play Jemima takes over, like the usual wifely Philistine, and makes Magnus hurry off to dress for dinner: "Come on, like a good little boy." Shaw's last stage direction reads: "The King, with a grimace of hopeless tenderness, allows himself to be led away."

The presence of so many women of this type in the Shavian dramatis personae is in itself a refutation of Duffin's too sweeping generalization about the "scarcity of conjugal bliss" in Shaw's plays and of his further dogmatizing that "no marriage is likely to be permanently happy." Though incompatibility frequently exists between husband and wife, only a highly cynical interpretation of the Jemima-Magnus sort of relationship could conclude that it is a "practically inseparable feature of marriage," and that man and woman are "naturally inharmonious." For the Shavian portrait gallery, like life itself, demonstrates that many men and women can get along happily together even though they are utterly unlike in temperament and interests. Indeed, they are more likely to get along satisfactorily if they are not alike, and if each can contribute a separate and different quality to the partnership so that there can be no conflict or rivalry between them.

In this gallery of affection and sweetness, however, probably such a wife and mother as Lady Britomart in *Major Barbara* would not be quite at home. For Lady Brit, who was modeled on Gilbert Murray's mother-in-law, Lady Carlisle, is the domineering woman, the matriarch, who has driven her husband, the great munitions manufacturer, Andrew Undershaft, from the house by her dogmatism and vigorous personality, and is now having a little difficulty in keeping her children under her thumb. Yet she is womanly to the extent of using Ann Whitefield's technique of often putting the responsibility for what she herself wants on somebody else's shoulders, and even of indulging in "a little gust of tears" on occasion. She is practical and materialistic and not at all sensitive to nuances of feeling. Her conception of motherhood is essentially negative. As she says to her obtuse son Stephen, bidding for his sympathy against the glamor of his suddenly returned father: "A woman has to bring up her children; and that means to restrain them, to deny them things they want, to set them tasks, to punish them when they do wrong, to do all the unpleasant things. And then the father, who has nothing to do but pet them and spoil them, comes in when all her work is done and steals their affection from her." Yet even she is won over to the idea of family unity again at the end of the play, when she sees the opportunity which her husband's model town offers to her managerial instincts.

It is also possible for the expression of the instincts of motherhood to become so excessive as to overreach themselves and destroy their objects. Mrs. Collins, the greengrocer's wife in *Getting Married,* is one of these unfortunates. Her husband's description of her must suffice, since she never appears on the stage. According to him she is another of those to whom marriage "came natural." In fact, "she's a regular old hen . . . a born wife and mother . . . That's why my children all ran away from home." As Collins analyzes her case, she had never been brought up to understand how much freedom means to some people or to realize that married people need to "take holidays from one another if they are to keep at all fresh." Collins has therefore decided that his best course is never to tell her anything for fear of hurting her feelings. "You see, she's such an out-and-out wife and mother that she's hardly a responsible human being out of her house, except when she's marketing." In his preface Shaw discusses at great length the discrepancies between the real and the ideal in marriage. But Mrs. Collins would not be capable of perceiving that there could be any difference.

At least twice Shaw has invented women who are frankly symbolical, or they are nothing. They are Mrs. George (Zenobia Alexandrina) Collins, sister-in-law of Mrs. Greengrocer (Mathilda) Collins in *Getting Married,* and Eve in *Back to Methuselah.* Both are striking, dominant figures, and Mrs. George is outright fantastic. As Shaw summarized the role in a letter of 1908, nominating the actress Fanny Brough for the part, it "demands an actress who can combine inspiration with the broadest comic characterization." To Stella Campbell in 1915 he described the role as "the most wonderful of all my serio-comic woman's parts." Any actress would have to be a genius to make believable a woman who is at the same time the wife of a coal merchant, the mayoress of the town, the mysterious and anonymous "Incognita Appassionata" who has been writing to Bishop Bridgenorth, a promiscuous and romantic lover, and a clairvoyant and seeress who is likely to go into a trance and vaticinate at any moment — and does. Eve has a

somewhat similar oracular function, but Shaw ungallantly allows Lilith to
steal away the culminating speech.

Preliminary warning of the uniqueness of Mrs. George is given by her
brother-in-law the greengrocer, who regards her with mingled awe and
admiration. He describes her to the Bishop's wife as "a very fine figure of a
woman," but very changeable and susceptible. In fact, whenever in her
younger days she fell in love, which was frequently, she would apparently
lose all control of herself. After moping and crying for a couple of days,
she would say to her husband, no matter who else was there to hear her,
"I must go to him, George," and off she would go. Innumerable times she
abandoned home and husband in this way. Three out of four times the men
would bring her back the same evening, pretending to be too noble to take
advantage of her; the fourth time they would run away themselves. And
always her husband took her back. Ultimately she learned her lesson and
took his advice that if she'd only "stay at home and hold off a bit they'd be
at her feet all day long." The result was that George always had plenty of
change of company, and his wife became "wonderful interesting" because
of the width and variety of her experience. And the older she grew, the
younger were her fascinated victims, like Sinjon Hotchkiss, the philanderer.
But Mrs. George is to Shaw much more than an amazing nymphomaniac,
who can "get around anybody if she wants to." Duffin dismisses her too
easily when he summarizes her as "sex incarnate." Collins prepares for her
symbolic function when he warns that not only is she "particular about
religion" but also goes into trances, where she utters "not things about herself, but as if it was the whole human race giving you a bit of its mind."
Only after the play is three-fourths over does she put in an appearance, and
steal the show. There is "nothing quiet" about her stylish dressing; she is
"not afraid of colors." Indeed, she is not even a lady in Lesbia's class sense
of the term. More important, "she proclaims herself to the first glance as
the triumphant, pampered, wilful, intensely alive woman who has always
been rich among poor people . . ." In other words, though her beauty is
now wrecked, her cheeks wasted and lined, her mouth twisted and piteous,
she remains one of Shaw's favorite "vital" women, with the vestiges of her
former beauty still upon her, and still with a sense of humor. Though she
desires a renewal of the old feelings of youth, her passions are now sufficiently burned out so that she prefers to talk to Hotchkiss "like a mother,"
and wants to call him "Sonny."

In her inspired ecstasy, she is transformed into Woman, speaking to and
accusing Man in love, personified in the Bishop and his chaplain, Soames.
"I've been myself," she proclaims. "I've not been afraid of myself. And at
last I have escaped from myself, and am become a voice for them that are
afraid to speak . . ." Reproachfully she addresses her listeners, anticipating
Hesione Hushabye, "When you loved me I gave you the whole sun and

stars to play with. I gave you eternity in a single moment . . . A moment only; but was it not enough? Were you not paid then for all the rest of your struggle on earth? Must I mend your clothes and sweep your floors as well? . . . I carried the child in my arms: must I carry the father too? . . . We possessed all the universe together; and you ask me to give you my scanty wages as well . . . I gave you your own soul: you ask me for my body as a plaything. Was it not enough? Was it not enough?"

This — and much more — is all too confusing for poor ascetic Soames to comprehend, but the Bishop admits that, thanks to his wife, he is following Mrs. George's rhapsodies very easily. Yet, in spite of this emblematic treatment of the Lady Mayoress as Woman personified, and in spite of her orphic references to childbearing, Shaw for some mysterious reason has apparently made her sterile herself. Nowhere, at least, does he indicate that she has any children of her own. At the end she is prepared to allow Hotchkiss the run of her house on the filial terms that he pretends to despise, and she remarks serio-facetiously that she will adopt Soames as a father; but in her own person she is presented as the pursuer, the mistress, and the wife. Only in her trance does she become the universal mother.

Eve, then, is in a sense a completion of Mrs. George; at least she represents a clearer and more comprehensible conception of the Mother Woman. In the first section of *Back to Methuselah,* entitled *In the Beginning,* Eve is immediately described as the creative element, and the theme of woman the creator versus man the destroyer runs through the entire play. She does not think about herself, but about Adam, whom she mothers. Unlike Adam she hears voices not merely from within herself but from all sides. She gives to things the names which the wise Serpent (whom Shaw pictures as a female being and in whose voice, according to a letter he wrote Mrs. Campbell in 1929, he always heard his Stella's voice) whispers to her. Taking advantage of her continual question "Why?" the Serpent transforms her curiosity into "Why not?" and, explaining the miracles that can be achieved simply by the power of the will, instils in her the idea of birth, with its stages: desire, imagination, will, creation.[18] A few centuries later the human race is well established, and Eve is fully occupied with her tasks as wife and mother. She is now better humored than Adam, "having given up worrying." She is shrewd in her estimates of her husband and children, denying that "the true nature of woman" is to pamper man. Since she has higher aspirations than either Adam or Cain, she is angered by both men: "I hardly know which of you satisfies me least, you with your dirty digging, or he with his dirty killing. I cannot think it was for either of these cheap ways of life that Lilith set you free." But in spite of the dreariness of life she still lives on because there is hope of "the coming true of your dreams and mine. Of newly created things. Of better things." She is the one who speaks of some of her descendants who have showed promise as poets, musicians, sculptors, scientists, and priests, although all of them have been hampered or ruined by the spirit of the soldier-destroyer, Cain. As the curtain goes down on the first play in the series, she becomes Shaw's raisonneur: "Man need not always live by bread alone. There is something else. We do not yet know what it is; but some day we shall find out; and then we will live on that alone; and there shall be no more digging nor spinning, nor fighting nor killing."

No more is seen of Eve, except through her tomboy reincarnation in Savvy Barnabas, and a flitting resemblance in Zoo,[19] until the ghosts of the Garden of Eden gather in the year 31,920 or *As Far As Thought Can Reach*. The Life Force having at last partly realized itself in the creation of the new race of longlivers, Eve expresses herself as satisfied and "fades away," leaving the stage empty except for Lilith. For in his usual puckish fashion, Shaw has robbed the mother of mankind of his climactic speech and assigned it to a creature who is popularly regarded as a female demon. But to Shaw Lilith is not the Talmudic first wife of Adam; she is the original creative element, "in whom father and mother were one." She is the force which labored and split itself into two, with separate functions for male and female: "I brought life into the whirlpool of force, and compelled my enemy, Matter, to obey a living soul." In a long soliloquy, almost as mystic in its way as Mrs. George's, she confesses her satisfaction with the manner in which life is evolving toward "pure intelligence," and sees only unpredictable possibilities in the "beyond." Yet of this elemental spirit, the mother-and-father of life in the Shavian biological Genesis, Shaw admitted to Pearson that he invented her merely out of dramatic necessity, as something "all in the day's work." To destroy any ideal misconceptions that might arise, he gleefully asserted: "Lilith's 'great speech' at the end of *Methuselah* was ground out as pure argument, as Lilith wasn't anybody, and there was no character to express."

### 4. *The New Woman*

When Shaw first began to write in the latter part of the nineteenth century, one of the phenomena which impressed him most was that the age (like most ages, if the truth were told) was obsessed with the idea of its own "newness." He was, naturally, sympathetic toward any such breaking away from the past, but at the same time his irresistible comic sense told him that here was fruitful material for satire. In the original preface to the Independent Theatre edition of *Widowers' Houses,* for instance, he had quoted from his quondam collaborator, William Archer's, review of his play in December 1892, which referred, among plenty of other things, to "the New Drama, the New Criticism, the New Humour, and all the other glories of our renovated world." Similarly, narrowing the field somewhat, when Shaw delightedly saw himself faced with the opportunity to write a preface for his volume of *Unpleasant Plays,* he referred to the following year, when he wrote *The Philanderer,* as the one in which "the discussion about Ibsenism, 'the New Woman,' and the like, was at its height." Indeed, "we of course called everything advanced 'the New.'" Nor could all the changes be regarded as improvements. For instance, because of the dominance of the new business bourgeoisie, the men, although "natural, amiable, and companionable enough," were narrow in their interests and "incredibly ill-mannered," and the women were even worse — "graceless, ignorant, narrow-minded to quite an appalling degree." In the middle classes particularly, however, a revolt against the home ("nobody has yet done justice to the modern clever Englishwoman's loathing of the very word 'home'") was beginning to have some broadening effects, even if it were only a "single clever daughter" who was rebelling. Thus Shaw, in his review of Elizabeth Robins's acting the role of Ella in Ibsen's *John Gabriel Borkman* in 1897, regarded her as representing "the impetuous, imaginative New Woman in her first youth." So rapidly did these new views sweep through the intellectual world that when Shaw composed his "Epistle Dedicatory to Arthur Bingham Walkley," another of his fellow dramatic critics, as a preface to *Man and Superman* in 1903, he was impelled to explain his choice of a heroine for the contemporary frame of his Don Juan drama by remarking, "You would laugh at me if at this time of day I dealt in duels and ghosts and 'womanly' women," and by going on to point out that women of all social classes are now "become equally dangerous: the sex is aggressive, powerful." Archibald Henderson once suggested that Shaw had a sort of forerunner of the modern new woman in his own household. This was his mother — in Henderson's phrase, "independent, self-reliant, indifferent to public opinion"; in her son's, "constitutionally unfitted for the sentiment of wifehood and motherhood." Mrs. Shaw once claimed humorously to Henderson that her son owed all his success to none other than herself.

So the new woman, sometimes also known as the unwomanly woman or the Bashkirtseff sex, was the object both of Shaw's admiration and of his satire, according to the degree of appropriateness or naturalness with which the role suited her character. In a typical Ibsen play, he had generalized in his discussion of *Brand* in *The Quintessence,* "the leading lady is an unwomanly woman, and the villain an idealist . . . a villain by his determination to do nothing wrong." But some of his own unwomanly women are by no means always leading ladies. Both his attitudes are illustrated in *The Philanderer.* Charteris reminds Julia that, when they first met, the position she took up "was that of a woman of advanced views," but it soon becomes evident that these are merely a fashion she has picked up and that they do not really belong to her at all. She is therefore merely a pseudo-new woman. But Grace is a genuine specimen. She affects a business-like, sensible dress and manners. Charteris early puts the question to her as "an advanced woman" concerning whether Julia belongs to him, and she gives the right answer, that "A woman belongs to herself and to nobody else." He congratulates her later on having "a thoroughbred heart." He points out to Cuthbertson and Craven that "The unwomanly women who work for their living and know how to take care of themselves never give any trouble," although Craven is of the opinion that the tone of the Ibsen Club is rather low "because the women smoke and earn their own living and all that." But Grace scandalizes even the presumably sophisticated Charteris when, at the end of the second act, she quietly tells him, "I'm what my father calls a New Woman. I quite agree with all your ideas." In fact, she informs him that she is really in earnest about them, whereas he is not; and that she will never marry a man she loves too much, since she would be utterly in his power, and no new woman would permit herself to be in anybody else's power. She also sensibly realizes that a philanderer, like an artist, will not make a good husband. To her, a man's respect is more important than his love; and in the end both she and Julia, in their diametrically opposite ways, show Charteris that they can live without him. It might be noted that Grace is already a widow, who admits that she married more because Tranfield was in love with her than because she was in love with him.

In *The Irrational Knot* Shaw had shown what some of these advanced ideas are likely to lead to if their possessor does not have discipline and self-control. Here Susanna Conolly, the popular "Lalage Virtue" of the Bijou burlesque, pursues Marmaduke and offers herself to him without marriage, much as Madge does to Owen Jack in *Love among the Artists*. Marmaduke, however, though initially shocked, accepts her, whereas Owen rejects Madge. Susanna is utterly independent and careless of what others think of her. She is a spitfire, she has brains, and she gains Nelly McQuinch's early respect for her ability to support herself. She preaches the Rev. George Lind a very good sermon comparing legal marriage conditions and her own independence, and her exposition of the new morality makes a profound impression on the poor clergyman, who protests that she seems to "see everything reversed — upside down." But Shaw, unfortunately for the attractive and clever Susanna, has determined to use her as an object lesson for a temperance theme. Susanna drinks. Liquor degrades and ruins her. She decides to leave her lover and child and go to America, where, after contracting delirium tremens, she commits suicide amid conditions of the utmost squalor.

Vivie Warren, however (of whom Praed exclaims almost at first glance, "You modern young ladies are splendid — perfectly splendid!"), although she smokes cigars and likes a shot of good whisky, has self-control and self-respect as well as self-confidence, aplomb, and independence. Her total lack of interest in art as well as her practicality, however, also smacks of the Philistine; in fact, Frank actually calls her one.

It is *You Never Can Tell* which at one time furnishes two interesting and amusing sub-species of the type in the Clandons, mother and elder daughter. Mrs. Clandon, supposedly modeled in part on Shaw's own mother, but in even greater part on Mrs. Annie Besant, Shaw's Socialist-Theosophist friend who had published some of his novels in her Socialist magazines, is the old new-woman, or once-new woman. She has always regarded herself as ahead of her era. Though it is only 1896 she has already gained great fame as the author of a series known as *The Twentieth Century Treatises,* on Cooking, Creeds, Clothing, Conduct, Children, and Parents. In dress and manner she looks distinctly old-fashioned for her age, but, winks Shaw, "she belongs to the forefront of her own period (say 1860–80)." Although she is actually kindly and humane, "displays of personal sentiment secretly embarrass her." In other words, "she feels strongly about social questions and principles, not about persons." Her manner is that of "the Old Guard of the Women's Rights movement." Much like Roebuck Ramsden, she holds to all her old opinions and favorite authors, like Darwin, Mill, Huxley, Tyndall, and Eliot, but can prove incontrovertibly that "Socialism is a fallacy." Although she has three children, she has never been in love, but believes that "a life devoted to the Cause of Humanity has enthusiasms and passions to offer which far transcend the selfish personal infatuations and sentimentalisms of romance." All in all, she is an "advanced woman, accustomed to defy public opinion," whereas her husband, who has deserted her, "had a great horror of anything getting into the papers." Duffin, even though he admits that he is using his terms "in the abstract," certainly misreads Shaw's intentions when he suggests that Mrs. Clandon "is indeed, perhaps, Shaw's ideal wife and mother," and Hamon is merely being ludicrous when he calls her "the realist educationist, . . . the heroine of the play, . . . thoughtful, cautious, and well-balanced," although we may admit her "frank and sincere temperament."

This is the kind of new woman who has spoiled her younger daughter Dolly, but has applied her advanced theories of education to her other two children, Philip and Gloria (especially Gloria), with varying success. Gloria is described by her brother and sister, the terrible twins (suggested, thinks Rattray, "by a pair of very spritely real twins, Maurice and Bonté Amos, members of a distinguished legal family"), as "The Woman of the Twentieth Century," "Nature's masterpiece," "Learning's daughter," and "Beauty's paragon." Shaw, however, presents her as "the incarnation of haughty high-mindedness, raging with the impatience of an impetuous, dominative character paralyzed by the impotence of her youth." That is, her new woman-ishness is all veneer. Unlike her mother, she is "all passion," and the conflict between her pride and her passion results in "a freezing coldness of manner." Yet Gloria is an attractive woman, whose full lips and muscularly plump figure "appeal with disdainful frankness to the senses and imagination." Shaw might as well have put it in his favorite single word, "vital," and let it go at that. But he adds that she might be a "very dangerous girl . . . if the moral passions were not also marked, and even nobly marked, in a fine brow."

Her first attempt at revolt against her mother in the question of how to treat their newly discovered father is abortive. She can still state her advanced opinion that the conditions of marriage at present are not such that any self-respecting woman can accept them. She at first wants to be friends with Valentine "in a sensible and wholesome way," argues that she is a "free woman" and is therefore not afraid to tell him that she likes him, but when he kisses her she breaks down, and throws the blame for her dilemma on her mother: "Why didn't you educate me properly?" Here, then, is the theme of the play. Valentine goes on to describe the new sort of scientific education being given to modern girls as "unwomanly" according to the old-fashioned man, but shows how it has actually left Gloria unguarded against attacks by his kind. He blames Mrs. Clandon openly for having given her daughter this "Higher Education of Women." He even informs Gloria, "I didn't respect your intellect: I've a better one myself: it's a masculine specialty."

The result is that Gloria is made over under Valentine's attack. She turns into a natural, even womanly, woman. She becomes intensely jealous when she learns of his previous affairs — and then the twins divulge that she has had several of her own, or at least has been frequently pursued by men in Madeira. But her illusions about herself begin to disappear, and she admits that her "miserable, cowardly, womanly feelings" are now on her father's side, though her conscience is still on her mother's. And at the end of the play Nature, the Life Force, the mother woman, the pursuer, and the terrified quarry all jam up together in this exposé of what happens to a "new woman" when she is really intended to be an old-fashioned womanly woman after all. Ellen Terry, whom Shaw wanted to play the role of Gloria, thought it "delightful. They are all immense." But she still stuck to Irving.

As Shaw got older the new woman seemed to him to get younger, narrower, and brasher. He followed her with eager interest and endowed her with many of his own favorite ideas, but a note of asperity began to creep into his characterizations, and this annoyance deepened into a positive distaste as the gap between his generation and hers widened.

Edith Bridgenorth, the youngest of Bishop Bridgenorth's daughters, is a relatively minor example, but since the action and the discussion of the entire play, *Getting Married,* which Shaw subtitles "A Disquisitory Play," revolve around her impending match, she is an important cog. Shaw uses her as a means of focusing his attack on the legal and domestic aspects of marriage as established in England. For Edith has locked herself into her room on her wedding morning, after having received through the mail a staggering and engrossing pamphlet, entitled *Do You Know What You Are Going To Do? By a Woman Who Has Done It*. Edith is "the typical spoilt child of a clerical household: almost as terrible a product as the spoilt child of a Bohemian household" (an example of which Shaw was to provide later in Ariadne Utterword in *Heartbreak House*). In other words, as Shaw puts it, all Edith's "childish affectations of conscientious scruple and religious impulse have been applauded and deferred to until she has become an ethical snob of the first water." Her humanitarianism is shown by her being engaged in all kinds of social work — "organizing shop assistants and sweated work girls and all that," as her fiancé, poor Sykes, protestingly puts it. For her "impetuous temper and energetic will, unrestrained by any touch of humor or skepticism, carry everything before them." She is enslaved by her sense of duty, but it is the new social duty, and not the old moral duty. So she insists that Slattox and his firm must be exposed, regardless of the consequences to herself. And after she and the rest have thoroughly investigated and then rejected the idea of substituting a mere alliance or simple legal contract for the orthodox marriage, she sneaks the docile Sykes off to a church wedding anyhow, in full knowledge of all the dire legal consequences it may entail on both of them. She has first insured him against any libel actions brought against him on her account, and he has agreed that if he ever commits any actionable crime he'll knock her down before witnesses and go off to Brighton with another lady to provide her with suitable grounds for divorce. This is one solution which Shaw's advanced young women find for their marriage problems.

Hypatia Tarleton in *Misalliance* is a more fully developed young rebel. She is "a typical English girl of a sort never called typical." Her dark hair, brows, and eyes contrast with her white skin. Before Bentley's arrival she has had many other chances to marry, but none of these men had enough brains or distinction for her; in fact, like Edith, she raises all kinds of questions about marriage, such as whether it is as much a matter of "fancy" as it used to be. Like Grace Tranfield, she can understand a woman's falling in love, but not marrying for love. Because of her vitality, she is sick of hearing people talk, talk, talk. She wants "something to happen." She shows the frequent cruelty of youth toward age when she informs sensitive old Lord Summerhays that she's got "a feeling . . . almost a ghastly sort of love for him." When he calls her only a "glorious young beast," she is flattered and says that that is exactly what she likes to be. Fed up with "nice things" such as respectability and propriety, and yearning to be "an active verb" (that is, according to the standard grammatical definition, to be, do, or suffer), she loathes the concepts of home, family, parents, and duty. The antithesis of Gloria Clandon, she is regarded by her proud father as the happy product of his educational methods, which, unlike Mrs. Clandon's, let her do whatever she wanted. But unfortunately, as Hypatia ironically points out, there wasn't anything for her to do. After she gets her eye on Joey Percival, however, she knows what she wants, even if she won't admit that she loves him. She preaches giving way to impulse to attain happiness, and catches him by playing tag through the garden and letting him catch her. But she ends on a most advanced note, nevertheless, by agreeing with her bewildered father that he and she, and all parents and children, could be friends if only the "family were rooted out of civilization." Henderson describes Hypatia as "an ultra-postwar girl divined four years before the war," and adds that she horrified even Shaw's mother "by her callous audacity." Irvine is so moved that he cries that she is "an incredible monster of female savagery," and cannot believe that her parents deserved anything like her. Duffin is just as deeply stirred, and ejaculates that, even if Shaw approves her, "to everyone else she is simply repulsive." Along with her, as emancipated but unpleasant women, he would place Margaret Knox, Gloria Clandon, the younger Bridgenorth women, Mrs. Warren, Blanche, and Susanna Conolly. The only ones who have retained their charm for him are Grace Tranfield, Barbara Undershaft, and — of all people! — Candida. Broadmindedness, it would seem, does not always go with the emancipated college professor. In the case of Hypatia, particularly, Duffin misses the whole point of her remark about her friend who refused to marry a man she loved in order to marry a man who loved her. Duffin comments, "Surely the whole point of this doctrine (of woman as the pursuer) is that when a woman 'loves' a man she never lets him rest till she *has* married him." Of course, the "whole point" really is that she is looking for a good husband and father, not a sweetheart, and so Hypatia discards Bentley just as Grace frees herself from Charteris.

Fanny in *Fanny's First Play* is an even more fully developed case, since her views include the new politics as well as a revolt against the home. She has just finished her education at Cambridge, where she was a member of the university Fabian Society. Impudent and utterly lacking in respect for age as she is, she does not fear to shock her father morally, but hesitates to shock him artistically. Trotter shrewdly guesses that Margaret Knox, in the gaol scene in Fanny's play, is really Fanny herself, and that Fanny was one of the Suffragets on the Deputation and spent a month in gaol with Lady Constance Lytton. Fanny proudly admits the charge. Though her father, the Count's, idealistic dreams of her are wrecked, she cries, "I'm prouder of it than I ever was of anything or ever shall be again." She has boldly met Hypatia's challenge to action.

Even Clara Eynsford Hill felt the call of the new intellectual life after the final curtain of *Pygmalion* had descended. At first Clara, like the young Bernard Shaw, was marked by "the bravado of the shabby genteel," and had "acquired a gay air of being very much at home in society." Her desire to be always in the forefront of the newest fashion makes her reprimand her mother for being disturbed by Liza's astounding "new small talk," and her assumed modernity lets her go off the stage "radiant, conscious of being thoroughly up to date," after she has commented scathingly, "Such nonsense, all this Victorian prudery . . . Such bloody nonsense!" This up-to-the-minuteness, however, is merely a surface finish through the play, and it is only in the epilogue, after her snobbery goes "bang" following her discovery that Liza had really just graduated from the gutter, that she is sincerely converted to the new movement. The instrument of conversion is her reading of the novels of H. G. Wells. She also discovers Galsworthy. As a result, she is no longer too proud to go to work in a furniture shop. When she meets Wells in the flesh, her modernization is complete.

Like Hypatia, Cynthia Barnabas in *Back to Methuselah* is a "glorious young beast." In fact, her nickname, Savvy, is merely short for "Savage." She flies impetuously onto the stage, a "vigorous sunburnt young lady with hazel hair cut to the level of her neck." She "seems to have nothing on but her short skirt, her blouse, her stockings, and a pair of Norwegian shoes." She smokes. In short, says Shaw, she is the "Simple-Lifer" of the twenties — or, we might say, the boyish girl. Savvy is already "out" at the age of eighteen, and has become a Socialist and a Bohemian, but she hasn't yet read a word of Conrad's new book on biology, and she knows even less about artistic matters than Fanny did — Horace being her particular blind spot, as the "Stagirite" was Fanny's. Like Liza and Clara, Savvy uses the latest slang, like "Cheese it" and "Come off it." But she does not regard herself as a "flapper." In fact, she maintains, "I am dowdy and serious," and goes on to prove her claims by insisting that she is interested in the Labor movement, theosophy, and reconstruction after the war. She refuses to flirt with the elderly ex-Prime Minister Lubin, and informs him with youthful dogmatism that his *laissez faire* textbook ideas are "obsolete rot," that Karl Marx's economics are "all rot," and that Darwin is likewise "all rot." After listening to the stupid, shortsighted recriminations of Burge and Lubin, however, she asks like a juvenile realist, "Why are these two ridiculous people to be allowed to come in and walk over us as if the world existed only to play their silly parliamentary game?"

But Shaw is not through with Savvy when he leaves her in *The Gospel of the Brothers Barnabas*. He has already linked her with the first play in his series when he has her confess to Conrad, "I believe the old people are the new people incarnated, Nunk. I suspect I am Eve." Conrad supports her theory, "You are Eve, in a sense. The Eternal Life persists . . . You are only a new hat and frock on Eve." But in spite of her hypothetical age, Savvy is still intellectually immature (to Shaw's mind), for she is not convinced by the Gospel of the Brothers Barnabas when it is explained to her and it is suggested that even the parlormaid might be the first of the new race.

But Shaw's disillusionment over what the once hopeful new woman has turned into reaches its aggrieved height in three young women whom he drew in the middle and late thirties: Aloysia Brollikins in *On the Rocks*, the Young Woman in *The Simpleton of the Unexpected Isles*, and Begonia Brown in *Geneva*. They are all marked by exaggerations of the worst traits which characterized the new women of the preceding decades, and Shaw's teeth are set on edge by their crassness and mere smartness.

Alderwoman Aloysia is "an unladylike but brilliant and very confident young woman in smart factory-made clothes after the latest Parisian models." Old Hipney, the sensible old skeptic, sums her up to Sir Arthur Chavender as full of Marx and conceit, but admits that she has some right to be vain since, "as to examinations and scholarships and certificates and gold medals and the like, she's won enough of them to last your whole family for two generations. She can win them in her sleep." And he goes on to comment on the difference between Sir Arthur's class and Aloysia's: "Your hearts are not in your education; but our young people can lift themselves out of the gutter with it." She is capable of lecturing the gentlemanly Duke of Domesday violently about the "Domesday Clearances," which, he gently points out, took place long before he was born, and she vituperates Sir Broadfoot Basham, D.S.O., K.C.M.G., O.B.E., of the police force, and informs him that in the Class War his "myrmidons will be well paid." It's she, representing the proletariat, who, according to the Duke, "spews out" what seems to him to be Sir Arthur's program of "first rate Platonic Communism" after the Prime Minister has won all the propertied classes to his side. Aloysia, however, refuses to melt before his flattery and fine manners. She relates her own thumbnail biography: "I started out as a school teacher; but when they cut my salary I went into a factory. I organized the girls there and became a trade union secretary. Wherever I went I rose because I couldn't keep down." And now, suddenly, she is, womanlike, attacked by the Life Force, though she handles it in her own independent way. Viscount Barking points out to Sir Arthur that she intends to marry Sir Arthur's son David, although David doesn't yet know it. She is confident that she can reform young David, since she is "a reading thinking modern woman," understands all about psychoanalysis and Oedipus complexes, and knows how to look at things "objectively and scientifically." As soon as she saw David she admits she said to herself, "Evolution is telling me to marry this youth." Nevertheless, in the finale even Aloysia turns herself into a temporarily womanly woman, and when David, making a dying effort at masculine independence, speaks impolitely and angrily to her in front of his mother, she returns his abuse with interest and "storms" out of the door — with David of course in hot and imploring pursuit.

The unnamed Young Woman in the prologue to *The Simpleton* is more briefly sketched. When she is first met in the "tropical port" badgering the emigration officials, she is clearly a talker, a plain-speaker, a critic of everybody and everything, and even an evangelist of a sort, slightly vulgar and breezy. And, when she reappears as Mrs. Hyering in the main play, although she is twenty years older and "better drilled socially," she is still "very much her old self." At the end of the play, in hope of avoiding the disintegration overtaking the useless members of society on the imminent Judgment Day, she goes off to work crossword puzzles, explaining, "It cultivates the mind so, don't you think?" As a specimen of the modern young woman she is innocuous enough.

Begonia Brown in *Geneva,* however, receives as much of Shaw's concentrated venom as he ever puts into his usually good-natured satire. In her outward manners she is surprisingly like Aloysia Brollikins, but in her opinions she is utterly different. Addicted to smoking and putting her heels on the table, she "is a self-satisfied young person, fairly attractive and well aware of it. Her dress, though smartly cut, is factory made; and her speech and manners are London suburban." Begonia, it soon transpires, is ambitious, and has won a London County Council scholarship. Yet she is prudish, for the first thing she thinks of when the Jew offers her another position than her present one as the typist and only active member of the International Committee for Intellectual Co-operation, with headquarters in Geneva, is that it be "all right . . . Morally, you know. No hanky panky. I am respectable; and I mean to keep respectable." She is also materialistic; she won't give up her present job, dull as it is, but sure for twenty-five years, for anything "chancy."

Begonia is particularly distinguished by her intense local pride and narrow parochialism. When the Germans inform her that she is an Aryan like themselves, she says she always retorts that she is an Englishwoman — "Not a common Englishwoman, of course; I'm a Camberwell woman; and though the West End may turn up its nose at Camberwell, Camberwell is better than Peckham any day in the week." In fact, she has a sort of xenophobia even on the local level: "I never could abide Peckham people. They are disliked everywhere. It's instinctive, somehow." When the Jew reminds her that "All peoples are disliked in the lump: English, Germans, French, Protestants, Catholics, Freemasons," she condescends tolerantly toward the Jews by remarking that she's known lots of nice Jews. She is obviously a chameleon, with no character of her own, since she is reduced to "nervous abjection" when the imposing Widow arrives. She is superficial, since her interest in dancing tournaments is greater than in the news that Germany has withdrawn from the League and that Britain has declared war on Russia — though only a war of sanctions. Still her xenophobia asserts itself, and she automatically wants to "give those Bolshies the bayonet." She has an utterly unthinking empire loyalty, as well she might have, since when she was at school she was "chosen five times to recite on Empire Day"; and in her very first year, when she was the smallest child present, she "presented the bouquet to King George's sister," who came to the prize giving. "Say a word against the empire, and you have finished with Begonia Brown." In fact, she never missed a day in seven years at school, and got fourteen prizes for regular attendance. On hearing the news that the British flag has been insulted in the Republic of the Earthly Paradise, she rises "in a fury," but she is not disturbed by the information that three convents and two churches have been burned down there, because, after all, "That's nothing: they're only Catholic churches." When the Secretary of the League informs her that her letters to the Hague have been responsible for several international upheavals, she is merely flattered: "I seem to be having a big success; and I won't pretend I'm not gratified."

To Shaw, Begonia is the embodiment of the British electorate and new governing classes. With modest pride she elucidates the reasons for her success: "You see, I have such a good memory: examinations are no trouble to me . . . You know, although I was always at the top of my class in school, I never pretended to be clever. Silly clever, I call it . . . If you want to know what real English public opinion is, keep your eye on me. I am not a bit afraid of war: remember that England has never lost a battle." She is delighted when the Conservatives want her to stand in a by-election for Camberwell, and has her practical reasons all ready for wanting to run and thinking that she will win: her newspaper publicity first, then the attractive salary, her well-known patriotism, and the split vote between Labor and the Communists. Benjy, the wealthy young Conservative candidate and the nephew of Sir Orpheus Midlander, foreign secretary, has by this time overcome his bashfulness and has become engaged to Begonia; so he proudly offers to withdraw in her favor and pay all her expenses. Sir Orpheus, too, is sure she will get in, to the amazement of the Secretary of the League, for to Sir Orpheus she has "courage, sincerity, good looks, and big publicity as the Geneva heroine. Everything our voters love." Moreover, he candidly admits, she doesn't need to have "a political idea in her head," since the party will see her through. And when she gets to Parliament, she will be a big success there too, because she "will say pluckily and sincerely just what she feels and thinks . . . The House of Commons is exactly like Camberwell" in plenty of respects. So she wins the election, is made a Dame of the British Empire, and sues a blackshirt who pretends to forget her name and calls her Mongolia Muggins, with the result that she clears about £4,000 from him and the sixteen newspapers who quoted him. After the Judge has heard her discuss her bigoted and ignorant sympathies, prejudices, and intentions, he proclaims that she and the Russian Commissar are kindred spirits in essential agreement. Both angrily protest, but he sticks to his point.

The astute Secretary's ironic summation of Dame Begonia Brown may stand as her epitaph: "she would have made a most comfortable wife. Pleasant-looking, good-natured, able to see everything within six inches of her nose and nothing beyond. A domestic paragon: a political idiot. In short, an ideal wife." And therefore, he might have added, a perfect Philistine.

5. *The Younger Generation*

The development in character and conduct of Shaw's new woman raises the allied question of his attitude toward the younger generation in general, male as well as female. So far as their behavior and their treatment of the older generation are concerned, as a matter of fact, Shaw makes little or no differentiation according to sex. His adolescents as well as his young men and women are almost without exception marked by a self-sufficiency and self-confidence, a contempt for age and experience, and a hardness and even boorishness of manners which have disturbed, annoyed, and sometimes even infuriated many readers. Hamon, writing with only Shaw's first twenty years of dramatic composition on which to base his opinions, commented mildly that, with the exceptions of Mrs. Clandon and Sir Patrick Cullen, the older people in the plays — and especially the fathers and mothers — were "presented in such a way as to make them appear ludicrous and often disagreeable." Duffin, writing some years later, realized more trenchantly that, as Shaw grew older, his picture of both youth and age changed: that in the earlier plays, although there are a few "young blockheads" like Johnny Tarleton and a few "wise old fellows" like Caesar and Summerhays, Shaw's dramatis personae may be divided into two main groups — "a crowd of cool, steady-visioned, emancipated young men and maidens, balanced by an equal crowd of hot-headed, hidebound, half-witted old and middle-aged people." True as these generalizations are, it should be noted that in at least certain important respects Shaw's picture of youth does not change: its brashness, its energy, its confidence in itself, and its insensitiveness to the feelings of others persist. It is his picture of the older generation that shifts to a greater sympathy, understanding, and approbation as the oldsters continue to meet the bumptious and impudent onslaughts of the youngsters. There are, of course, the inevitable exceptions, like Ellie Dunn, in which intelligent youth is drawn to experienced age, but they are not typical. Shaw, like Galsworthy, as he grew older, became more and more bewildered and disillusioned by the younger generation whose cause of revolt and self-realization he had once espoused and glorified. With the best of good will and inclination toward tolerance, both men confessed that they had been outdistanced and defeated in their quest for a new, sane, and forward-looking freedom through the leadership of the young. In his latter years, however, Shaw's knowledge of the young must have been gained by pure divination, since all his intimate associates, such as Blanche Patch and Stephen Winsten, agree that he had not met any young people in ages — and, in fact, avoided meeting them (as well as children) if possible.

In *Man and Superman* Shaw put into doctrinal terms the theory that he had already been illustrating in the novels and early plays. Here the irrepressible Tanner, "working himself up into a sociological rage" over Ann's sweetly hypocritical assurance that "I love my mother, Jack," bursts out: "Oh, I protest against this vile abjection of youth to age!" He rants about the marriage market, and calls for a revolution of the children. "I tell you, the first duty of manhood and womanhood is a Declaration of Independence: the man who pleads his father's authority is no man: the woman who pleads her mother's authority is unfit to bear citizens to a free people." Mrs. Whitefield in her negative way also bears her evidence of the true state of parental-filial relationships when she complains to Tanner: "I don't know why it is that other people's children are so nice to me, and that my own have so little consideration for me. It's no wonder I don't seem able to care for Ann and Rhoda as I do for you and Tavy and Violet." Yet Mrs. Whitefield is too conventional to draw the obvious conclusion from the situation she has described, and when she still insists that she loves her children it is Tanner's agreeable task to deliver himself of another shocking *bon mot:* "I suspect that the tables of consanguinity have a natural basis in a natural repugnance." (Shaw forgot that he had once said just the opposite in *The Quintessence of Ibsenism,* in discussing the question of incest as involved in the attraction between Oswald Alving and Regina.)

This parental-filial repulsion, however, had been well established in the novels. Robert Smith in *Immaturity* was nauseated by the "solemn humbug" that his parents used to inflict on him; Adrian Herbert and his mother in *Love among the Artists* had completely incompatible views and possessed nothing important in common; Elinor McQuinch in *The Irrational Knot* "resented her parents' tyranny," and Mr. Lind once smiled at Marmaduke, "happily forgetful, worldly wise as he was, of the inevitable conspiracy of youth against age"; in *Cashel Byron's Profession* there is an utter lack of sympathy and understanding between Cashel and his actress mother, Adelaide Gisborne, and for a long time Lydia and her father did not get along very well, although eventually they came to respect one another; and when Shaw metamorphosed the last novel into *The Admirable Bashville* he still related how Cashel had run away from home to escape the "importunate relationship" with his romantic mother.

In the early plays there are, for a less extreme example, the terrible twins, Dolly and Philip, in *You Never Can Tell.* Shaw describes them as "a very pretty woman in miniature, . . . hardly eighteen yet," and "a handsome man in miniature, obviously the young lady's twin." She is marked by "a rapidly clearing cloud of Spartan obstinacy on her tiny firm set mouth and quaintly squared eyebrows." He is distinguished by decisive movements, a speech which is "unexpectedly deeptoned and trenchant," and manners which are finished, mature, but prepossessing. Yet, stamped by suavity and precociousness as the pair are, they promptly inform the astonished and somewhat dubious Valentine that they prefer people with unimproved minds: "Our own minds are in that fresh and unspoiled condition." Shortly afterward they announce that their mother does not realize that they have grown up, and demand to be taken into her confidence about their unknown father, whereupon she lectures them on the two kinds of family life, the one that she feels she has brought them up to, based on mutual respect and recognition of individual rights in the family, and the husband-and-father dominated one, which consists of "detestable tyrannies" and "duties." When, shortly thereafter, they meet their soured old father, Crampton, they produce such an unhappy impression on him that he exclaims of Dolly to Valentine: "That's a spoiled child, Mr. Valentine. That's one of your modern products." As Henderson once put it, Shaw "created the flapper before she existed in real life." The twins' unabashed mercenariness and practicality are demonstrated when they learn, however, that their despised father has money. Finally, of course, sufficient domestic readjustments are made so that the play can be said to have a happy ending. As Duffin remarks, the dispute between the parents as to how the children were to be brought up accounts for some of the twins' eccentricities.

Revealingly enough, Shaw himself admitted at this time that even to him the prime characteristic of youth was that it had no soul. For in a letter to Terry, grumbling at the difficulty of casting the twins, he outlined his requirements for the pair as follows: "The boy must be attractive, with a smart diction, an inimitable self possession, a refined gravity when mocking his elders, and an exquisite impudence. The other twin is Winifred Emery, who is youth personified (having no soul) and will hit off the callous prettiness of the sister to perfection."

The young people of the inner play in *Fanny's First Play* are only slightly older than the twins, but they lack the veneer of glossy precociousness which characterizes their predecessors. Margaret Knox, a "strong, springy girl of eighteen, with large nostrils" and "an audacious chin," is vigorously serious in her revolt in spite of her outwardly gay manner. Margaret has finally kicked over the traces, run away from home, and ended in jail. As a result, her previous standards of judgment have become so upset that, as she frankly tells her parents after her release, she doesn't know what sort of people they really are either. All she knows is that when she was "set free" she was set free for "evil as well as good," and that she is now a "heroine of reality," not of romance. She denounces society's conceptions of respectability as just "pretending, pretending, pretending," and tells her mother, who is doing her best to understand: "I know now that I am stronger than you and Papa. I havn't found that happiness of yours that is within yourself; but I've found strength." There are to be no masks for her any longer. To her father's horror, she is going to tell everybody what has happened; in fact, she is going to "tear it all down."

Naturally, with this new sense of power and self-realization, she throws over Bobby Gilbey, to whom she has been practically engaged by the two families. Bobby, who is a "pretty youth, of very suburban gentility, strong and manly enough by nature but untrained and unsatisfactory," has also been rebelling, in a flabbier, less sensational way, against his family. In fact, Darling Dora Delaney, "a young lady of hilarious disposition, very tolerable good looks, and killing clothes," has been giving him the education that his tutor, Holy Joe Grenfell, has only abetted him in. Bobby, it is true, had dominated Holy Joe and released all Joe's inhibitions, but it is Dora who is really doing the job of emancipation. As she tells Bobby's parents, "You see, you've brought Bobby up too strict; and when he gets loose there's no holding him." Miss Delaney, however, is confident that if she marries him she can finish his education, and, with the support of Mrs. Knox and Juggins, seems about to be given the chance to prove her claim at the end of the play.

The Patient in *Too True To Be Good* is even more extreme in her revolt and voices views which are as drastic as Tanner's own. Although she and her mother agree to give each other another chance at the end, Mops first dogmatizes: "No woman can shake off her mother. There should be no mothers: there should be only women, strong women able to stand by themselves, not clingers. I would kill all clingers." Later, this homicidal urge is somewhat lightened by her rather unrealizable wish that she had been born an orphan. "I want a world without parents: there is no room for them in my dream." Nevertheless, Aubrey at the very end of the same play is allowed to put a matching shoe on the other foot when he orates at considerable length on the disgusting manners and conduct of the young postwar generation.

Shaw treats the Patient with at least a touch of fondness. He has considerably less affection for Flavia and David Chavender in *On the Rocks,* both of whom Duffin regards as "irresponsible to the point of imbecility." They are not quite that bad, but they are bad enough. Flavia, nineteen years of age, first "bursts violently into the room," shouting, "I will not stand Mamma any longer. She interferes with me in every possible way out of sheer dislike of me. I refuse to live in this house with her a moment longer." This Declaration of Independence she extends by proclaiming that she has simply no individuality left because her mother is always telling her what to do. Lady Chavender, by no means a devotee of motherhood, knows that her fault has been just the opposite of the one charged, and she confesses sadly to her husband, "It serves us right . . . for letting them bring themselves up in the post-war fashion instead of teaching them to be ladies and gentlemen." Later Flavia goes to a meeting for the unemployed, where she meets Viscount Barking ("Toffy"), who falls in love with her. In the true spirit of the new democracy she warns him that she wouldn't be seen at a wedding with a "lousy" viscount, and that she wants to marry a poor man, because, as Toffy explains to Sir Arthur, her "ideal of a delightful husband" is one who is brutal and violent, and uses filthy language. Toffy cures her of this "girlish illusion" by taking her to another meeting and showing her what nice men with good manners poor men really are. Then he proves to her that he is "a real he-man" by calling her "the foulest names until she gave in."

David Chavender, eighteen years old and rather small for his age, is slight and refined in appearance, but follows his sister's lead in the attack on their parents. He too goes to the meeting for the unemployed, is arrested, and falls unemphatically in love with Aloysia, who promptly takes the lead and proposes for him. To her Sir Arthur explains that his son doesn't really hate his mother, as would seem to be the case. What has happened is that, like other modern young people, David has merely read too many books on psychoanalysis and Oedipus complexes, and has got his head "filled with nonsense." Although Aloysia pretends to be greatly upset by David's awful language to her, she is grimly resolved to reform him, in spite of Sir Arthur's warning about women who marry men in such hopes. If anyone can reform David, Aloysia will — though the skeptic might well fear that his second state may be worse than his first.

It is not surprising to find the Margarets, the Mopses, and the Flavias in rebellion when even a Stephen Undershaft can be goaded in his flaccid way into announcing the same stand. His not quite dead spirit flames up a little fairly early in *Major Barbara* when he begs his mother: "For Heaven's sake either treat me as a child, as you always do, and tell me nothing at all; or tell me everything, and let me take it as best I can." Lady Britomart of course insists that she has never treated any of them like children and that she has always made them her "companions and friends." Stephen knows better, and finally asserts himself against his mother by refusing to become a "man of business in any sense." Politics, he thinks, are right for him. When, however, he declares his conviction that it is "the best elements in the English character" that really govern England, Undershaft decides that his son is a born journalist, and so advises him.

Even when Shaw "refinished" the last act of Shakespeare's *Cymbeline*, he made Guiderius and Arviragus, the King's newly discovered sons, voice his own views of filial un-duty when they learn their true parentage. When Guiderius demands militantly of his father, "Can I change fathers as I change a shirt?" Arviragus supports him just as impudently:

> *Well, we have reached an age*
> *When fathers' helps are felt as hindrances.*
> *I am tired of being preached at.*

Old Belarius, embarrassed, tries to assume responsibility for the pair's rudeness, but has to admit that

> *not you nor I*
> *Can tell our children's minds.*

In A.D. 31920 the conflict is still going on, just as it was in 1429 when the Dauphin and his young son in *Saint Joan* hated one another. In the twentieth-century act in *Back to Methuselah* Conrad Barnabas had lamented that his daughter Savvy didn't trust her father any more. "She doesn't talk about things to me. She doesn't read anything I write . . . I am out of it as far as Savvy is concerned." And in the thirty-second millennium (that is, "As Far As Thought Can Reach") youth still does not understand age. The young folks make fun of the Ancients and their way of life. They call them names like "You old fish!" and flippantly accuse them of not knowing "the difference between a man and a woman." They vow "never to become as the ancients." But time, after all, is not a matter that even the Superchildren can control. They grow up. They lose their interest in clothes, love, and dancing. Chloe finally just wants to sit down by herself and meditate on the properties of numbers. This, apparently, is the only way in which Shaw thinks the conflict can be resolved.

As for the problem in our own day, Henderson once had an enlightening colloquy on the subject with his Dr. Johnson. And he learned that Shaw was at least consistent, if not paternal, in his views. For, in spite of the indignant passage in *The Quintessence* about the forcible separating of some children from their parents by the idealists in the state, Shaw still followed the Socialist line closely enough to defend the right of the government to act as it did in the cases of both Shelley and Mrs. Besant. "There may," asserted Shaw, "be some doubt as to who are the best people to have charge of children, but there can be no doubt that the parents are the worst."

## 6. *The Manly Woman*

In discussing what he called "The New Element" in *The Quintessence* Shaw had remarked incidentally of one of the characters of his favorite, Dickens: "Betsy Trotwood is a dear because she is an old bachelor in petticoats: a manly woman, like all good women: good men being equally all womanly men." In the following plays he did not forget this last of his main

types of the female species; in fact, although most of his manly women are
not at all like Betsy Trotwood, he was to use this conception for some of his
most powerful, as well as some of his most farcical, characterizations. Bi-
sexuality, it seems, is the next best thing to having practically no sex at all,
like the Ancients.

Young Sylvia Craven in *The Philanderer* represents the manly woman
in her youth and at an early stage of her Shavian development. As a new
woman, Sylvia not only demands individual freedom but also insists on
actual equality in manners, language, and social treatment with the male
sex. At eighteen, she wears a smart tailor-made dress, a jacket, and a white
blouse with "a man's collar and watch chain so arranged as to look as like
a man's waistcoat and shirt-front as possible without spoiling the prettiness
of the effect." Like most of the women in the Ibsen Club, who keep the
smoking room far too full for Cuthbertson, she smokes cigarettes (and rolls
her own) as a badge of her freedom. But she is still sensitive about her
position, and often feels that she is being slighted because of the "respect"
due to her sex. She therefore affects a blunt, "manly" language, and demands
that she be called by her surname at the Club, just as men are. She is delighted when Charteris slaps her on the shoulder and calls her "old chap"
and "old boy." Even when the news of her father's recovery from Paramore's
Disease is announced (since there is no Paramore's Disease), she declares
that she's not going to be sentimental about it — but pets him nevertheless.
Her womanly sister Julia, as a matter of fact, has reduced her Christian
name to the affectionate diminutive, "Silly."

Vivie Warren, one of the "modern young ladies" who seem so "splendid"
to Praed, is "an attractive specimen of the sensitive, able, highly educated
young middle-class Englishwoman." She is prompt, strong, confident, and
self-possessed, and affects a dress which is plain and business-like, though
not dowdy. At her belt she even wears a chatelaine, with a fountain pen and
a paper knife among its pendants. She has a hearty grip, with which she
not only numbs the aesthetic Praed's fingers but also surprises the robust
Crofts when she squeezes his hand. Like Sylvia Craven and Dolly Clandon,
she likes tobacco, but is not satisfied with anything so delicate as a cigarette.
Perfect content to her when she is tired means "a comfortable chair, a cigar,
a little whisky, and a novel with a good detective story." At Cambridge
Vivie proved that a woman's brain is as good as a man's by tying with the
third wrangler — although she admits that she did it on a bet and wouldn't
do it again because she has found that the money and the kind of education
she got weren't worth the effort. Nevertheless she uses her mathematical
training to set up as an actuary, and the indications are that the accounting
firm that she and her friend Honoria Fraser organize will be a success. She
admits that she was bored when she went to the National Gallery, the

Opera, and a concert where Beethoven and Wagner were played all evening. When Frank Gardner remarks that she looks "quite happy — and as hard as nails," she agrees.

In *The Music-Cure* the positions of the sexes are actually reversed, in one of Shaw's lowest farces. Strega Thundridge, the famous pianist, is "a hard, strong, independent, muscular woman," as anyone who has heard her play would realize. Timid Lord Reginald Fitzambey, an M.P. and even an under-secretary, who loathes music, somehow finds that he has proposed to her, using such arguments as "I am a poor little thing, Strega; but I could make a home for you." As Shaw had written in the preface to his *Pleasant Plays,* "domineering women marry weak and amiable men who only desire a quiet life and whose judgment nobody respects, rather than masterful men." Probably, nevertheless, neither of these caricatures would meet Shaw's highest conception of the perfect manly woman or womanly man, but in them he shows once more how he can have fun at the expense of his own types — more fun, sometimes, than his audiences do.

In *Press Cuttings* the manly woman and the manly man are somewhat more evenly matched. Here Mrs. Rosa Carmine Banger, secretary to the Anti-Suffraget League, is ludicrously contrasted with her president, Lady Corinthia Fanshawe. Lady Corinthia is "beautiful and romantic"; Mrs. Banger is "a masculine woman of forty with a powerful voice and great physical strength." Her theory, indeed, is that "All the really strong men of history have been disguised women." So impressed is General Sandstone that he proposes marriage to her, announcing that he "has met his ideal at last, a really soldierly woman." When Mrs. Banger accepts him, General Mitchener laments that "the British Army is now to all intents and purposes commanded by Mrs. Banger." The only hope is to oppose Mrs. Banger with Mrs. Farrell, to whom he proposes, and is accepted. Perhaps the empire may be saved.

So far only two or three of Shaw's manly women have been recognizable human beings; the rest have been burlesques. Lina Szczepanowska, the Polish acrobatess who steps calmly out of the wreckage of John Tarleton's glass pavilion and Joey's Percival's aeroplane in *Misalliance,* falls somewhere in between, but Shaw's conception of her is basically serious. Lina's profession, her family tradition of running risks, and her at-homeness in male dress all delight Hypatia, who describes her as "the man-woman or woman-man or whatever you call her." Yet Lina's vitality makes her highly attractive to males. She has a "dainty little book" in which she sets down the names, ages, and offers of those who have made propositions to her, but she has rejected them all after showing her superiority to the proposers. The precipitate John Tarleton meets the same fate, but is admitted to her "friendship," and addressed as "old pal." As a matter of fact, she speaks for her author when she fulminates disgustedly against the single topic of conversation and interest in the household — love. It is unhealthy. Male incontinence is universal. And to her Shaw gives the privilege of delivering the lengthy manifesto of the "free woman." Why should she yield to any man, even to marry him? "I am an honest woman," she cries. "I earn my living. I am a free woman: I live in my own house. I am a woman of the world: . . . every night crowds of people applaud me, delight in me, buy my picture, pay hard-earned money to see me. I am strong: I am skilful: I am brave: I am independent: I am unbought: I am all that a woman ought to be." With all these virtues, and more, why, she asks, should I "take my bread from the hand of a man and make him the master of my body and soul?" Thus to Lina Szczepanowska, a Polish acrobat, and to Mrs. George Collins, the wife of a coal dealer, Shaw has given his two most elaborate and eloquent speeches on the relationship between man and woman and the essential superiority of woman to man.

In the preface to *The Millionairess* Shaw explains that his heroine represents the *maitresse femme* type of woman, and goes on at considerable length to discuss the characteristics of the "boss," male and female, and the relationship of the type to society. It is fortunate that he does so, for otherwise the reader might well miss the significance of this farce, which makes him feel that for the first two acts he has been belabored gleefully with a clown's bladder (which makes a lot of noise but has no weight — and which the clown enjoys much more than the victim does); that in the third act he has been knocked down with the blackjack of a doctrinaire; and that in the fourth he has been plied with smelling salts in the hope of sending him home smiling in the delusion that he has tremendously enjoyed being batted all over the place.

Epifania Fitzfassenden, somewhat reminiscent of Lady Britomart, is a millionairess and a managing woman, who has not yet discovered how to make use of her money and her talents. As Shaw wrote playfully to his good friend Lady Astor, with whom, along with her husband and Lord Lothian, he had recently taken a trip to Russia, where they had had a stimulating interview with Stalin himself: "People will say you are the millionairess. An awful, impossible woman. . . ." Irvine, however, sees in Epifania a combination of Beatrice Webb and Lydia, from *Cashel Byron's Profession.* Eppy promptly admits that although she may not be a great woman, she is at least "an unusual woman" — as how could the daughter of her father, the famous financier, now dead, help being? In fact, she seems to have something of an Electra complex, for she constantly quotes his maxims and advice, and acts as she thinks would please him, in spite of the fact that he has left her practically a pauper, with only thirty millions instead of the two hundred he had promised her. She is also "a woman who must always want something and always get it."

So Eppy is introduced as a romantic, domineering, vain female, a snob, thoroughly acquainted with the laws, especially of libel, lacking in a sense of humor, dominating the conversation and other people's lives, given to breaking furniture when balked, and even exchanging blows when driven to extremes. Polly classifies her among "people that no one can live with," even though they may be "very goodlooking and vital and splendid and temperamental and romantic and all that; and they can make a man or woman happy for half an hour when they are pleased with themselves and disposed to be agreeable." And when Eppy abruptly decides that the man she really wants is the Egyptian doctor, he is unimpressed by her attempt to appeal to his sense of romance and adventure. He diagnoses her in his turn: "Enormous self-confidence. Reckless audacity. Insane egotism. Apparently sexless," because "You talk to me as if you were a man. There is no mystery, no separateness, no sacredness about men to you." Her reply that men, except her father, are "a very different and inferior species" does not improve their relations.

The trouble with Epifania, according to Shaw, is that she is frustrated. She has found no suitable outlet for her energy and ability to manage and direct. Convinced that she belongs to the only real aristocracy, the aristocracy of money, and that she is "a plutocrat of plutocrats" (plutocracy being the real social menace, according to the preface of *The Apple Cart*), she has taken money alone as power, security, and pleasure, without demonstrating that she herself has the ability to make it and to do something for society in the process. As a result, she and the Doctor accept each other's challenges to go out into the world with only a few shillings and prove themselves there. Of course, Eppy succeeds without the slightest trouble. Shaw takes us back to the days of *Mrs. Warren* by getting her a job in a sweatshop, through threats of exposure and blackmail. She refuses to do manual work, but insists on "Brain work . . . Managing work. Planning work. Driving work." In spite of the fear and opposition of the wife she shows the proprietors how to buy their own lorry and deal directly with wholesalers. Not finding enough to occupy herself with in this shop, she becomes a scullery maid at the old Pig and Whistle, and soon transmogrifies it into an attractive riverside hotel, the Cardinal's Hat. It is true that she liquidates the old couple, the owners, in the process, but they were outdated anyhow. Because the son saw she was right and backed her up, she takes him on as manager. In fact, he admits freely that she's always right.

Yet Eppy remains the womanly woman as well as the manly woman. She lies about assaulting Adrian and claims loss of memory due to shock. She still fights to keep every penny she has. As her lawyer, Sagamore, says, "She knows the privileges of her sex to a hair's breadth and never oversteps them . . . No woman can be more ladylike — more feminine — when it is her cue to play the perfect lady." When Sagamore assures Alastair that there is no justice for a man against a woman, especially a millionairess, she declares that there is no justice for a millionairess either — she can't keep anything but her money.

And what does all this mean? It means, states the prefatory Shaw, that society is at fault for not giving the plutocrats, and especially rich managing women like Epifania, something useful to do with their brains and organizing powers. There is much to be said for bosses, even for dictators like Mussolini — though Shaw does not speak so well of Hitler, chiefly because of his fallacious racial theories. Shaw even hedges slightly on the desirability of liquidation or extermination by the time he came to write the preface, in contradiction to the implications of the play itself. Ah, preaches Shaw, "Communism is the fairy godmother who can transform Bosses into 'servants to all the rest'; but only a creed of Creative Evolution can set the souls of the people free."

Most people would not see much similarity between Epifania Fitzfassenden and Saint Joan; but Shaw does. At the end of his preface he remarks: "But . . . when all these perfectly feasible equalizations are made real, there still remains Epifania, shorn of her millions and unable to replace them, but still as dominant as Saint Joan, Saint Clare, and Saint Teresa. The most complete Communism and Democracy can only give her her chance far more effectively than any feudal or capitalist society." For in the preface to Saint Joan many years before Shaw had described Joan as not only a "genius and a saint" but also "a born boss." She was an "unwomanly woman" like Rosa Bonheur and George Sand — the "sort of woman that wants to lead a man's life." Although she was too young and ignorant to be a full-fledged "managing woman" as yet, she belonged to the "hardy managing type." Not pretty or attractive, she "was the pioneer of rational dressing for women." In war, maintains Shaw, "she was as much a realist as Napoleon" — forgetting that in the notes to *Caesar and Cleopatra* he had written: "At all events, Caesar might have won his battles without being wiser than Charles II or Nelson or Joan of Arc, who were, like most modern 'self-made' millionaires, half-witted geniuses, enjoying the worship accorded by all races to certain forms of insanity." So even Shaw sometimes changes his mind. To him Joan was to become the supreme example of the manly woman, combining many of the leading qualities of both sexes.

In the play itself, Shaw portrays her out of her own mouth: "I have arranged it all: you have only to give the order." "I will never take a husband . . . I am a soldier: I do not want to be thought of as a woman. I will not dress as a woman. I do not care for the things a woman cares for." "I am such a coward. I am frightened beyond words before a battle; but it is so dull afterwards when there is no danger." She would like to nurse Dunois for a while: "Soldiers always nurse children when they get a chance." "They all say I am mad until I talk to them."

The problem of Joan's sanity and her visions Shaw attempts to solve by classifying her as a "Galtonic vizualizer," to whom the conceptions of the imagination are reflected in the mind's eye as in a magic lantern. Joan, of course, is convinced that the things she sees and the orders she gives are straight from "her Lord . . . the King of Heaven." Although sure almost to the end that God will not let her be beaten, in spite of the skepticism of Dunois and others, she feels her isolation and uniqueness: "Yes: I am alone on earth: I have always been alone . . . France is alone; and God is alone . . . I see now that the loneliness of God is his strength." This sense of mystical union, however, sometimes extends to her bond with "the common people," from whom she has sprung and on whom she often depends for spiritual as well as physical support and encouragement. Two of the leading ideas which Shaw focuses in Joan are associated with her sense of oneness and representativeness — her Protestantism and her nationalism. As Cauchon complains, "She acts as if she herself were The Church . . . It is always God and herself." In such a conception, obviously, the church loses its powerful position as an intermediary. As for her nationalism, in preaching the unity of France ("France for the Frenchmen") she is also undermining the universality of Catholicism, not yet being prophetic enough in her vision to conceive the picture of one world in the political sense.

The tragedy of the death of a leader like Joan, too simple, direct, and sincere to realize the nature of the forces arrayed against her, is mitigated partly by her perception of her future as a martyr. When she tells the Archbishop, the King, Dunois, and the rest that if she goes through the fire she will go through it to the hearts of the common people for ever and ever, she is perhaps being faced in her instinctive and unintellectual way with the same problem that Thomas à Becket had faced: the problem of the relationship between *hubris* and martyrdom. She, however, solves it with the same problem that Thomas à Becket had faced: the problem of [20] canonization she recapitulates to Charles, now called the Victorious: "I was no beauty. I was always a rough one: a regular soldier. I might almost as well have been a man. Pity I wasn't . . . But my head was in the skies, and the glory of God was upon me." And after the final magnificat from all the cast she puts a question to them ironically and astutely: "Woe unto me when all men praise me! I bid you remember that I am a saint, and that saints can work miracles. And now tell me: shall I rise from the dead, and come back to you as a living woman?" In consternation they all spring to their feet and exit one by one, each with his particular excuse. Joan is left alone, once more addressing God: "O God that madest this beautiful earth, when will it be ready to receive Thy saints? How long, O Lord, how long?"

# V I

## ... THAN THE MALE

SHAW'S WOMEN have left a somewhat equivocal impression in the minds of many of his critics. How do his women compare with his men? Which sex is he fonder of portraying, and which does he portray more successfully? And which does he seem to have a higher opinion of in the social scheme? In attempting to find an answer to these questions, Duffin, for instance, conducts an analysis and reduces his findings to what he calls "facts and figures." Somewhat unhappily, he admits that the initial impression left by Shaw's women is not "inspiring." Women play the "less worthy part" in more plays than men do; there are more "unpleasant" women than "unpleasant" men; the "great men" outnumber the "great women." Nevertheless, he concludes with the triumphant paradox that "the supreme characters on the Shavian stage are women," and cites, as a rather feeble climax, Candida, Eve, Lilith, Lysistrata, and Joan in proof.

Generalization is always risky. If, for example, one were to base his conclusions on the mere proportion of the sexes in Shaw's highest character category, the realist, one would have to declare a virtual tie. In the plays, Shaw's male realists, on the whole, seem surer of themselves from the beginning, whereas his females more often have to undergo a disillusioning process to achieve realism; in the novels, however, there are more natural-born female realists in proportion than in the plays. On the other hand, when one reviews the outstanding characters in Shaw's three basic categories, one is forced to the conclusion that his most memorable men are usually realists, whereas his most memorable women are usually either Philistines or idealists. But, despite this situation, as C. E. M. Joad points out in his excellent article on "Shaw's Philosophy" in *G.B.S. 90*, over and over again there occur covert hints and overt remarks which indicate that, in cases like Eve and Lilith, Shaw would rate the importance of woman — particularly, of course, the mother woman — above that of man in the evolution of life; femaleness is more primitive, and thus more fundamental, than maleness — that is, woman is biologically primary, whereas man is biologically secondary. In this sense woman, to Shaw, must perforce be greater than man. In his dramatis personae, too, there are a greater number of distinctive female types than there are male, though the male have their significant varieties too.

1. *The New Man*

The emergence of the new woman in the latter part of the nineteenth century impressed Shaw as one of the most striking social phenomena of the age. His sense of symmetry also told him that there ought to be a new man to parallel this new woman, and his observant eye soon differentiated this type for his creative use. But, although the new male type possessed very great social and economic meaning, Shaw never became a tenth as much interested in it as he did in the female and therefore produced very few well-developed specimens of it in his writings. In fact, Tanner, in *Man and Superman,* is the only one of Shaw's characters to note and comment specifically on the type, in the person of his remarkable chauffeur, Enry Straker. It is to the bored Octavius, who is much more concerned with Ann, that Tanner breaks the news of his discovery. "That's a very momentous social phenomenon," he exclaims after an enlightening discussion of labor, education, and Socialism with Straker. "Here have we literary and cultured persons been for years setting up a cry of the New Woman whenever some unusually old fashioned female came along; and never noticing the advent of the New Man. Straker's the New Man."

As a matter of fact, though, Shaw himself had perceived the coming of the new male type many years before, without attaching the label to it. Edward Conolly, the protagonist of *The Irrational Knot* and later a prominent minor figure in that much more amusing and credible novel, *Love among the Artists,* was the crude material from which Shaw was to distil the comic essence of Enry twenty or so years later. The supercilious clergyman, Mr. Lind, describes Conolly as "only a workman" — which would probably be Tavy's attitude toward Straker. But Lord Jasper, Earl of Carbury, Conolly's employer, "a man with no sort of turn for being a nobleman," but one with a great interest in experimental science, calls him "a genius as an electrician," and treats him with the same democratic camaraderie as Tanner treats his chauffeur. As an American boy of Irish ancestry, Conolly was apprenticed to an electrical engineer, and finally came to England to work as an electrician — as Shaw in his preface points out that he himself did in his first job with the Edison Telephone Company, established in London with a staff which was mostly American. With his mechanical ability, his practicality, and his plans for a cheap electro-motor, Conolly soon becomes a great success in applied science and business, and enters the social world as well, a world for which he has a withering contempt.

Like so many of Shaw's favorite heroes, Conolly is a diabolonian. He is not only a plain speaker, but he has no manners — and prides himself on the fact. He has no ambitions to be a "gentleman." He defends his sister Susanna's conduct in establishing a liaison with Marmaduke, and does not consider it immoral. He tells Marian Lind that he has never had the usual "ideals" about relatives or patriotism. His letter of proposal to her is drawn up along purely rational lines. After their marriage Marian epitomizes him as a pure scientist and realist even in human relations. In fact, even though he betrays slight philandering proclivities (and, like Bompas in *How He Lied to Her Husband,* likes other men to make love to his wife), he shows more humanitarianism toward the servants than toward his wife. Only once, after his marriage has clearly gone on the rocks and Mrs. Leith Fairfax tries sincerely to intervene, does his "inhuman self-possession" vanish long enough for him to speak kindly and gratefully to her for a moment; later, when Elinor McQuinch tells him some home truths about himself and shows him his wife's letter about running away, he is imperturbable. Although Marian perceives that her husband "sees and feels everything by instinct," she diagnoses his creed as "to believe in nature as something inexorable, and to aim at being as inexorable as nature." Thus all sentiment disappears in his presence — and all feeling too.

Yet Conolly is not a narrow man. Mr. Lind describes him to Mrs. Douglas as "a practical man . . . but highly educated." Lind not only is impressed by the other's ability to speak French and Italian fluently, but also admits that he is a "remarkable musician" and is "by no means deficient in culture." Conolly's musical taste and knowledge are, like Shaw's own, so self-assured that he cannot bear amateurism, and he is therefore publicly irritated by his wife's playing the piano, because, as he says, music is merely "pretty" to her and she "patronizes it to the best of her ability." Marian therefore plays no more, but he continues to sing. In a fifteen-minute oration to Elinor on the subject of his divorce, he explains to her the importance of artistic understanding to a whole man, and points out that, although he started as a workman and still regards himself as one, the difference between himself and his colleague Jackson, whom they all call "the Yankee cad," is that he was lucky enough to get an aesthetic training while he was young, whereas Jackson, who is not a cad at all when in his proper place at the works, did not, and therefore is taken in by all the sham refinements he now sees around him. Yes, admits Conolly, "it was not until I had made a *mésalliance* for Marian's sake that I realized how infinitely beneath me and my class was the one I had married into." Yet his inordinate pride in being a worker is no greater than that of Sam Gerridge, the independent plumber of Tom Robertson's *Caste* in 1867, who brags truculently about being a mechanic and not being ashamed of his paper cap.

At the end of the novel, Conolly holds out inexorably for the repudiation of all duties, but his world is too rarefied for Marian to live in. In the curtain lines she comments, with more perspicacity than Shaw gives her credit for, "You are too wise, Ned." But Ned replies, "It is impossible to be too wise, dearest." Then he "unhesitatingly turned and left her." Irvine sums Conolly up as a "Benthamite robot," like Bluntschli. But Bluntschli, after all, had some feeling and romance still left in him. West discounts the significance of Conolly as a "champion of the social eligibility of the new scientific intelligentsia," since the latter was "fighting a battle which to all intents and purposes was already won." Conolly's own sister was content to sum him up as "a man in a thousand—though Lord forbid we should have many of his sort about!" One in a thousand, it will be remembered, was Shaw's proportion of realists to Philistines and idealists in *The Quintessence*. In his preface to the novel Shaw defended his work as "a fiction of the first order," not the second order, because "it is one of those fictions in which the morality is original and not ready made." It remains a fiction nevertheless.

In Enry Straker twenty years later Shaw cut his canvas considerably smaller, but created a much more recognizable and appealing human figure on it. Enry has little of Conolly's broad claims to "culture," but it is noteworthy that he is quick to set Tanner right when Tanner attributes to Voltaire a saying that his chauffeur knows is to be found in "Bow Mar Shay." Straker is the efficient mechanic, the man who does things with his hands, that the new kind of technological education is producing. For, after Board School, Enry has gone to the Polytechnic, which, as Tanner playfully points out, is Enry's university, better than Oxford, Cambridge, Durham, Dublin, or Glasgow. But Enry, as Enry sees himself, is no snob. He admits that Oxford is probably a very nice sort of place "for people that like that sort of place. They teach you to be a gentleman there. In the Polytechnic they teach you to be an engineer or such like." Enry is as proud of his class as Sam Gerridge ever was. According to Tanner, "This man takes more trouble to drop his aitches than ever his father did to pick them up. It's a mark of caste to him. I have never met anybody more swollen with the pride of class than Enry is." Straker takes the chaffing good-naturedly, but is nevertheless intensely serious about the machine age. When Octavius, who apparently knows his Ruskin, announces that he believes "most intensely in the dignity of labor," Enry, unimpressed, replies, "That's because you never done any, Mr. Robinson. My business is to do away with labor. You'll get more out of me and a machine than you will out of twenty laborers, and not so much to drink either." Whereupon Tanner begs Tavy not to get Enry started on political economy, about which he knows more than they do, for Tavy is only a "poetic Socialist" —Enry is a "scientific one." Yet Straker's horizon is too limited for him to be a true Shavian realist. In fact, when Mendoza offers to tell the story of his life and Enry is doubtful, Tanner reprimands him jocosely: "Tsh-sh:

you are a Philistine, Henry: you have no romance in you." Joad in *G.B.S.* *90* suggests that Straker, as well as Alfred Doolittle in *Pygmalion,* with their "fund of instinctive rule-of-thumb philosophy," devoid though it is of any culture and most intellectual attainments, are the lineal descendants of Shaw's favorite, Samuel Butler's, Mrs. Jupp in *The Way of All Flesh* and Yram in *Erewhon.*

In his preface Shaw admits that the original model for Straker was Leporello, valet to Mozart's Don Giovanni, whose metamorphosis "into Enry Straker, motor engineer and New Man, is an intentional dramatic sketch for the contemporary embryo of Mr. H. G. Wells's anticipation of the efficient engineering class which will, he hopes, finally sweep the jabberers out of the way of civilization." But the important matter, of course, is not that here we have a servant with ideas not only of equality but of superiority, but that here is a doer and a maker of the machine age contrasted with the — presumably — outmoded talker, theorizer, and intellectual. Irvine concludes that Shaw's implication is that Straker, being a doer and not a talker, "will inherit the earth." Perhaps, however, remembering Shaw's own propensity for talking as well as his scorn of the material and scientific in his super-civilization, one might hesitate to draw quite such a comprehensive inference. It is enough that Enry is a characteristic phenomenon of our modern age.

This type of new man, then, did not hold out quite such a rosy hope for the future as did Shaw's first, and best, type of the new woman. Shaw also presents another, and later, type of the new man which proved to be as disappointing as the later type of new woman. Most representative of this type is Gunner in *Misalliance;* at least, that is the name which the exuberantly imaginative Tarleton gives him after he flushes him in the portable Turkish bath, though later Gunner names himself John Brown, and finally admits that he is really Julius Baker, the son of Tarleton's old and discarded flame, Lucinda Titmus. But Gunner, like Straker, had a sort of precursor in the novels, since Bashville, the footman in *Cashel Byron's Profession* and later the title character in *The Admirable Bashville,* is in a way a new man, though not a mechanical man. For Bashville, as the echo in the title of Shaw's later play suggests, was a sort of Admirable Crichton. Not only was he deferred to in the stables as "an authority on sporting affairs, and an expert wrestler in the Cornish fashion," but "At the sign of the Green Man in the village he was known as a fluent orator and keen political debater." He was fond of poetry, and loved to recite it to his fellow-servants, especially the women. His mistress, Lydia Carew, however, although she realized his smartness, "had no suspicion that she was waited on by a versatile young student of poetry and public affairs, distinguished for his gallantry, his personal prowess, his eloquence, and his influence on local politics." Nor did she have any suspicion that, in his new democracy, he aspired to love her. When he learns that she prefers Cashel Byron, that famous practitioner of the sister art of boxing, to himself and his wrestling, he takes the blow with the good grace of a "man of honor," but determines never to go "into service" again. In fact, he is so impressed by her kind and polite dealing with him that he wakes from his dream and sees himself only as "a very young, very humble, and very ignorant man, whose head had been turned by a pleasant place and a kind mistress."

Gunner, too, thinks much better of himself than he deserves, but his whole character is coarsened. The "strong expression of moral shock" on his face while he witnesses the conduct of Hypatia and Percival from his eyrie in the Turkish bath shows that he is an idealist. He is obviously also an idealist in regard to his mother, much like Brassbound. Like Brassbound, too, he comes to Tarleton demanding justice, not money. He is a cashier, and he draws a deadly picture of the life "in a stuffy little den counting another man's money," but he feels that he has "an intellect: a mind and a brain and a soul"; and these need to be fed. He is therefore rebelling. So he has been reading books at one of Tarleton's free libraries — not the novelettes that Tarleton suspected in his remark, "Judging from your conversational style, I should think you must spend at least a shilling a week on romantic literature," but books on Russia and the new social experiments there. He hates bourgeois holidays and the kind of recreation they afford, and denounces the morals of "your rotten bourgeoisie." Under the influence of sloe gin (he is a teetotaler by conviction) he announces himself as "one of the intellectuals . . . a reading man, a thinking man." In reply to Tarleton's query as to whether there are "chaps of this sort in Jinghiskahn," experienced old Summerhays admits that "they exist everywhere: they are a most serious modern problem," and goes on to analyze Gunner's type of thinker and education by calling him "a troublesome person" with "neither sense enough nor strength enough to know how to behave yourself in a difficulty of any sort." Gunner's sort of anarchism, says Summerhays, is the kind that the police can best deal with. And finally motherly Mrs. Tarleton, remembering her friendship with Lucy Titmus, leads Gunner away, still blustering in loud-mouthed, drunken independence about "not knuckling down to any man here" and affirming his "manhood all the same." Obviously the new education has done no good to a man like this, whose shallow Marxism even Shaw has to expose.

In all this, indeed, there is a queer echo of Snobby Price, one of the "undeserving poor" in *Major Barbara*. Snobby is another man with a grievance against society, especially capitalism. To the skeptical Rummy (short for Romola) Mitchens he calls himself "an intelligent workin man," whose father was "a Chartist and a reading, thinking man: a stationer, too." But Snobby can't get a job at his trade of painting because, as he explains, he is "intelligent beyond the station o life into which it has pleased the

capitalists to call me; and they don't like a man that sees through em."
Moreover, like a good labor unionist, "I stand by my class and do as little
as I can so's to leave arf the job for me fellow workers." Finally, being "fly
enough to know wot's inside the law and wot's outside it," he does inside
it as the capitalists do: "pinch wot I can lay me ands on." So it is the "state
of society" on which he lays the blame for his milking the Salvation Army
for handouts, though he is able-bodied and perfectly capable of working.

Compared to spineless social "rebels" of this type, the self-respecting
though spiritually limited mechanic like Enry is infinitely to be preferred.
It is very strange that Shaw never pursued the history of Enry's type any
further.

## 2. *The Philanderer*

When even a cold rationalist like Ned Conolly is once caught by his
wife looking back along the street at a woman, "doubtless a pretty one,
probably dark," it is no wonder that lesser men are frequently professed
philanderers, though they may consider themselves realists at the same
time. Marian Conolly's comment on her husband's extra-curricular activities, which showed him "always ready to make love to any one that will
listen to him," was that "He only does it to amuse himself. He does not
really care for them: I almost wish he did, sometimes." But Shaw was
only maliciously trying to make Marian out as a bit of a hypocrite, since
only a few minutes before, when her old flame, Sholto Douglas, had called,
she had received him in such a way that he at once realized that "he was
clearly welcome to philander." Sholto, a poet whose sonnets used to breathe
"real, romantic, burning, suicidal love," is an old hand at this art, but
temporarily meets a just fate when he finds himself eloping with Marian,
who even at this serious juncture cannot resist flirting "a little" with the
ship's doctor. Douglas, however, accomplishes a marvel of self-justification
when at the end he refuses to marry Marian, runs out on her, and apologizes to his mother for his misbehavior.

Sidney Trefusis, the unsocial Socialist, also reflects some of his author's
amatory proclivities. Although already married to Henrietta, Sidney amuses
himself by making love to the schoolgirl, Agatha Wylie, in order to make
her happy, and then forgets all about her. When he finds that she has taken
his flirtation all too seriously, he watches her "with the curiosity of a vivisector." After Henrietta's melodramatic love-death, he informs his friends
Brandon and Erskine that he keeps a portrait of her constantly before him
to "correct his natural amativeness." Although he has fallen in love once
or twice since, a glance at the picture of his lost wife is enough to cure
him of any desire to marry. In fact, he does not believe that "any human
being was ever foolish enough to love another in the story-book fashion,"
or that any "latter-day man has any faith in the thoroughness or perma-

nence of his affection for his mate." Woman, he believes, is playing exactly the same comedy. But the "strain of gallantry which was incorrigible to him" eventually is transformed into love, or at least into the determination to marry, partly because Agatha insists she is no longer in love with him. After analyzing his attitude and situation realistically and scientifically, he is even pleased to find "a consoling dash of romance in the transaction." So, after persuading Gertrude Lindsay to transfer her love from him to Erskine by pulling out all the old stops about duty, self-sacrifice, and renunciation (appealing to a woman "according to her womanishness," as he candidly and gleefully puts it to Jansenius), he finally wears Agatha's opposition away, and marries her so as "not to let the individualists outbreed me." To this godlike, omniscient mind it is no surprise that the marriage turned out "much as I expected it would," although he confesses that his wife's "views on the subject vary with the circumstances under which they are expressed." But at least the philanderer has been tamed, largely by his own impulse.

Charteris, title character of *The Philanderer,* is a more consistent study. Always laughing at his own "amative enthusiasm," admitting that he could love any pretty woman, playing selfishly and egotistically on women's credulities and old-fashioned ideals, saying that he cares for all women equally and talking to them as if they were "any other fellow," he has a powerful fascination for the other sex. He frankly advises Grace to marry someone else, so that he can come and philander with her; but at the end she decides not to remarry at all. Her wise advice, as she takes the rejected and almost fainting Julia in her arms, is: "Never make a hero of a philanderer." But Shaw has tried his best to do so, for his final stage direction reads, in part: "Charteris, amused and untouched, shakes his head laughingly." Henderson is considerably out of sympathy with Shaw on this point, for he calls Charteris "the type of degenerate male flirt — the pallid prey of the *maladie du siècle,"* and refers to his "bloodless Don Juanism."

Charteris is rather exceptional among Shaw's philanderers, most of whom follow the course of Shakespeare's Benedick and ultimately, after considerable protestation and experimentation, succumb to Hymen. Closest to Charteris is St. John Hotchkiss, in *Getting Married,* whom for some obscure reason Shaw associated with the playwright St. John Hankin in a letter to Mrs. Campbell in 1915. "Sinjon" is so uncircumspect as to allow himself to get engaged to Leo Bridgenorth even before her divorce from Rejjy seems about to go through. Sinjon is also so forgetful, so susceptible, and so gallant that he offers to take Cecil's place with Edith before he recalls his "prior engagement." He is, moreover, deeply involved with Mrs. George, whose mature charms infatuated him the very first day that he met her in her husband's coal shop. Although at one point she sarcastically characterizes him as "only one of those poor petticoat-hunting creatures that any woman can pick up" and complains that "the habit of falling in love with other men's wives is growing" on him, he remains primarily true to his allegiance to her. At the end of the play, following his haughtily selfish declaration that he doesn't believe in anything but his own will and pride and honor, and his insistence that he has no regard for the superstition of marriage or middle class morality, he admits that he would be unable to steal George's wife, even if she were willing to be stolen. All his radical and advanced philosophies were mere words, and he is content to have the privilege of calling on her in her home, where he can enjoy the company and conversation of her and her husband. Ruefully he confesses, "This marriage bond which I despise will bind me as it never seems to bind the people who believe in it, and whose chief amusement it is to go to the theatres where it is laughed at." Obviously, Hotchkiss will never marry.

But the rest of Shaw's major philanderers are either already married or are on the verge of getting married during the course of the plays. Sergius, in *Arms and the Man,* gets a gleam in his eye as soon as he glimpses the tail of Louka's double apron, in spite of — or perhaps because of — the fact that he has just completed a very noble love scene with Raina in the highest romantic tradition. Twirling his moustache, Sergius admits that he finds it very fatiguing to keep the "higher love" up for any length of time and that "One feels the need of some relief after it." Yet Sergius is happily entrapped by Louka before he is many weeks older.

Valentine, the handsome "Duellist of Sex" in *You Never Can Tell,* falls in love at first sight with Gloria Clandon, but yet bluntly admits that he has felt this way many times before. He is no novice at the game, and has been interviewed by many mothers about their daughters. He explains glibly, however, that "a man's power of love and admiration is like any other of his powers: he has to throw it away many times before he learns what is really worthy of it." From the outset he is "in search of amusing adventures," and does not aspire to marry. But in spite of his terrorized struggles to escape at the last moment, the net falls over him, and he is ready to be exhibited as a domesticated husband a short time after the curtain falls.

John Tanner, Shaw insists, is his reincarnation of Don Juan Tenorio, and *Man and Superman* is a Don Juan play, "in which not one of that hero's mille e tre adventures is brought upon the stage." A Don Juan, admits Shaw in his preface, is, "Vulgarly, a libertine." But he prefers to take the term in a philosophic sense, as applying to a man who "follows his own instincts without regard to the common, statute, or canon law." The modern Don Juan is no mere Casanova, but has read Schopenhauer, Nietzsche, and Westermarck, and "is concerned for the future of the race instead of for the freedom of his own instincts." Having thus stacked the

cards in favor of his conception, Shaw lets Ann exclaim: "What a shocking
flirt you are, Jack! . . . You are always abusing and offending people; but
you never really let go your hold of them." And Tanner himself contradicts
Tavy, who has accused him of never having been in love: "I! I have never
been out of it. Why, I am in love even with Ann. But I am neither the
slave of love nor its dupe." In the play, however, he philanders with nobody; in fact, only in his reminiscences with Ann about his boyhood and
his affair with the mysterious "dark-eyed girl named Rachel Rosetree" does
he even seem to have any philandering history. He goes so far as to remark
jocosely to the shocked Octavius, "I believe we were changed in our cradles,
and that you are the real descendant of Don Juan." The missing affairs
are discussed only by Don Juan himself in Hell. So perhaps it is not so
surprising after all that Tanner, finding himself in the strangely pleasant
coils of the boa constrictor, decides to coöperate with the Life Force and
do his share for the future of the race.

Similarly the philandering activities of Hector Hushabye, more or less
happily married to Hesione in *Heartbreak House,* have been prodigious.
As he apologizes to his wife for having kissed her sister so strenuously,
"And as women are always falling in love with my moustache I get landed
in all sorts of tedious and terrifying flirtations in which I'm not a bit in
earnest." In *The Millionairess* Epifania dissects her unsatisfactory lover,
Adrian Blenderland, to the Egyptian doctor, while delivering a dissertation on the various kinds of unfaithfulness in marriage: "This disappointed
philanderer tries to frighten you with my unfaithfulness. He has never
been married: I have." Even the canny and definitely happily married King
Magnus in *The Apple Cart* admits to the predatory Orinthia, "women
like you are dangerous to wives. But I don't dislike your sort: I understand
it, being a little in that line myself."

*Overruled* is entirely a farcical comedy of philandering — or "the gallant-
ries of married people" — and Shaw provides it with a disquisitory preface
of some length on monogamy, jealousy, morality, sex, and nature, in which
he even calls for a sort of Kinsey Report so that the world can know the
truth of what really goes on after marriage. The playlet is a kind of pre-
Cowardian *Private Lives,* in which Shaw illustrates the difference between
the theoretical and the practical libertine. His two couples are more theoretical than applied. Mr. Juno believes that "passion is not real passion
without guilt," and insists that the conventions of illicit love be lived up
to — but he never passes the conventions of licit love after all. Gregory
Lunn is a thwarted and conscience-ridden philanderer, always thinking of
his promise to his mother never to make love to a married woman. Mrs.
Juno is also afraid of going "too far," but is enough of a pursuer to say,
"I think you ought to go . . . but if you try I shall grab you round the
neck and disgrace myself." Mrs. Lunn (née Jenkins) is very respectable,

but men are always falling in love with her. She never reciprocates, but likes to be amused by the experience. In her Shaw extends somewhat the idea in *How He Lied to Her Husband* when he has her remark, without any jealousy, that she's "naturally rather particular" about the women her husband falls in love with. Eventually, after they have all had their temporary fill of philandering, they go out to dinner together, paired off with each other's husbands and wives.

From the preceding cases it is clear that Shaw does not confine his philanderers to men, although they are in the majority. Besides Mrs. Lunn and Mrs. Juno, Ariadne Utterword — according to Hesione — is a desperate philanderer, who "has never been in love in her life, though she has always been trying to fall head over ears." And Sweetie in *Too True To Be Good* is as much a philanderer as a pursuer. The mercurial Aubrey tattles on her by saying: "I have known her to fall in love with a new face twice in the same week." Sweetie has a special taste for commercial travelers, and was kicked out of the hospital during her nurse's training because she had too much sex appeal for the patients. The conclusion is that most human beings have the philandering instinct in them to a greater or less degree. But it is more prominent and characteristic in the male because the Life Force makes most females take their love affairs with full seriousness. The males can afford to wait, or amuse themselves first before succumbing to marriage.

### 3. Art and the Artist Man

In the first act of *Man and Superman* the omniscient Tanner further bewilders the already bewildered Octavius by informing him: "Of all human struggles there is none so treacherous and remorseless as the struggle between the artist man and the mother woman." This dogma Shaw reinforces in his preface, so that its significance in understanding the whole truth about art and artists cannot be overlooked. The difference between prosaic people and artistic people, says Shaw, is that the prosaic man puts money and nourishment first and the prosaic woman puts children first, whereas the artist is always straying "in all directions after secondary ideals." The artist yearns to create, in his sense of the word, but his sense is not the woman's sense. Money, food, marriage, children are nothing to the real artist, for they stand in his way, which he pursues with the same unscrupulousness and selfishness, disguised as "self-sacrifice," as the woman uses in pursuing hers. Thus, for his purpose, the artist will feed on women as on everything else, for his purpose is "as impersonal, as irresistible as her own." Consequently, when the two purposes meet, as they often do, "the clash is sometimes tragic."

So far in his argument Shaw has assumed that the artist is a man, as he generally is — and always is in Shaw's plays, though not always in his novels. But of course he realizes that there are female artists too, and he savors the dramatic possibilities by adding that when the situation is "complicated by the genius being a woman, then the game is one for a king of critics: your George Sand becomes a mother to gain experience for the novelist and to develop her, and gobbles up men of genius, Chopins, Mussets and the like, as mere hors d'oeuvres." It is astonishing that a connoisseur like Shaw, perceiving the opportunities in such a combination, left them to a Philip Moeller to exploit instead of adding Madame Sand to his own historical portrait gallery.

Before examining in any detail the many Shavian dramatic specimens of the artist man, often engaged in the internecine struggle with the mother woman, actual or potential, it is desirable to explore further Shaw's conceptions of art and the artist, his function, methods, and aims. I say "conceptions" rather than "conception," because, as most critics, such as Bentley, fail to note clearly, Shaw's views on the subject altered as time went on, and he shifted the focus of his camera considerably. His philosophy during the period when he was writing his novels, especially, had quite a different emphasis from the one, or the ones, when he was writing his plays.

From the beginning of his writing career Shaw had a particular interest in the various forms of art and their practitioners. In his first novel, *Immaturity,* he introduced Jim Vesey, a superannuated landscape painter, and Cyril Scott, a promising young artist; Hawkshaw, an unprincipled society poet; and Lady Geraldine Porter, a rich and strong-minded patroness of the arts. In *Cashel Byron's Profession,* Mr. Carew, the shrewd but disappointed critic, sociologist, and philosopher, leaves a letter warning his daughter Lydia: "Beware of painters, poets, musicians, and artists of all sorts, except very great artists. Self-satisfied workmen who have learned their business well, whether they be chancellors of the exchequer or farmers, I recommend to you as, on the whole, the most tolerable class of men I have met." In the same vein, in the preface to *The Irrational Knot* Shaw candidly presents himself as "a stupendously selfish artist leaning with the full weight of his hungry body on an energetic and capable woman" — i.e., his mother. In the novel itself, the philandering Sholto Douglas is a minor romantic poet, who won the Newdigate prize while at Oxford. Sholto is a poseur, and he and his mother maintain "toward one another an attitude which their friends found beautiful and edifying; but, like artists' models, they found the attitude fatiguing, in spite of their practice and its dignity." It is no surprise, then, that this pseudo-artist turns out to be a cad when Marian elopes with him. Of course, Conolly's standards of art, as of everything, are always inhumanly high.

The same harsh treatment of the artist class in general occurs in *An Unsocial Socialist.* When the snobbish Henrietta Trefusis reminds her husband Sidney that they belong to the artistic and cultured classes, and can therefore keep aloof from shopkeepers, he catches her up promptly with, "And as to your friends the artists, they are the worst of all." And he goes on to charge them with inflated conceit because they are such great "sticklers for the arbitrary dominion of genius and talent" over the non-artist. They are never satisfied, and they are more mercenary than most business men: "high priests of the modern Moloch." This socialistic attack on the social contribution of art Trefusis supplements by anticipating the coming accusation of artists' degeneracy by Shaw's future enemy, Max Nordau: "Nine out of ten of them are diseased creatures, just sane enough to trade on their own neuroses." Yet, lecturing to his friends Sir Charles Brandon and Chichester Erskine, both devoted dilettantes in art, on the future of art (mechanized), he concludes with the wisest dictum he has yet uttered: "Art rises when men rise, and grovels when men grovel."

This is, in a way, the thesis of Shaw's most earnest and intensive early discussion of the matter — *Love among the Artists*. This lively, though clumsy, novel is a thorough study of the relationship between art and life, of the various attitudes toward art, and of the various types of artist. It contains a truer, because a more comprehensive, view of Shaw's younger conception of art and its place in civilization than the other novels do. The whole problem revolves around the question of the difference between the true artist — the genius — and the pseudo-artist, or pretender. And no one could have a greater admiration than Shaw for the real artist, just as no one could have a greater contempt than he for the second-rater and self-deluded charlatan. It is noteworthy, too, that it is pure art that commands his allegiance at this time — art untouched by any hint of didacticism or utility.

The pure and complete artists in the story are the terrible Owen Jack, the uncouth Welsh bolshevik of a composer,[21] and Aurélie Szczympliça, the great Polish pianist. Jack never marries, though once he temporarily loses his head and proposes to Mary Sutherland. When rejected, he quietly rejoices and swears, "Hence I shall devote myself to the only mistress I am fitted for, Music. She has not many such masters." And later he lectures to Madge Brailsford on their two kinds of art (she now seems natural only on the stage; in real life she seems to be acting): "We two are artists, as you are aware. Well, there is an art that is inspired by nothing but a passion for shamming; and that is yours, so far. There is an art which is inspired by a passion for beauty, but only in men who can never associate beauty with a lie. That is my art. Master that and you will be able to make true love." It is a bit of a surprise to hear Shaw's mouthpiece reiterating that beauty is truth and truth beauty, and that that is all men need to know about art.

Aurélie, although she unwisely gives in and marries the effeminate painter, Adrian Herbert, and is still married to him at the end of the book, is so devoted to her art that she tells him that he is very injudicious to care so much about love. To her, who infinitely prefers music, love is the most stupid thing in the world. "What madness possessed me, an artist, to marry?" she laments. "Did I not know that it is ever the end of an artist's career?" And yet she admits a sort of deficiency in herself when she says that she envies Mary, now Mrs. Hoskyn, the power to be in love. "I cannot love. I can feel it in the music — in the romance — in the poetry; but in real life — it is impossible . . . I see people and things too clearly to be in love." So here again is another clear-sighted spokesman of Shaw asserting that art is in romance and poetry.

Poor Adrian, who insists to the skeptical Mary that he has really been in love in "the story-book fashion," has made the important discovery that "life is larger than any special craft." Mary, too, has discovered "that the world is larger than Art, and that there is plenty of interest in it for those who do not even know what Art means." But Mary has adjusted herself successfully, and has become the normal woman of artistic leanings and interests; Adrian cannot adjust himself, and loses his feeble grip on both art and life. The baby which is born to him and Aurélie and which looks "very sad and old" is obviously symbolical of their sort of incompatible union.

Shaw's aesthetic creed thus revealed in the eighties, that great art demands the utmost devotion for its own sake, and that its highest aim is the creation of beauty, receives confirmation from his own pen in his *Self Sketches*. Here, in describing his first phase as an author, he refers to the five novels which nobody would publish, and adds: "I began a profane Passion Play, with the mother of the hero represented as a termagant, but never carried it through. I was always, fortunately for me, a failure as a trifler. All my attempts at Art for Art's Sake broke down: it was like hammering nails into sheets of note paper." Thus Shaw admits that it was only after his discovery that the practice of "Art for Art's Sake" was getting him nowhere that he changed his theory and adopted his own variety of Ruskin's "Art for Life's Sake." As he narrates a little later in the *Self Sketches,* his first success as a public speaker came when the Zetetical Society decided to pay a tribute to "Art, of which it was utterly ignorant," by "setting aside an evening for a paper on it by a lady in the esthetic dress momentarily fashionable in Morrisan cliques just then." The way in which he "wiped the floor" with that paper was the first thing that made many of his fellow-members "reconsider their first impression of me as a bumptious discordant idiot."

Vociferously, Shaw announced his new stand on art in the prefaces to his first plays. *Widowers' Houses,* he apprised his readers, was to be regarded as a work of art, it is true, but a work of art with a purpose, as

are all "the world's acknowledged masterpieces." Although he admitted
that his play was a "mere topical farce, . . . not beautiful or lovable," he
still insisted that it was to be considered a "propagandist play," intended
to make Progressive votes. His art, like Molière's, he cried, was not the
expression of his sense of beauty, but of his sense of moral and intellectual
perversity. Thus he challenged head-on the critics who damned his play
as a mere "discussion" or "sermon," and took his stand on the didacticism
of art. Amusedly he pointed out that the people who found his sociology
wrong almost without exception also found his craftsmanship bad, and
vice versa. Though the two things are far from inseparable, it is, in fact,
impossible to appreciate a work of art without a sufficient knowledge of
its subject matter. Matter is always much more important than manner, and
in the preface to *Three Plays for Puritans* Shaw defied anyone "to prove
that the great epoch makers in fine art have owed their position to their
technical skill," for generally they have begun to create before their new
ideas have taken hold of them sufficiently to demand a constant expression
by their art.

Continuing his campaign in the preface to *Mrs. Warren's Profession,*
Shaw set down his credo that "art is the subtlest, the most seductive, the
most effective instrument of moral propaganda in the world, excepting
only the example of personal conduct." Even this exception, however, he
retracted in the case of his own art, the art of the stage, since the theater
"works by exhibiting examples of personal conduct," and thus has a
double force. In the preface to the *Pleasant Plays,* however, he indicated
that he had not completely abandoned some of his older conceptions, but
had, rather, merely put them in their proper relationship. Though the
function of the artist is to see by instinct and then reflect his vision to
the common man, Shaw somewhat inconsistently insisted that his object
of making the audience laugh with tears in their eyes could not be achieved
"except through an artistic beauty of execution unattainable without long
and arduous practice." Beauty of technique and an appeal to the more
serious emotions are, then, still part of the Shavian credo.

In a discussion of this sort the question of the morality of art must
inevitably arise. And, as Shaw reminded his readers proudly in the preface
to *Three Plays for Puritans,* he had always been a Puritan in his attitude
toward art. Love, and sensuousness in general, have been the conventional
subjects of the romantic artist, but, he asserted, fine music, architecture,
and the rest must never become the "instruments of a systematic idolatry
of sensuousness" or of a "deification of Love." Sooner than let this happen
he would deal with art far more violently than even the most fanatical
of Cromwell's major generals were able to. Not having put all his op-
ponents to flight in this preface, with its valiant attack on the current
plays of his fellow-dramatists from Pinero down, Shaw returned to the

charge in his preface to *Overruled,* with some sarcastic remarks on "The Pseudo Sex Play" and "Pruderies of the French Stage." As for art and morality, "It is ridiculous to say, as inconsiderate amateurs of the arts do, that art has nothing to do with morality. What is true is that the artist's business is not that of the policeman," who must be kept out of the fine artist's "studies of sex and studies of crime." Sex is never dealt with realistically or sincerely on the English stage or in English art in general. Similarly, in his 1913 additions to *The Quintessence,* he wrote concerning the degradation of civilized woman: "Ibsen's reply is that the sacrifice of the woman of the Stone Age to fruitful passions which she herself shares is as nothing compared to the wasting of the modern woman's soul to gratify the imagination and stimulate the genius of the modern artist, poet, and philosopher."

Most Englishmen, particularly the Philistines, would have enthusiastically supported Shaw's insistence on the morality of art, even though his ideas of morality and theirs would certainly not have coincided. Many people, however, were more excited about immorality and art than they were about morality. Dr. Max Nordau's *Entartung,* or *Degeneration,* had served to focus the controversy in 1893, and in 1895 Shaw had replied with *The Sanity of Art: An Exposure of the Current Nonsense about Artists Being Degenerate.* Nordau's thesis, as summarized by Shaw, was "that all our characteristically modern works of art are themselves symptoms of disease in the artist, and that these diseased artists are themselves symptoms of the nervous exhaustion of the race by overwork." This charge (an amusing echo of Sidney Trefusis' opinion a decade before), Shaw is compelled to admit in both his original reply and in the preface to his reprinted pamphlet in 1907, has some truth in it. "I do not see how any observant student of genius from the life can deny that the Arts have their criminals and lunatics as well as their sane and honest men." But a distinction should be made between uttering unorthodox and scandalous ideas and indulging in outrageous conduct; the first is permissible, if not essential; the second wrong. True art has a very severe discipline, but in creative art there are no ready-made rules to guide one to the right expression for his thought except his own sense of beauty and fitness, which is often in conflict with past precedents. From this source rises the impression of degeneration in the minds of the thoughtless. Though this explanation should be self-evident, Shaw is sure that in England, at least, Nordau's errors will not be perceived, since England is a place "where nothing but superstitious awe and self-mistrust prevents most men from thinking about art as Nordau boldly speaks of it; where to have a sense of art is to be one in a thousand, the other nine hundred and ninety-nine being either Philistine voluptuaries or Calvinistic anti-voluptuaries." Here is the realist peering around the corner again in the guise of the true artist. Yet one must remember, as Shaw notes in his preface, that in real life "your genius is ever one part genius and ninety-nine parts Tory." But this one part is frequently enough to bring him into conflict with himself and the life he is forced to live in the family and in society.

From some of the above remarks it will be noted that Shaw does not believe that art is democratically intelligible or appreciable. This position is sustained in the preface to *Major Barbara* where, after indulging in some irony at the expense of the aesthetic conception of the relationship between life, work, and art held by Ruskin, Morris, Kropotkin, etc., Shaw corrects their idealism by remarking: "The poor do not share their taste nor understand their art criticism . . . they want to wallow in all the costly vulgarities from which the elect souls among the rich turn away with loathing." In his introduction to *Three Plays by Brieux* he is even more categorical: "the majority of men of all nations are not merely incapable of fine art, but resent it furiously." Nevertheless, he reiterates, "Now great art is never produced for its own sake." It is "the identification of the artist's purpose with the purpose of the universe, which alone makes an artist great."

The reader may have noticed that when Shaw reprinted *The Sanity of Art* in 1907 he was classifying himself as an "artist-philosopher," and not merely an "artist-with-a-purpose." This new phase had begun at least as early as 1903 when, in dedicating *Man and Superman* to Walkley, he had written: "That the author of Everyman was no mere artist, but an artist-philosopher, and that the artist-philosophers are the only sort of artists I take quite seriously, will be no news to you." As a matter of fact, after finishing *Captain Brassbound's Conversion* in 1899 Shaw had written to Ellen Terry about his plans for the future: "And now no more plays — at least no more practical ones. None at all, indeed, for some time to come: it is time to do something more in Shaw-philosophy, in politics and sociology. Your author, dear Ellen, must be more than a common dramatist." *Man and Superman,* completed in 1903, was the first product of this new period, in which he thought of himself primarily as a thinker and controversialist.

The preface is rife with pronouncements repeating Shaw's "contempt for belles lettres." The main thing is that the writer should have "opinions." "But 'for arts's sake' alone," he shouts, "I would not face the toil of writing a single sentence." And he lumps all the aesthetes together by declaiming that when the academician declares "that art should not be didactic, all the people who have nothing to teach and all the people who don't want to learn agree with him emphatically." He gives a list of some of the writers "whose peculiar sense of the world I recognize as more or less akin to my own." They include Bunyan, Blake,[22] Hogarth, and Turner first among the English; then Shelley and Morris; and among the foreigners Goethe, Schopenhauer, Wagner, Ibsen, Tolstoy, and Nietzsche. Admitting his addiction to Dickens and Shakespeare, and analyzing some of their characters, he concludes that they are not in a class with "the works of the artist-philosophers," such as Bunyan, Nietzsche, and the rest.

Particularly, however, he attacks the concentration of most of the so-called artists on sex, whereas the works of the great geniuses in all fields of art "are free of the otherwise universal dominion of the tyranny of sex." Don Juan, in his autobiographical speech singing "the philosophic man" in the dream scene, explains the role that the artist filled in his own development. After the doctors of medicine, the doctors of divinity, and the politicians had tempted him and preached to him in vain, "Then came the romantic man, the Artist, with his love songs and his paintings and his poems; and with him I had great delight for many years, and some profit; for I cultivated my senses for his sake; and his songs taught me to hear better, his paintings to see better, and his poems to feel more deeply." And the culmination of all this was that "he led me at last into the worship of Woman." All the beauty of the song, the painting, and the poem became focused in her. But whereas the artist was often too poor or too timid to learn to know beautiful or refined women intimately, Juan was "more favored by nature and circumstance." He learned the truth, and the ideal was shattered. She taught him much in the process, but she, like art, was only a way-station on his road to a philosophy.

But art can become a valuable means of education in another way. Shaw devotes a lengthy section of his preface to *Misalliance* to a discussion of the importance of teaching fine art to children. From the point of view of results, he says, "fine art is the only teacher except torture," for a person cannot really listen to a lesson or a sermon unless the teacher or the preacher is an artist. Unhappily children come into contact with too much bad art in school and "even acquire the notion that fine art is lascivious and destructive to the character" (note, for example, the attack of Johnny Tarleton on writers in the play itself). After all, the estimation of what is good art is relative. In fact, there "is no good art, any more than there is good anything in the absolute sense." Therefore people must be allowed to range through all fiction, pictures, music, and drama as they wish, in order to find the best. In this way, too, children will be delivered from any dangerous "idolatry of the artist," while "the enchantment of art" itself is still preserved for them; "on the contrary, we shall teach them to demand art everywhere as a condition attainable by cultivating the body, mind, and heart." The world, however, as might have been expected, did not heed this sage advice, and when Shaw wrote *The Millionairess* we still find him complaining in his preface: "Our schools and universities do not concern themselves with fine art, which they despise as an unmanly pursuit."

But Shaw had far from reached the final stage in his conception of the artist. Developing from the "artist-philosopher" in *Man and Superman* and passing through an intermediate stage in the preface to *Major Barbara* in which he referred to writers as "we paper apostles and artist-magicians," he was to come to the conception of the "artist-prophet" in the 1921 preface to *Back to Methuselah,* and then to the idea of the "artist-biologist" in the new postscript that he wrote in 1944 for the Galaxy Edition of the same play.

As Shaw grew older, he came to be more and more convinced that religion was the most important theme he could write on; he also became increasingly convinced that science must be put in its place, and made to contribute as much as possible to religion. Art, of course, was to be the instrument in the process. Thus he wrote in 1921: "It will be seen that the revival of religion on a scientific basis does not mean the death of art, but a glorious rebirth of it. Indeed art has never been great when it was not providing an iconography for a live religion. And it has never been quite contemptible except when imitating the iconography after the religion has become a superstition." Drawing many examples from his great knowledge of music and painting, Shaw decided that "until we have a great religious movement we cannot hope for a great artistic one." In a section entitled "The Artist-Prophets," using Michael Angelo and Beethoven as his chief examples, he excoriated himself because his previous plays "did not constitute me an iconographer of the religion of my time, fulfilling my natural function as an artist." Thus in the *Methuselah* cycle, presenting this previously lacking iconography, Shaw offered himself as an artist-prophet of the present, preaching the new "twentieth century religion" of Creative Evolution.

By 1944, after having had over a score of years to reflect on the results of his missionary work, he had not changed his mind about his credo, though he was disappointed in the number of converts. Encouraging himself by recalling the obstacles against which all "heresies" must make progress, he concluded: "The moral of this is that heretical teaching must be made irresistibly attractive by fine art if the heretics are not to starve or burn." To this end, he was now willing to concede, "the metaphysicians and artist-philosophers must cooperate with the astronomers and physiologists." Thus he now saw his function as "an instrument in the grip of Creative Evolution": "Like Shakespear again, I was a born dramatist, which means a born artist-biologist struggling to take biology a step forward on its way to positive science from its present metaphysical stage." That he still considered "artist-biologist" the best term to describe himself is shown by his use of it in his *Self Sketches* to answer questions asking him to define his religion. Nevertheless, for some reason he was apparently not yet ready to take the physicist into the combination, for in the preface to *In Good King Charles's Golden Days,* explaining why he had been forced to bring Godfrey Kneller into his play instead of Hogarth, whom he would have preferred, he remarked: "There is another clash which is important and topical in view of the hold that professional science has gained on popular credulity since the middle of the nineteenth century. I mean the eternal clash between the artist and the physicist." Physics, it seems, is harder for art to assimilate than is biology.

Finally, to Shaw the mystic, art has always been a process of inspiration, almost in the vatic sense. His approval of Wagner's speculation about the intuitive quality of the operation of the artist's instinct has already been recorded. This view is reflected in even such incidental remarks as this one in the preface to *Geneva:* "When I am not writing plays as a more or less inspired artist I write political schoolbooks." Indeed, in the preface to one of his last plays, *Buoyant Billions,* he repeats his old confession about his method of composition: "When I write a play, I do not foresee nor intend a page of it from one end to the other." He mentions "moments of inexplicable happiness" that come to him sometimes as he writes, but he admits rather sadly that they have not come to him oftener than once in every fifteen or so years. He is not ashamed, indeed, to go so far as to compare his writings to the experiments that his mother used to make with a ouija board and a planchette. Is Shaw actually only an automatic writer being used by the Life Force for its revelations to man?

It is against this setting of Shaw's general views of art and the artist that the specific specimens in his plays need to be examined. They are always presented in some relationship with women, but this relationship is not always equally fundamental. As might be expected, the cases illustrating the clash between the artist man and the mother woman are the most interesting, because of the dramatic conflict involved. Some of Shaw's relatively unentangled artists, however, illuminate certain of his general theories.

Praed, for instance, in *Mrs. Warren's Profession,* reflects Shaw's first contempt for the art for art's sake man. Praed is immediately described as having "something of the artist about him," but it is not until some time later that we learn that he is an architect. The shrewd Vivie soon begins to watch him "with dawning disappointment as to the quality of his brains and character." In his function as artist Praed regards himself as being committed to having a sensitive soul; thus when Vivie describes to him her practical, masculine tastes, he cries out in pain, "I am an artist; and I can't believe it." And he continues to reiterate, "The Gospel of Art is the only one I can preach."

Praed, although not capable of engendering active dislike from anybody, is obviously not a very appealing character. Apollodorus, the Sicilian in *Caesar and Cleopatra,* is one of Shaw's most ingratiating minor personages. The very fact that Caesar likes to have him around and calls him "an amusing dog . . . Give me a good talker — one with wit and imagination enough to live without continually doing something," is evidence enough of Shaw's own admiration. And yet Apollodorus is a "patrician." He is "dressed with deliberate aestheticism." He is "a votary of art," and announces proudly, "I do not keep a shop. Mine is a temple of the arts. I am a worshipper of beauty . . . My motto is Art for Art's sake." When Caesar defends Apollodorus to the Philistine Britannus as "a famous patrician amateur," Britannus, in what Shaw wishes the audience to take as truly British smugness, responds, "I crave the gentleman's pardon. I understood him to say he was a professional." It should be noted, however, that Apollodorus is not, in the strictest sense, an artist at all. He is a collector, a connoisseur, an appreciator, but not a practitioner.

Apollodorus, however, unlike Praed, is masculine. Apollodorus is a doer as well as a talker — and Shaw, with ironic self-consciousness, always praises doers and runs down talkers. Apollodorus is no coward, as his bold actions on the causeway, in the lighthouse, and in the ocean prove. He swims expertly. The sword he carries, and knows how to use, is especially beautiful, as "the only weapon fit for an artist." As he quips, somewhat loosely, "Who says artist, says duellist." He even dares to argue with Caesar, when he takes the side of Cleopatra after the murder of Pothinus: "Caesar, what you say has an Olympian ring to it: it must be right: for it is fine art. But I am still on the side of Cleopatra." And when Caesar, who earlier in the play had displayed a somewhat skeptical attitude toward literature, returns to Rome, he leaves the art of Egypt in Apollodorus' charge, with the promise: "Remember, Rome loves art and will encourage it ungrudgingly." Apollodorus, anticipating history, responds, "Rome will produce no art itself, but it will buy up and take away what the other nations produce," thus giving Caesar his chance to complete the judgment of posterity: "Is peace not an art? is government not an art? is civilization not an art? All these we give you in exchange for a few ornaments. You will have the best of the bargain." And the realist, not the artist, has the last word.

In spite of Shaw's profuse use of allusions to artists and works of art, Godfrey Kneller, in *In Good King Charles's Golden Days*, is the only historical representative to appear in his plays. Kneller, like the Musician who protests that "true art will not be thus forced" when Cleopatra insists that he teach her to play the harp in a fortnight on pain of being flogged for each wrong note, has high standards for his art. His dispute with Isaac Newton about straight lines and curves, and their relation to the theories of the universe, takes up a large section of the play, and Kneller with complete seriousness cites the shocked Barbara Villiers as a proof of his belief that "The right line, the line of beauty, is a curve." Kneller's further very up-to-date theory of the curved universe upsets Newton so completely that he recants his acceptance of Archbishop Ussher's chronology of creation. But Kneller's major speeches have to do with his conception of God himself as an artist. He tells the King, "Your Majesty: the world must learn from its artists because God made the world as an artist. Your philosophers steal all their boasted discoveries from artists . . . artists do not prove things. They do not need to. They KNOW them." To sober George Fox's scandalized comment that it is plain to him that the painter is claiming that his hand is the hand of God, Kneller eloquently responds: "And whose hand is it if not the hand of God? . . . But the hand that can draw the images of God and reveal the soul in them, and is inspired to do this and nothing else even if he starves and is cast off by his father and all his family for it: is not his hand the hand used by God, who, being a spirit without body, parts or passions, has no hands?" Though Newton is allowed the last ironical word to "you, who know everything because you and God are both artists," the victory really lies with Kneller, whose arguments are of course easily recognized as the arguments of Bernard Shaw, even if in giving the preëminence to the artist over the mathematician and philosopher they may seem to come close to retracting Shaw's ranking of the different kinds of artists. It should be remembered, however, that in his preface Shaw had explained that his Kneller, because of historical necessity, was really only a substitute for Hogarth, whom he would have preferred to use, but had to reject because he was not yet born. And Hogarth, of course, was one of Shaw's chief artist-philosophers.

It is the artist man-mother woman combat, however, that engages Shaw's main interest. In *The Philanderer* the struggle between Julia and Charteris, whom she describes as "a far crueller, more wanton vivisector" than Dr. Paramore, has been essentially such a conflict, since the "Ibsenite philosopher" has most of the characteristics of the dilettante artist. The same explanation can be given for the epic battle between Higgins and Liza in *Pygmalion*. In a sort of travesty, the fencing between Henry Apjohn, the "very beautiful" young poet and pugilist, and Mrs. Aurora Bompas in *How He Lied to Her Husband,* echoes the eternal conflict. And of course the Candida-Marchbanks situation resolves itself naturally into the same elements.

The prize cases, however, cases which are in violent contrast with one another, are those of Octavius Robinson in *Man and Superman* and Louis Dubedat in *The Doctor's Dilemma.* Octavius has worried many people because he, like Praed, is such a feckless specimen of an artist, and they cannot understand how Shaw, with such views on the greatness of art as he puts into the mouth of Tanner, could offer Tavy to represent art in the play. The answer of course is that Octavius is not being portrayed as a great artist — or, indeed, as an artist with any real prospect of success in his vocation. Taken over "unaltered" from Mozart's Don Ottavio, Ana's conventional and faithful lover, as Shaw points out in his preface, Octavius is described as "really an uncommonly nice looking young fellow." His elegant mourning clothes, his slim, shapely figure, his "pretty little moustache," all "announce the man who will love and suffer later on." He is amiable, sincere, and eager to be of service to others. Even in school he "was always a really good boy," and Ann never thought of tempting him as she did the others to see "what a boy might be capable of." And yet Tavy has a devoted, doglike love for Ann. He represents, then, romantic, idealistic woman-worship. He is the would-be artist who wants to "count for something as a poet," who wants "to write a great play" — with Ann, of course, as the inspiration and heroine. Yet, with all his yearning, he is not practically ambitious and never expects to be "a big success of some kind."

It is necessary for the benevolent and yet purblind Tanner to take Tavy aside and lecture to him about the truth of his courtship of Ann. Jack insists that his friend is "an artist," but when he goes on to explain how a "great" or "true" artist would behave, it is quite obvious that Octavius has none of the qualities of even potential greatness. To women, the true artist, says Tanner, is "half vivisector, half vampire." He is a "bad husband, . . . a child-robber, a blood-sucker, a hypocrite and a cheat." For "the artist's work is to shew us ourselves as we really are," and so, with this purpose, "In the rage of that creation he is as ruthless as the woman, as dangerous to her as she to him, and as horribly fascinating." This treacherous and remorseless struggle between the artist man and the mother woman "is all the deadlier because, in your romanticist cant, they love one another." Octavius resents the picture; in fact, he refuses to admit its truth, though — true to his conventional conceptions — he tries to point out to Tanner that "it is out of the deadliest struggles that we get the noblest characters." Similarly conventional is his reaction to the discovery of his sister Violet's supposed predicament. Later Tanner implies that Tavy is unlike such great poets as Petrarch and Dante, who wrote first-rate poetry even though much of it was love poetry, because "they never exposed their idolatry to the test of domestic familiarity."

The practical Ann, when she is sure she has Jack securely in her grasp, is given the final verdict on Tavy after she knows that she is safe in discarding him as a possible second choice. She tells him that he is getting "a sort of satisfaction already in being out of danger," and that he's the kind of poet who should only dream about women. She diagnoses him to the astonished Tanner as the sort of man that never marries, but lives in a bachelor apartment with a broken heart and is idolized by his landlady, whereas Tanner is the kind that always gets married. "The poetic temperament," she dogmatizes, is "a very nice temperament, very amiable, very harmless and poetic, I daresay; but it's an old maid's temperament." And Tanner, convinced, finally chimes in acquiescently, "Barren. The Life

Force passes it by." It should be noted, however, that the Statue informs the thrilled Don Juan that there are neither any beautiful women nor any artistic people (nor, apparently, any marrying, or giving in marriage) in heaven, the home of the masters of reality, where Juan is now going. The parallel between Juan and Tanner is not quite complete.

Except for Eugene Marchbanks, Shaw's only full-length portrait of the artist in action is that of Louis Dubedat. Eugene, however, is merely on the brink of his career as a poet; Louis is well embarked on his as a painter. Eugene is the hero of his play; Louis is the villain — or at least the villain-hero — of his. Eugene has been misunderstood by many critics; but Louis has put most of them to the extreme limits of their vocabularies to find suitably explosive epithets to launch at him.

Dubedat is only twenty-three, "physically still a stripling, and pretty, though not effeminate." He has an engaging personality; though he is "all nerves," he is not at all shy and, as Shaw puts it, "his artist's power of appealing to the imagination gains him credit for all sorts of qualities and powers, whether he possesses them or not." He is soon revealed to the somewhat gullible doctors as perfectly unscrupulous in borrowing money and exploiting his wife (as Shaw boasts he did his mother). Louis is a conscienceless liar and cheat, completely lacking in any normal ethical sense; and he even cheerfully suggests blackmail. On the discovery of his so-called "marriage" to Minnie, the hotel maid, Sir Patrick Cullen labels the imperturbable young man "a damned young blackguard," and Ridgeon agrees, but with this qualification: "I'm not at all convinced that the world would not be a better world if everybody behaved as Dubedat does than it is now that everybody behaves as Blenkinsop does." (Blenkinsop is the pathetic, poverty-stricken, over-humble doctor whom Ridgeon decides to cure rather than Louis.) Yet Louis is not a coward, as is seen in the casual, even proud way in which he meets death; and he never pretends to be any better than he is. Some would call him merely an impressive poseur when he tells Jennifer that she is to gain his immortality for him by marrying again, in order to become the vehicle of a tradition of beauty, wonder, and romance which will bring more of an aura to his name than even his paintings will. Shaw leaves it a more or less open question as to whether Louis has been deluded about his own egoism. In a magnificent dying speech, which in length rivals that of any perishing opera singer, Louis examines himself, and from his own point of view decides that he has not been found wanting: "With all my faults I don't think I've ever been really selfish. No artist can: Art is too large for that . . . I'm not afraid and I'm not ashamed. I know that in an accidental sort of way, struggling through the unreal part of life, I haven't always been able to live up to my ideal. But in my own real world I have never done anything wrong, never denied my faith, never been untrue to myself . . . I believe in Michael Angelo, Velasquez, and Rembrandt; in the might of design, the mystery of color, the redemption of all things by Beauty everlasting, and the message of Art that has made these hands blessed. Amen. Amen." And with this credo on his lips — a credo which because of its wording some people thought blasphemous and which at the same time shows him to be an idealist in spite of his claiming G.B.S. as his master — the artist dies. Ridgeon's epitaph is: "The most tragic thing in the world is a man of genius who is not also a man of honor." Sir Patrick's is: "A blackguard's a blackguard; an honest man's an honest man; and neither of them will ever be at a loss for a religion or a morality to prove that their ways are the right ways. It's the same with nations, the same with professions, the same all the world over and always will be."

The complex and extraordinary character of Dubedat is composite in origin, as Henderson, Pearson, Shaw's own dramatic reviews, etc., show. The major source was Edward Aveling, D. Sc., a brilliant but perfectly incredible swindler, teacher, Socialist, atheist, and seducer, because of whom Karl Marx's daughter Eleanor finally committed suicide. Max Beerbohm saw a strong resemblance to Henry James's Roderick Hudson in Dubedat; and Henderson caught "here and there, too, a suggestion of . . . Oscar Wilde." Certainly in his review of Wilde's *An Ideal Husband* in 1895 Shaw had described the artist's distinguishing mark, the refusal to work, in his characteristic manner; and in his review of *Trilby* in the same year he had imputed to du Maurier himself "all the artist's charm, and all his dishonesty," while dubbing "the original Svengali, the luckless artist-cad (a very deplorable type of cad)." Louis's suggestion about the worthless check, according to Henderson, was based on an actual proposal once made to Shaw himself by a mysterious man "whose name, because of its association with that of one of the greatest thinkers of the nineteenth century, is known all over the world." A "well-known sculptor" had had a similar pecadillo in not feeling any obligation to finish a work which a trusting admirer had paid for before completion. The sardonic passage in which Dubedat asserts that he has always done his best to be a disciple of Bernard Shaw was founded on the behavior of a young scamp who tried to blackmail his own father. Finally, Rattray quotes Shaw's own statement that he "turned a person, now an M.P.," into a character in the play, and that this person then sent him £50 "in payment of an old debt." [23]

Out of this welter of material from real life Shaw constructed his study of an artist husband preying on an unsuspecting and adoring wife — as well as on anyone else in range — for the benefit of his art. The expected conflict, however, is only partly developed because Jennifer, as has already been shown, is only a mother in embryo. She is content to be a mother to her husband, the artist, but not, so far, to any children; and so Shaw describes Louis as "younger than Jennifer," but yet as patronizing her "as a matter of course."

At the exhibit of Louis's paintings in the epilogue Ridgeon still acts "as if constrained to admit the extraordinary fascination and merit of the work" he is viewing. This, to me, is the strangest aspect of Shaw's handling of the character of the artist. For everyone in the play, all the critics, and the author himself agree without question that as an artist Dubedat is a great genius. In the first scene, as soon as Ridgeon looks at one of the drawings that Jennifer insists on showing him, he exclaims, "Yes, this is the real thing." Soon afterward, "devouring" a sketch of Jennifer with his eyes, he calls it "a wonderful drawing," and wants to buy it. When Jennifer proudly adds that she did not bring the best pictures with her — "so few people like them" — the susceptible Ridgeon suggests as his fee, "Shall we say a beautiful drawing of his favorite model for the whole treatment, including the cure?" The sensible Sir Patrick agrees with his colleague's admiration of Louis's art. B.B. and Walpole at the dinner, equally impressed, promptly ask the artist to sign his sketches of them. Schutzmacher is apparently the only one with reservations. Ultimately, however, it is learned that he also admires the drawings, but because of the way Louis had privately talked about the Jews being the only people "who knew anything about art," had said that he had to put up with the "Philistine twaddle" of the rest, and had then tried to borrow money from him, he had refused to lend money to such a stranger. Finally, however, implying that, as a Jew, he is the only one who can really understand Louis's work, he takes the picture. And yet what are we actually told about the type and significance of Louis's art? Ridgeon calls it "very clever." B.B. says, "Ah, charming, charming." Walpole says, "Very sweet. You're a nailer at pastel." Ridgeon later adds that Louis is "a genuine source of pretty and pleasant and good things." But are these comments, even granting that doctors are not expected to have the art critic's knowledge and vocabulary, sufficient to entitle Dubedat to be described as having "the creative power of a god," as Duffin puts it, or to be referred to as "a great artist," as Henderson calls him?

As a matter of fact, from all that we can learn about Louis's subjects, style, methods of work, etc., he seems to be little more than a superior sidewalk or sand-beach picture-maker, dashing off a pencil sketch of a pretty woman or coloring a romantic landscape in a fashion that would never qualify him, even at a distance, for the company of Michael Angelo, Rembrandt, or even Velasquez.

The most comprehensive discussion and resumé of Shaw's views on the nature and place of art in life may be found in the first and the last parts of *Back to Methuselah*. In *In the Beginning* Shaw furnishes his explanation of how art, science, religion, etc., came into existence, when the main functions in the creation of life and the management of the family were delegated to the woman, and the man was thus freed for contemplation, invention, and other kinds of creativeness. Though Adam and Cain do not profit much from their opportunities, Eve still has the hope that her dreams of better things will come true. She describes others of her descendants as already being poets, musicians, sculptors, scientists, and priests, and contrasts their occupations with the destructiveness of Cain, the war-maker. "When they come, there is always some new wonder, or some new hope: something to live for. They never want to die, because they are always learning and always creating either things or wisdom, or at least dreaming of them."

The scene of *As Far As Thought Can Reach* opens on the youth's Festival of the Artists in the year 31920. The celebrants, dressed in the Greek style of the fourth century B.C. and bearing names from Greek pastoral poetry, are none of them over four years of age, and none looks older than eighteen. Strephon inadvertently propounds the theme of the debate when he asks, "What use are the artists if they cannot bring their beautiful creations to life?" Only adolescents would be interested in such a question in the world of the future, as we see when the just-arrived She-Ancient tells the Newly Born, a beautiful girl just hatched, that her companions will teach her how to keep up an imitation of happiness during her four years of immaturity by showing her what they call arts, sports, and pleasures. The old criticomachia then ensues among the older young folks about whether one has the right to criticize art if one cannot create it. When opinion divides, Ecrasia takes her stand on the principle that "the business of the artist is to create beauty." She is therefore disgusted by the fact that the sculptor Arjillax's new busts, instead of being "ideally beautiful nymphs and youths," are "horribly realistic studies" of the Ancients — the "one subject that is by universal consent of all connoisseurs absolutely excluded from the fine arts." Arjillax, however, argues against the "smirking nymphs and posturing youths" and all "the pretty confectionery you call sculpture" in favor of the "intensity of mind that is stamped" on the Ancients, and tells the story of the development of the art of painting and sculpture, and of romanticism versus realism, from none other than the Archangel Michael — for the ages have strangely distorted the names of even the greatest persons in history.

The silent and meditative Martellus now remarks that he has already gone through all Arjillax's phases, but grew tired of merely dead art. He explains how the other's disillusionment with works of mere fleeting beauty marks the beginning of his dissatisfaction with all images, and adds that the striving to get nearer to truth and reality will eventuate in his intellectual conscience's turning to the eternal and therefore in his desertion of art altogether, since "art is false and life alone is true." Then Martellus springs his surprise. He has brought with him an artist even greater than himself: Pygmalion, the scientist — a "laboratory person," as Ecrasia interjects indignantly. Pygmalion wears an expression of "eager benevolent interest" in everything and everybody, but he is no fool, for, using the modeling which Martellus has done, he has created "the two most wonderful works of art in the world," which, predicts Martellus, will "inspire a loathing that will cure you of the lunacy of art forever." Pygmalion has created artificial human beings — not supermen, of course, nor yet prehistoric creatures, but somewhere in between.[24] So he proceeds to lecture his somewhat restless comrades on biology and vital forces, on the superiority of science to art, because it uses the intellect, and on his own process of producing something to "fix high-potential Life Force." His first creations were apparently Golems or Frankenstein's monsters, but now he has a pair of human beings "who are all reflexes and nothing else" — something like the Newly Born, he remarks with scientific detachment. Martellus calls them only automata, responding to external stimuli alone, but Pygmalion maintains stoutly that they are conscious and human in a primitive sort of way. Admitting that no true artist would be content with "less than the best," he confesses that he failed to make longlivers, as he would have liked — and brings on his figures.

They are a man and a woman "of noble appearance, beautifully modeled and splendidly attired," and their names are Ozymandias and Semiramis. Impressive as they are and responsive to the general applause as they dance, they soon turn out to be vain, jealous, and quarrelsome — and Darwinian determinists, not Shavian vitalists, in philosophy. Their quick and angry brawling results in the accidental death of their creator, and thus Martellus is presented with a promptly seized chance to moralize: "They are masterpieces of art. And see what they have done. Does that convince you of the value of art, Arjillax?" The Ancients, following Shaw's theory that the dangerous criminal should be killed without anger, therefore mesmerize the pair to death with their powerful emanations. Semiramis dies with a little more honor than Ozymandias, and Ecrasia therefore voices Shaw's judgment that the "woman is more sensible than the man." Henderson, incidentally, sees a similarity between these electronic rays that all Shaw's longlivers are able to emit in varying degrees, and the power called Vril possessed by the "subterranean sages" in Bulwer-Lytton's *The Coming Race*. The development of such a power is also one of the experimental fantasies of Captain Shotover in *Heartbreak House*.

So for a moment the argument between Ecrasia and Arjillax is resumed — she continuing to play her role as "an artistic little animal," and he persisting in his wish to make studies of the Ancients, even though he would "idealize them a little." Consequently the Ancients step to the middle of the circle to instruct their young charges on life and art. If, in their present stage of immaturity, they must still create artistically, they should be content with making rag dolls — that is, lifeless toys — and should not attempt to make living beings. But even rag dolls are dangerous, for those who make them always want to go beyond them. So they paint pictures, make up stories, and even act plays. The result is, according to the She-Ancient, that "you take them so very very seriously that Ecrasia here declares the making of dolls is the holiest work of creation, and the words you put into the mouths of dolls the sacredest of scriptures and the noblest of utterances." The He-Ancient concludes that, after all, "you can create nothing but yourself." Art may be all right for the immature, but it is not necessary for the Ancients. Admirable as it may be in its way, it is only an elementary means to its end. And the end is seeing one's soul. To the Ancients, with their "direct sense of life," the body itself is the last doll to be discarded, so that eventually only thought will be left. This sort of metaphysical speculation, with its prospect of a bodiless future, is too boresome to the young people — all except Martellus, who is now practically five years old. He is ready to give up art for contemplation.

Apparently Shaw, the artist-philosopher, if he were completely true to his theory, would prefer to discard the artist in himself and let only the philosopher remain. Fortunately he was not able to achieve the fission.

# VII

## RACES AND NATIONS

AS SOON AS SHAW'S OPINIONS of races and nationalities are mentioned, most playgoing and playreading Americans immediately think of his contemptuously derisive, but only slightly exaggerated, dictum, "The one hundred percent American is ninety-nine percent idiot." And, unless they are superhumanly tolerant, and self-controlled, or are communistically inclined themselves, the temperature of their patriotic blood promptly begins to rise. What right, many Americans have demanded, does a man who has taken more money out of their country than he has out of his own have to snap like this at the hand that has fed him? Is it polite? Is it humane? Is it fair? Shaw himself remarked that Americans didn't have to go to see his plays or read his books if they didn't want to, and raised the question of whether perhaps there is a streak of masochism in the national character which makes them kiss the whip. But he also pointed out that he is actually no harder on Americans than he is on other nationalities, and that if Americans would only look as carefully at what he has said about the English and the Irish, for example, as they do at his criticisms of them they would be grateful for his mild and gentle handling.

Shaw's technique of characterization, like that of all satirists and caricaturists, calls for attacking through the chink in the armor, for selecting and magnifying the manifest weaknesses and disproportions until only an inherently or wilfully blind person can fail to see where the reform should begin. If the patrioteers are the most unduly sensitive, that is their misfortune; if many of them are impervious to the truth, that is our misfortune. Back in 1878, when young George Bernard Shaw was just getting a foothold in London, W. S. Gilbert had struck at the same sclerotic human type in the Boatswain's song in *H.M.S. Pinafore*:

> He is an Englishman!
>  For he himself has said it,
>   And it's greatly to his credit,
> That he is an Englishman!
> For he might have been a Roosian,
> A French, or Turk, or Proosian,
> Or perhaps Itali-an!

> *But in spite of all temptations*
> *To belong to other nations,*
> *He remains an Englishman!*

And the chorus joins in lustily with a "Hurrah! For the true-born Englishman!"

In the course of a seventy-year polemical writing career Shaw naturally had something to say about most of the races and nationalities that populate, or infest, the earth. Sometimes he is the mosquito, sometimes the vulture, but his instinct usually leads him pretty straight to the vulnerable spot, and he makes his attack, sometimes directly, sometimes indirectly, through short dialogistic jibes, through prefatory exegeses, or through the portrayal of whole illustrative characters.

## 1. *The Englishman*

Shaw's central accusation against these "true-born" English is that they are, even more than the Americans, incorrigible idealists, who are so utterly incapable of seeing real facts and essential truths that they usually become hypocrites, unable to perceive the beams in their own eyes while only too aware of the motes that are in others'. Although they too, like the Americans, generally remain children, with perhaps a few months' advantage in age, they always mask their selfish and often predatory actions under pious platitudes and altruistic pretendings which are so beautifully and sententiously phrased that they take in even their inventors.

In 1897, when Shaw was reviewing a new edition of George Meredith's *Essay on Comedy,* he was full of the idea of national characteristics, and especially English characteristics, as a subject for comedy, and found himself disagreeing with Meredith on the subject, in spite of his generally high admiration for the other's work as a critical authority. No matter whether you take the English generally or particularly, Shaw writes — "Whether in the lump or sectionally as playgoers, churchgoers, voters, and what not" — they are always distinguished and united by "the bond of their common nonsense, their invincible determination to tell and be told lies about everything, and their power of dealing acquisitively and successfully with facts while keeping them, like disaffected slaves, rigidly in their proper place: that is, outside moral consciousness." It is this quality in the Englishman, much more than his "half-diffident, half-contemptuous" attitude toward fine art, that is responsible for making him "the most successful man in the world" so far as money and social precedence go. This point enables Shaw to introduce a very interesting statement of his conception of comedy, according to which the Englishman's sort of common sense, based on "unscrupulousness and singleness of purpose," is, contrary to Meredith, "not only not 'the basis of the comic,' but actually makes comedy impossible, because it would not seem like common sense at all if it were not self-

satisfiedly unconscious of its moral and intellectual bluntness." The true
function of Comedy, Shaw believes, lies in dispelling this unconsciousness
"by turning the searchlight of the keenest moral and intellectual analysis
right on to it." Then, contrasting the true, common sense Briton with
"the Frenchman, the Irishman, the American, the ancient Greek" on the
score of the latters' "accurate and complete consciousness of things — of
intellectual mastery of them," he proceeds to praise their "positive enjoyment of disillusion (the most dreaded and hated of calamities in England),
and consequently a love of comedy (the fine art of disillusion) deep
enough to make huge sacrifices of dearly idealized institutions for it." This
kindness to the French, Irish, Americans, and Greeks is undoubtedly due
not so much to love of them as to the desire to use them as sticks with
which to beat the British, but the statement shows at least that Shaw had
a sound and consistent theory behind his own comic writing.

Thus even the terrible twins in *You Never Can Tell,* having been
brought to England for the first time from Madeira, "think that every
Englishman they meet is a joke," and young Philip announces to the dum-
founded McComas, "I find it impossible to take the inhabitants of this
island seriously." The Lady in *On the Rocks* taxes the English with frivolity, which, she says, is not only a "common English failing" but "almost a
national characteristic." Adolphus in *Poison, Passion, and Petrifaction* confesses honestly, "I warn you that I am an Englishman. You may laugh at
my manners, at my brains, at my national institutions; but if you laugh at
my clothes, one of us must die." The Englishman, moreover, is as vain of
his physical prowess (including his ability to drink; *vide Great Catherine*)
as he is of his taste in dress. Nor is this characteristic confined to the male.
Thus the French lieutenant, M. Duvallet, in *Fanny's First Play,* comments
sardonically after watching Margaret's and Bobby's impromptu wrestling
match, "The athletic young Englishwoman is an example to all Europe."
Similarly Ermyntrude informs her Inca that, as an Englishwoman, she is
"perfectly capable of tackling ten Incas if necessary." Sibthorpe Juno in
*Overruled* voices the national conviction that, when obliged to, "Every Englishman can use his fists," but when his statement is challenged by his wife
it is discovered that neither he nor Gregory Lunn has ever learned or tried
to do so. Nevertheless, as Shaw charged in the preface to *Three Plays for
Puritans,* "The well-fed Englishman, though he lives and dies a schoolboy,
cannot play. He cannot play cricket or football: he has to work at them."
This is the same charge, of course, that the ordinary Englishman, or European, levels at American sport.

When Confucius in *The Thing Happens* deflates Burge-Lubin's claims
for the greatness of England's contributions to government, democracy, and
world history, the President cheerfully admits that "the real life of England
is from Friday to Tuesday," rather than from Tuesday to Friday. It is the

long week-end that really counts. "Is there a jollier place on earth to live in," he demands, "than England out of office hours?" After all, he wonders, why should the English drudge when they can get other people to do their work for them? That ability is a sign of their brains. Archbishop Haslam, who has said that in his youth in the twentieth century the Englishman's thinking, organizing, directing, etc., were done for him by "Jewish brains, Scotch brains, Italian brains, German brains," whereas now in the twenty-second century it is done by "yellow brains, brown brains, and black brains," concludes that English amusements are still "the amusements of boys and girls," and tells Burge-Lubin that their countrymen are essentially a non-adult race, whereas "the Irish and the Scots, and the niggers and the Chinks, as you call them, . . . do somehow contrive to grow up a little before they die."

As a matter of fact, many of those who are thought to be most representative of English life and thought are not really Englishmen at all. In *The Apple Cart,* it is learned, all the members of the Cabinet came from families "from Scotland or Ireland or Wales or Jerusalem or somewhere." Proteus, in particular, is a Scotchman by ancestry, and is therefore determined to "force this issue to its logical end," even though that attitude is "unEnglish." "God help England," he exclaims, "if she had no Scots to think for her." In *The Thing Happens,* Scotchmen now man the public services of China, while Chinamen manage England. Charles II remarks feelingly, "For brains and religion you must go to Scotland; and Scotland is the most damnable country on earth . . . I sometimes think brains and religion are the curse of the world." Thus the missionary, Rankin, in *Captain Brassbound's Conversion,* is a Scotchman, "a convinced son of the Free Church and the North African Mission," though he has "a faithful brown eye, and a peaceful soul." Harriett Russell, the charming but highly rational heroine of *Immaturity,* is also Scotch. On the other hand, the excitable musician, Owen Jack, in *Love among the Artists,* is Welsh, and the romantic Jennifer Dubedat in *The Doctor's Dilemma* is Cornish.

English taste, especially that of the rich manufacturer, is invariably bad. Thus, Shaw asserts, the beauty of the Egyptian decoration of the hall in *Caesar and Cleopatra* makes "the place handsome, wholesome, simple and cool, or, as a rich English manufacturer would express it, poor, bare, ridiculous and unhomely. For Tottenham Court Road civilization is to this civilization as glass and tattoo civilization is to Tottenham Court Road." In other words, there has been no aesthetic progress in England. In the same way the English in *The Dark Lady of the Sonnets* show their bad literary taste in making Shakespeare's worst plays his most popular. Yet the English are snobs, as Hotchkiss proudly boasts in *Getting Married:* "The whole strength of England lies in the fact that the enormous majority of the English people are snobs. They insult poverty. They despise vulgarity. They love nobility . . . They will not obey a man risen from the ranks. They never trust one of their own class . . . If he's not a gentleman, I don't care whether he's honest or not." The Devil in *Man and Superman,* who has just called attention to the fact that the country where he has the largest following is England, explains the situation wherein, although most of "the best people" are to be found in hell, a number of people, "almost all English," prefer to go to heaven, much as the rows of weary listeners at English concerts are to be found in the concert hall, "not because they really like classical music, but because they think they ought to" be there. Fundamentally, however, the typical Englishman distrusts brains. Thus Cecil Savoyard in *Fanny's First Play* doesn't think that any Englishman would like to be called an Intellectual; and Charles II dogmatizes, "the English will not be ruled; and there is nothing they hate like brains."

So independent that, like the Emigration Officer in *The Simpleton of the Unexpected Isles,* they claim the right even to commit suicide where and when they please; so narrowly patriotic that in *Saint Joan* Warrick informs Cauchon that in his country the word "traitor" does not mean "betrayer" as it does in French, but rather "simply one who is not wholly devoted to our English interests"; so backward and conservative that, according to *The Dark Lady of the Sonnets,* England will set up a National Theater only after all the other nations have done so — and then only to be in fashion, "to do humbly and dutifully whatso she seeth everybody else doing"; so blindly vain of the ability of the average Englishman to think like Newton and Shakespeare or construct a steam engine or "lay a cable t' th' Antipodes" that Cetewayo, the Zulu chief in *The Admirable Bashville,* has to disillusion Lucian as to the truth; so sentimental that Sir Arthur Chavender in *On the Rocks* makes a speech all to himself about the Englishmen's love of peace and their being above all a "domestic nation" — "the heart of England is the English home"; so distrustful of the common people that the Newcomer in *Geneva* insists that "Plebiscites are unEnglish, thoroughly unEnglish"; so naively unscrupulous in money matters that they will promise anything or sign anything without thinking that anyone, such as the Jew in the same play, would really hold them to their agreement if anything went wrong; so practical and prosaic in their stupidity and vitality that, according to the preface to *Man and Superman,* they become positively dangerous when they place "nourishment and children first, heaven and hell a somewhat remote second, and the health of society as an organic whole nowhere" — the English as a race are essentially moral hypocrites who always manage to better themselves somehow in their proclamation of the highest principles and their indulgence in the most hard-headed of actions. Tanner describes it to Tavy as "your pious English habit of regarding the world as a moral gymnasium built expressly to strengthen your character in." Even when Juno is trying to push an amour in spite of Mrs. Lunn's "respectability," he announces, "But I'm an Englishman; and I think you ought to respect the conventions of English life . . . I may be doing wrong, but I'm doing it in a proper and customary manner. You may be doing right; but you're doing it in an unusual and questionable manner." Or, in the words of the Statue, "An Englishman thinks he is moral when he is only uncomfortable." But, the Statue might have added, he would be still more uncomfortable if he weren't being moral. It's the face that you put on a thing that counts. Even if "You have no hearts, you English," as Patiomkin asserts in *Great Catherine,* you must pretend that you have and are using them for the best interests of your victims.

All this is especially applicable in the English imperialist's interpretation of Kipling's "white man's burden" as really meaning the "Englishman's burden." As Captain Brassbound's faithful Drinkwater puts it, more or less intelligibly, in explaining the presence of the gang in Africa, "It gows agin us as Hinglishmen to see these bloomin furriners settin ap their Castoms Ahses and spheres o hinfluence and sich lawk hall owver Arfricar. Daownt Harfricar belong as much to huz as to them? . . . Waw, it's spreadin civlawzytion, it is." So the pirates rob, as the traders exploit. Tarleton, the successful business man who is so full of ideas in *Misalliance,* draws a similarly idealized picture of the benefits of imperialism to both the English and the natives, as illustrated by what happened at Jinghiskahn: "Ah yes. Good thing the empire. Educates us. Opens our minds. Knocks the Bible out of us. And civilizes the other chaps." To the correction of Lord Summerhays that it civilizes them and uncivilizes us, Tarleton argues that it all averages out the human race, making the nigger half an Englishman and the Englishman half a nigger, and cites the good Spain did for South America and the benefits that the Romans brought to Britain, in spite of what happened to themselves in the process. "That's the good side of Imperialism: it's unselfish," he maintains. "I despise the Little Englanders: they're always thinking about England. Smallminded. I'm for the parliament of man, the federation of the world. Read Tennyson." And he is "hugely amused" when he agrees with Summerhays that the English are "Awful hypocrites, ain't we?" In the same fashion Burge-Lubin sounds the imperialistic note of the Englishman's responsibility: "If there was ever a race divinely appointed to take charge of the non-adult races and guide them and train them and keep them out of mischief until they grow up to be capable of adopting our institutions, that race is the English race." And he is undeterred by the assertion of Confucius that it is the English who have the non-adult mind. The typical Englishman, like Chavender before his conversion, simply puts forward his ideal image of the English character and refuses to look further. Thus when Old Hipney exposes the real stupidity and ignorance of the average English working man, Sir Arthur merely replies: "But surely you recognize, Mr. Hipney, that all this is thoroughly wrong — wrong in feeling

— contrary to English instincts — out of character, if I may put it that way."
Yet there is also the English genius for compromise, which wins a position
little by little. Thus the "Genuinely English Brigands" applaud Mendoza
when he says that he agrees with both sides in the dispute between the
Anarchist and the Socialists about the distribution of wealth.

In view of these characteristics, it is no wonder that Private Meek in
*Too True To Be Good,* paraphrasing Hamlet, announces that the Union
of Federated Sensible Societies in Beotia "won't admit any more English
. . . : they say their lunatic asylums are too full already." Charles II also
confesses his distaste for his male subjects in this apostrophe: "No: give me
English birds and English trees, English dogs and Irish horses, English
rivers and English ships; but English men! No, No, NO!" When Catherine
roguishly queries whether he feels the same way about English women,
however, he has to admit, "Ah! there you have me, beloved."

At least twice Shaw has arraigned the English character in general at
some length. Pra in *The Simpleton* describes England as "a strange mad
country where the young are taught languages that are dead and histories
that are lies, but are never told how to eat and drink and clothe themselves and reproduce their species. They worship strange gods; and they
play games with balls marvellously well; but of the great game of life they
are ignorant." So in his country the English, being basically unteachable, are
not encouraged to stay alive. But Napoleon's analysis of the English to the
Strange Lady is the most explicit and complete of all. To him, the English,
a "nation of shopkeepers," are "a race apart." Although none of them are
too low to have scruples, while at the same time none are too high "to be
free from their tyranny," all Englishmen are born with "a certain miraculous power" which makes them masters of the earth. For when an Englishman "wants a thing, he never tells himself that he wants it. He waits
patiently until there comes into his mind, no one knows how, a burning
conviction that it is his moral and religious duty to conquer those who have
got the thing he wants. Then he becomes irresistible." Aristocrat or shopkeeper, he grabs what he wants, but is "never at a loss for an effective moral
attitude." Pretending to champion freedom and national independence, he
"annexes half the world, and calls it Colonization." Wanting a new market
for his cheap Manchester goods, he sends a missionary to preach the gospel
of peace to the natives; then when the natives kill the missionary, he con-
quers them in defense of Christianity "and takes the market as a reward
from heaven." Even at home, boasting that "a slave is free the moment his
foot touches British soil . . . , he sells the children of his poor at six years
of age to work under the lash in his factories for sixteen hours a day." All
in all, says the astute Napoleon in evaluation of the race that he already
knew were to be his chief rivals and obstacles, there "is nothing so bad or
so good that you will not find Englishmen doing it; but you will never find

an Englishman in the wrong," for, with his perennial watchword of "duty," he will do everything "on principle": fight you on patriotic principles, rob you on business principles, enslave you on imperial principles, bully you on manly principles, support his king on loyal principles, and cut off his king's head on republican principles. With this analysis, he diagnoses the Lady as being English on the basis of her technique as recently applied to him — though he cannot thus account for her brains. This mystery is cleared up, however, by his discovery that her grandmother was Irish.

But Shaw leaves even the English with just a touch of hope. As Mrs. Lutestring says in *The Thing Happens,* as she looks far back into her long past, "we had the possibilities of becoming a great nation within us." And the philosophical but practical Confucius develops the same idea when he shrewdly explains to Burge-Lubin that his statement about the English mind not being an adult mind should really have been taken as a great compliment, meaning that the English would be the greatest nation on earth if they could only live long enough to attain maturity.

Concrete specimens of the "true-born" Englishman in the round are best sought for abroad, or at least show up best away from home. After all, most of Shaw's characters are Englishmen, who display all sorts of mixed qualities according to their types; but several times he has apparently gone to special pains to depict the most representative characteristics of the Englishman in one — usually a man — who is out of his native environment and therefore contrasts strikingly with his new surroundings. Thus Begonia Brown, the complacent Briton and brummagem new woman, is first introduced in Geneva, and only later develops into an exemplary Dame of the British Empire. Iddy the curate, with his simple mind and conventional morality, is displayed against the backdrop of the Unexpected Isles, and when tempted by oriental "Nature" reminds himself, vainly, that he is an Englishman: "In this sign I shall conquer." Another churchman, Chaplain de Stogumber, reveals his English essence in France at the trial of Saint Joan. One of his most deeply felt accusations against her is: "But this woman denies to England her legitimate conquests, given her by God because of her peculiar fitness to rule over less civilized races for their own good." He is convinced that if Saints Margaret and Catherine were genuine they would have spoken to Joan in English. Even after his despairing repentance he thanks God that the soldier who gave the burning Joan two sticks tied together for a cross was an Englishman, and insists that the people who laughed at her death were French. Ladvenu, however, hopes and believes that they were English.

Eighteenth-century Russia also serves, in *Great Catherine,* to bring out the egregious Englishness of Captain Edstaston and his fiancée, Claire. Edstaston, "a handsome strongly built young English officer, . . . evidently on fairly good terms with himself, and very sure of his social position," has

served against the American rebels and is now on a mission to St. Peters-
burgh. A very proper and easily shocked young man, he surprises the casual
Russians by wanting to dress for his audience with the Queen, feels personally disgraced by being bundled off to the audience in the drunken
Patiomkin's arms, and acknowledges blushingly that he finds Catherine's
hussar uniform "very becoming," but "perhaps a little unfeminine." He has
scruples about taking presents — the "scruples of a gentleman," he calls
them; but the astonished Patiomkin remarks, "You are the first Englishman I ever saw refuse anything he could get." In discussing politics, he
flatters himself that he speaks like "a practical man," but he is surprised to
hear that "foreigners" too have a policy, for he always thought that policy
was only Mr. Pitt's business. As any "member of the Church of England"
should, he regards Voltaire as an "abominable infidel," but he recants under
the pressure of Catherine's tickling. Under ordinary circumstances, however,
he is brave enough, and is not intimidated by his possible danger. His sense
of humor is so insular and primitive that he bursts into convulsions of
laughter at the name "Popof." When Varinka taps her forehead significantly,
Patiomkin explains patiently, "No: only English." To get free of Catherine's
tickling, he finally admits that he loves her, whereupon she promptly and
gladly returns him to Claire. Gratefully he proceeds to give her "a word
of plain wholesome English advice," in which he suggests that she marry
"some good man who will be a strength and a support" to her old age, so
that she can sit happily with her little ones at her knee and her man by the
fireside in the long winter evenings. "Home! duty! happiness! they all mean
the same thing; and they all flourish best on the drawing room hearth rug."
As he leaves, Catherine, sputtering with what Patiomkin cannot be sure is
fury or laughter, but which turns out to be the latter, cries out her wish that
she might only preserve the Englishman for her museum.

Claire, "a robust young English lady," will obviously make the captain
a suitable mate. She is jealous and snobbish, even snubbing the Queen at
one point. With typical English antipathy to the overt expression of emotion,
she and her lover are "awkward and shamefaced" when the Russians put
them in one another's arms. But she too has English courage, and dashes
bravely to Edstaston's rescue when she thinks he is in danger.

Lord Augustus Highcastle, who does his bit in prolonging the First
World War, is an even broader caricature. Augustus is the Colonel Blimp
of his day, and, as he says, "Whilst England remains England, wherever
there is a public job to be done you will find a Highcastle sticking to it."

The only one of these true-born Englishmen whom Shaw shows any
genuine fondness for is Britannus, Caesar's secretary, but this fondness too
is tinged with condescension. Caesar is continually delighted with the man's
Briticisms. Britannus is a first-century B.C. Dundreary, "about forty, tall,
solemn, and already slightly bald, with a heavy, drooping, hazel-colored

mustache trained so as to lose its ends in a pair of trim whiskers." He is "carefully dressed in blue," and later admits that when he was captured in Britain by Caesar he was painted blue all over, for "Blue is the color worn by all Britons of good standing. In war we stain our bodies blue; so that though our enemies may strip us of our clothes and our lives, they cannot strip us of our respectability." The first speech of Britannus reminds Caesar of his "duty to his country" in collecting back debts from Egypt, and from there he goes on to cite the "duty to Rome," the "honor of Rome," "peace with honor," and similar idealistic slogans. Caesar, however, delights in "the moral eye-to-business of his British secretary." As could be predicted, Britannus denounces Cleopatra's marriage to her brother Ptolemy as "not proper" — in fact, a "scandal." He reproaches his master for his Roman levity, and laments, "if I could but persuade you to regard life seriously, as men do in my country! . . . These are moral questions with us." He too, however, is brave as a lion, as he shows in fighting against the Egyptians, and so impresses Caesar that the latter decides not to free him from his slavery after all, but as a reward to keep him forever at his side as a friend.

In a special note on the character of Britannus, Shaw remarks that those who have read his play in manuscript have evinced "a strong conviction that an ancient Briton could not possibly have been like a modern one," but that he himself rejects this "curious view." To him, Britannus represents "the unadulterated Briton who fought Caesar and impressed Roman observers much as we should expect the ancestors of Mr. Podsnap to impress the cultivated Italians of their time." For Britannus was born — and here again Shaw repeats his persistent belief in the influence of climate not only on physiology but also on character — before "the Roman and Norman conquests must for a time have disturbed the normal British type produced by the climate." Britannus is then the aboriginal, the prototypical Englishman, more likable and less reprehensible than his descendants, perhaps, because he appears in the mere dawn of the race.

## 2. The Irishman [25]

It may seem a little peculiar to begin a discussion of Shaw's Irishman with a discussion of another Englishman. But in *John Bull's Other Island* the Irish are so mixed up with the English and the English with the Irish that it is a bit hard at times to tell which characteristics are which. As Shaw asserts in his prefatory section entitled "What Is an Irishman?" "Ireland is the only spot on earth which still produces the ideal Englishman of history" — that is, "clearheaded, sane, hardily callous to the boyish sentimentalities, and credulities." Though the Irishman may also at times illustrate every corruption, vice, and folly on the list, he is still "never quite the hysterical, nonsense-crammed, fact-proof, truth-terrified, unballasted sport of all the bogey panics and all the silly enthusiasms that now calls itself 'God's Englishman.' " This "Preface for Politicians" was written in 1907 when the Home Rule question was stirring the two countries to new heights of fury.

Unfortunately Tom Broadbent, the Englishman of the play who goes to Ireland and is accepted by the Irish in Rosscullen as their representative, is scarcely the ideal Englishman of history. Although the English audiences laughed inordinately at Broadbent to show their tolerance and "largeminded good humor," they failed to understand the real seriousness of the portrait of an Englishman "infatuated in politics, hypnotized by his newspaper-leader-writers and parliamentary orators into an utter paralysis of his common sense, without moral delicacy or social tact, and above all, a successful muddler-through in business and love." In the prosperous business partnership between the English Tom Broadbent and the Irish Larry Doyle all that the former contributed was "the strength, self-satisfaction, social confidence and cheerful bumptiousness that money, comfort, and good feeding bring to all healthy people," whereas the latter possessed "the freedom from illusion, the power of facing facts, the nervous industry, the sharpened wits, the sensitive pride of the imaginative man who has fought his way up through social persecution and poverty." Yet the electorate in Rosscullen accepts Broadbent after Doyle, a plain speaker who offends all with his home truths about Irish politics, religion, and domestic life, has refused to run.

Illustrating the frequent confusion in the use and application of Shavian terms, West goes so far astray as to assert that Broadbent is a realist and Doyle an idealist, and that the play as a whole symbolizes the "new era of co-operation between Ireland's dreamer and England's man of action." Such a conclusion may represent the actuality, but if so it completely overlooks the fact that the capitalistic partnership is scarcely effected with Shaw's benediction, for, as West inconsistently admits, Father Keegan is present as the dreamer — the apparent idealist but actual realist — who does not give up his dreams.

In the play itself Broadbent, based on several Liberal politicians, with some traits from A. B. Walkley, who fell in love with the Irish accent of the Abbey Players as Broadbent does with Nora's, is described as a mass of contradictions — "sometimes eager and credulous, sometimes shrewd and roguish, sometimes portentously solemn, sometimes jolly and impetuous, always buoyant and irresistible, mostly likeable and enormously absurd in his most earnest moments." Doyle warns his partner that the latter is simply going on a "sentimental expedition for perfectly ridiculous reasons, with your head full of political nonsense that would not take in any ordinarily intelligent monkey." After his arrival Broadbent preaches a Liberal doctrine of retrenchment, reform, and Home Rule in such a grandiloquent fashion that he seems in some ways more anti-English than the Irish. He would like to become a naturalized Irishman, he tells his wished-for constituents. "The ideal is what I like," he cries. He gets drunk on poteen, forces his romanticized love on fragile Nora Reilly and browbeats her into agreeing to marry him, and makes a fool of himself with a pig. Nevertheless, as Larry says, "He'll never know they're laughing at him; and while they're laughing he'll win the seat." Keegan sums up the secret of "the conquering English" as: "Let not the right side of your brain know what the left side doeth." And yet even Keegan is forced to admit that perhaps, if the Irish have any future at all, it will probably be the industrial and residential future that business men and engineers like Broadbent are bringing it to replace its "empty enthusiasms and patriotisms, and emptier memories and regrets." In his preface, Shaw confesses, "Personally I like Englishmen much better than Irishmen."

As for Larry Doyle, he is an expatriate, like Shaw himself, and makes no bones about his "instinct against not going back to Ireland." Most Irishmen who have left, he maintains, haven't really wanted to go back, in spite of their noisy patriotism. Larry's "cold grey eyes, strained nose, fine fastidious lips, critical brows, clever head, . . . with a suggestion of thin-skinnedness and dissatisfaction" make Tim Haffigan at first take him for an Englishman. Doyle admits that he has probably "learnt something in America and a few other remote and inferior places" which has helped him to realize the truth about Ireland. Roughly, as Shaw puts it in his preface, the main difference between the Englishman and the Irishman is that the former "is wholly at the mercy of his imagination, with no sense of reality to check it," whereas the latter, "with a far subtler and more fastidious imagination, has one eye always on things as they are." This differentiation fits Larry neatly. Thus he is able to deliver his long, mystic, and bitter aria on the weaknesses of the Irish character, dwelling with loving pain on "the dreaming! the dreaming! the torturing, heartscalding, never satisfying dreaming, dreaming, dreaming, dreaming!" Yet, somewhat contradictorily, Shaw makes him go on about the average Irishman: "An Irishman's imagination never lets him alone, never convinces him, never satisfies him; but it makes him that he can't face reality nor deal with it nor handle it nor conquer it." The Irishman can't be truly religious nor intelligently political; and he takes to drink and telling stories. Larry himself, obviously, has been strong enough to break away from this and from the climate, on which he, like Shaw, blames so much of the tragedy. Yet ex-Father Keegan sums him up as "this Irishman, so foolish in his cleverness."

It might well seem that Larry Doyle's Irishmen are all under the domination of the Celtic myth which Matthew Arnold was largely responsible for setting up in his lectures on Celtic literature. As Shaw said of himself in the preface to *Man and Superman,* "I know the vanity of the poetic qualities of which Englishmen teach Irishmen to be proud." Thus, in spite of the prevailing melancholy in Doyle's picture of Ireland, Shaw in his preface to *John Bull* insists, "There is no Irish race any more than there is an English race or a Yankee race." But, he adds, "There *is* an Irish climate, which will stamp an immigrant more deeply and durably in two years, apparently, than the English climate will in two hundred." Larry, it would seem, has got away from that climate in time to salvage some of his realistic sense; Broadbent will soon be a servile subject to its influence.

The other Irish specimens furnished by Shaw in his play, with the conspicuous exception of Keegan, create an even more unfavorable impression, though Nora Reilly has deceived others than Broadbent. Notable among these are Duffin, who praises Nora's "delicacy of apprehension" as well as her negatively refined qualities, and John Corbin, the critic who, according to Henderson, called her Kathleen ni Houlihan (remembering Larry's sardonic reference to Yeats's symbolic playlet in his aria speech) and said: "The real drama of the piece centres in the story of how the Irishman loses Nora and the Briton wins her . . . In his heart Larry loves his countrywoman, as she has always loved him, and she has no real affection for the Briton. Here lies the comic irony of the denouement, the very essence of Shaw's comment on his problem." But if Larry really loves Nora, he does a remarkably skilful job of concealing the state of his feelings; for to the ordinary observer he seems positively callous and cruel to her. He gives no overt sign of recognizing what Henderson calls her "quintessence of graceful coquetry, larmoyant piquancy, and Celtic charm." Her appearance of aristocracy, sneers Larry, comes from the fact that she is a woman "who eats not wisely but too little," and her charm is merely that of a dream. She is anemic, prudish, and easily shocked. She has pride and tenacity, but in the end she proves to be like Julia Craven: her main quarry escapes, but she does get a husband. At the end of the play, Larry "with curt sincerity" predicts all the good things that a marriage with Broadbent will do for her. The skeptically minded critic, however, will be inclined to wonder.

An assortment of minor figures, not including the priest, Father Dempsey, and the unfrocked priest, ex-Father Keegan, whose profession relegates them to the next chapter, round out this varied Irish portrait gallery. Tim Haffigan, who strikes the innocent Broadbent in London as an Irishman of Irishmen, is "stunted, shortnecked, smallheaded, redhaired," with "furtive eyes" and an appearance as if he might be "a tenth-rate schoolmaster ruined by drink," but is soon shown up by the expert Doyle as no Irishman at all, since he was born in Glasgow and sponges on "romantic duffers" like Broadbent with his "stage brogue" and flattery in order to get a few drinks. Tim, however, does have a couple of genuine Irish uncles, Matt and Andy Haffigan, in Rosscullen. Matt turns out to be an "oldish peasant farmer, small, leathery, peat-faced, with a deep voice and a surliness that is meant to be aggressive, and is in effect pathetic." He and his brother Andy, brought to a niggardly independence through the Land Purchase, represent the obstinate, unintelligent, driving, deadening labor of the Irish peasantry.

Cornelius Doyle is the small-business man of the country town, elderly and wiry, with a "rather worried face." Barney Doran has enormous energy, but is intolerant and vulgar, and is given to practical jokes; it is he who goes almost hysterical telling the story of Broadbent and the pig. Patsy Farrell, the astonished eavesdropper on Keegan's dialogue with the grass-hopper, is the kind that "Englishmen think . . . half-witted, which is ex-actly what he intends them to think." Finally, there is Aunt Judy, "a con-tented product of a narrow, strainless life" — a woman "who is in no way remarkable, lively and busy without energy or grip, placid without tran-quillity, kindly without concern for others." With such a group Shaw, it would seem, feels that he has a sufficient cross-section of life in Ireland itself to convey the truth of the picture.

Just as Shaw wrote only two plays, one long and one short, in which the action takes place *in toto* in America, so he confined himself to two of similar lengths dealing with his native land. *O'Flaherty V.C.*, besides being a "recruiting Pamphlet" against all wars, carries on the depiction of Ireland as a nation which can never agree with itself and which is split into quar-relling factions that divide even families into bitter groups. General Sir Pearce Madigan is the Irish country squire who is more English than the English. He has married an English wife, who is in London. An "elderly baronet in khaki, beaming with enthusiasm," he lectures O'Flaherty on patriotism, and reminds him, "After all, he is our king; and it's our own country, isn't it?" He tells the cynical O'Flaherty that "that little Cross of yours gives you a higher rank in the roll of glory than I can pretend to" and assures him patronizingly that "I'm proud to have you for my guest here today." To him there is a "gratifying side" to parades and such things, and he is convinced that the war "has uplifted us all in a wonderful way." But Sir Pearce is kind to the poor.

The disillusioned O'Flaherty, however, is fed up with parades, speeches, and all the rest, nor does he feel about his country quite as Madigan does. "And as to the king, God help him, my mother would have taken the skin off my back if I'd ever let on to have any other king than Parnell." He calls himself a "ready liar," however, having learned at home. Although he admits that in spite of his fighting and being decorated (which was just luck) he doesn't know what the war is all about, he confesses one gain: that it has taught him to talk plain to people like Sir Pearce. So he viciously attacks the results of the English rule of Ireland, and informs him roundly that "No war is right" and that "You'll never have a quiet world til you knock the patriotism out of the human race." Even though he expects people to go back to their "natural divilment" when the war is over, it has at least set him thinking for the first time in his life, and has made him independent enough to tell even his termagant of a mother that from now on he'll fight for whom he pleases.

To Sir Pearce's stupefaction, Mrs. O'Flaherty, who has been his tenant all her life and whom he has thought all along to be completely loyal to king and country, turns out to be, in her son's words, the "biggest kanatt from here to the cross of Monasterboice" and the "wildest Fenian and rebel" in the county. So blindly devoted to republicanism is she that she thought all along her son was fighting against the English because he told her he was going to "fight for the French and for the Russians." "Oh, she's the romantic woman is my mother, and no mistake," boasts O'Flaherty apologetically. Not only has she prayed for Sir Pearce to be converted to Roman Catholicism, but she maintains that all the English generals, poets, and great men in general were actually Irish. But so, she believes, were the Lost Tribes of Israel and Venus herself. In fact, as her son explains her, "She's like the English: they think there's no one like themselves. It's the same with the Germans, though they're educated and ought to know better." Such a comparison naturally did nothing to increase Shaw's popularity with either the English or the Irish during the war.

Though Shaw was never exactly a vociferous proponent of Ireland for the Irish, the idea of Home Rule continued to creep into his plays.[26] In *The Apple Cart,* the proposal that America rejoin the British empire came as a result of the recent establishment of the Irish Free State and of the visit of its President, Mike O'Rafferty, to the United States. As Queen Jemima says, "Our own best families go so much to Ireland nowadays . . . They never come back . . . it is not the climate. It's the Horse Show." Contrarily, in *The Simpleton,* when England tries to withdraw from the empire, the Free State President issues a statement declaring that Ireland cannot permit England to destroy empire unity. "Ireland," he proclaims, "will lead the attack on treason and disruption." The later history of Irish nationalism is carried to its fantastic conclusion in the Elderly Gentleman's romantic and garbled account in *Methuselah.* (It should be noted, incidentally, that the state of the longlivers is first established in Ireland, "described by the earliest bards as an emerald gem set in a silver sea!") For, according to the Elderly Gentleman, when the empire finally transferred its capital to Baghdad, and said "to the turbulent Irish race which it had oppressed but never conquered, 'At last we leave you to yourselves; and much good may it do you,' the Irish as one man uttered the historic shout 'No: we'll be damned if you do,' and emigrated to the countries where there was still a Nationalist question, to India, Persia, and Corea, to Morocco, Tunis, and Tripoli." Here the world continued to ring with the stories of their "sufferings and wrongs," until, after two hundred years, "the claims of nationality were so universally conceded that there was no longer a single country on the face of the earth with a national grievance or a national movement." This utopia naturally put the Irish in a serious predicament, since they had nothing left to agitate for and were in danger of losing their position "as the most interesting race on earth." They were boycotted everywhere as intolerable bores. So to regain their prestige they announced that they were the Lost Tribes of Israel and claimed Jerusalem — whereupon the Jews "abandoned the city and redistributed themselves throughout Europe." Disappointed here in their search for a quarrel, the Irish were counseled by an English archbishop to go back to their own country, which none of them had ever seen. But when they landed in Galway Bay, the younger folk, more realistic than their parents, who were passionately kissing the soil of Ireland, looked about them and said, "There is no earth, only stone." So they "all left for England the next day; and no Irishman ever again confessed to being Irish, even to his own children; so that when that generation passed away the Irish race vanished from human knowledge."

Once more, then, Shaw did not essentially modify his ideas on a subject between his youth and his old age. In a review of a revival of Boucicault's *The Colleen Bawn* early in 1896, he anticipated his more lengthy description of the truth about the Irish character and manners in *John Bull's Other Island* and other later works, and wrote: "I am quite ready to help the saving work of reducing the sham Ireland of romance to a heap of unsightly ruins. When this is done, my country can consider the relative merits of building something real in the old country, or taking a hint from that other clever people, the Jews, and abandoning their Palestine to put on all the rest of the world as a shepherd putteth on his garment." Either or both of these alternatives offered by the young prophet seem to be distinct possibilities for the Irish problem. For that is the leitmotif of Shaw's treatment of his compatriots: though among the cleverest people in the world, they are problems, and will probably remain so.

## 3. *The Jew*

The similarity that existed in Shaw's mind between the Irish and the Jews has already been suggested. They are both problems, and they are both clever. They both have reputations as being artists and dreamers, and they both have a strong vein of practicality and even realism. They quarrel among themselves, and yet there is a kind of unity and loyalty among them. They are both, therefore, paradoxes.

In his preface to the Shaw-Terry correspondence, Shaw wrote that in the theater of the mid-nineteenth century, "Actors, like Jews, were a race apart; and like all segregated races they preserved manners and customs peculiar to themselves." Mendoza explains Louisa Straker's charge that "every Jew considers in his heart that English people are dirty in their habits" by saying, "Our elaborate sanitary code makes us unduly contemptuous of the Gentile." Perhaps this very sense of separateness is largely responsible for the attitude of other races toward the Jews. From this point of view their responsibility for the Crucifixion, so often thrown in their faces by Christians, such as the

Widow in *Geneva*, is not primarily to blame for their ostracization. Even before the birth of Christ Shaw makes Apollodorus say of Caesar in Alexandria, at the end of *Caesar and Cleopatra*, "He was settling the Jewish question when I left." But not even Caesar could make it stay settled. Shaw has no confidence in such modern attempts at solution as Zionism. Epifania, maintaining that though she is a millionairess she is a Christian to the last drop of her blood, explains the difference between Christians and Jews: "Jews throw half their money away on charities and fancies like Zionism." Mendoza, called a "sheeny" by the Rowdy Social-Democrat, replies "with crushing magnanimity," admitting that he is a Jew, but claiming to be an exception to all rules. Nevertheless, Shaw ironically has him assert that "when the Zionists need a leader to reassemble our race on its historic soil of Palestine, Mendoza will not be the last to volunteer." So far, however, he is merely the leader of a band of brigands — and the Devil in the dream scene.

Often the very consciousness of their Jewishness not only sets the Jews apart from others but also divides them from themselves. Shaw's earliest Jew, Jansenius in *An Unsocial Socialist*, in spite of his imposing presence, handsome appearance with his aquiline nose, dark eyes, and massive brow, and his business success as a banker, is secretly so ashamed of his Jewish origin that to the bewilderment of his friends, "who naturally believed he was proud of it," he has permitted his children to be educated as Christians. Though Shaw does not specifically label Sartorius in *Widowers' Houses* a Jew, the latter's "strong aquiline nose" and general air of importance, as well as his reticence and sensitivity about his past, give rise to some suspicion on this point.[27] Mendoza is unhappy because Louisa, instead of responding to his love, recommends that he marry "an accursed barmaid named Rebecca Lazarus," whom he loathes. (Note that Lazarus is also the name of Undershaft's aesthetically inclined Jewish partner in *Major Barbara*.) Yet Mendoza, boasting of his position as head of the syndicate of brigands, "as the Jew always becomes leader by his brains and imagination," admits honestly, "with all my pride of race I would give everything I possess to be an Englishman." Similarly, Dr. Leo ("Loony") Schutzmacher, also known as Shoemaker, in *The Doctor's Dilemma*, though middle-aged, well dressed, and with "a friendly but propitiatory air," is not quite sure of his reception by the gentile doctors with some of whom he has gone to school. "His combination of soft manners and responsive kindliness, with a certain unseizable reserve and a familiar yet foreign chiselling of feature, reveal the Jew: in this instance the handsome gentlemanly Jew." Schutzmacher's ingratiating apartness is further emphasized by his sardonic confession that he has always liked Englishmen better than Jews because to him the latter seem unusual, different, and "foreign."

But the unnamed Jew in *Geneva* is naturally the most complete study of the type. A "middle-aged gentleman of distinguished appearance, with a blond beard and moustache," he has come to Geneva to ask the Committee to apply to the Court of International Justice at the Hague for a warrant charging the "responsible ruler" of Germany with assault and battery, burglary, and "attempting to exterminate a section of the human race." When he somewhat truculently informs Begonia Brown that he is a Jew, she replies incredulously, "I don't believe you. You don't look like one." With a characteristic combination of pride, self-consciousness, and self-immolation, he goes on to instruct her in detail: "I am not a primitive Hittite. You cannot draw my nose in profile by simply writing down the number six . . . I have all the marks of a German blond. German is my native language: in fact I am in every sense German. But I worship in the synagogue; and when I worship I put my hat on, whereas a German takes it off. On this ground they class me as a non-Aryan, which is nonsense, as there is no such thing as an Aryan." Although he believes that "All peoples are disliked in the lump," he goes on to admit that there are good reasons for disliking Jews. In fact, he dislikes most of them himself.

Such Semitic anti-Semitism is further supplemented in the play by the non-Semites, the Newcomer and the Widow. The Newcomer maintains that the Jew ought to have been born in Jerusalem; he had no right to be born in Germany. The Widow, like Stogumber in *Saint Joan,* who "would not leave a Jew alive in Christendom if I had my way," at first would shoot all Jews, "because they crucified my Savior"; but when the Jew invites her to dine with him, because "Only a Jew can appreciate your magnificent type of beauty," she demurs only temporarily and then accepts, agreeing that the Jews have taste and are "vital" in their "oriental fashion." Gentile antipathy to Jews is also revealed in the slurring epithets that spring to gentile lips, such as Wilks's disillusioned admission just before he commits suicide in *The Simpleton* "that any Jew boy could do all I do here and do it better," and the Junker, General Strammfest's, ashamed confession in *Annajanska* that he has been made Commander-in-Chief by his own solicitor, "a Jew . . . A Hebrew Jew!" The Sergeant in *Too True* objects to much in the Old Testament because he feels that, although it may have gone down with "those old Jews," it is not really religion.

Gentile jealousy, particularly in money matters, of course accounts for much of the bad feeling. In *Geneva* the Jew accuses Ernest Battler of excluding Jews from Germany because the Germans cannot compete with them, and on the news of the approaching end of the world he rushes to the telephone to call his stockbroker. Schutzmacher, a retired "g.p." (general practitioner), has made his money by advertising, not "Consultation Free," but, on a shop window, "Dr. Leo Schutzmacher, L.R.C.P. M.R.C.S. Advice and medicine sixpence. Cure Guaranteed." On the Shavian theory that "most people get well all right if they are careful and you give them a little sensible advice," he has made enough money to make many of his more famous colleagues envious of him. When Epifania tells the Egyptian doctor that her ancestors were moneylenders to all Europe five hundred years ago, his automatic comment is, "Jewess, eh?" Warwick, however, defends the race against his chaplain's charge of extortion by asserting, "The Jews generally give value . . . In my experience the men who want something for nothing are invariably the Christians." Undershaft, in speaking to Dolly Cusins of his partner Lazarus, also feels that the Jews have often been maligned: "Lazarus is a gentle romantic Jew who cares for nothing but string quartets and stalls at fashionable theatres. He will get the credit of your rapacity in money matters, as he has hitherto had the credit for mine."

There are, therefore, types of Jews just as there are types of other races, and the stereotype is not to be trusted. As Shaw said in the preface to *Three Plays for Puritans,* "I can see no validity whatever in the view that the influence of the rich Jews on the theatre is any worse than the influence of the rich of any other race . . . All that can fairly be said of the Jewish influence on the theatre is that it is exotic." Their reputation for sensitiveness and aestheticism along with their materialism, however, is attested by Louis Dubedat's attempt to flatter Schutzmacher as being *ipso facto* an art connoisseur because he is a Jew, while at the same time trying to borrow money from him, knowing that for the same reason he has it.

## 4. *The American* [28]

Though Shaw had dealt at some length with America and Americans in a couple of his early novels, his first reference to them in his plays occurs in *Widowers' Houses,* his first dramatic production. Here, within the first minute after the curtain has risen, he makes young Dr. Trench sum up the other tourists on his Rhine trip: "Pooh! The steam boat people were the scum of the earth — Americans and all sorts. They may go hang themselves, Billy. I shall not bother about them."

Although the excessively contemptuous snobbishness of the first part of this remark is perhaps more attributable to Trench than to Shaw himself, in the last part certainly there is no similarity. Shaw did bother a great deal about Americans, as the large number of general references to them in his various writings attests. His actual American characters are relatively few, but his conclusions about American characteristics are frequent, sharp, dogmatic, and unequivocal. To sum up bluntly the impressions left after reviewing his various pronouncements on the theme, Americans are all millionaires, fond of extravagance and display, often disposed toward showy philanthropy, though their methods of money-making are likely to be somewhat shady. American society is a materialistic society, with a mass production of cheap goods, like cloth and alarm clocks, which drive out better things on the foreign as well as the domestic market. American bars, night clubs, and motor cars have invaded the world. Americans are a speedy and mechanically inventive race, but they have done little for civilization. They are vulgarly talkative, rapacious, and imperialistic. They love to brag about their democratic institutions, which are not really democratic at all, for democracy has not worked, either socially, politically, racially, or morally. And they are at the same time sentimentalists and idealists — though of a different stamp from the English.

Shaw always insisted that he was fond of Americans.

So far as the American characters in his plays and novels are concerned, however, the only one whom he seems to show any real affection for is his first, Edward Conolly, the Irish-American electrical engineer who has come to England and makes his fortune there, as seen in *The Irrational Knot* and *Love among the Artists*. But enough has already been said about Conolly as a Shavian realist and diabolonian to suggest the impression that he creates on most people other than the author. The Crawfords, the rich American acquaintances of Conolly's wife Marian, who befriend her in New York, are much more typical. General Crawford and his wife are good-hearted enough, under certain circumstances, but they are also naïve and rather vulgar. And the three visitors, "a gentleman, with his wife and brother," to whom they introduce her, soon show their shallowness. The lady simply eats, listens to the others' conversation, and admires Marian's dress. The husband is polite, but when Marian compares him with the English gentlemen she knows, he seems "rather oppressively respectful, and too much given to conversing in little speeches." He has traveled, and can describe his impressions "in correct narrative style"; but that is as far as his talents go. The brother falls in love with her at first sight, and becomes so "recklessly talkative" that he soon convinces her that "American society produced quite as choice a compound of off-handedness and folly as London could." All in all, the whole company "were not exactly what Marian considered the best sort of people; but New York was not London."

Captain Hamlin Kearney, of the American cruiser *Santiago* in *Captain Brassbound's Conversion,* "a robustly built western American, with the keen, squeezed, wind beaten eyes and obstinately enduring mouth of his profession," is a "curious ethnological specimen, with all the nations of the old world at war in his veins." Even stranger, "he is developing artificially in the direction of sleekness and culture under the restraints of an overwhelming dread of European criticism, and climatically in the direction of the indigenous North American Indian, who is already in possession of his hair, his cheek-bones, and the manlier instincts in him which the sea has rescued from civilization." To this confession of his environmentalist belief in the influence of climate on racial physiognomy, Shaw adds dubiously, "The world, pondering on the great part of its own future which is in his hands, contemplates him with wonder as to what the devil he will evolve into in another century or two." Kearney, obviously an efficient naval officer, marked by a "genial American courtesy," is otherwise epitomized by such remarks, delivered in good Shavian Americanese, as "The United States navy will have no hand in offering any violence to the pure instincts of womanhood," and "You recall me to my dooty, Lady Waynflete." Shaw, however, chivalrously gives him an opportunity at a small counterattack when Kearney, hinting at the English idealization of the Nelson-Hamilton affair, remarks, "Yours is an extraordinairy country — to an Amerrican."

Some of Kearney's characteristics, notably his sentimentalism toward women and his moralizing and sententiousness, are reflected in reverse in *Blanco Posnet,* Shaw's second play to have its entire setting in America — the only other being *The Devil's Disciple.* When Blanco affronts Feemy Evans by calling her a slut, she flames back at him with all the outraged innocence of a woman who knows he is right, "You're no true American man, to insult a woman like that." And shortly afterward Blanco jeeringly defies the Sheriff and the rest of the townsfolk by informing them, "I stand on the honor and virtue of my American manhood."

This is the kind of talk also attributed to the Hector Malones, senior and junior, in *Man and Superman.* The father, an Irish-American "whose native intonation has clung to him through many changes of place and rank," is the biggest office furniture man in the world — and a large stockholder in Mendoza, Limited, the nature of whose activities he has not bothered to learn. Malone's formal dress suggests that he is probably "a man whose social position needs constant and scrupulous affirmation without regard to climate." As a result, "he looks vulgar in his finery, though in a working dress of any kind he would look dignified enough." He has a hard mouth, a dogged chin, and the "self-confidence of one who has made money, and something of the truculence of one who has made it in a brutalizing struggle." On the whole, he is a man "to be pitied when he is not to be feared"; there is "something pathetic about him at times." He is actuated always by a prejudice against the English middle class. His materialism is revealed by his insistence that his son's marriage must show a "social profit somewhere." As young Hector tells Violet, the old man would show his own son the door for marrying "the most perfect lady in England merely because she has no handle to her name." The astute Violet, however, calls old Malone "romantic" to his face, and winds him around her efficient finger.

Violet also calls her husband-in-secret, Hector, "romantic," and Shaw agrees, for he says that Hector gets along best with "romantic Christians of the amoristic sect," like Octavius. The young man is "an Eastern American, . . . but he is not at all ashamed of his nationality." Therefore the English, protectively, approve of him and are kind to him, as if he were a child or an animal. On his side, he feels that the British are apt "to represent their various incapacities as points of good breeding," in such matters as their lack of what he calls "moral tone," their "want of respect for womanhood," the very vulgar failure of their pronunciation "in tackling such words as world, girl, bird, etc.," their coarseness in using what they regard as plain speaking, and their inability to enliven social intercourse by such pastimes as games and stories. He himself has the most chivalrous manners toward women, and is full of "elevated moral sentiments." In fact, according to Shaw's indictment, "Hector's culture is nothing but a state of saturation with our literary exports of thirty years ago," which is positively "dumbfounding." His devout and fundamental religiosity, his intellectual poverty, and his despising of politics offset "the engaging freshness of his personality." At least, he is "careful not to talk commercial shop, in which department he is probably much in advance of his English capitalist friends." Certainly he is a Shavian "manly man," shocked at the dishonor of his father's opening his son's letter, and trying to disown his father and insisting that he is going to get his own job to support his wife. Observing him, Tanner concludes, "No wonder American women prefer to live in Europe!" After all the marital problems are worked out at the end of the play, Mrs. Whitefield confidentially advises Violet, "Don't let him take you to America. Promise me that you won't." Violet's reply, made "very decidedly," is foregone: "I should think not indeed."

Such pictures of American men — Shaw has apparently not been sufficiently impressed, even unfavorably, by American women to draw their portraits in any of his plays — reflect the opinions that he had been presenting in his dramatic reviews in the nineties. For example, in 1896 he wrote that the hero of Gattie's *The Honorable Member* "is a high-toned young man of the American ethical sort"; in 1897, of a revival of *Antony and Cleopatra,* that if any passage in Shakespeare is stripped "of that beauty of sound by prosaic paraphrase, . . . you have nothing left but a platitude that even an American professor of ethics would blush to offer his disciples"; and, later in the same year, of Musset's *Lorenzaccio,* that to the romantic man a woman is "not a human being or a fellow-creature, but simply the incarnated divinity of sex. And I regret to add that women rather liked being worshipped on false pretenses at first. In America they still do."

Whether in business, politics, or the professions, to Shaw the American is always cut from the same bolt of cloth. Take Vanhattan, the American ambassador to England in *The Apple Cart.* Without having arranged an audience in advance, he enters "in an effusive condition" and salutes the Queen "with a handshake so prolonged that she stares in astonishment." Announcing that the Declaration of Independence has been canceled and that the United States is proposing to rejoin the British Empire to enjoy Dominion Home Rule, he talks magniloquently about this being "a great historic scene." When Magnus cannily perceives that this union would mean the end of English independence and that England would become "a mere appendage of a big American concern," Vanhattan points out that the change would be merely nominal, since American goods, ideas, money, amusements, etc., are already "at home" in England, and much of England, both tangible and intangible, has been transplanted to America. The Queen, reflecting that the way American women behave at court shows that they already recognize the English as "their natural superiors," at first feels that the change would be a "very good thing . . . We shall civilize these Americans." The uxorious Magnus admits that she may be right, and that he may end as "an American Emperor" just to keep her amused. The play concludes with the question of "annexation" left an open one — but, with another of those frequent flashes of Shavian prophetic insight, a distinct future possibility. The "old England," certainly, is gone forever.

The last Shavian American is the Journalist in *Geneva*. He is "a smart young American gentleman," afflicted with the worst case yet of Americanese language. He is flip, pushing, and clever in a boyish sort of way, but his vulgarity offsets his vitality. Although he fades out partway through the play, we have seen enough of him to realize that Shaw has not yet relented in his portrayal of Americans for comic purposes.

## 5. *The German*

Although the sergeant in *The Devil's Disciple* is careful to point out that the Hessian troops are German, and therefore stupid, Shaw's presentation of the Germans is confined chiefly to their treatment of the Jews and to German-English relationships before and during the First World War. The Jew's resentment of his ostracism by his blond fellow-countrymen in *Geneva* is typical of the first point, which is developed at some length in the preface, wherein Shaw damns Hitler for his racial theories and his persecution of the Jews. This is all simply part of German nationalism and the glorification of the Aryan. Mrs. O'Flaherty, for instance, it will be remembered, points to German national pride, which, she says, is like the English, except that the Germans should know better, since they're better educated.

Even in 1909, to the average Englishman, Germany was already the Enemy, and in *Press Cuttings* Shaw satirizes the excesses to which the jingoistic Englishman was going in his claims to English supremacy. Balsquith, the Prime Minister, shows some common sense in his estimate of the probable results of the rivalry. Although he realizes that the fact that Germany has laid down four more dreadnoughts challenges his country's position as mistress of the seas, he also realizes that the new compulsory military service law in England increases the danger of war tenfold, because it increases German jealousy of English power. The militaristic General Mitchener, however, is not dismayed, since "patriotism" to him is more significant than war. Suggesting that "in these days of aeroplanes and Zeppelin

airships the question of the moon is becoming one of the greatest importance," he demands, "Can you, as an Englishman, tamely contemplate the
possibility of having to live under a German moon? The British flag must
be planted there at all hazards." Such a fear of the military use of the moon
seemed much more absurd in 1909 than it does a half-century later. But
even the Orderly, an anti-militarist, can be aroused from mildness to blood-
thirstiness by the mere mention of Germany. "Shew me a German," he
vows, "and I'll have a go at him as fast as you or any man."

Consequently, when war broke out Shaw felt justified in crying, "I told
you so," and the nation retaliated by calling him "Pro-German." In *Major
Barbara* he had indirectly extolled the German genius in manufacturing
munitions by having Undershaft explain that the reason he did not want to
pass his business on to his son Stephen was that he feared Stephen would
carry it along only "until the real Undershaft — probably an Italian or a
German — would invent a new method and cut him out." Although the
Princess in *The Inca of Perusalem* fears that if she marries the Inca she
will "be an alien enemy everywhere except in Perusalem, because the Inca
has made war on everybody. And I shall have to pretend that everybody
has made war on him," Shaw allows the Inca himself, obviously modeled
on the Kaiser, to utter some pretty convincing speeches of self-justification.
In the notes which he wrote to *Androcles* during the war Shaw indulges
in some scorching irony at the expense of the treatment of the Germans by
the churches, especially the Church of England; but at the same time he
related an anecdote about how the Crown Prince when the play was first
performed in Berlin ostentatiously left the theater, "unable to endure the
(I hope) very clear and fair exposition of autocratic Imperialism given by
the Roman captain to his Christian prisoners." Another scathing attack on
the anti-German war excesses during the war is made in the preface to
*Heartbreak House,* where Shaw charges that "the impact of physical death
and destruction, the one reality that every fool can understand, tore off the
masks of education, art, science, and religion from our ignorance and
barbarism, and left us glorying grotesquely in the licence suddenly accorded
to our vilest passions and most abject terrors." But in *Augustus Does His
Bit* Shaw allows Augustus to make one of his few sensible remarks when
he states his conviction, based on his observation of one of his brothers-in-
law, who is on the German general staff, that the "Hun" War Office is as
badly run as any other War Office. On the other hand, Augustus is naïvely
proud of the Germans' insistence on sending him back to the English without exchanging him for a similar English prisoner because the German who
captured him "was kind enough to say he could not believe a German
officer answering to that description existed."

Just as Shaw sometimes uses the Germans as a stick with which to beat
the English, so sometimes he also uses them as a means of contrast with

the Russians. The stiff-minded officers who are outsmarted by Annajanska, the Bolshevik Empress, are given German names like Strammfest and Schneidekind; and Patiomkin, speaking for Shaw, announces that although Catherine is a German he has "given her a Russian heart." Ernest Battler — with the minor exception of the Inca, the only actual German character in Shaw's plays — is unfavorably contrasted with the Commissar in *Geneva,* and will be discussed at more length as helping to illustrate one of Shaw's leading types of politicians. Even Vanhattan, the American ambassador in *The Apple Cart,* is allowed to become truly prophetic when, in commenting on those "queer old geographical expressions which you use here from old family habit," he adds: "I suppose you mean by Germany the chain of more or less Soviet Republics between the Ural Mountains and the North Sea. Well, the clever people at Moscow and Berlin and Geneva are trying to federate them" — a move the at-least-partial success of which even Shaw probably did not anticipate within such a relatively short time.

## 6. *The Slav*

Among the Slavic races Shaw has been attracted only to the Bulgarians, the Poles, and the Russians. It is true that Bluntschli, the realistic mercenary in *Arms and the Man,* has sold his services to the Servian army, and is first taken by Catherine Petkoff to be a German because of his name, but he soon identifies himself as a Swiss. And to Shaw the Swiss seem to be especially associated with hotels, since not only is Bluntschli's family in the hotel business, but the Clerk in *Augustus* refers ostentatiously to the waiter who "calls himself a Swiss."

Shaw's Bulgarians, also all found in *Arms and the Man,* are parvenus in the society of Western nations. Catherine Petkoff, energetic and imperious in her way, "might be a very splendid specimen of the wife of a mountain farmer, but is determined to be a Viennese lady." Her husband, vain over the rank of major which the war has won for him, even if the Russians are running the war itself, is cheerful, insignificant, and unpolished, "naturally unambitious except as to his income and his importance in local society." Raina Petkoff and Sergius Saranoff are both intelligent, handsome, and romantic, and are being acted upon — to their ultimate gain — by the coming of the Western civilization which they have not yet assimilated. The intermediate status of the household, including the servants, is indicated by its pride in its uniqueness, for the house has almost the only inside staircase in Bulgaria — to say nothing of a special room for a library, whose shelves are practically untenanted, but which possesses an electric bell. Petkoff's contact with "civilized people" — that is, foreigners such as the Russians and the Austrians — makes him embarrassed when he finds the family wash hanging on the bushes to dry, although his wife assures him that "really refined people" don't notice such things.

Shaw's Poles, on the other hand, are certainly not untutored, semi-barbarian innocents, since his two main specimens are both — each in a different way — artists. Aurélie Szczympliça in *Love among the Artists,* in fact, epitomizes art for art's sake, for she is utterly devoted to her music, to the exclusion of any significant interest in her personal or domestic life. And Lina Szczepanowska, the new woman and acrobat in *Misalliance,* is just as devoted to her profession, which she and her family have always regarded as an art, so that she also disdains any personal entanglements which would interfere with its practice.

*Great Catherine,* Shaw's only play with a Russian setting, gives his picture of a rather primitive Russian society, just beginning to feel its power in European politics. *Geneva,* through the person of the Commissar, permits him to present his view of Russia at present, together with his even more sanguine hopes for its future. In between, including high praise for Tchekov and Tolstoy in the preface to *Heartbreak House,* are allusions to Russia, almost invariably flattering, even when their utterers hate the Soviets on principle; but, astonishingly enough, there are no other Russian characters in his plays.

Life in Russia in the eighteenth century, according to *Great Catherine,* was exuberant, extravagant, vital, dirty, and disorderly. But the Russians, though undisciplined, really loved living. Patiomkin, whom Shaw greatly admires, is typical of his country. Shaw thinks him worth describing at length: "Superficially Patiomkin is a violent, brutal barbarian, an upstart despot of the most intolerable and dangerous type, ugly, lazy, and disgusting in his personal habits. Yet ambassadors report him the ablest man in Russia . . . He has a wild sense of humor, which enables him to laugh at himself as well as at everybody else . . . In fact, he actually is an outrageous ruffian . . . but . . . a man to be reckoned with." When necessary, this ruffian can turn into a "pale, fragile nobleman, aged and quite sober, extremely dignified in manner and address." Generally, however, he is happily drunk, absurdly generous with diamonds, and full of grotesque exaggeration, emotionalism, sentiment, and amorousness. His abilities as a diplomat are only shadowily suggested in his farcical handling of the relationship between Edstaston and Catherine. Seemingly even the congenial Shaw felt somewhat apologetic about the boisterousness of the character he had drawn, for in reply to criticism he wrote in his preface that he might honestly plead that "the apparently outrageous Patiomkin is but a timidly bowdlerized ghost of the original."

As for Catherine, a German by birth but a Russian by marriage and adoption, she is the Queen, according to the sub-title, "Whom Glory Still Adores." Nevertheless, in the preface Shaw states that he doubts whether either she or "the statesmen with whom she played this mischievous kind of political chess had any notion of the real history of their own times or of the real forces that were moulding Europe," since she was overwhelmed and shocked by the French Revolution. He admits that in his play, written especially for Gertrude Kingston to act, he mainly adopts Byron's conception of Catherine in *Don Juan*, substituting "an English country gentleman" for the original Spanish nobleman. His Catherine, he explains, is "by no means barbarous or intemperate in her personal habits. She not only disputes with Frederick the Great the reputation of being the cleverest monarch in Europe, but may even put in a very plausible claim to be the cleverest and most attractive individual alive." She speaks of herself as a "Liberal Empress" and a "philosopher," "frank and original in character, like an Englishman," the only person in Russia who gets no fun out of her being Empress. Although on occasion she can speak "like a fishfag," with a strong German accent, she is building a new museum for her "enlightened capital," and even when annoyed or angered she remains conscious of her desire to make Russia great and dignified in the eyes of the world. "Europe is looking on," she reminds herself and the rest. Nevertheless, she finally allows herself to be hugely amused by the trick which Patiomkin plays on Edstaston and lends herself to extracting the full amount of fun possible out of it.

This desire not only to make Russia great but also to have her recognized abroad as great even if this means the destruction of her rivals, has of course marked the activities of most of Russia's leaders, particularly of the twentieth century. Thus some of the British journalists in *The Simpleton* at first attribute the disappearances on Judgment Day to a Russian "plot to destroy our most valuable citizens." Boanerges in *The Apple Cart*, although he wears a Russian blouse and peaked cap, remains patriotic enough to expostulate, in connection with the probable future shifting of the British capital to either Washington or Moscow: "Moscow thinks a lot of itself. But what has Moscow to teach us that we cannot teach ourselves! Moscow is built on English history, written in London by Karl Marx." Even the chauvinistic Admiral Hotspot in *On the Rocks* is impressed by Russian advances. He talks admiringly of what the Russian fleet and sailors did for the Revolution, and points out that the Russians are the only nation which has a special Cabinet for thinking — a Cabinet which has "knocked the whole place to pieces." Both the Duke of Domesday and Sir Arthur Chavender, he suggests to them, would be in the dustbin if they lived in Russia today, even though, as he admits, Sir Arthur has at least tried to think. Hipney, too, reminds them all that the English voters can be stampeded into almost anything simply by telling them that the Russians are coming. Shaw himself, of course, seizes the opportunity in his preface to make an extended defense of Soviet political theory, government, and even of the Ogpu and its purges. In *Too True*, Private Meek (one of whose middle names is Trotsky) also becomes Shaw's mouthpiece when he announces that everybody within fifty miles is asking him to get a passport visaed for Beotia — "The Union of Federated Sensible Societies . . . The U.F.S.S. Everybody wants to go there now, sir." This utopia is already so idyllic that the only Englishman it will admit is the reformed Colonel Tallboys, because "their people have so much leisure that they are at their wits' end for some occupation to keep them out of mischief." They've seen some of the Colonel's water color paintings, and want to make him "head of their centres of repose and culture." It's only the Colonel's lady who keeps him from accepting.

But the Commissar represents the culmination of Shaw's Russophilia. The English Bishop is aghast when he discovers that this affable and understanding acquaintance at Geneva, this "very smart Russian gentleman," is actually "Commissar Posky of the Sovnarkom and Politbureau, Soviet delegate to the League Council." Posky assures the Bishop that his "hands are not bloodstained." Recalling that his government has agreed not to propagandize to overthrow the British National Government, he objects to the establishment of a British organization in Russia, the Society for the Propagation of the Gospel in Foreign Parts, to overthrow the Soviet system and establish instead the Church of England and the British Constitution. In this *reductio ad absurdum* of the situation, the Bishop is almost as simpleminded as Shaw, though in reverse, in refusing to see anything wrong in these methods. After the Bishop has dropped dead, the Commissar continues to propagandize the other members of the group. He tells them that a Communist state is "only possible for highly civilized people, trained to Communism from their childhood." He explains that the Soviets shoot only exploiters and saboteurs — and they have shot only relatively few people anyhow. He finds it very difficult to accustom himself to the exaggerated importance attached to sex in the western countries. Russians are not hypocritical about claiming freedom of speech, as the English are. In fact, "The future is for Russian ideas," not English.

The perfection of the Commissar's ideas, however, is not left unchallenged. The Secretary cries that he hates Communism because the present government "has declared for Socialism in a single country," and is not abashed when the other dubs him a Trotskyite. The Judge joins in, and charges that as a matter of fact Dame Begonia's intentions and sympathies are just the same as the Commissar's. "None of you seem to have any idea of the sort of world you are living in." But the Judge explains his attitude further by pointing out that Russian politics are only fifty years behind her political and social philosophies, whereas the politics of other nations are five hundred to five thousand years behind. There are at least hopes in Russia. The Commissar, however, remains nationalistic enough to maintain that these ideas can flourish only under the guidance of Moscow, and he proclaims that when the other peoples have eaten each other up, Holy Russia will save the soul of the world by teaching it to feed its people instead of robbing them. Though the Commissar is comparatively silent during the trial itself (note that Stalin is not summoned to be questioned along with the other dictators), he warns Battler that when Germany has finished its conquest it will have to settle with Russia as to how much it can keep. Again, the prophet Shaw has at least approximated the future.

## 7. *The Romance Races*

Shaw has not been much attracted to the Romance races, either as characters for his plays or as objects of his satiric commentary. Napoleon, as a Corsican, is both French and Italian. Except for Bombardone, the Innkeeper in *The Man of Destiny,* and the Romans in *Caesar and Cleopatra,* the only other Italian in the plays, Marzo, one of Captain Brassbound's band, turns out to be, in Drinkwater's words, only a "hawce barrer an street pianner Hawtellian," born in Hatton Gardens. Shaw, however, gives the Italians credit for some inventiveness. Not only does Undershaft praise their potential ingenuity in the cannon business, but Hipney remarks that he has heard that they "are tapping their volcanoes for cheap power."

The French have made a little deeper impression. The setting and most of the characters in *Saint Joan* are of course French. Louise de Kéroualle, Charles II's mistress, is a transplanted Frenchwoman, with all the traditional guiles and temperament of her race and sex. The captivating Strange Lady whose wiles overcome Napoleon reveals, however, that she has English as well as Irish and French ancestors. Voltaire in *The Black Girl* is of course French.

In general Shaw's treatment of the French is pretty well confined to some contrasting pictures between the traditional Englishman's notion (or perhaps "ideal") of the nation, with the truth (or "reality"). When Margaret Knox introduces her befriender, the French marine officer, M. Duvallet, to her father, Knox exclaims with despairing suspicion, "A Frenchman! It needed only this." A little later, still scandalized, he wails, "Do you mean to tell me that my daughter laughs at French jokes?" and his friend Gilbey, in spite of Juggins's protests, chimes in, "We all know what French jokes are." Like Duvallet, one of the bandits in *Man and Superman* is an "unmistakable Frenchman." Chaplain de Stogumber is sure that "there is no faith in a Frenchman." The long-headed Vanhattan recalls the legendary French mercenariness: "So long as Paris is full of Americans, and Americans are full of money, all's well in the west from the French point of view." But at the same time the French pride themselves on their refinement and culture. Thus Patiomkin, who drinks "too much French brandy and too little Russian kvass," in conformity with the Francophilia of the Russia of his day, laments, "No wonder the French sneer at us as barbarians." Catherine herself, after refusing to be flattered by the Princess Dashkoff's remark that the Empress's brain is just like Voltaire's and informing the Princess that she would not "give a rouble to have the brains of all the philosophers in

France," nevertheless praises Voltaire soon afterward as "a wonderful author," who has (shades of Henry George!) lucidly exposed "the folly of this crazy plan for raising the entire revenue of the country from a single tax on land!"

But Shaw naturally knows that there is another France than this one of popular tradition, the exposition of which he entrusts, by a sort of process of comic inversion, to characters like O'Flaherty and Duvallet. The Irishman, although impressed by the low pay of the French army, has decided that if he survives the war and ever marries, he will marry a Frenchwoman (in fact, he has been "as good as married to a couple of them already"), and settle down on a French farm. For French women can cook better meals than anyone ever found in Ireland, and French fields are so big that ten of the dirty little Irish fields wouldn't fill one of their ditches. (Incidentally, too, O'Flaherty thinks that the Belgians are also pretty good men, and that the French ought to be more civil to them; both nations know how to till their land properly.)

Duvallet takes a different and somewhat enigmatic line. By praising the English and derogating his own countrymen, he shows how most people tend to idealize the foreign. He admires the freedom and independence of English and American girls, and laments the narrowness of the French. He is favorably struck by the fact that "home life can hardly be said to exist in England," so that "everywhere in these islands one can enjoy the exhilarating, the soul-liberating spectacle of men quarreling with their brothers, defying their fathers, refusing to speak with their mothers." Paying his respects to English morality, military genius, and lack of "false ideals of patriotic enthusiasm," he concludes that if all Frenchwomen were like Margaret Knox, "if all Frenchmen had the good sense, the power of seeing things as they really are, the calm judgment, the open mind, the philosophic grasp, the foresight and true courage, which are so natural to you as an Englishman that you are scarcely conscious of possessing them, France would become the greatest nation in the world." From this sort of irony, neither nation emerges with much credit.

As for the Spanish and the Portuguese, the latter, if judged by Shaw's sole Portuguese character, Charles II's queen, Catherine of Braganza, come off better than any of the other Romance countries, since Catherine is sensible, motherly, domestic, and practical. The Spaniards in the dream scene in *Man and Superman* are of course only slightly altered Englishmen, though some Spanish characteristics and tendencies are attributed to Don Juan, Ana, and the Statue. Of the bandits, only one might be Spanish, since he looks like "a bullfighter ruined by drink." The scenery of the last two acts is marked by "Spanish magnificence and Spanish economy everywhere." That is the paradox that Shaw strikes in his treatment of most of the Mediterranean countries: profuseness, even flamboyance, contrasted with narrowness of mind and shrewd practicality, such as is seen in Flanco de Fortinbras of *Geneva.*

### 8. *Etc.*

Though the Dutch are represented by the upright Judge in *Geneva,* there are, strangely enough, no Scandinavians of any consequence in any of Shaw's plays, nor any important references to them. Nevertheless, in his prefaces, notes, letters, reviews, etc., he is continually referring to such Scandinavian playwrights as Ibsen and Strindberg — and invariably with approval. Typical is his remark in his preface to his correspondence with Ellen Terry, in which, after asserting, "Now I claim that no male writer born in the nineteenth century outside Norway and Sweden did more to knock Woman off her pedestal and plant her on the solid earth than I," he goes on to cite Ibsen and Strindberg as notable examples and collaborators. And he is almost as niggardly in his treatment of South America, the Widow from the Republic of the Earthly Paradise being that continent's only prominent — and not very flattering — representative.

Opposed as Shaw is to the dangerous fallacy of racial purity and superiority, he has always displayed an attraction to and fondness for those races whose skin pigmentation differs from that of the Occidental nations. Africa, the Near East, and the Far East have placed their representatives in his works far more frequently than have Scandinavia and South America.

Shaw's high regard for Mahomet (he once almost started to write a play about the Prophet, but turned to Saint Joan instead) undoubtedly has helped to turn his attention to the Arabs, the Egyptians, and the Moors. The discussion of Mahometanism in the latter part of *Getting Married* is of course motivated partly by the subject of the play, but the flavor of Shaw's commendations is not merely to be accounted for thus. In the preface to *The Simpleton* he calls Mahomet unqualifiedly "one of the greatest of the prophets of God," and he makes Warwick remark liberally in *Saint Joan* that in some respects the conduct of the followers of the Arab camel driver "compared favorably with ours." For, indeed, they "profess great respect for our Lord." The mere fact of Mahometan polygamy does not bother Shaw, since it is simply a matter of *mores.* Thus he allows the already married Inca of Perusalem, in proposing to Ermyntrude, to offer "to embrace the Mahometan faith, which allows a man four wives. . . . It will please the Turks." In *Methuselah,* in fact, by A.D. 3000 the capital of the British Commonwealth has been moved to Baghdad. Alexandria, the beautiful capital of Egypt in *Caesar and Cleopatra,* harbors some emotional Egyptians, including its husband-seeking (though ethnologically Greek) queen. The Egyptian Doctor in *The Millionairess,* however, fights against matrimony, but vainly. "A serious looking middleaged Egyptian gentleman in an old black frock coat and a tarboosh, speaking English too well to be mistaken for a native," he operates a clinic for penniless Mahometan refugees, and assures the predatory Eppy that he is married to Science and that he has to reserve himself for "poor and useful people." Nevertheless, becoming interested in spite of himself in her father fixation, her excess of money, and her magnificent pulse, he permits himself to fall into her toils. After all, as Drinkwater puts it with his usual originality, "Hooman nitre is the sime everywheres. Them eathens is jast lawk you an me, gavner." He is talking about the Porter, but his remarks can apply almost equally well to the other Moroccan Moors in *Captain Brassbound,* particularly Osman, the Sheikh, and the Cadi.

Sir Jafna Pandranath, the elderly Ceylonese plutocrat in *On the Rocks,* proves that an Indian can take an honored place in white society, though underneath the surface the whites may resent his success and finally reveal their essential racial snobbery. On his first entrance all the others rise "as if to receive a royal personage." Although "evidently too much occupied and worried by making money to get any fun out of spending it," he supports Sir Arthur's proposal to nationalize the land so that a stop will be put to "this shameless exploitation of the financiers and entrepreneurs by a useless, idle, and predatory landed class." He also is willing to adopt certain principles of Communism in the name of capital and private enterprise. But Sir Dexter Rightside's angry and jealous lashing at him as "only a silly nigger pretending to be an English gentleman" insults his racial pride, and blows down Sir Arthur's whole flimsy house of cards. Sir Jafna denounces the entire assemblage, and informs them that he has so far supported England's connection with India, believing that Indian brains would eventually take over England, but that now he will work for separation. Archbishop Haslam in *The Thing Happens* has a similarly high regard for "brown brains," as he calls them, for he tells Barnabas, Burge-Lubin, and the rest that, because of his maturity and experience, "If you were to kill me as I stand here, you would have to appoint an Indian to succeed me . . . We are letting all the power slip into the hands of the colored people." The doctrine of colored superiority to supplant white superiority is also voiced in *The Simpleton,* whose "natives" are probably Indians (called "niggers" by the Emigration officer). In reply to the Young Woman's suggestion that he marry a "colored woman" Hyering answers that "now that they're all educated they won't look at a white man." Besides, they say that he's ignorant and smells bad. The political situation, too, has changed. Pra is responsible for the news that "Since India won Dominion status Delhi has been the centre of the British Empire." Apparently the shift to Baghdad is to come later. It is in Pra and Prola, the brown priest and priestess in the play, that Shaw focuses his theme and his hope for a new future race, in spite of the failure of their present hybrid brood of beautiful but stupid golden-skinned children.

To some one hundred percent Englishmen as well as Americans, all colored peoples are "niggers." Shaw not only regards the future of the brown races optimistically, but he has an equally high respect for the black. Old Captain Shotover, for instance, advises Mangan to "marry a West India negress: they make excellent wives. I was married to one myself for two years." And he goes on to prove his seriousness by crediting her with redeeming him from being "damned" in this period of his life. In *The Thing Happens* England has imported negresses and Chinese to perform the real work of governing her. The Minister of Health is a "handsome Negress," who comments on the attractiveness of a rich, dark skin to men, is amused by Burge-Lubin's prudery when he plugs in his television switchboard on her and is shocked at finding her in dishabille, and mischievously sharpens the appetite of her conscience-impeded lover by telling him that distant flirtations teach self-control. It is Burge-Lubin who mentions the new book by the librarian of the Biological Society which suggests that "the future of the world lies with the Mulatto." And of course the heroine in Shaw's last "novel," *The Adventures of the Black Girl in Her Search for God,* is a negress, marked from the first by her inquisitiveness and skepticism — and a Creative Evolutionist by instinct. She confesses frankly that neither she nor any other intelligent person can love everybody, and she knows that some dangerous people must be killed. At first, when Voltaire, at the end of her allegorical and theological adventures, suggests that she marry the red-headed Irish Socialist, the Irishman protests, but he finally surrenders and discovers that family life with her and their "charmingly coffee-colored" pickaninnies is quite happy. She gives up her search, for "by that time her strengthened mind had taken her far beyond the stage at which there is any fun in smashing idols with knobkerries." Halfway through the story the lady ethnologist in the English expedition to Africa has predicted, "I keep telling you that the next great civilization will be a black civilization."

As for the yellow races, Confucius is the only representative in the flesh. Yet Shaw's more or less random observations about the Japanese and the Chinese suggest that they hold certain standard associations and stereotypes for him. Probably Undershaft's reference to the Russo-Japanese War as an opportunity for testing his new "aerial battleship" is merely topical, since it was made in 1905. But Japanese military and naval efficiency continued to impress Shaw, or at least Admiral Hotspot, who announces in *On the Rocks,* "I have my eye on Japan." Chavender, too, in discussing the current disarmament plans (which practically amount to rearmament plans), remarks that his secretary will fill in a blank which he has left in the manuscript of a speech he is preparing by inserting "whatever number of ships the Japanese are standing out for." Nevertheless, Japan also has quite a different association for Sir Arthur. For to him it stands for art as well as militarism; and in contemplating the voyages that he hopes some day to make he confesses that he looks forward especially to Japan, where he expects to "pick up some nice old bric-a-brac."

Both the Japanese and the Chinese help to focus the immigration and labor problems for Shaw. The Newcomer in *Geneva* reminds the rest that Australia will not allow "a yellow man" to enter, and that the United States will not let a Japanese into California. Hipney, while analyzing the chronic English unemployment situation in *On the Rocks,* points out that a "Chinese coolie can live on a penny a day"; and the Jew in *Geneva* asserts that the British exclude the Chinese because they are better and cheaper workmen than the whites. Moreover, the Chinese, according to the Judge, have unexpectedly developed a new revolutionary quality. Although in his preface Shaw repeats the old idea that "Men are what they were," and never really learn from the past, he somewhat inconsistently has his Judge in the play admonish the others that "as late as the nineteenth century the world believed that the Chinese could never change. Now they are the most revolutionary of all the revolutionists."

Confucius, the Chief Secretary to the President of the British Islands in *The Thing Happens,* presents Shaw's most fully considered view of the Chinese characteristics. "Ever since the public services have been manned by Chinese," he reminds Burge-Lubin, "the country has been well and honestly governed." On the theory that "Only strangers are impartial," the Chinese have decided that reciprocal trade in public servants is the only way to solve the problem of honest government; and he is careful to point out that they have imported Scotchmen to govern China, and not Englishmen, who are not "fitted by nature to understand politics." Knowing more English and world history than President Burge-Lubin, he reminds his boss that democracy is "an institution peculiar to China," though never a real success there. Like Shaw, he is another authoritarian, and reminds the rest blandly, "I am the government." Naturally, as he realizes, nobody likes him, and he is "held in awe" rather than loved. Yet even this pragmatist and sage has his philosophic limitations. He is stunned and fearful when he learns that the first longlivers have appeared, and predicts a dire future for the old race. Although he admits that he has "come to regard some such development as this as inevitable," he nevertheless counsels strict secrecy about the discovery. After he has had a few minutes to think the thing over, however, he concludes that the inevitable must be accepted, even though it will destroy all family life and social relationships as now practised, and he ends his conversation with the adolescently worried Burge-Lubin by stating, "We cannot stop it, since the vital force that has produced this change would paralyze our opposition to it."

So Confucius, like the Black Girl, Pra, and Prola, decides that the best thing is to get into harmony with Creative Evolution and not to fight it. The colored races, on the whole, seem to be naturally more receptive to the doctrine than the white races. There is a broader streak of mysticism in them than in their neighbors, so that through them a brighter promise of salvation is held out.

# VIII

## DOCTOR, LAWYER, MERCHANT, CHIEF . . .

IN THE *Self Sketches* one of Shaw's comments on Duffin's *The Quintessence of Bernard Shaw* runs as follows: "There is a great deal of truth in your description of democracy as 'stupidity armed with a gun'; but you miss the fact that in my sense 'the lawyer, the priest, the literary man, and the politician' are on the whole more dangerous than the common folk who have not been stultified by the process which we call secondary education." In this typically Shavian generalization reappear not only his disesteem of democracy and his scorn of formal education, but also his penchant for hurling satirical darts and spears at the professional, artistic, and genteel classes in general. Though Shaw, while a Socialist-into-Communist, was all for aristocracy in his sense of the term, he was always intensely disappointed in the failure of our educational and political systems to select the best men to teach us, to govern us, and to care for our mental, physical, spiritual, and legal ills. This human stupidity is at the root of his satire on the professional classes. In fact, the very word "profession" early attained a very questionable connotation in his mind. Not only did he introduce it into two of his early titles — *Cashel Byron's Profession* and *Mrs. Warren's Profession* — to apply to activities which were outside the pale of the law, though patronized hypocritically by the respectable, but he also confessed that he would have liked to use it ironically as a title to describe Andrew Undershaft's munitions industry if he had not used it twice already.

A similar cynicism appears in his attitude toward a still larger class, within which most members of the professions are, or would like to be, found. In the marvelous preface to *Immaturity,* one of the most amusing and revelatory short autobiographies ever written, Shaw caustically celebrates his own birth and family thus: "I sing my own class: the Shabby Genteel, the Poor Relations, the Gentlemen who are no Gentlemen." Perhaps this rankling sense of social stratification and even modified ostracism in his younger days had something to do with his later selection of one of the targets that he most delighted to perforate: ladies and gentlemen.[29] In spite of the fact that, as West insists from the Marxist point of view, the struggle over the meaning of the word "gentleman" as one of the centers of the bourgeois revolution was already well past when Shaw began to write, it is nevertheless a subject that he never lets go of, from the first of his writings to the last; in fact, after a time, one gets the feeling that he is worrying it to death, especially in farce. Yet this is not to say that there is not a strong element of seriousness in his flippancy. For — reversing Arnold — just as Arnold saw more danger to his chosen people, his people of light, in his Philistines than in his barbarians or aristocrats, so Shaw was really more concerned by what his ladies and gentlemen were doing to society than by what his Philistines were, or were not, doing. The fact should not be overlooked, however, that plenty of ladies and gentlemen are also Philistines, in Shaw's sense.

Appended to "The Revolutionist's Handbook," itself an appendix to the dramatic text of *Man and Superman* in 1903, Shaw placed his more or less uneven collection of aphorisms and epigrams which he entitled "Maxims for Revolutionists." One section of this collection, headed "The Perfect Gentleman," contains since various apothegms tacitly based on the assumption that the automatic adherence to a standardized code of manners, clothes, thought, and conduct is the key to the whole group of ladies and gentlemen, and therefore usually to the professions as well. Most of the basis of the trouble is to be found in the discrepancy between the externals of the code and the actual actions of those who pretend to follow it. These aphorisms deal with such matters as false standards of honor, consumption without production, parasitism, patriotism, education, and certain specific types such as the "sportsman warrior gentleman" and the "intellectually and artistically cultivated gentleman," and they should not be overlooked in estimating Shaw's opinions of the various professional types.

Yet, consistent as Shaw's ostensible attitude of amused scorn toward ladies and gentlemen remains throughout his works, he cannot conceal his own equally consistent and essentially aristocratic point of view. It is always obvious, to anyone who can read between the lines and weigh the turns of his characterization, that he continues to retain his own predilections toward gentlemanly behavior. He is ever sensitive toward coarse and vulgar traits in his characters, whether they are traits of dress, manners, or inner personality, or whether these characters command his overt respect for what they represent in their social milieu. Irvine, in discussing Shaw's devotion to street oratory and public agitation, makes a revealing comment when he states that Shaw "was also shy, sensitive, proud, and even snobbish. Later he confessed that he felt, quite as keenly as Morris, the humiliations of the gentlemanly agitator." Those who knew Shaw intimately in his latter years, like Blanche Patch and Stephen Winsten, depict him as thoroughly enjoying his life and position as a country gentleman, and as even lauding this type of idealist by defining it thus: "A gentleman is a man, more often a woman, who owes nothing and leaves the world in debt to him. It is better to die a gentleman than a martyr."

## 1. *Doctor*

Toward the end of the first act of *The Doctor's Dilemma,* after Sir Colenso Ridgeon, who is receiving his first congratulations on the announcement of his knighthood in the new birthday honors list, learns that the distinction has come to him because his colleague, Sir Ralph Bloomfield Bonington, successfully misused Ridgeon's new discovery of the opsonin treatment in tuberculosis, he exclaims ruefully to Sir Patrick Cullen, "So that's why they made me a knight! And that's the medical profession!" But sane, old-fashioned Sir Patrick reproves him gently, "And a very good profession, too, my lad. When you know as much as I know of the ignorance and superstition of the patients, you'll wonder that we're half as good as we are." Ridgeon, still a bit deflated, improves on Sir Patrick's hint: "We're not a profession: we're a conspiracy." Whereupon the other sums up and broadens out Shaw's opinion on professions in general: "All professions are conspiracies against the laity."

It is a doctor who is the first professional man to appear in one of Shaw's plays, and it is a doctor who is one of the earliest men to receive the brunt of his satire in his novels. Although it is not clear just how much the education and profession of Dr. Harry Trench in *Widowers' Houses* had to do with his behavior in the real estate deal, it might at least have been expected that his experience among the out-patients in the slums while he was an interne would have made him fight a little harder for the interests of the poor than he did. Trench, however, is still quite young — only "about 24, stoutly built, thick in the neck, with close-cropped and black hair, with undignified medical student manners, frank, hasty, rather boyish." The excuse of youth, however, cannot serve for the titled specialist, called simply Sir Francis, who is summoned to attend the dying Henrietta Trefusis in *An Unsocial Socialist.* A "grey-whiskered gentleman, scrupulously dressed and mannered," the physician hedges and fences against Sidney's pointed inquiries as to the relative significance of the various possible causes of his wife's death. "His conscience," writes Shaw, "was not quite at rest. Henrietta's pain, had not, he thought, served any good purpose; but he did not want to say so, lest he should acquire a reputation for impiety and lose his practice." Moreover, he felt that professional etiquette required him to mask his real opinion of the general practitioner and family doctor who had first been called in on the case. In fact, though the other's treatment had been very unskilful, "sooner than betray his colleague's inefficiency, he would have allowed him to decimate London." And when the family doctor, whom Shaw contemptuously refuses even to give a name to, comes on the scene, he proves to be so weak and fatuous that the reader is forced to admit that the specialist was right in his estimate, though the family had had confidence in the other for many years.

Shaw's famous and unshaken prejudice against the medical profession is a striking example of what conditioning can do to a generally free and inquiring mind. Harris traces his friend's lack of reverence for doctors back to his childhood days in Dublin when George John Vandaleur[30] Lee once "cleared the apothecary out of the house" when Shaw "was an overdosed child and cured his mother by mesmeric induction of his own vitality." Henderson and Pearson tell how, when Shaw was vaccinated in 1881 in the midst of a smallpox epidemic, he caught the disease nevertheless. Although this attack not only left him unscarred but also helped his self-advertizing campaign by greatly stimulating the growth of his beard, his faith in inoculation as a means of prevention promptly vanished and never returned, in spite of all the later evidence in the medical world. Not long afterward the death of one of his best friends, the author, Socialist, and fellow-vegetarian, James Leigh Joynes, left such an indelible impression on him that over half a century later he could still write bitterly in his *Self Sketches* about "the death of Joynes, who, having a disordered heart, was slaughtered by medical immobilization and alcoholic stimulation: a treatment so grossly and obviously lethal that I have never forgiven the medical profession for it."

Shaw brooded upon such events so angrily that he could not keep his criticisms out of even his theater reviews. For instance, the opening paragraphs of his account of a revival of *Henry IV* in 1896 are devoted to this "miserably incompetent world." In it, the "average doctor is a walking compound of natural ignorance and acquired witchcraft, who kills your favorite child, wrecks your wife's health, and orders you into habits of nervous dram-drinking before you have the courage to send him about his business, and take your chance like a gentleman." Similarly, to Shaw, the "average lawyer is a nincompoop, who contradicts your perfectly sound impressions on notorious points of law, involves you in litigations when your case is hopeless, compromises when your success is certain, and cannot even make your will without securing the utter defeat of your intentions if anyone bothers to dispute them." And so he goes on, slashing at *The Lancet* and *The British Medical Journal,* raging at the use of mercury, salicylic acid, "hashed thyroid," and "vivisected rabbits," and shouting that, like the medicine-mad and the law-mad, "the military-mad and the clergy-mad stalk at large throughout the kingdom. Men believe in the professions as they believe in ghosts, because they want to believe in them." And then, after accusing mankind of fact-blindness, "the most common sort of blindness," he admits gamely that his own weakness is not in "any of the respectable departments of bogusdom": it is in the theater. Fatefully, in the very next year, his conviction of the bogus nature of medicine was confirmed, for he suffered a general breakdown in health, precipitated by an abscess on his foot caused by a tightly laced shoe. Necrosis of the bone developed. When the wound was dressed, according to the accepted medical belief of the time in Lister's antiseptic theory, iodoform gauze was always left in the cavity. Naturally the wound refused to heal, and Shaw almost lost his foot. Only in 1899 was this treatment stopped, and what Pearson calls "pipe water" (whatever that is)[31] was substituted. Shaw's foot recovered, but from then on he was as much anti-Lister as he was already anti-Jenner. Still later, so rumor has it, another breakdown and generally anemic condition could be arrested only by a surreptitious dosage of liver extract — a great blow to the pride of a vegetarian. And yet this fragile, long-suffering enemy of Aesculapius became a nonagenarian.

In the massive preface to *The Doctor's Dilemma,* in which every aspect of medicine from private operations to Public Hygiene through Socialism is discussed, Shaw nevertheless, with the greatest good nature, defends himself against the charge of prejudice against doctors — and Blanche Patch confirms this assertion on the basis of her thirty years' association with him. Whenever he really needed a doctor, he immediately went to one. It is true, Shaw reiterates in his preface, that doctors "are like other Englishmen: most of them have no honor and no conscience . . . As a matter of fact, the rank and file of doctors are no more scientific than their tailors . . . Doctoring is an art, not a science . . . Doctoring is not even the art of keeping people in health . . . : it is the art of curing illnesses." On the other hand, he confesses that even if doctors are no better than other men they are certainly no worse, and finally focuses in his play: "I was reprimanded during the performances of *The Doctor's Dilemma* at the Court Theatre in 1907 because I made the artist a rascal, the journalist an illiterate incapable, and all the doctors 'angels'! But I did not go beyond the warrant of my own experience. It has been my luck to have doctors among my friends for nearly forty years past (all perfectly aware of my freedom from the usual credulity as to the miraculous powers and knowledge attributed to them) . . ." This, then, is Shaw's diagnostic question for distinguishing between a (relatively) good and a bad doctor: how skeptical is he as to the nature, methods, and results of his own profession?

Dr. Paramore, Shaw's earliest full-length medical portrait, of course has no skepticism. An experimenter and, especially, a vivisector, the discoverer of the non-existent "Paramore's Disease," he has the fashionable bedside manner and a "conscientiously sinister appearance." Although "not intentionally insincere," he is "highly self satisfied intellectually," and when he reads of the disproof of the existence of his disease his reaction is purely selfish and not at all humanitarian. No longer will he and Colonel Craven be celebrated in the medical schools for the newest sort of liver complaint, with its non-meat, non-alcohol, non-tobacco treatment. Even when Julia is concerned, he gravely assures the incredulous Charteris that his self-respect is dearer to him than she is: "I cannot trifle with scientific questions for the sake of a personal advantage." As Charteris exclaims, "The nonconformist conscience is bad enough; but the scientific conscience is the very devil." Nevertheless, it is in Paramore's mouth that Shaw puts his counterattack on war and hunting in the argument against vivisection.

The unnamed doctor in *The Music Cure* and the Waiter in *The Inca of Perusalem,* an ex-doctor out of a job because of the war, similarly have no doubts about their profession. In *The Millionairess,* however, the again unnamed Egyptian doctor (it is noteworthy how many of Shaw's doctors are so unimportantly typical that he does not think them deserving of being given names), shows some glimmerings of a saner attitude toward his job. He works in a hospital and keeps a clinic for penniless Mahometan refugees. But though at first he refuses to attend Epifania, since he has to reserve himself for "poor and useful people," and though he sees through her imaginary ailments, he eventually gives in to the attractions of her irresistible pulse and agrees to marry her. The doctor in the first act of *Too True To Be Good* is also unnamed, and at first seems to be merely another specimen of the conventional Shavian medical nincompoop. When he arrives to treat the Patient he is "indifferent, but keeps up his bedside manner carefully." Although he has already given her "a dose of the latest fashionable opiate," he has actually, according to the Monster (that is, the incarnated measles microbe), mistaken measles for influenza. The doctor knows that he would lose his patient if he told Mrs. Mopply that there is no measles microbe, so he admits privately that "when there is no microbe I invent one." Under her pressure the doctor agrees to write another prescription because she won't be happy without one, lies about the Patient's temperature, prescribes diet as well as medicine, and even consents to an inoculation, although he knows that it will be useless since the girl is already infected. But finally, in a private self-communion with the microbe, he admits that he can't cure any disease, but gets the credit when the patients cure themselves. He continues pragmatically, "I am a faith healer . . . Faith is a humbug. But it works." In a further burst of candor he adds that he calls the process science because "people believe in science," and he diagnoses human credulity by explaining, "you see, it's easier to believe in bottles and inoculations than in oneself and that mysterious power that gives us our own life and that none of us knows anything about."

Valentine, the dentist in *You Never Can Tell,* is a much more open and plausible rebel against the fraternity. According to his autobiographical confession, he twice "set up as a respectable medical practitioner in various parts of England." But on both occasions he acted conscientiously and told his patients "the brute truth instead of what they wanted to be told. Result: ruin." Consequently, he has now set up as "a five shilling dentist," and is done with conscience forever. Valentine, the relapsed doctor, is the hero of the play.

Shaw's only other doctor-hero is Sir Colenso Ridgeon, patterned after his friend Sir Almroth Wright, as he admiringly explains in his preface. Ridgeon is a shy and sensitive man of fifty who has never shaken off his youth — as is proved by the fact that, still "extremely susceptible to the beauty of women," he is dumbfounded at the end to discover that Jennifer regards him as "an elderly man," and could never conceive of his being in love with her or she with him. In his professional aspects, however, he is of the questioning, doubting type. "Even the lines in his face," says Shaw, "are those of overwork and restless skepticism, perhaps partly of curiosity and appetite, rather than that of age." Unlike Dr. Paramore, he does not feel irrevocably committed to his own theories, and he realizes that, in his experiments with opsonin and the phagocytes, "inoculation that ought to cure sometimes kills." The controlling factor, he speculates, is timing and the phases of the disease. Nevertheless, he sometimes lets himself be swayed by personal motives even in his professional actions. It is worth noting, for instance, that when he tries to reject Dubedat as a patient with the excuse that his resources are limited, the previous description of his treatment and cure does not indicate that it is really so hard to administer. Practically speaking, Ridgeon is actually so unethical as to be willing to take advantage of the opportunities of his profession and murder his rival for love. Even at the end he remains something of a pitiable idealist, since he still loves Jennifer in spite of his realization of the truth about her. He has saved her illusions, even though he ultimately does everything he can to destroy them. But as a doctor, if not always as a man, he comes closer than anyone else in the play, except perhaps Sir Patrick Cullen, to meeting Shaw's standards for the profession.

Sir Patrick also represents skepticism and common sense. He believes that all the great "discoveries" in modern science are in reality leading "right back to my poor dear father's ideas and discoveries. Most discoveries are made regularly every fifteen years." As for Sir Colenso's epoch-making work, Cullen reminds the others without giving offence that it is after all only a form of inoculation, which Sir Patrick's father "practised until it was made criminal in eighteen-forty." B.B. "archly" calls Cullen "the bow-wow of the old school defending its drugs," but this "bow-wow" inspires confidence in most of the audience because of his very simplicity.

B.B. himself — or, more formally, Sir Ralph Bloomfield Bonington — is a good-natured, uncritical, "colossal humbug," who "knows just as much (and just as little) as his contemporaries." His distinguishing medical trait is that he opposes all drugs, and preaches "Nature's remedy. Nature and Science are at one." His slogan is "Stimulate the phagocytes." The only possible use for anti-toxins is to help this stimulation. Loving the sound of his own musical voice, he "radiates an enormous self-satisfaction, cheering, reassuring, healing by the mere incompatibility of disease or anxiety with his welcome presence." He is, indeed, a "born healer, as independent of mere treatment or skill as any Christian scientist." Nor does he, like Ridgeon, believe in examining the social value of his patients before treating them, for if he did he would not be the wealthy man that he is, with the smart practice that he has.

Opposed to this inspirational type of physician is Cutler Walpole, who prefers to be called plain "Mr." As Shaw classifies him, Walpole is "one of your chloroform surgeons." Medicine, to him, is a racket, and all that can be depended on is cutting and operating. Working on the fear principle among his patients, he has discovered that the cause of practically all illness is blood-poisoning, centering in the nuciform sac, and he therefore has turned a pretty penny by making its removal the fashionable operation of the day. It is true that B.B. maintains that only two and a half percent of the population have such a sac, whereas Cutler maintains that ninety-five percent do; but Cutler usually manages to find something to remove when he gets inside. Although he has had some misadventures with sponges and opera singers, he "seems never at a loss, never in doubt." He is one of the less "angelic" of Shaw's doctors.

Ending the list and contrasting with one another are Drs. Blenkinsop and Schutzmacher, known as "Loony" in medical school, but now calling himself Shoemaker. Schutzmacher, a "handsome, gentlemanly Jew," has just retired, after making a comfortable fortune by a very simple device as a general practitioner in a Midlands manufacturing town. All he had to do was to advertize in a shop window: "Advice and medicine sixpence. Cure guaranteed." He gave all his patients Parrish's Chemical Food, and they practically always got well. "You see," he explains to Ridgeon, "most people get well all right if they are careful and you give them a little sensible advice." Shaw is rather sympathetic toward Schutzmacher.

Blenkinsop, another "g.p.," is — unlike the ex-Loony — decidedly not prosperous. He has "the lines made by a conscience between his eyes," but he admits that he hasn't opened a book in thirty years. He hasn't had time to do so, in his scrubby little practice. Yet, although he has forgotten all his "science," he has had great "clinical experience," as he puts it. Blenkinsop is the fulcrum of the play, for he poses Ridgeon's choice between himself and Dubedat. B.B. calls him "that honest decent man," and Ridgeon agrees. In fact, when Jennifer refers to him as "that elderly man — that rather silly — " Ridgeon interrupts her by reiterating that Blenkinsop is "an excellent honest man, whose life is as valuable as anyone else's." Nevertheless, though Ridgeon is obviously Shaw's mouthpiece in this estimate, Blenkinsop is actually pretty nauseating in his humble independence and apologetic unwillingness to be patronized.

All in all, it is a remarkably lively medical portrait gallery that Shaw has got together in *The Doctor's Dilemma*. Yet Emmy, the be-moled but popular ancient servant who opens the door to patients and takes care of Ridgeon himself, gives ample warning of Shaw's honest opinion of them all when at the very outset she remarks to Dr. Redpenny, Ridgeon's wide-eyed, credulous, worshiping young assistant: "Oh, I don't think much of science; and neither will you when you've lived as long with it as I have." On the other hand, James Bridie — himself a doctor — sums up his verdict on the play in *G.B.S. 90* by deciding that, although Shaw took Rowlandson, Gilray, and others as models for his satire on B.B. and the rest, he "attempted to use the bludgeon. Unfortunately he was not sufficiently informed as to where to hit his adversary." Presumably Dr. Bridie could have done a better job in this respect, though it is hard to see how he could have written a better comedy on the subject — at least for the first four acts.

Except for the rather ambiguous Egyptian doctor in *The Millionairess* Shaw's last doctor of any significance is the Lady in *On the Rocks*. She is described as a doctor but not a "proper doctor," although she charges twenty guineas for diagnosis and twelve more a week for treatment at her sanatorium in the Welsh mountains. Entering mysteriously, like a sort of ghost, she proves to be a "rather interesting and attractive woman," dressed in gray robes — somewhat like the Oracle in *Methuselah*. Contemplating the puzzled and confused Sir Arthur Chavender "gravely and pityingly," she describes herself as both "a messenger of death" and a "healer." What she does is "read men and women." She is, she announces, "a ghost from the future . . . men and women who are ahead of their time." She soon has Sir Arthur half-hypnotized, a condition in which he agrees to go to her in her Welsh retreat for a "thinking cure" — which turns out to consist mostly of a study of the principles of Marxism. It is in this Lady, however, that Shaw seems to have found the only kind of doctor of whom he can really approve. As she informs Sir Arthur (with a strangely perverse echo of B.B. and the doctor in *Too True*), it is "the mind that makes the body: that is the secret, and the secret of all true healers." That is Shaw's theory of the Life Force, too.

## 2. *Lawyer*

There are actually far fewer lawyers in Shaw's plays than one would expect from the impression those works leave on the reader, but these few usually fall into a recognizable type — or stereotype. For Shaw's general opinion of the law, as represented by its operatives and agents, is little higher than his view of the other professions, and is expressed with his habitual dogmatism and pungency. The Patient's remark to Aubrey abridges the customary Shavian judgment thus: "If you have no conscience about what you preach, your proper job is at the bar."

Only four times in his whole portrait gallery has Shaw drawn the legal affiliations of a character with sufficient prominence to make that character significant as a member of his profession, though several times he has introduced sketchy portraits of only minor interest. Both Juno and Lunn of *Overruled,* for example, are incidentally described by Mrs. Lunn as solicitors, but except for their pedantry and word-chopping there is little else in them attributable to their profession. Lawyer Hawkins in *The Devil's Disciple,* although he looks "as much squire as solicitor," has the usual lawyer's fussy distress about the "bad phraseology" of Timothy Dudgeon's will. In *The Fascinating Foundling* Shaw spoofs the very unimpressive Lord Chancellor, Sir Cardonius Boshington, as a flabby handler of the problems of wards and orphans and as a sort of political shuttlecock. Julius Sagamore in *The Millionairess* is "a smart young solicitor," with an office "which suggests opulence." He knows all the ins and outs of such things as the arguments and tricks of opposing lawyers in damage suits, he is clever at handling suicide threats, but even he is paralyzed by the proposed terms of Eppy's will. Shaw allows Sagamore "a little" sense of humor, but adds that he tries "to keep it in check." Naturally Sagamore, like the fashionable doctor, always takes the client with the most money. Sir Ferdinand Flopper, the Buoyants' latest solicitor in *Buoyant Billions,* is a grave and not unlikable, but baffled, figure.

None of these barristers is memorable in the slightest way. But in one of his earliest plays, *You Never Can Tell,* Shaw lavishly provided no less than two attorneys, whose contrasted outlines are as sharp and distinct as any sketches — if not caricatures — Shaw has ever drawn. Finch McComas is stamped at once as a "gentleman," whose professional sense of respectability has made the corners of his mouth turn down "purposely, as if he suspected them of wanting to turn up, and was determined not to let them have their way." Everything in McComas is under control, and yet there is something friendly and disarming about him. Like his mouth, he has "a brow kept resolutely wide open, as if, again, he had resolved in his youth to be truthful, magnanimous, and incorruptible, but had never succeeded in making that habit of mind automatic and unconscious." Yet there is "no sign of stupidity or infirmity of will about him: on the contrary, he would pass anywhere at sight as a man of more than average professional capacity and responsibility." McComas, however, has a past. Once, before he became respectable, he wore a beard and a sombrero, and attended meetings of the Dialectical Society. Treated much more sympathetically than Roebuck Ramsden, he nevertheless somewhat anticipates that gentleman because, although he insists that he has actually changed none of his views on religion and the rights of the individual, he is now "indulged as an old fogey," because he has "refused to bow the knee to Socialism."

There is something likable about Finch McComas, even though Shaw finds it necessary to warn the reader that he "is by no means to be laughed at." Walter Bohun, Q.C., on the other hand, is a travesty on the pompous man of law, although he tries hard at the masquerade to be one of the boys, and actually takes in critic Augustin Hamon, who regards McComas as "a little ridiculous," but describes Bohun as "a distinguished barrister, a realist." As a matter of fact, Bohun actually turns out to be the son of the waiter William Boon — an instance of "modern democracy," brags McComas; no, only of education, corrects William: "He never had any turn for real work." Valentine describes him in advance to Gloria, with "gay malice," as "the very incarnation of intellect. You can *hear* his mind working." Whereupon Bohun appears at the window, a "grotesquely majestic stranger, in a domino and false face, with goggles." But after Shaw has let the audience be convulsed at this farcical reversal of expectation, the counsellor removes his mask and is revealed as "physically and spiritually, a coarsened man: in cunning and logic, a ruthlessly sharpened one." He has a bearing which in itself is "sufficiently imposing and disquieting; but when he speaks, his powerful, menacing voice, impressively articulate speech, strong inexorable manner, and a terrifying power of intensely critical listening raise the impression produced by him to absolute tremendousness." Valentine, dazed but gamely fighting Bohun's domineering legal dogmatism, protests that the other's technique is "simply breaking a butterfly on a wheel," but Bohun blasts him and McComas with a "My specialty is being right when other people are wrong." Nevertheless, in spite of the heavy caricature, Shaw has decided that in this play everybody is going to be happy, and so at the end he assigns Bohun to dance with Dolly Clandon "in a most powerful manner, but with studied grace and propriety," and finally to decide the Clandon-Crampton case in a sensible though categorical fashion.

Of all Shaw's lawyers Sir Howard Hallam, who turns out to be Captain Brassbound's uncle, furnishes the clearest explanation of the Shavian diagnosis of what is wrong with the law. Hallam, who is now "one of Her Majesty's judges," has had a long career from the time when he was "a struggling barrister," through a period as Attorney General with influence at the Colonial Office, to his present status. When he turns up in Morocco with Lady Cicely he "is trying to take life more genially and easily in his character of tourist," but it is not a simple task, for, says Shaw, he is a "gentleman, more than elderly, . . . facing old age on compulsion, not resignedly." As in Bohun, intellect and dogmatism mark his manners, as one would expect from his "brainy rectangular forehead, . . . resolute nose with strongly governed nostrils, and . . . tightly fastened down mouth which has evidently shut much in temper and anger in its time." When any question of moral delinquency arises, he takes on a "tone of cold disgust," and his eyes and mouth become "intrepid, resolute, and angry." Yet, Shaw warns in a letter to Terry, Sir Howard "must be gentleman enough to be dignified when he's crusty."

It is Lady Cicely who becomes the solvent for this harshness, which melts before her femininity and honesty, just as in the case of Brassbound himself and the other men she meets. Naturally and candidly spilling out home truths, she points out early in the play, "You always think . . . that nothing prevents people killing each other but the fear of your hanging them for it," and in this way broaches the main theme, which links it directly with *Caesar and Cleopatra,* which had just preceded it: justice in its relationship with law, punishment, and revenge. Gently and humorously she clarifies to Brassbound the process which has made Hallam what he is: "Bless me! your uncle Howard is one of the most harmless of men — much nicer than most professional people. Of course he does dreadful things as a judge; but then if you take a man and pay him £5,000 a year to be wicked, and praise him for it, and have policemen and courts and laws and juries to drive him into it so that he can't help doing it, what can you expect?" In other words, it is society which perverts justice, and often prevents the potential rehabilitation of the criminal by its primitive notions of punishment as a camouflaged revenge.

By the time he wrote *Geneva,* Shaw had mellowed much more concerning judges, for he presents the unnamed Senior Judge of the Court of International Justice at the Hague with considerable respect. It is true that the Judge, a Dutchman, is young and male enough so that at first Begonia Brown makes something of a conquest of him. Yet, although the Judge is susceptible to women, and is also at first taken in by Sir Orpheus Midlander, the Widow, the Jew, and the Newcomer (for the Judge is inclined to see good in everybody), his instinct ultimately leads him to the truth. Shaw describes him as much younger than a British judge would be, but still as "very grave and every inch a judge." He himself admits that, unlike English judges, he has had no experience at the bar, but he swears that, differing from most modern statesmen, he is dedicated "to the reign of law based on the eternal principle of justice." This seems a bit highfalutin to the practical Sir Orpheus, who confesses, "I am afraid you are a bit of an idealist." As we shall see, it is really Sir Orpheus who is a Shavian idealist, and so the Judge, who is more of a Shavian realist, can reply without embarrassment, "Necessarily, Justice is an ideal; and I am a judge."

Actually, the Judge, along with the Secretary, becomes Shaw's raisonneur. And to this just and upright judge Shaw assigns the last speech in his play, denying the Secretary's charge that the trial has been simply a farce, and insisting that the mere appearance of the dictators in public before such an international bar has been for the good of the world. In 1938 Shaw's proposal did not seem quite so naive as it did a decade or so later.

## 3. *Soldier and Sailor*

As the curtain rises in *Caesar and Cleopatra,* the silver stars and the cloudless sky look down, as Shaw puts it, on "two notable drawbacks of civilization: a palace, and soldiers." Don Juan a few years thereafter corroborates his creator, for he almost provokes the Statue in *Man and Superman* to a second duel by twitting him about "that vulgar pageant of incompetent schoolboyish gladiators which you call the army," and reminding him that "When the military man approaches, the world locks up its spoons and packs off its womankind." Again, in the preface to *John Bull's Other Island,* Shaw inveighs against the soldier as "an anachronism of which we must get rid," for through him is produced "moral imbecility, ferocity, and cowardice." Two world wars failed to make Shaw change his mind, for he devoted two angrily ironical chapters in *Everybody's Political What's What?* to a discussion of "War and Its Great Men" and "The Military Man" — although unfortunately he blunts the point of one of his favorite examples by confusing the experiences of the artilleryman with those of the infantryman. Yet his impressions from watching a group of soldiers on a modern battlefield are at least partially sound, for he concludes that it is laughable to imagine that "these heavily bored men were being heroic, or cruel, or anything in the least romantic or sensational," and that it is "the civilians and the women who keep up the romantic prestige of war, not the soldiers." Sir Patrick Cullen had already tilted against the idealist cult of "Dulce et decorum est pro patria mori" by complaining, "Every fool that runs his nose against a bullet is a hero nowadays, because he dies for his country. Why don't he live for it to some purpose?"

Yet, although Shaw sometimes hates and sometimes merely despises those who have anything to do with the inception or prosecution of war in any of its forms, it is also obvious that some of his favorite heroes have been military men, and that at times he has even preached war as one means of eliminating the unfit and the unproductive. The ambivalence of his mind on this subject goes even beyond the qualification that he introduces into the aforementioned preface to *John Bull's Other Island* when he admits: "I am not forgetting the patent fact that the military mind and the humane mind can exist in the same person." Both minds can exist, and have existed, in Bernard Shaw.

The military caste in its lowest form is typified, for example, by General Mitchener in *Press Cuttings.* Mitchener is farcically intolerant, vain, stupid, and bloodthirsty. He reminds his orderly that "when a man enters the army he leaves fear behind him," but he himself is scared to death by the invasion of the Suffragets. Mitchener has two character tags. When a problem of administration, discipline, or control proves too much for him, he shouts loudly, "Shoot them down!" And when a subordinate backs him mentally into a corner, all he can think of is to command, "Attention. Right about face. March." His favorite talk is about a soldier's "duty," and everything must proceed according to "regulations" and "channels." His very egotism, however, dominates his convictions, for because of his hatred of the anti-Suffragets and their methods he allows himself to be converted to democracy and women's suffrage, and in order to discomfit General Sandstone and Mrs. Banger he proposes to Mrs. Farrell, the charwoman, and is accepted.

It is their unwillingness to have minds of their own that lies at the root of the inadequacies of so many of Shaw's militarists, and this is often summarized in their fanatical devotion to "duty." Thus the sub-lieutenant in *The Man of Destiny,* a young man "without fear, without reverence, without imagination, without sense, . . . stupendously egotistical . . . , yet of a vigorous babbling vitality," admonishes the Strange Lady, "You mustn't delay me, you know. Duty, madame, duty." The innkeeper Giuseppe suggests to Napoleon that the only way to improve the Lieutenant is to make him a general, whereupon everything that he now does wrong will automatically become right. Yet the Lieutenant himself unconsciously becomes the voice for some of Shaw's own ironical satire on military operations when he maintains that his horse really won the Battle of Lodi because it was the horse that found the ford that let the cavalry turn the Austrians' flank. Here he somewhat resembles his predecessor by a year, Major Sergius Saranoff, who won a "battle the wrong way when our worthy Russian generals were losing it the right way."

"Duty's duty," insists the Sergeant in *The Devil's Disciple,* and so he arrests Dick as a matter of duty. But while protesting high-mindedly to Judith, *"Me* take money in the execution of my duty!" he "shoots the money dexterously into his pocket," and grants her request by a subterfuge. Major Swindon, "a very conscientious looking man of about 45," has a higher rank, but perhaps even fewer brains, for he drives Burgoyne to impatient desperation when all he can advise in a dangerous situation is that "the British soldier will give a good account of himself" and that the troops will do their "duty." He is brave and stupidly self-reliant, however, and does not hesitate to inform Burgoyne, "It is my duty to tell you, sir, that I do not consider the threats of a mob of rebellious tradesmen a sufficient reason for our giving way." British officers are of course always gentlemen far above the commonalty, like Colonel Craven in *The Philanderer,* who has had "an entirely thoughtless career as an officer and a gentleman," but imperturbably faces death from Paramore's Disease.

The Sentinel and the Centurion in *Caesar and Cleopatra* have no other criterion than duty for their actions. "We know our duty," the Sentinel assures Apollodorus, just as the Centurion has sulkily answered Cleopatra, "I do my duty. That is enough for me." Apollodorus's comment is apt: "Majesty: when a stupid man is doing something he is ashamed of, he

always declares it is his duty." Two thousand years and a difference of many
grades in rank cannot change the military mind in this respect, for General
Boxer Bridgenorth in *Getting Married* also always has the word "duty" on
his sentimental lips. Boxer, as Shaw describes him, has "large brave nostrils,
an iron mouth, faithful dog's eyes, and much natural simplicity and dignity
of character. He is ignorant, stupid, and prejudiced, having been carefully
trained to be so . . . , but one blames society, not himself, for this." Thus
the responsibility for the soldier as well as the lawyer is society's own, as
any good Socialist would hold. Yet one cannot help feeling even sorrier
for poor Boxer than for Sir Howard Hallam, for Boxer is highly conscious
of his own deficiencies and at one point with childish pettishness admits
that he is "only a silly soldier man," not at all clever like the rest of the
family.

Shaw's typical soldiers, in fact, are almost legion. In *Caesar and Cleopatra,* Belzanor, the captain, is "a typical veteran, tough and wilful; prompt,
capable and crafty where brute force will serve; helpless and boyish when
it will not: an effective sergeant, an incompetent general, a deplorable dictator." The twelve other soldiers of the guard are all "highly aristocratic
young Egyptian gentlemen . . . , very unEnglish in point of not being
ashamed of and uncomfortable in their professional dress." Rufio, the Roman
officer, is "very blunt, prompt and rough." He opposes Caesar's proposed
clemency, and explains, "I mean no harm by killing. I do it as a dog kills a
cat, by instinct." Shaw's approval of his motive in killing Ftatateeta to protect himself is shown by Caesar's announcement that he is going to leave
the astounded Rufio behind him as Roman governor in Egypt. Achillas,
Ptolemy's general, is "apparently not a clever man, but distinguished and
dignified." Lucius Septimius represents the military opportunist. He offers to
change sides when his shrewd prophetic sense tells him that Caesar is finally
going to win, and Caesar, also a pragmatist, accepts him. Caesar, in fact,
is the only military man in the play who would have intelligence enough
to understand Bernard Shaw, and whom Shaw could therefore accept as a
full and rounded man as well as a soldier. Henderson not only goes so far
as to select Caesar as Shaw's greatest character, next to Joan of Arc, but also
sees in him definite similarities to Shaw himself. For to Henderson, Caesar,
although a dreamer in politics and "in private a trifle vain and rhetorical,"
is still a man of business sagacity in practical affairs, sufficient to himself and
"strong enough to dispense with happiness." To these Shavian traits add
that, "like the ageless Shaw, he is boyish, exuberant, humorous," and it is
easily seen how the artist has reflected himself in the conqueror.

With a leader like this, commonplace officers such as Major Petkoff in
*Arms and the Man* can scarcely compete. Yet the Major has the highest
rank that the Russians have allowed any Bulgarian to hold in the Bulgarian
army, and he is greatly flattered by his distinction. On the whole, he is

simply an officer who is "cheerful, excitable, insignificant, unpolished . . . , naturally unambitious except as to his income and his importance in local society."

Colonel Tallboys, V.C., D.S.O., of *Too True To Be Good,* although "every inch a commanding officer," turns out to be merely a water-color artist at heart. "He won his cross as a company officer," explains Shaw in introduction, "and has never looked back since then." With a high sense of his own dignity and importance and an insistence on absolute military protocol, he is convinced at first that Private Meek is half-witted, but after he receives a demonstration of the little man's efficiency in an emergency, he decides he was wrong in his theory that "if you treat a private soldier as a human being the result is disastrous to himself," and arranges to turn over the troops to Meek and devote himself to sketching. After all, "the secret of command, in the army and elsewhere, is never to waste a minute doing anything that can be delegated to a subordinate." Tallboys graciously accepts a K.C.B., knowing that everything he is cited for doing is imaginary; but, knowing also that the government is preparing for an election, he accepts the honor because he really deserved it earlier but never got it. He finally confesses that he envies Meek as a private, and laments that he cannot become one himself because his wife would never let him.

There is also Sinjon Hotchkiss in *Getting Married,* "a very smart young gentleman," correct to the last thread, condescending, "preoccupied with his ideas," and proud to be a snob. Because of a certain episode which took place during his military career in South Africa, he impudently inscribes his calling cards: "Mr St John Hotchkiss, the Celebrated Coward, late Lieutenant in the 165th Fusiliers."

And so the list could go on: Captain Edstaston, the ineffable English prig of *Great Catherine;* General Sir Pearce Madigan, the Anglicized Irish country gentleman of *O'Flaherty V.C.;* Colonel Augustus Highcastle, the Colonel Blimp of *Augustus Does His Bit,* who was struck on the head by a shot, and still carries "the flattened projectile as a trophy . . . Fortunately we have strong heads, we Highcastles. Nothing has ever penetrated to our brains"; General Strammfest of *Annajanska, the Bolshevik Empress,* who was made a child forever by Nature and the dowager Panjandrina, who once dandled him on her knee; Captain Robert de Baudricourt and Captain Le Hire, of *Saint Joan,* one of whom is "a military squire, handsome and physically energetic, but with no will of his own," and the other "a war dog with no court manners and pronounced camp ones"; the Roman Captain in *Androcles and the Lion,* who first appears to be simply a typical Roman line officer, but proves to have more in him by the end; King Edward III of *The Six of Calais,* blustering but uxorious, whom his consort describes as "this one big soldier, the greatest baby of them all"; General Flanco de Fortinbras, the correct, ultra-conservative dictator of *Geneva;*

and Sir Broadfoot Basham and Admiral Sir Bemrose Hotspot, representing the army and the navy respectively in *On the Rocks.*

Sir Broadfoot, who is now Chief Commissioner of Police, is a "capable looking man from the military point of view," a gentleman with "fairly pleasant" manners, which are still "not in the least conciliatory." As a general turned policeman, Sir Broadfoot is surprisingly progressive on the surface, but most of the stigmata of his caste are still visible underneath.

Admiral Hotspot, who, together with the "manly" Captain Kearney of the *U.S.S. Santiago* in *Captain Brassbound's Conversion,* represents the navy in the Shavian dramatis personae, is less intelligent and therefore less attractive. Shaw calls him "a halfwitted admiral; but the half that has not been sacrificed to his profession is sound and vigorous." Although he is a Conservative in politics, Sir Bemrose, like Sir Broadfoot, approves of the Prime Minister's new Socialistic plans because of the increased appropriations for the navy. As First Lord of the Admiralty, he assures Chavender that the navy will keep things straight. But his way of taking care of "these Labor chaps and Red flaggers" would be to "put their ballot papers behind the fire," and he finally approves openly of Sir Dexter Rightside's fascism.

Shaw's highly abbreviated gallery of sailors as opposed to his extensive collection of soldiers is filled out slightly by the charming, half-mad Captain Shotover in *Heartbreak House.* Shotover, however, is not a navy man, but only a superannuated sea-captain, now retired to the country, where he dwells in a house with a living-room "which has been built so as to resemble the after part of an old-fashioned ship with a stern galley," and occupies himself in seeking the "seventh degree of concentration" through his rum bottle and in inventing patent life boats, ships with magnetic keels to suck up submarines, dynamite to "kill fellows like Mangan," and a "psychic ray that will explode all the explosives [in the world] at the will of a Mahatma." Described by Shaw as an "ancient but still hardy man with an immense white beard," by Ellie as a "wild-looking old gentleman," and by Hector as "a supernatural old man," Shotover is a kind of Shavian Lob, who insists that nobody ever quarrels with him because nobody ever takes him seriously, but who has ideas about modern civilization that would blow most of it to fragments. He believes that destruction is necessary because of the way other people use their power. His dynamic idealism and aspiration are so intense that Ellie tells him, "You must never be in the real world when we talk together." Yet the Captain is something of a diabolist too; in fact, according to Nurse Guinness, "They say he sold himself to the devil in Zanzibar before he was a captain." As a Shavian mouthpiece he proclaims at the air raid: "Stand by, all hands, for judgment. . . . Courage will not save you; but it will shew you that your souls are still alive."

It took Shaw a long time to make up his mind about Napoleon. At first, as in *The Man of Destiny,* Napoleon was a hero because he was a realist and an iconoclast, who presumably did not understand the "classic" art of war and yet revolutionized warfare by developing the use of artillery in a way that had never been done before: Yet by the time of *Everybody's Political What's What?* Shaw's admiration for Napoleon had vanished. The winning of battles became such child's play to him, wrote Shaw, that he came to regard himself as invincible, and "millions perished to gratify his ambition and exercise his talent before the European nations combined strongly enough, and found a commander able enough, to extirpate him." And yet Napoleon, like Hitler, was idolized for the ruin he brought to all Europe. This changed Shavian attitude, of course (one of the very few times when Shaw changed his mind as he grew older), had been adumbrated by his picture of Cain Adamson Charles Napoleon of *Tragedy of an Elderly Gentleman,* who looked "very like Napoleon I" with his "compact figure" and "clean-shaven, saturnine" face, his "measured steps," and his hand placed in his lapel "in the traditional manner." This Napoleon of the year 3000 immediately makes his presence known by announcing portentously, "I am the Man of Destiny . . . I go until I am stopped. I am never stopped . . . I belong to myself . . . I never wait." But the Oracle refuses to be impressed by these echoes of Shaw, Ibsen, and Sergius Saranoff, although she does admit that his "mesmeric field, . . . feeble as it is, . . . is the strongest I have yet observed in a shortliver." Nevertheless, Napoleon is unable to endure her direct radiation, to his great discomfiture. Although he makes a devastating dissection of the motives which lead men to fight, as opposed to their cowardice, he is swept away into such self-idealizations as "If you kill me, or put a stop to my activity (it is the same thing), the nobler part of human life perishes." And so he comes to his problem: "War has made me popular, powerful, famous, historically immortal. But I foresee that if I go on to the end it will leave me execrated, dethroned, imprisoned, perhaps executed. Yet if I stop fighting I commit suicide as a great man and become a common one . . . How am I to satisfy my genius by fighting until I die?" The Oracle's answer is to try to shoot him so that he will "die before the tide of glory turns," but she, being a woman, misses him at five yards — and Shaw promptly introduces the audience to the Falstaff monument, which was erected as the "last civilized thing" done by the "pseudo-Christian civilization" as a tribute to the first man to preach that "cowardice was a great patriotic virtue."

Warwick, the hard, suave, practical soldier-politician of *Saint Joan,* compels Shaw's unwilling admiration for his ability to appraise a military and political situation from his own limited point of view. Fearing Joan's undermining of the feudal system by establishing her new nationalism and setting up the King directly under God, and understanding what he labels her Protestantism, he is determined that she die, no matter what attitude or action the church may take. Although he is the only one at the trial and after the execution who has no doubts or qualms about what has been done, Joan herself in the vision-epilogue assures him that she bears no malice against him when he tells her that he acted purely from political and not personal motives. Shaw bears her out in his preface by asserting to the reader, "There are no villains in the piece."

An agreeable contrast with Warwick in the play is "Jack" Dunois, the commander of the French troops at Orleans, described with envious sarcasm by Gilles de Rais (none other than "Bluebeard" himself) as "the brave Dunois, the handsome Dunois, the wonderful invincible Dunois, the darling of all the ladies, the beautiful bastard." Joan's "only friend . . . among all these nobles," as she herself puts it, Dunois is a sort of second-class combination of the early Napoleon and Julius Caesar. He is, says Shaw, "a good-natured and capable man who has no affectations and no foolish illusions." He is something of a realist, and has no superstitious trust in miracles to. carry him through, in spite of his respect for Joan. The canniest military head of them all, distrusting mere "pluck and impetuosity," he finally succeeds in driving the English out of France. His devotion to his profession, indeed, overcomes his slightly uneasy conscience when he half-apologizes to Joan in the epilogue: "Perhaps I should never have let the priests burn you; but I was busy fighting; and it was the Church's business, not mine."

The prototype of Shaw's blunt, realistic, professional soldier is of course Captain Bluntschli, in *Arms and the Man*. He lays claim to no high, romantic motives for fighting, and boasts modestly, "I am only a Swiss, fighting as a professional soldier. I joined Servia because it was the nearest to me." He carries chocolate instead of cartridges. He admits that all soldiers are afraid of death. He too has his conception of duty, but it is a frankly cynical one: "It is our duty to live as long as we can, and kill as many of the enemy as we can." He realizes that "nine out of ten soldiers are born fools." All the proof necessary is to note how the Bulgarians won their battle by "sheer ignorance of the art of war"; that is, by making a thoroughly "unprofessional" and almost accidental cavalry charge against machine guns, which happened to be unprovided with ammunition.

Gentlemanly Johnny Burgoyne, however, is, by far, Shaw's most interesting portrayal of a military officer. As Shaw maintains in his lengthy note, the general "is not a conventional stage soldier, but as faithful a portrait as it is in the nature of stage portraits to be." Henderson regards him as "an eighteenth-century Shaw" — "suave, sarcastic, urbane, . . . the high comedian." Burgoyne was a man of many parts — not the least of which was that he had aspirations and some accomplishments as a comic dramatist, a fact which certainly did not lessen Shaw's attraction to him, since he mentions it in a characterizing stage direction. Burgoyne is also a gentleman of fashion, a gallant who has made a distinguished marriage through elopement, and a man with enough aristocratic connections to have had many opportunities of military distinction given to him. His "large, brilliant, apprehensive, and intelligent" eyes are his most remarkable feature, for they help to redeem his fastidiously fine nose and small mouth, which suggest "less force than go to the making of a first rate general." Notable among his peculiarities is his conviction "that English soldiers should be treated as thinking beings"; yet he is delighted by Dick's retort, "I never expect a soldier to think, sir." Shaw praises Burgoyne's military reports as "very clever as criticisms, and humane and enlightened within certain aristocratic limits," and singles out for special comment the fact that "in America, where Burgoyne was an enemy and an invader, he was admired and praised." When Swindon remarks to him at the end of the play, "You look defeated, General Burgoyne," he is candid enough to reply, "I am, sir; and I am humane enough to be glad of it."

Nevertheless, the casual reader is likely to miss the ambivalence of Shaw's attitude toward "Gentlemanly Johnny." The key is to be found in the adjective; but without a knowledge of the Shavian opinion of gentlemen the reader might well fail to perceive at least a thin vein of satire running through the bedrock of friendliness. Burgoyne, it is true, is a real gentleman, not a fake one, and quickly recognizes Dick Dudgeon as a fellow. Nevertheless, Dick admits that he really is "not obliged" to Burgoyne for arranging to hang him "in a gentlemanly manner." It is Judith Anderson, however, who brings out the General's essential humanity when she cries, "Is it nothing to you what wicked thing you do if only you do it like a gentleman?" Burgoyne, thereupon, is "visibly shaken by Judith's reproach," and later, when Dick is rescued, is obviously pleased to be relieved of his disagreeable duty. Shaw's own comment on his intentions in creating the role of Burgoyne is to be found in a letter he wrote to Terry in 1897 on her own qualities as a lady: "And so you don't know what a gentleman is. Oh my third act, my third act! Ellen: Burgoyne is a gentleman; and that is the whole meaning of that part of the play. It is not enough, for the instruction of this generation, that Richard should be superior to religion and morality as typified by his mother and his home, or to love as typified by Judith. He must also be superior to gentility: that is, to the whole idea of modern society." Then Shaw comes to particulars: "Burgoyne pleads all through for softening and easing the trial by reciprocal politeness and consideration between all the parties, and for ignoring the villainy of his gallows, the unworthiness of his cause, and the murderousness of his profession. The picture is completed by the band playing Handel's music, and the Christian clergyman reading the Bible to give the strangling an air of being an impressive ceremony." Against this array it is surprising that any sympathy for Burgoyne remains at all, and yet some undoubtedly does.

By this time it should have become evident that Shaw's interest in soldiers and sailors is confined largely to the officers' ranks. Is this because he is, paradoxically, actually snobbish himself, or because they afford a more fruitful field for his satire or his intellectual comedy? Something of a case might be made out for either point of view. Even among the very few well-developed enlisted men in his gallery there is no real Tommy Atkins. These few men, too, like O'Flaherty, V.C., are generally treated more sympathetically than their superiors, and have qualities which entitle them to a position distinctly above the one that they hold.

In proof, the briefly appearing Orderly in *Press Cuttings* may be compared with the fully drawn Private Meek and Sergeant Fielding of *Too True To Be Good*. The Orderly, like the Orderly in *Augustus Does His Bit,* has been conscripted, and regards himself as a civilian by nature. In fact, he complains, "The service is a disgrace to me. When my mother's people pass me in the street with this uniform on, I hardly know which way to look." He also is never sure whom to obey, especially officers, and is democratically unintimidated by Mitchener; in fact, he regards himself as "the voice of old England."

This Orderly is shrewd but illiterate; the Sergeant in *Too True* is also a bit crass, but no one could call him unlettered, for he carries a Bible and *The Pilgrim's Progress* always with him, and is now mainly occupied in finding his way out of the religious "mess" his mind has previously been in to a philosophy that will fit the state he and the world are now in. Although he admits to Sweetie that a man of his figure can have his pick of women, he asserts, to her initial horror, that he is most interested in getting a woman's opinions. "I like to explore her mind as well as her body." In the Shavian topsyturvydom of this play, the Sergeant is the lay preacher. He explains that when the officers "won't do their military duties I have to do them. It's the same with our religious duties. It's the chaplain's job, not mine." But since a good chaplain "doesn't believe any of the old stuff" any longer, the Sergeant has to puzzle it all out for himself. To the Patient, who has already expressed her desire to strangle all women who won't join her in her crusading sisterhood of reform, he expounds his military philosophy, which, strangely enough, parallels Shaw's very closely: "You see, miss, the great principle of soldiering, as I see it, is that the world is kept going by the people who want the right thing killing the people who want the wrong thing. When a soldier is doing that, he is doing the work of God." Though the Sergeant qualifies the ferociousness of this statement by explaining that his theory is not the same thing as the English killing the Germans, neither he in the play nor Shaw in the preface gives any satisfactory basis on which it can be indubitably decided when the thing that you want is the right thing, and when the thing wanted by the enemy you are exterminating is the wrong thing.

Just as General Burgoyne is Shaw's most appealing military creation among the officers' ranks, so is Private Meek — Napoleon Alexander Trotsky

Meek, to be exact — the most ingratiating among the enlisted men. But why should he not be, since he was patterned with loving, whimsical care after Shaw's familiar friend, the fabulous T. E. Lawrence of Arabia, who later changed his too-famous name to T. E. Shaw?[32] In every significant respect, from his comically unmilitary yet wholly correct appearance to his strategic omniscience, from his ominously prophetic motorcycle to his expertness as a layer of bombs, from his command of native dialects to his change of rank, Private Meek is a hugely amusing parody on Colonel Lawrence. As Shaw describes him after he has roared up to Colonel Tallboys on his "very imperfectly silenced motor bicycle," he is insignificant, dusty, and windbeaten, yet there is nothing in him which an inspecting officer could specifically find fault with: "his tunic and puttees are smart and correct, and his speech ready and rapid." With his "long head and Wellingtonian nose," there is, nevertheless, "something exasperatingly and inexplicably wrong with him." Although "very prompt, concise, and soldierly in his replies, he somehow suggests that there is an imprescriptible joke somewhere by an invisible smile which unhappily at times produces an impression of irony." Irvine sees Meek as a somewhat less witty Bluntschli; but as a practical soldier he at least equals the Swiss, if he does not excel him. Whereas Meek confesses cheerfully to Tallboys that his "nerves" have always made him flunk the examination when his superiors have wanted to promote him to corporal, he finally reveals that in a previous campaign he has been a brevet colonel, but resigned his commission in order to become his own man. Even in this inferior incarnation, however, he remains the whole British army and the native tribes rolled into one. At the outset Tallboys is merely infuriated when Meek humbly informs him that Colonel Saxby "addressed me as Lord of the Western Isles," but by the end, in his admiring envy, Tallboys gives him the final accolade: "I see this man Meek doing everything that is natural to a complete man."

. But it is the man that Tallboys and Shaw praise — not the soldier.

## 4. Teacher

In the preface to *Misalliance,* a "disquisitory" play dealing with the way children should, or should not, be brought up, Shaw blithely tells a story about a friend of his who caught a schoolmaster striking a child and who, yielding to a sudden humanitarian impulse, gave the teacher a black eye. Hauled into court on a charge of breach of the peace, he asked a nearby police officer what would probably happen to him. "What did you do?" the officer asked. "I gave a man a black eye," was the answer. "Six pounds if he was a gentleman: two if he wasn't," the constable estimated. "He was a schoolmaster," pondered Shaw's friend uncertainly. "Two pounds," the policeman informed him promptly — and two pounds it was. From that time on, Shaw says, he has always advised "elementary schoolmasters to qualify themselves in the art of self-defence, as the British Constitution expresses our national estimate of them by allowing us to blacken three of their eyes for the same price as one of an ordinary professional man."

Thus, it would seem, the "ordinary professional man," whatever his other shortcomings, is officially a gentleman; the schoolteacher — or at least the elementary schoolteacher — is not. Though, according to the usual Shavian standards, this might be considered a point in his favor, the teacher has an even greater deficiency; he is a talker, not a doer. As Cashel Byron preaches in *The Admirable Bashville,*

> . . . *Bid the professor quit*
> *His fraudulent pedantry, and do i' the world*
> *The thing he would teach others.*

Or, according to "The Revolutionist's Handbook" on "Education," "He who can, does. He who cannot, teaches." The cynic, remembering Shaw's own loquacious and advisory propensities, might suggest adding, "teaches — or writes."

In Shaw's novels there are several pedagogical portraits — all unfavorable. The opening chapters of *Cashel Byron's Profession* itself present two conventionally unflattering glimpses of the teaching staff of "Moncrief House, Panley Common. Scholastic establishment for the sons of gentlemen, etc.," in the masters, Dr. Moncrief and Mr. Wilson; and later on the reader is introduced to Wallace Parker, Alice Goff's cousin and would-be lover, a prig and and pedant who has just been made second master of Sunbury College. On the girls' side of the fence there are Miss Maria Wilson and the other members of the faculty of Alton College in *An Unsocial Socialist.* Miss Wilson, the headmistress, practises the progressive educational theory of "government by moral force" alone. Opposed to Miss Wilson is Mrs. Miller, old-fashioned, narrow-minded, unsympathetic with the girls, but still not ill-natured, who takes out her affectionate impulses on a large cat rather than on her students. Yet Shaw, through Trefusis, approves of Miss Wilson's system almost as little as of Mrs. Miller's, for Sidney tells the headmistress roundly that, in spite of her "moral force," hers is still "the old system of making laws and enforcing them by penalties." The superiority of Alton to other schools, he explains, is due only "to the comparative reasonableness of its laws and the mildness and judgment with which they are enforced." When she protests and would argue with him, he beats her down by blaming her for his "absurd marriage" with Henrietta Jansenius, one of the school's graduates, because Henrietta's training at Alton gave her a "superficial culture" which trapped him into believing that she was his equal in mind as well as body.

In the early plays the picture is similarly vinegary. Theodotus, Ptolemy's tutor in *Caesar and Cleopatra,* is "a little old man, whose features are as cramped and wizened as his limbs, except his tall straight forehead, which occupies more space than the rest of his face." Theodotus is another super-cilious scholar, who "maintains an air of magpie keenness and profundity, listening to what the others say with the sarcastic vigilance of a philosopher listening to the exercises of his disciples." Theodotus can be moved by "gen-uine literary emotion: the passion of the pedant" when he finds that the library of Alexandria is in flames, but he is incapable of understanding Caesar's meaning when the latter, unmoved, asserts that "it is better that the Egyptians should live their lives than dream them away with the help of books." In the same play the old Musician, "with a lined face, prominent brows, white beard, moustache and eyebrows twisted and horned at the end, and a consciously keen and pretentious expression," informs Cleopatra, who wants to be taught to play the harp, that it won't take her long to learn — only about four years. Asked why, he states that she "must first become pro-ficient in the philosophy of Pythagoras." When she inquires impatiently whether it has taken the slave girl that long to learn, the Musician explains that a slave can learn much faster because she "learns as a dog learns." Al-though he assures Cleopatra that "all other teachers are quacks," she decides that she will learn as a dog learns, since the slave can play better than her master, and she promises him a flogging for every false note she strikes after he has given her a lesson a day for a fortnight. Music teachers too, it would seem, preach better than they practise.

As Shaw grew older, however, he began to discover that all teachers are not perfect fools. Take, for instance, Dr. Conrad Barnabas, Professor of Biology at Jarrowfields University, in *The Gospel of the Brothers Barnabas*. Conrad, who enters relatively little into the political discussion in the play, modestly recognizes his own limitations, and is therefore the more insistent on the value of living three hundred years. If he could live as long as Methuselah, he is convinced, he could make himself a real biologist, instead of what he is now, "a child trying to walk." Conrad is a realist, not shocked by Savvy's crudities, as her father is. He quotes Flinders Petrie on the failure of previous civilizations which have gone under, noting that the "signs of the end are always the same: Democracy, Socialism, and Votes for Women," but also pointing out that the latter two are not true signs of decay, but simply difficulties which "haven't yet been properly organized." He agrees with the affable, loose-talking Lubin that in the last fifty years "the men of science have always been wrong," but explains his meaning by qualifying, "Yes: the fellows you call men of science. The people who make money by it, and their medical hangers-on." And Conrad concludes trium-phantly, "Ever since the reaction against Darwin set in at the beginning of the present century, all scientific opinion worth counting has been con-verging rapidly upon Creative Evolution . . . Nature always proceeds by jumps."

For a man with such a thoroughly Shavian philosophy, it is hard to understand what has happened to his continuation, Barnabas, in *The Thing Happens.* He has now become "a thin, unamiable man, . . . harsh and querulous," and "younger and more commonplace" than Conrad. As Accountant General, he "is the greatest living authority on the duration of human life," but all he thinks of is his accounts and the social security records. In fact, completely contradicting his progenitor, he wants to kill or sterilize all the longlivers, and argues that Nature dictates this act. Strangely, therefore, Barnabas displays more Shavian intelligence as a teacher than he does as a practical man. Perhaps, however, Shaw would call him, in his reincarnation, merely a politician.

It should not be stretching the classification too much to count Henry Higgins of *Pygmalion,* and perhaps even Colonel Pickering, as teachers. Indeed, Shaw actually subtitles his preface to the play "A Professor of Phonetics," and the Sarcastic Bystander in the first scene directly addresses Higgins as "teacher." Higgins, recognized at once by Pickering as the author of Higgins's Universal Alphabet, a man whom he has come all the way from India to meet, was the product of a long process of imaginative creation on Shaw's part. Although, comments the preface, "Pygmalion Higgins is not a portrait of Sweet, to whom the adventure of Eliza Doolittle would have been impossible; still, as will be seen, there are touches of Sweet in the play." But in addition to the traces of the great Oxford phonetician and comparative philologist, Henry Sweet, Shaw acknowledges a slight indebtedness not only to Robert Bridges, the poet laureate, "to whom perhaps Higgins may owe his Miltonic sympathies," but also to his own perennial interest in and practice of the Pitman system of shorthand, his expertness in which is attested in *G.B.S. 90* by Dr. Daniel Jones, Professor of Phonetics in the University College, London. As a matter of fact, Shaw's concern with phonetics and dialects, manifested in characters like Lexy and Burgess in *Candida,* and even discussed in a long note on "English and American Dialects" in *Captain Brassbound's Conversion,* as applied especially to Felix Drinkwater and Captain Kearney, originated as early as 1879 in the old Zetetical Society, where he met James Lecky. Soon thereafter, in *Love among the Artists,* he created Owen Jack, whose interest in all the problems of elocution from pronunciation to enunciation goes so far beyond his chief profession as a musical performer and teacher that he undertakes to tutor the stage-struck Magdalen Brailsford, and is so successful that she eventually becomes a famous actress. Jack, in his methods and general conduct, is a clear precursor of Higgins, for he not only has a highly acute ear for slight distinctions in pronunciation, but he is also so exacting, sharp, and critical that he tires Magdalen out at every lesson and sometimes even unsympathetically makes her break down and weep. Still, like Liza, after she has profited and recovered from his unmannerly abuse, she is eternally grateful to him for his coaching, falls in love with him (in her fashion), but is unceremoniously rebuffed.

In *Pygmalion* Shaw goes to considerable pains to describe Higgins in detail for his actor and his readers. A "robust, vital, appetizing sort of man," Higgins belongs to the "energetic, scientific type, heartily, even violently interested in everything that can be studied as a scientific subject, and careless about himself and other people, including their feelings." He acts, in fact, "rather like a very impetuous baby," and he has a manner which "varies from genial bullying when he is in a good humor to a stormy petulance when anything goes wrong." Even in these least reasonable moments, however, "he is so entirely frank and void of malice that he remains likeable." He makes little or no distinction between men and women, except that when he is neither bullying nor swearing he sometimes "coaxes women as a child coaxes its nurse when it wants to get anything out of her." This preliminary analysis Higgins completely lives up to in his unsusceptibility to Liza, as well as to the score of American millionairesses he has taught "to speak English," in his boorishness, his bad language, and lack of table manners, in his use of intimidation and reward as his methods, and in his persistence until he gets his way. The explanation of his attitude toward women is to be found in the fact that he is suffering from a slight Oedipus complex (though generally Shaw is contemptuous of Freud and the "new psychology"). As Higgins confesses to his mother (who certainly is no Jocasta), "Oh, I can't be bothered by young women. My idea of a lovable woman is somebody as like you as possible." Selfish and insistent that *he* won the bet, with no recognition of the part played by Liza herself, he has a thoroughly independent, realistic, tough-minded, outspoken philosophy, so that she is justified in calling him "a born preacher." When Liza, stung past endurance, but still attracted to him, although realizing that he could never make a good husband, tells him that she is going to marry Freddy Hill, he ends by bursting into a gale of incredulous laughter. As Shaw says, "His cheerful, careless, vigorous voice shews that he is incorrigible." In fact, Higgins might be described as a successful Tanner, who escapes the coils of the boa-constrictor as Tanner did not. There is no doubt that Shaw regards this professor as his hero, for in his expository epilogue he makes it clear that although he calls his play a "romance" the term does not necessarily mean that the heroine must marry the hero.

There is, however, some question as to whether Higgins is really the title-character in the play, as most people too easily assume and as Shaw implies in his use of the phrase "Pygmalion Higgins." (The sculptural analogy had perhaps come to Shaw's mind because of his great new friendship with Rodin.) Liza herself insists that Colonel Pickering, an "elderly gentleman of the amiable military type," the author of *Spoken Sanskrit* and an accomplished student of Indian dialects, is really responsible for her transformation. Antithetical to Higgins in all but his interest in linguistics, Pickering is gentle and courteous always. He is immediately touched by Liza's vulgarity and innocence, and even offers to pay for her lessons himself. He works on her mind and soul; Higgins confines himself to her oral cavity. Pickering is shocked when his friend refers to the past as an "experiment," and protests impulsively when Liza quotes Higgins's description of her as "a squashed cabbage leaf of Covent Garden." The real beginning of her education occurred, she tells the pleased but embarrassed colonel, when he called her "Miss Doolittle" the day she first came to Wimpole Street. All Higgins did was to teach her to speak, but it was Pickering from whom she "learnt really nice manners; and that is what makes one a lady, isn't it?" Higgins, she charges, would have taught her just the opposite. Shrewdly, Liza states her theory that "the difference between a lady and a flower girl is not how she behaves, but how she's treated." Nevertheless, though from this point of view Pygmalion Pickering is more important than Pygmalion Higgins in molding Galatea Doolittle, it should be noted that Mrs. Higgins is the only one who has really understood Liza and her problem all along. Both men, in their obtuse male fashion, fail to realize the difficulties that they are creating for Liza's future, and both at first think only selfishly of the victory they have achieved. Colonel Pickering, however, is genuinely "conscience-stricken" when Mrs. Higgins points out how selfish they have been; Professor Higgins never shows any signs of having a conscience.

As a matter of fact, the only consistently attractive teacher in the Shavian repertory is Adolphus Cusins of *Major Barbara,* whom Eric Bentley, flagrantly disregarding Shaw's own statement about Undershaft, persists in calling the hero of the play. Cusins, as everyone at once recognized, was a reflection, artistically distorted, of Shaw's favorite Greek scholar, Gilbert Murray, the translator of Euripides, who also later dedicated his book on Aristophanes to "My old Friend G.B.S., Lover of Ideas and Hater of Cruelty; Who has Filled Many Lands with Laughter and whose Courage has Never Failed." Like Murray, Cusins was born in Australia. Even to the practical but mystical Undershaft, he is a poet, who quotes his translations of Euripides, slightly adapted from Murray's, on every appropriate occasion. Adolphus is "a spectacled student, slight, thin haired, and sweet voiced," with an intellectual and subtle sense of humor which is complicated by an appalling temper that contrasts paradoxically with his usually gentle manner. As Lady Britomart democratically remarks of his suit for her daughter's hand, "After all, nobody can say a word against Greek: it stamps a man at once as an educated gentleman . . ." Although Dolly proclaims himself as a collector of religions, who can believe in all of them, even in that of the Salvation Army while Barbara is a member, he prefers to avoid family prayers since he doesn't agree that he has done the things that he ought not to have done, et cetera. His proficiency on the bass drum (the name of the conductor of the Philharmonic Society from the late sixties to the eighties, Rattray points out, had been Cusins), his admission that he is "as mad as a hatter," and his frankness about his fear of marriage despite his feeling that he and nobody else must marry Barbara convince Undershaft that "you are a young man after my own heart." Cusins is at first idealistically attracted by the romance of the love of the common people, but he is weaned away by the creed of his prospective father-in-law, who talks him out of his scruples about pity and love, and points out that according to Plato himself society cannot be saved until either the Professor of Greek takes to making gunpowder or vice versa. This version of Plato's philosopher-warrior so tickles and per-suades Cusins that he agrees to make war on war in spite of his hatred of war. Wanting to make power for the world and agreeing with Barbara that all power is spiritual, he concludes: "I want a democratic power strong enough to force the intellectual oligarchy to use its genius for the general good or else perish." Having already turned into a shrewd but lucky busi-ness bargainer, and having been discovered to be a technical foundling be-cause his father married his deceased wife's sister, which was perfectly legal and moral in Australia, though not in England at the time, he is adopted by Undershaft as his heir to the munitions business — a man who, Shaw hopes, will find "the way of life . . . through the factory of death." Adol-phus Cusins is, indeed, a remarkable college professor.

The preceding census of the genus, however, will scarcely support Irvine's witty but overhasty generalization, following his suggestion that Lina in *Misalliance* "is by nature a schoolmistress, worthy of all the fiery execrations heaped on that tribe in the Preface," that nevertheless "schoolmasters are nearly as often the heroes of Shaw's plays as the villains of his prefaces."

## 5. *Journalist and Critic*

Not only did Shaw himself get his literary start as a journalist, but he always had an exalted conception of journalism, in the higher sense of the word at least. For in this sense all his plays have been journalism, since they have dealt with topics that, directly or indirectly, have concerned the in-stitutions, problems, or social types of the day, and have aimed to stimulate thought and action on these matters. Yet most of the journalists in his plays (there are none of any consequence in his novels) have been presented with scathing contempt or good-natured superciliousness. Obviously, something happened fairly early in his career to sour him on the whole profession — the profession that, to his apparent delight, and up to his very deathbed, hounded his every footstep and eavesdropped on his every word, so that practically nothing could happen at home or abroad without eliciting a printed comment or footnote by G.B.S.

Irvine finds the key to Shaw's disillusionment with the world of the

newspaper in the Boer War and in the behavior of popular democracy during this agonizing and embarrassing period. For, says Irvine, "The spectacle
of a whole nation driven blind and mad with rage . . . by a gigantic spree
of yellow journalism is not calculated to reassure a democratic idealist." So
Shaw, who in the nineties had been generally proud of his profession, after
the war hated the newspapers for what they could do and had done to the
public mind. If Irvine is right, then Shaw's reaction against journalism during the war had even profounder repercussions, for it helped to poison his
great hopes for democracy. Mitchener in *Press Cuttings* expresses Shaw's
own opinions when he asserts confidently, "You know that if we need public
opinion to support us, we can get any quantity of it manufactured in our
papers by poor devils of journalists who will sell their souls for five shillings."
Nor did time soften Shaw's view, for many years later he had King Magnus
in *The Apple Cart* remark: "You know that I have no control of the Press.
The Press is in the hands of men much richer than I, who would not insert
a single paragraph against their own interests even if it were signed by my
own hand and sent to them with a royal command." And Proteus goes even
further, pointing out that nevertheless the journalists are still taken in by
the King's cleverness. Newspaper men, then, are both venal and prepossessed
as well as stupid.

The anonymous reporter in *The Doctor's Dilemma* is a ludicrous but
horrible example. As Shaw describes him, he is "disabled for ordinary business pursuits by a congenital erroneousness which renders him incapable of
describing accurately anything he sees, or understanding or reporting accurately anything he hears." He has therefore become a journalist, because
this is the "only employment in which these defects do not matter." Walpole,
comparing journalism with medicine, echoes Shaw by calling it "an illiterate
profession, with no qualifications and no public register." And the Newspaper Man lives up to the standards set for him. Utterly callous, or at least
insensitive and unseeing, he barges in on Dubedat's death scene looking
for a story, and within a few seconds of that death has completely reversed
Louis's dying wishes and final words in trying to get them down in his
notebook. A few seconds after that, all he can think of is trying to get a
feature article out of Jennifer on "How It Feels To Be a Widow." This
complacent irresponsibility is a variation on that attributed to Stephen
Undershaft, whose assertion that, even though he may not be very bright,
he knows that it is character and not money that governs England, is
turned by the ironical Andrew into the conclusion that his son is a born
journalist, and is clinched by his offer to start him off "with a high-toned
weekly review." The journalist-friend of Begonia Brown in *Geneva,* "a
smart young American gentleman," is only a slight improvement. Slangy
and breezy, he at least knows his Shakespeare and his Swinburne, and corrects others who do not know them so well. But it is the Journalist who is

really responsible for Begonia's well-phrased letters to the Hague, and who therefore helps to set the whole world imbroglio in motion.

Shaw's favorite type of journalist, however, is the dramatic critic, whom he came to know so intimately through his own experience in the profession. As Savoyard remarks disparagingly of Flawner Bannal in *Fanny's First Play,* he is, after all, "only a pressman." In preface after preface to his early plays Shaw reveals his disdain for most of his colleagues. In trying to account for the hostile reception of *Widowers' Houses,* for instance, he discusses the relations of the "new drama" to the critics. Beginning by conceding that it has "no malice to fear from the serious critics," he points out, however, that "the fairness of the criticism is one thing, its adequacy quite another." And he goes on to charge that the reason so many of his critics have been "completely beaten" by his play is that they are utterly ignorant of the realities of society and the contemporary social system. For the world that they live in, the world of their theater, is not a real world at all. Similarly, in discussing the reaction of the critics to *Mrs. Warren's Profession,* he remarks with some pride: "I have once more shared with Ibsen the triumphant amusement of startling all but the strongest-headed of the London theatre critics clean out of the practice of their profession." As he expected, they have all behaved like perfect idealists. Even J. T. Grein, the manager and impresario of the Independent Theatre, which produced Bernard's first play, had exclaimed that Shaw had "shattered his ideals." Nevertheless, Shaw maintains that he would not hesitate to submit his play to a committee from the Salvation Army, the Central Vigilance Committee, or any organization of that sort, because its members would know enough about real life to understand it. It is the same criticism of benighted innocence and old-fashionedness that he puts into the mouth of McComas, who remarks to Mrs. Clandon in *You Never Can Tell:* "There is only one place in all England where your opinions would still pass as advanced" — and that is the theater. The clash, then, was between the romantic morality of the critics and the realistic morality of the plays, as the editor of *Plays Pleasant and Unpleasant* phrased it.

Cuthbertson in *The Philanderer* is Shaw's first specimen of the dramatic critic. Dear old Cuthbertson takes everything that he sees both on and off the stage quite seriously, but he interprets everything as if it were straight out of one of his favorite sentimental and melodramatic dramas. He has, in fact, spent his whole life "in witnessing scenes of suffering nobly endured." Obviously, then, although he has joined the Ibsen Club because it was the thing to do, he has "never approved of it," and has found himself completely out of place and unhappy in it. Cuthbertson, it will be remembered, is an idealist, like nearly all his colleagues.

It was in the outer framework play — the play-without-a-play, one might say — of *Fanny's First Play* that Shaw really concentrated his lampooning of

his fellow critics. To understand this satirical comedy, one of the most popular of all Shaw's plays on its initial run, it is necessary to recall that it was
announced anonymously, as the work of " Mr. Xxxxxx Xxxx," although the
secret of the author's identity was a more or less open one. Thus the mystery
of the authorship of the entire play presumably paralleled the mystery of
the authorship of the play-within-a-play. In the outer play the audience at
once learns that Count O'Dowda, the romantic idealist, has hired Mr. Cecil
Savoyard to direct a private performance of a play written by his daughter
Fanny, just out of Cambridge, and that, in order to make the atmosphere
authentic and to profit from professional criticism, Fanny has requested that
a number of representative London critics be invited to the Count's country
house. Savoyard has been able to oblige rather easily; in fact, all the critics
but Flawner Bannal have, for various reasons, agreed to come free; and
even Bannal, who originally asked for fifty guineas, has actually come for
ten and expenses.

   Savoyard, who admits that he would be insulted if anyone called him an
intellectual, hymns Bannal in advance as "the man in the street," who
"really represents the British playgoer. When he likes a thing, you may take
your oath there are a hundred thousand people in London that'll like it if
they can only be got to know about it." In fact, Savoyard confesses, "if we
hadn't got him we might just as well have had nobody at all," and he
further puffs his friend's "inside knowledge" of the theater, since "We know
him; and he knows us." It is therefore a bit of a shock to the audience to
discover that this paragon is a very young man of about twenty, "quite unlike the others, who can be classed at sight as professional men whilst Bannal is obviously an unemployable of the business class picking up a living
by an obtuse courage which gives him cheerfulness, conviviality, and bounce,
and is helped out positively by a slight turn for writing, and negatively by
a comfortable ignorance and lack of intuition which hides from him all the
dangers and disgraces that keep men of finer perception in check." It is no
surprise to learn that Bannal approves the Count's romanticism, but with all
his brashness he refuses to deliver an opinion of the play until he knows its
author and its classification, whether comedy, tragedy, farce, melodrama,
"repertory theatre tosh, or really straight paying stuff." Nevertheless, di-
agnosing the author as a person with "intellect without emotion," "a giant
brain . . . ; but no heart," he finally selects Shaw, though he would have
preferred something by Pinero. After the truth is divulged, he decides that
it's a "jolly good little play," although not quite "like one of Shakespear's —
Hamlet or The Lady of Lyons, you know."

   Gilbert Gunn, who writes plays himself, is one of the young intellectuals,
according to Savoyard; that is, he is one of the "chaps that go for the newest
things and swear they're oldfashioned." After the performance, Gunn, "with
studied weariness," pronounces that to him the play seems "the most ordinary

sort of old-fashioned Ibsenite drivel," a touched-up "rotten old-fashioned domestic melodrama," with a "feeble air of intellectual pretentiousness" about it which suggests Granville-Barker.

Vaughan is a drama critic who doubles in music. He has no sense of humor, but, says Savoyard rather astutely, this is not because he can't see a joke, but because a joke positively hurts him and a "comedy scene makes him sore all over," so that he goes away and "pitches into the play for all he's worth." But at least he's honest and says what he feels, no matter whether it pleases anybody else or not. The audience is therefore prepared to hear him disagree bluntly with the Count about the incredible nature of the play, but he is even farther afield than the rest about its author. After rejecting Barrie, because it is "intensely disagreeable," in spite of the fact that its footman is cribbed from *The Admirable Crichton* (which, with congenital inaccuracy, he describes as a play in which a footman turns out to be really an earl), he chooses Pinero, whom he despises. He excludes Shaw, because in his articles he has proved many times that Shaw is "psychologically incapable of the note of passion." Vaughan is the man who maintains that all Shaw's characters "are himself: mere puppets stuck up to spout Shaw," whereas these characters are easily distinguishable from one another.

Vaughan has consented to come to the Count's just to keep his friend Trotter company. And Trotter, though generally standoffish, has come because Savoyard has told him that Fanny wanted him to, and he has a daughter of his own. Trotter, the author of *Playful Impressions,* is fifty, the oldest of the lot. He wears "diplomatic dress, with sword and three-cornered hat," the uniform of the new Academic Committee, like the French Academy's. Trotter is a dear, fatherly old flatterer and innocent, susceptible to women and impressionistic in his critical theories. Yet he swears by Aristotle, and inveighs against the new repertory drama of discussion, dialogue, conversation, and exhibition of character, which he refuses to accept as plays at all. He is supposed to be very witty and very French, and pretends to despise art and the theater. Fanny naively and ironically shocks him when she informs him that at Cambridge and among the Fabians he is regarded as "a *bel esprit,* a wit, an Irresponsible, a Parisian Immoralist, *très chic.*" The imputation that he is "a Nietzschean! perhaps a Shavian! ! !" is almost more than he can bear for he considers that he is really "on the serious side." Nevertheless, he is the only one who is shrewd enough to guess Fanny's authorship, perhaps because, as he has told the Count, "Any clever modern girl could turn out that sort of thing by the yard."

In these four men, then, Shaw has summed up his verdict on modern dramatic critics. As Savoyard tells the Count, "All you want is a few sample opinions. Out of a hundred notices you won't find more than four at the outside that say anything different." And none of these four, even, displays much critical intelligence.

Perhaps one more portrait should be added to this literary gallery — Adrian Blenderbland, of *The Millionairess*. Adrian, jibes Alastair Fitzfassenden, is a "chap that sets up to be an intellectual because his father was a publisher." The elder Blenderbland was chairman of *Blenderbland's Literary Pennyworths;* but Adrian is only on the board, and has never contributed an idea to its policies. He is "an imposing man in the prime of life, bearded in the Victorian literary fashion, rather handsome and well dressed." To him money is a "vulgar bore and a soul destroying worry," but he always needs it. Blenderbland's chief occupation is to be Eppy's "Sunday husband," with whom she can discuss subjects that are beyond her legal husband's mental grasp, as she loyally puts it. But she ends by calling him "a spoilt old bachelor" as well as a bore, after she has been smitten with the Indian doctor. Blenderbland certainly contributes nothing to the raising of the level of Shaw's impressions of people who live by the driving of a pen or typewriter, either their own or somebody else's.

## 6. *Priest*

The casual reader is usually astounded when he hears Shaw referred to by a Shavian as "essentially a religious writer," and, recalling several outstanding evidences of the playwright's unorthodoxy and skepticism of institutional religion and its human representatives, is even led to protest feebly against the description. Yet, as Shaw remarked to Winsten, "I often get letters addressed to the Reverend George B. Shaw. You can deceive people some of the time, but they ultimately discover your true vocation."

The mere number of ecclesiastics of one sect or another in Shaw's clerical portrait gallery (there are actually nearer three dozen of them than the "nearly a dozen" that Duffin allows) indicates his abiding interest in the subject. Among the professions there are far more churchmen gracing his casts than there are representatives of any other pursuit except politics. Moreover (a point worth making), these clergymen actually do grace these casts more often than they disgrace them. Shaw despises and hates surprisingly few of his captive specimens — though at the same time there are relatively few that he admires without reservation either. The great majority lie somewhere between the extremes. Sometimes Shaw contemplates them with a gentle amusement; sometimes he shows how their utter devotion to an ideal has led them astray; and sometimes he suggests that their vocation was not really for the church at all. But only three or four times has he really dipped his pen in vitriol.

In the novels the pair of blushing curates in *An Unsocial Socialist* reveal Shaw's early classification of his types. Mr. Josephs, a sort of lean, close-shaven, studious scarecrow, pretends to asceticism. Mr. Fairholme, whiskered, robust, and aggressive, is the secular type, suffused with "an air of protest against such notions as that of a clergyman may not marry, hunt, play cricket, or share the sports of an honest layman." But both are easily reduced to flushed embarrassment by a pointed flash or two from the eyes of the girls from Alton College out for a stroll. The Rev. George Lind in *The Irrational Knot* is less shadowy, but more obnoxious. Stamped with the usual clerical morality and conventionality, and brimming over with the continuous impulse to tell other people how to improve their lives and characters, he is charged with hypocrisy by the sharp-witted Nelly Mc-Quinch, but defended by his nice sister Marian, who believes that he is sincere. Always rewarded by being given the dirty work to do, he is discouraged when his appeals to the various "duties" have no effect on Conolly, but he does not think of reassessing his position as a result; nor, when he finds that his ideal of his father has been mistaken, does he consider giving up that ideal. Although he is tremendously impressed and excited by his contact with Vice through his meeting with the actress, Susanna Conolly, he merely preaches a sermon about it. In fact, as he boasts, he has been educated to feel only in accordance with his duty. All he can think of when he learns that Conolly plans to divorce Marian is, "Consider the disgrace, the impiety." There is therefore no chance of his realizing that, to Shaw's mind, he has got his opinions "exactly upside down," as he has accused Conolly of doing.

If the Rev. George Lind is merely, as Miss McQuinch thought, a moral hypocrite, the Rev. Sam Gardner in *Mrs. Warren's Profession* is a physical one as well. Not only can his son Frank terrify him by twitting him about his "razzle-dazzle" past, but he can also get drunk and tell shocking anecdotes in the present. He buys his sermons, and is impressed by the importance of social position. He is also suspected of having fathered Vivie Warren. As Shaw describes him, he is "a pretentious, booming, noisy person, hopelessly asserting himself as a father and a clergyman without being able to command respect in either capacity." He has the "irresoluteness of a sheep and the pompousness and aggressiveness of a jackass." It is no wonder that Mrs. Gardner, described by her somewhat decadent son as "a genuinely intellectual, artistic woman," prefers to go to London when her husband gets convivial with Sir George Crofts. Nevertheless, in spite of the acidity of this portrait, Shaw insists in his preface that in the Rev. Sam he did not intend "an attack on religion." This precious father and son have been introduced, he says, "to set up a mordant contrast" between them and "the woman of infamous profession, with her well brought-up, straightforward, hardworking daughter." So even here Shaw has tried to protect himself against the charge of an anti-religious bias.

Elder Daniels, however, shews up still worse in *The Shewing-Up of Blanco Posnet*. The Elder, pious and unctuous, turns out to be the brother of the horse-thief Blanco, and was once known as "Boozy" Posnet. Now, however, his vindictiveness and fear of betrayal would lead him willingly into seeing his brother hanged — following the forms of the law first, if possible; but these are not essential. He is the worst villain — in fact, the only true-bred one — among the whole gang of Shaw's melodramatic frontier riffraff.

John Bowyer Spenser Neville de Stogumber, Bachelor of Theology, and Keeper of the Private Seal to His Eminence the Cardinal of Winchester (more simply identified as the Chaplain in *Saint Joan*), is a more delicate case. Although he insists that he is not an Englishman — explaining that he is a gentleman who happened to be born in England — the bull-necked, fifty-year-old Stogumber is presented as a summation of all that is most narrow and insular in the English character, a Francophobe and a Jew-hater. At the trial, his trivial, pedantic mentality is revealed in the list of sixty-four charges drawn up, with a fine lack of discrimination in degree and significance, by him and the French Canon de Courcelles. Yet, in spite of his dogmatism, resolution, and coarseness of fiber, the sight of the actual burning of Joan is too horrible for him to endure. He "staggers in from the courtyard like a demented creature," crying, "I shall be damned to all eternity." And, indeed, in the vision-epilogue, he reappears as "an old priest, white-haired, bent, with a silly but benevolent smile," admitting that he is not always in his right mind, perhaps, but maintaining that his parishioners say that "we know you are a kind man, and would not harm a fly." This combination of thick-headed stupidity and weak-minded simplicity marks several of Shaw's ecclesiastics.

There are, in fact, a whole group of clergymen who, like Stogumber, entered the church because they were young men of good family who had nothing better to do with their lives. As Shaw put it in the preface to *Mrs. Warren's Profession*, "many clergymen are in the church through no genuine calling, but simply because . . . it is the refuge of the fool of the family." Alexander, or Lexy, Mill, Morell's curate in *Candida*, is obviously one of this type. Lexy, "a conceitedly well intentioned, enthusiastic, immature person," has nothing "positively unbearable" about him except his habit of finicky enunciation with the corners of his lips drawn together, and a set of "horribly corrupt" Oxford vowels. Morell has plucked him from the nearest University settlement, "whither he had come from Oxford to give the east end of London the benefit of his university training," and he has repaid the rector of St. Dominic's with a "doglike devotion" and the compliment of attempted imitation.

The Rev. Bill Haslam, of *The Gospel of the Brothers Barnabas*, admits candidly, "If there's a living in the family, or one's governor knows a patron, one gets shoved into the church by one's parents." Bill "has nothing clerical about him except his collar," and "smiles with a frank schoolboyishness that makes it impossible to be unkind to him." Finding the church people as "dull as ditch water," he prefers a set of tennis with young Savvy Barnabas.

Disclaiming any pretensions to intellectuality, he asserts that the church is good enough for him, and will last his time. Nevertheless, even at this age he flashes some signs of intelligence. He realizes that his bishop is "the most priceless of fossils . . . , more than usually out of date," and he admits honestly, with a half-prophetic foresight, "If I thought I was going to live 960 years, I don't think I would stay in the Church."

Perhaps because young Bill Haslam has indicated his lack of belief in the new Gospel of the Brothers Barnabas, the audience is more or less prepared to find him turning up as the Archbishop of York in *The Thing Happens;* in fact, in the interim of two hundred and fifty years, he has also been Archbishop Haslam, Archbishop Stickit, President Dickenson, and General Bullyboy. Bill Haslam's "boyishness of manner is quite gone: he now has complete authority and self-possession"; and President Burge-Lubin "is a little afraid of him." For Bill Haslam, like Mrs. Lutestring, the ex-parlor maid and present Domestic Minister, has turned into one of the first long-livers, and his character has been seasoned considerably in the process. It seems a little strange that he has not been recognized in his transformations when the historians looked through the preserved photographs of his illustrious personalities, but he has at least attained a wisdom and an understanding which enable him to realize how he and his kind will be hated and feared as "unnatural" by the "normal" part of mankind, to allow for their attitude, but to go through with his marriage to Mrs. Lutestring nevertheless.

The Simpleton of the Unexpected Isles is Phosphor Hammingtap, affectionately named Iddy — short for Idiot — by his family back home in England. He is a young English clergyman, who freely admits that he is "weak-minded but not mad," but attributes his deficiencies to his parentage and upbringing as a "nitrogen baby." For his father, "a famous biological chemist" (based, Duffin is sure, on Sir Frederick Keeble), fed the family cows on nitrogen grass (not gas), which produced an unusual kind of milk and butter, which in turn, combined with a special nitrate wheat, helped to produce Iddy. Kidnapped by pirates one Sunday afternoon when he was doing locum tenens for the rector of St. Biddulphs, he was made their chaplain because he looked "so innocent and respectable." After finally being put ashore on the Unexpected Isles, he is offered a bishopric by Sir Charles Farwaters, and assured that the best bishops are usually the weak-minded rather than the strong-minded ones. Iddy's conscience, which has already made his life "one long remorse," begins to bother him when he finds that his heart is filled with "inexpressible longings" by Maya and Vashti, the beautiful but stupid offspring of the "eugenic experiment" consisting of a "family of six parents." When Pra, one of the three fathers, pronounces that, since the two girls have no consciences, a union between them and Iddy is "clearly indicated," the young man gives in to the call of the flesh and, although shocked at the prospect of having two wives, succumbs to the polygamous match which precipitates a civil war throughout the British empire, each country sending a navy to defend its own conception of the laws and sacraments of a decent marriage. After he has basked passively for some time in the monotony of what he thinks is a perfect reciprocal — but unproductive — love, he finally realizes that the girls are tired of him. And while it is still a moot question as to whether the Angel of Judgment Day will leave him in existence as one of those who are contributing positively to life, he decides that he wants to go home. "I am glad I am an English clergyman. A village and a cottage: a garden and a church: these things will not turn to nothing. I shall be content with my little black coat and my little white collar and my little treasure of words spoken by my Lord Jesus." And he goes out in search of this truly idyllic existence "like a man in a trance."

The Anglican Bishop in *Geneva,* though no longer young, must have been much like Lexy, Bill, and Iddy in his youth. Now "old, soft, gentle and rather infirm," he is overwhelmed by fear for the future of civilization when he learns that "they are actually preaching Communism in my diocese." Recovering from his first swoon, which struck him down when he learned the identity of Commissar Posky, he cannot see why the Commissar should object to the English carrying on their religious and political propaganda in Russia through the Society for the Propagation of the Gospel in Foreign Parts, although of course it is unthinkable that the Soviets should be allowed to carry on their parallel propaganda in England. He is incredulous when Posky explains that the English were examined and found to be "obsessed with tribal superstitions of the most barbarous kind," and faints again when the Commissar tells him that "the Komintern is the State Church in Russia exactly as the Church of England is the State Church in Britain." To Posky's astonished comment that "this man does not seem to know what sort of world he is living in," Begonia innocently explains, "He's an English bishop, you know," and caps the Russian's query as to whether the Bishop is not also "a rational human being" with an "Oh no: nothing so common as that." The Bishop recovers just in time to hear Posky assert, "There are no poor in Russia." This time he drops dead. Posky's epitaph — "Was he ever alive? To me he was incredible" — is followed by his remark that the only other British bishop he ever met "was nearly seven feet tall, an athlete, and a most revolutionary preacher." To this Sir Orpheus Midlander proudly replies, "That is what makes the Church of England so easy to deal with. No types. Just English gentlemen."

Not quite so naive is Aubrey Bagot, the Burglar-Preacher in *Too True.* But from the first announcement that Aubrey was ordained secretly at Oxford, through his tour of duty as a "sky pilot" in the Air Force, to his present uninhibited propensity for preaching, no matter whether what he preaches is true or false, Shaw emphasizes the ecclesiastical aspect. In fact, even Aubrey's bathing suit and robe are in black and white: "a clerical touch." After all, as the reformed Burglar says, "The only place where a man is safe from contradiction is the pulpit." After the Elder, on Sweetie's pleas, consents to let his son remain a preacher, the curtain goes down on Aubrey, like Dick Dudgeon and Blanco Posnet, still spouting away.

Sometimes Shaw's churchmen are too worldly. But sometimes they are too unworldly. Archdeacon Daffodil Donkin of *The Inca of Perusalem* has bowed the knee to Mammon in marrying his daughter Ermyntrude to an American millionaire instead of to his favorite curate, and is now being punished for his materialism. Father Dempsey of *John Bull's Other Island,* "stout and fatherly," is "far short of that finest type of countryside pastor which represents the genius of the priesthood; but . . . equally far above the base type." The charge against him is that he "is a priest, neither by vocation nor ambition, but because the life suits him." Yet he has "boundless authority over his flock" — partly, perhaps, because, as he remarks to Broadbent, "A theory? Me!" At the other extreme are the Missionary in *The Adventures of the Black Girl in Her Search for God* and the Deaconess in *Geneva.* The Missionary is "a born apostle of love." She is "a small white woman, not yet 30: an odd little body who had found no satisfaction for her soul with her very respectable and fairly well-to-do family in her native England and had settled down in the African forest to teach little African children to love Christ and adore the cross." There is, however, something symptomatic in the fact that she has been engaged to six different clergymen in succession, but couldn't bring herself to go through with it. The explanation of her trouble may perhaps be found in the Deaconess who comes to the trial at the Hague, carrying a bundle of tracts and insisting on addressing the Court without invitation. She is an "attractive and very voluble middle-aged English lady," who offers Christianity as the solution to all the world's woes. She has come because it is her "duty" to do so, and she is the only one present who admits to loving everyone else. Her worship of God has been a kind of selfish hedonism; and the failure of this kind of religion to console in the calamity of approaching annihilation is clear.

Thus many of Shaw's churchmen and women are well meaning, but ineffective through some defect or weakness in their spiritual or intellectual composition. Rankin, the missionary of *Captain Brassbound's Conversion,* is "an elderly Scotchman, spiritually a little weatherbeaten . . . , but still a convinced son of the Free Church and the North Africa mission." He is marked with "a faithful brown eye, and a peaceful soul," as well as "a twinkle of mild humor." But his "first and only convert" has been Drinkwater, the "stage tar" from the cockney slums — and, as Rankin himself freely admits, he hasn't made a very good job of it. Still, the audience feels kindly disposed and rather protective toward old Rankin.

The same thing is true of George Fox, the Quaker or "Friend" of *In Good King Charles's Golden Days.* Shaw's interest in the simple, single-hearted Fox goes back at least to the preface of *The Simpleton*. Of him and his "inner light" even Nell Gwynn can say, "I think you have God by the ear closer than the bishops." Fox, who believes that revelations still continue (although he is somewhat worried by the contradiction of yesterday's revelations by those of today), cannot reconcile the things being proclaimed by the Royal Society with "the word of God as revealed to us in the Holy Scriptures." The mere sound of a church bell brings a sort of crusading frenzy upon him, for he hates everything having to do with "steeplehouses" and their ecclesiastical occupants. Playhouses and actors, especially the new female players, have almost the same effect on him, but in a less pronounced degree. Yet he is always humble in his own ignorance, admitting that he finds the company of the King and his companions agreeable, "but very unsettling." His evangelical devotion is so strong that he pleads with Charles to throw his crown into the gutter and become a Friend. The King is at least polite and attentive.

The audience feels something of the same paternal protectiveness toward the Rev. James Mavor Morell, whom Shaw describes as "a first-rate clergyman" but withal "a great baby." Morell does not confine his activities to the chancel and the parish house, but, ironically, is a sort of fellow-traveler with Shaw himself, for he is an active member of the Christian Socialist Union and the Guild of St. Matthew. In fact, his practical, sociological zeal as a reformer exceeds his spiritual insights, and he has even, conscientiously but good-naturedly, exposed his father-in-law Burgess on a shady labor contract, much as did the invisible clergyman in *Widowers' Houses,* who opposed Sartorius and his methods in the vestry.

There is no hypocrisy either in Father Anthony of *Getting Married,* but only limited vision. Born Oliver Cromwell Soames, he has been a solicitor, but a spiritual convulsion turned him into a priest and he is now Bishop Bridgenorth's chaplain. But Father Anthony is utterly unlike his superior, who treats him with a sort of paternal, skeptical amusement. Anthony is an ascetic and a celibate, who fasts and observes all the High Church rituals. The full-blooded Mrs. George describes him as not a man and not a woman either. Father Anthony preaches that "Doing your duty is your business," and is convinced of his own particular duty of "taking the Christian vows of celibacy and poverty." He is repelled by real love, but delights in imitations of it in religious pictures. Yet he too is a sort of Shavian fellow-traveler, for he surprisingly admits, "I am a Christian. That obliges me to be a Communist." Mrs. George epitomizes him for the author when she warns him to "beware of an empty heart."

Father Anthony would perhaps have been more at home in the Roman Catholic communion than in his own, at least under a liberal Anglican like Bishop Bridgenorth. Yet Shaw is remarkably tolerant toward the Roman church too, all the way from Monsignor Grenfell, who deals rather humorously and shrewdly with the trace-kicking Bobby Gilbey in *Fanny's First Play*, to the whole hierarchy of ecclesiastics in *Saint Joan*.

The most humane and sympathetic of them all is Brother Martin Ladvenu, one of the "assessors," "a young but ascetically fine-drawn Dominican," who leaves no method or appeal untried in his effort to save Joan from her fate. Although even he feels it essential to break down her "terrible pride and self-sufficiency," he hides his face in his hands when the Inquisitor's final judgment is delivered. Like Stogumber, he is profoundly affected by the spectacle of the burning, but his grave and composed conviction that as she died "her Savior appeared to her then in His tenderest glory" finds a more useful outlet, for it is partly through his obstinate efforts that the judgment against Joan is reversed twenty-five years later.

Even Brother John Lemaitre, the acting deputy for the Chief Inquisitor, is utterly sincere in his devotion to what he considers the good of the church and of religion. Unlike Canon John D'Estivet, the Promoter or Prosecutor, who is "well mannered, but vulpine beneath his veneer," the deputy Inquisitor is "a mild, elderly gentleman, but has evident reserves of authority and firmness." He admits that at first he regarded Joan's case as one of politics, not heresy, but has now changed his mind. Shaw allows Lemaitre a long speech of eloquent but sincere casuistry in defense of the Inquisition, based on the contention that a good end justifies bad means, and quoting Athanasius to the effect that even those who cannot understand must be damned if they err. The fervor of his faith dominates his sorrowful admission that he realizes that Joan, from her point of view, is "quite innocent. . . . She does not understand a word that we were saying."

Even Peter Cauchon, Bishop of Beauvais, whose dead body was later exhumed, excommunicated, and cast into the common sewer, is actuated throughout — according to his own lights — by an all-consuming desire for justice. In the epilogue he swears to Joan, "Yet God is my witness I was just: I was merciful: I was faithful to my light: I could do no other than I did." Nor does Joan seem to bear him any more ill-will for his part than she does Warwick, with whom Cauchon treats to betray her. Yet Cauchon will not agree with the Englishman's guileful suggestion that she be destroyed as a sorceress. "She is not a witch," asserts the Bishop. "She is a heretic." His first duty, maintains Cauchon, is "to seek this girl's salvation." Acting up to the very end on his insistence that Joan have "a fair hearing," he is as sincere in his convictions and verdict as any churchly bigot could ever be.

Contrasting with the Bishop of Beauvais is the Archbishop of Rheims, "a full-fed political prelate with nothing of the ecclesiastic about him except his imposing bearing." Like Cauchon, however, he disbelieves Joan's popularly acclaimed miracles — largely, it seems, because she doesn't belong to the union. His definition of a miracle is that it is any "event which creates faith"—a viewpoint which under any other circumstances might allow him to make use of Joan. On the other hand, "It is for the Church to make saints." Yet even the Archbishop is capable of some delicacy of feeling. He is touched by Joan's adulation of him and his office, rebukes the courtiers for being amused by her naiveté, and "shakes his head in instinctive remonstrance" when "she kisses the hem of his robe fervently." There is no reason for disbelieving him when he tells La Trémouille: "Do not think that I am a lover of crooked ways. There is a new spirit rising in men: we are at the dawning of a wider epoch. If I were a simple monk, and had not to rule men, I should seek peace for my spirit with Aristotle and Pythagoras rather than with the saints and their miracles." Philosophy, it would appear, has a profounder appeal to the Archbishop than does his present profession.

As a matter of fact, this realization that they are misplaced in their calling marks several of Shaw's most admired churchmen. Notice the analysis of the Rev. Anthony Anderson as "a shrewd, genial, ready Presbyterian divine . . . , with something of the authority of his profession in his bearing. But it is an altogether secular authority, sweetened by a conciliatory, sensible manner not at all suggestive of a quite thoroughgoing other-worldliness . . . No doubt an excellent parson, but still a man capable of making the most of this world, and perhaps a little apologetically conscious of getting along better with it than a sound Presbyterian ought." Although Anderson talks often of "duties," they are real duties to him, followed because of his own inner impulses. Dick Dudgeon feels the man's true mettle before he fully understands him, and exclaims, "there is something in you that I respect, and that makes me desire to have you for my enemy." Thus, when Anderson learns what Dick has done, "the man of peace vanishes, transfigured into a choleric and formidable man of war," who, remembering his former life, can cry, "Minister—faugh!" and announce his conversion to his true profession as "the man of action" and a captain in the Springtown militia.

Perhaps to emphasize this theme of the unmatching peg and hole, Shaw has supplemented Anderson with Brudenell, the English chaplain in the same play. Brudenell, based, as Shaw tells us in his note, on a real character of the same name, is outwardly a conventional enough military chaplain, but has inner qualms. Not only does he gamble like a man with Dick in prison, but he is sincerely embarrassed by Dick's refusing his pious offices before the execution. With real sympathy he watches Judith pray in her distress, and offers his hand to help Dick from the cart. He is, as Shaw's note puts it, a "warrior chaplain, who, like Anthony Anderson in the play, seems to have mistaken his natural profession."

Franklyn Barnabas also represents the same viewpoint in a more advanced state. For Franklyn, along with his brother Conrad the first ardent proponent of Shaw's new program of extending the term of human life to three centuries, confesses to Bill Haslam, "I was in the Church myself for some years." As Franklyn explains his own history, "I felt it to be my vocation to walk with God, like Enoch. After twenty years of it I realized that I was walking with my own ignorance and self-conceit, and that I was not within a hundred and fifty years of the experience and wisdom I was pretending to." Nevertheless, in spite of his spiritual sensitiveness and political acumen and cynicism (he is a Socialist), he is still something of an idealist. He is shocked at his daughter Savvy's manners, and admits that he himself was "brought up in the old bourgeois morality." When his old associate Burge (who calls him "you old aristocrat you") comes in, he uses all the "false cordiality" he has just been denouncing. These, however, are only foibles; and essentially he earns Shaw's true admiration, for he is confident that in the hands of himself and his brother religion and science will again "come alive." The purpose of evolution to him, as to Shaw, is omnipotence and omniscience, the pursuit of an ultimate goal never quite attained. To him Shaw gives his confident prediction that Creative Evolution "is going to be the religion of the twentieth century."

*The Simpleton of the Unexpected Isles,* in its final scene a sort of postscript to *Back to Methuselah,* offers the native priest and priestess, Pra and Prola, who, as the Judgment Day begins to liquidate most of mankind, seem about to become a new Adam and Eve to usher in the civilization of the future. Prola, carrying "the fountain of life within her," is in the early acts "a very handsome young native priestess," and Pra, holding the "key" to that fountain, is "a handsome man in the prime of life," — a sort of "brown bishop." Although their bizarre but well-intentioned experiment in eugenics to unite the best in East and West is doomed to failure, they are intelligent, instinctive, and open-minded. Iddy rhapsodizes of Prola, whom he loves almost as well as he does her daughters, "You were never young and you will never be old. You are the way and the light for me . . . You have never loved anything human: why should you? Nothing human is good enough to be loved." And at the end, as she becomes more and more symbolical of the creative principle in woman, if not actually the Life Force, she announces that, except for Pra, her empire is not for such as they. Though perhaps the original union of Prola and Pra was that of "a mad woman" with "an extraordinarily clever fool," they have learned, with Shaw, that "in the Unexpected Isles all plans fail," but that "the future is to those who prefer surprise and wonder to security."

This power to discard the old and accept the new, no matter what the change may do to one's position and personal relationships, distinguishes all Shaw's favorite churchmen. Even the Elder, Aubrey's father in *Too True To Be Good,* a sort of clergyman in reverse, is happy in his pessimistic way. Discovered sitting in a seacoast grotto labeled "Sn Pauls" by some facetious

English soldiers, he is indeed a "very tall gaunt elder, by his dress and bearing a well-to-do English gentleman." He is in "deepest mourning; and his attitude is one of hopeless dejection." Although Aubrey has already described his parent as a devout atheist and hater of churches, the audience is only partially prepared to hear him admit that Einstein's destruction of Darwin's and Newton's deterministic world has left him nothing to hold on to. Although Sweetie calls him mad, he still maintains that he is the sane one "in a world of lunatics." Yet he offers himself as an example of "the supreme tragedy of the atheist who has lost his faith." And it is here that Shaw is having some affectionate but rather bitter fun at the expense of his friend, W. R. Inge, the "Gloomy Dean" of St. Paul's Cathedral. For here, in ironical reversal, is echoed all the disillusionment and loss of faith in the likelihood of human progress, coupled with a command of modern science and philosophy, which in Inge's writings have startled and upset so many of the faithful. To complete the circle, it should be noted that Dr. Inge has contributed the essay on "Shaw as a Theologian" to *G.B.S. 90,* in which he makes it clear that he thinks Shaw has completely misunderstood Christianity, but calls him "one of the kindest friends I ever had."

Much happier than the Elder in his disillusion with man-made creeds is Father Keegan of *John Bull's Other Island*. Nevertheless, Keegan, a "man with the face of a young saint, yet with white hair and perhaps fifty years on his back," is discovered in a "trance of intense melancholy." His looks at once arouse curiosity, since, although "rather more clerical in appearance than most English curates are nowadays," he "does not wear the collar and waistcoat of a parish priest." For Keegan, a modern Irish St. Francis, who is a sympathetic brother to all animals from pigs to crickets, has been unfrocked by the church because, after traveling and ministering devotedly in his profession, he once "confessed a black man and gave him absolution"; whereupon, according to the church's story, the Hindu put a spell on him and drove him mad. It is true that Keegan has some original theories about the earth, and Ireland especially, centering on his exquisite colloquy with the grasshopper, in which they agree that Ireland is really hell and wonder what they did when they were alive to be sent there to expiate their sins. Keegan also has a Shavian theory about the relationship between truth and jokes: "My way of joking is to tell the truth: it's the funniest joke in the world." Yet in spite of his melancholy, he betrays a sort of happiness as he presents his mystical conception of Ireland as opposed to the cynical and practical one of Larry Doyle and Broadbent. Even in his three-in-one speech, however, as Irvine says, Keegan is talking not only Morrisite Socialism, but also Comteism and Ibsenism, for his brand of mysticism, "with all its poetic madness and rhythmic incantation, is a very secular and rational mysticism." The simple Patsy, however, adores Keegan as a saint.

Of all Shaw's well-populated gallery of churchmen, finally, it is Bishop

Bridgenorth in *Getting Married* who is his obvious favorite. The Bishop is still in the church and, despite his heretical views on some subjects, seems to have a genuine vocation for it. But the Bishop is a diabolonian realist even before he is a bishop.

# I X

## THE POLITICIAN

ASTONISHED AS MANY PEOPLE ARE to hear Shaw described as a religious writer, there is practically no one whose eyebrows would rise in the slightest when the label "political writer" is applied. The process of Socialist-into-Fabian-into-Communist (tinctured with Fascist), the enticements of totalitarianism and dictatorship, the collision between democracy and aristocracy, culminating in the vision of the Superman, all took place with such pitiless self-publicity that the public watched the show with the fascination attending the old-fashioned three-ring circus. The wonder is that there were not more accidents, that the agile toe did not trip more frequently, that the prehensile foot did not lose its grip on the high wire more often, and that the skilled fingers did not drop more of the crystal balls in their juggled evolutions. But the most astounding wonder of all is that the box office held up so well — indeed, that the audience did not long ago desert the performer, not in mere boredom or bewilderment, but with loud and angry shrieks of protest and repugnance. The explanation of how a man, openly and proudly holding ideas which were so completely anathema to the vast majority of persons within his own immediate political and social orbit, still managed to retain not only their attention but also their affection is one of the many mysteries surrounding the powers and operations of any potent and picturesque personality.*

And yet, although Shaw has selected more of his characters from the political arena than from any other professional field, he has still generally worked according to the traditional conception of comedy and its methods: he has used the weapon of satire and sometimes of caricature to expose the foibles, the imperfections, the ridiculousness, the dangers, and even the menace of most of the fraternity; seldom has he presented a model of good political behavior, a pattern of a wise or perfect leader, for his audience to admire or imitate. This generalization holds pretty firmly, at least, for his politicians of the present. The past has produced, it would seem, more

* For a development of this idea, see my article, "The Schizophrenia of Bernard Shaw," in the *American Scholar*, Fall 1952.

figures of approximate greatness, like Julius Caesar, Mahomet, and — at any rate to Shaw's youthful eyes — Napoleon. In his utopia of the future, of course, the politician — as well as practically all the other professional types except the priest — will disappear. Like the state of Karl Marx they will wither away. There will no longer be any need or place for them. Shaw would probably agree pretty well with the Brobdignagian emperor of his fellow-Irishman, who "gave it for his opinion, that whoever could make two ears of corn, or two blades of grass, to grow upon a spot of ground where only one grew before, would deserve better of mankind, and do more essential service to his country, than the whole race of politicians put together."

## 1. *The Race*

If Shaw meant what he said about the British Envoy in his *Tragedy of an Elderly Gentleman,* the "typical politician . . . looks like an imperfectly reformed criminal disguised by a good tailor." The Envoy also admits freely, and even rather proudly, "I don't know any history; a modern Prime Minister has something better to do than sit reading books." His words and his deeds are of course completely at variance; for instance, he swears that he is for peace, but he does his best to keep his country ahead in armaments. He envies and distrusts his friend, the Emperor of Turania, who has accompanied him to consult the Oracle in Galway, and is sure that the Emperor has really come along only to spy on him. Inadvertently he admits that he has made the trip largely to impress the electorate, the "folks at home." So at the end, after the Oracle's scathing rebuke, he resolves to tell the exact truth, not the meaning of the truth: "I am going back to Baghdad to tell the British electorate that the oracle repeated to me, word for word, what it said to Sir Fuller Eastwind fifteen years ago." Needless to say, Sir Fuller, like a true politician, had not disclosed what the Oracle had really told him, but had invented an oracular revelation which could be symbolically interpreted to mean that he and his party needed to stay in power.

As Shaw explained of the Roman Emperor and his supporters in his notes to *Androcles,* they are "politicians who are pure opportunist Have-and-Holders." They have no ideas of their own, but profit from supporting the *status quo;* and their reactions are "much the same as those of a modern British Home Secretary towards members of the lower middle classes." Or, as Bishop Bridgenorth puts it in *Getting Married,* the politicians in office are always afraid of adopting and supporting progressive measures because of their fear of losing the next election — and then they lose it anyway. Mercer, the elderly clerk in *The Fascinating Foundling,* looks at the matter from only a slightly different angle when he reminds the Lord Chancellor: "Well, my lord; politics is politics; and after all, what is politics if it isn't shewing up the other side?" To the puzzled Anastasia's inquiry as to why the Lord Chancellor allows his clerk to be a Radical, he replies, "Well, madam, to make him a Conservative and an Imperialist I should have to raise his salary considerably; and I prefer to save money and put up with a Radical."

The factors that determine a man's politics, then, are not purely ideological. When Boss Mangan in *Heartbreak House* tells Lady Utterword that he was once asked by the Prime Minister "to join the Government without even going through the nonsense of an election, as the dictator of a great public department," she asks innocently, "As a Conservative or a Liberal?" The Boss's attempt to discomfit her with a "No such nonsense. As a practical business man," makes all the rest burst out laughing, but he confounds them quickly with the facts: "The syndicate found the money: they knew how useful I should be to them in the Government." And he adds that, dubious as he is about his positive achievements, he has at least "put a stop to the games of the other fellows in the other departments . . . I look like the fellow that was too clever for all the others, don't I? If that isn't a triumph of practical business, what is?"

Everyone in politics, then, is not necessarily a fool, though nearly everyone is a crook. But Lord Reginald Fitzambey in *The Music Cure,* an M.P. as well as an undersecretary in the War Office, is both, for he can't understand why he has done anything wrong when he bought more shares than he could afford in the British Macaroni Trust after learning, through his job, that the army was to be put on a vegetarian diet. Balsquith, the Prime Minister in *Press Cuttings,* however, is a cut above most of Shaw's politicians, even if he is an idealist. The fruit of the Prime Minister's long political experience can be put succinctly: "After twenty years in the army a man thinks he knows everything. After twenty months in the Cabinet he knows that he knows nothing."

Sometimes it is useful to be aware of one's ignorance, even if it is not always wise to admit it. Proteus, in *The Apple Cart,* acknowledges frankly, "I am Prime Minister for the same reason that all Prime Ministers have been Prime Ministers: because I am good for nothing else." In this admission he is more or less echoing Lysistrata, who has previously remarked, "Well, they say everybody's business is nobody's business, which is just what Joe is fitted for." Nevertheless, this is not a complete estimate of the versatile Joe Proteus. Impatient, variable, lazy, and temperamental as he is, he still manages to stay in his job. His main antagonist, the shrewd King Magnus, has a better opinion of his Prime Minister than the rest of the Cabinet do. He realizes that Proteus, like himself, is a first-rate actor, and that most of his behavior is carefully calculated. Magnus's tribute to the opponent whom he ultimately defeats in their struggle for political power is: "Proteus is a clever fellow: even on occasion a fine fellow. It would give me no satisfaction to beat him . . . But there would be some innocent fun in outwitting him." The "less considerate critics," as Shaw points out in his preface, overlooked speeches of this sort, and complained that the author had "packed the cards by making the King a wise man and the minister a fool." In so writing, however, they had misunderstood the real relationship between the two. "Both play with equal skill; and the King wins, not by greater astuteness, but because he has the ace of trumps in his hand and knows when to play it." Nevertheless, the general picture of politics presented is, in Shaw's own figure, that of a game played for the fun and excitement of winning more than for the good of the nation involved.

## 2. *The Conservative*

Shaw's Conservatives are, on the whole, a pretty piddling lot. Perhaps he does not think them important enough to waste much of his time on them. Trench, Cokane, and Sartorius in *Widowers' Houses* soon find themselves congenial in the matter of politics, and indulge in a mutual back-scratching as follows: "SARTORIUS. I assume, to begin with, Dr. Trench, that you are not a Socialist, or anything of that sort. TRENCH. Certainly not. I am a Conservative — at least, if I ever took the trouble to vote, I should vote for the Conservative and against the other fellow. COKANE. True blue, Harry, true blue! SARTORIUS. I am glad to find that so far we are in perfect sympathy. I am, of course, a Conservative; not a narrow or prejudiced one, I hope, nor at all opposed to true progress, but still a sound Conservative."

Thus the Conservative, though inclined to be apologetic about the label, is usually negative rather than positive, is against rather than for. The Lord Chancellor in *The Fascinating Foundling,* for example, is not so much afraid of Mercer's Radicalism as he is about raising his salary. But Lord Dunreen, named in *The Gospel of the Brothers Barnabas* as the Prime Minister and described as "the bitterest old Tory left alive," is defended by Franklyn Barnabas against the envious attack of Joyce Burge because Dunreen at least "has ascertainable beliefs and principles to offer. The people know where they are with Dunreen. They know what he thinks right and what he thinks wrong. With your followers they never know where they are." Though Lord Dunreen's principles are undoubtedly negative principles, he is laudably positive about them.

The pattern is further illustrated by Sir Dexter Rightside in *On the Rocks.* Sir Dexter, "evidently a person of consequence," proclaims that he will resist change because he knows "the country does not want change." He is indignant because he thinks that he, as the Conservative leader, should have been made Prime Minister instead of Foreign Secretary under the Coalition government. He is especially indignant at Sir Arthur Chavender, whom he brands as "your Bolshy Premier," and yet he is the only one of Sir Arthur's callers who sees the reformed Prime Minister's proposals as a whole and denounces them for this reason. Sir Dexter even darkly suspects that there may be "money from Moscow" behind the Healer herself. And to prevent the carrying out of Sir Arthur's plans he characteristically threatens to "put fifty thousand patriotic young Londoners into Union Jack shirts," with all the necessary discipline, money, and guns behind them. Here he is supported by Admiral Sir Bemrose Hotspot, who was made First Lord of the Admiralty because of his aggressive ultra-Conservatism.

On the whole, however, young Benjy in *Geneva* is more representative of the party. Originally the Government's Conservative candidate for Camberwell, he happily withdraws in favor of Begonia Brown when he becomes engaged to her. Her opinion of him, both before and after, is not very high. She first describes him as an "innocent young lad rolling in money," a "perfect gentleman," a "bit of a sucker," and a "jolly good catch." After she has got him she cheerfully admits that "dear Billikins is not very bright." Benjy himself, "a cheerful young gentleman, powerfully built, with an uproarious voice," freely admits that he only went into politics because his mother made him. During the trial at the Hague he is much more concerned with keeping his arm around Begonia's waist and "shamelessly enjoying their physical contact" than he is with the Court's proceedings. Even the news of the coming icecap doesn't change any of his values; all it accomplishes is to make him suggest to his uncle that they sell their property and have "a tremendous spree before the icecaps nip us."

Whatever Sir Orpheus's other deficiencies, he is not likely to be tempted by such a proposal. Although Shaw describes him as "a very welldressed gentleman of fifty or thereabouts, genial in manner, quickwitted in conversation, altogether a pleasant and popular personality," Sir Orpheus characterizes himself more modestly. "But for Heaven's sake," he pleads, "don't call me clever or I shall be defeated at the next election. I have the greatest respect for poetry and the fine arts and all that sort of thing; but please understand that I am not an intellectual. A plain Englishman doing my duty to my country according to my poor lights." Not ambitious or competitive, fairly well off (on money made by his grandfather), he wonders how he landed where he is. "I am quite an ordinary chap really." To prove his devotion to literature (he read poetry in his undergraduate days) he quotes from Swinburne, thinking him Oscar Wilde. On hearing for the first time of the International Committee for Intellectual Co-operation, he protests, "But we can't have literary people interfering in foreign affairs." A delightful optimist about the state of the world and international peace, he is actually as narrow a parochialist as Begonia. When the Judge criticizes the Powers for not using the League except for their own national purposes, he inquires naively, "But how else could they use it?" His prescription for civilization is: "There is only one way of reconciling all the nations in a real league, and that is to convert them all to English ideas." He believes that the world will one day be governed, not necessarily by the "most advanced race," but by the "race best fitted by its character . . . to govern justly and prosperously." Who can doubt that this race will be the English? Shaw's own first views on the subject of the League, like those of most Fabians and Laborites, were that, as Irvine puts it, "The greatest hope for world peace is in a federation of states organized against war on the basis of international socialism." But he later reacted against a loose, heterogeneous League in favor of an organization of peoples with similar traditions, forms of government, cultures, and even a common language. Certainly he foresaw no unity through British domination, as Sir Orpheus did.

Sir Orpheus also has other ideas quite antagonistic to Shaw's own. He disparages the Judge's idealism about justice, and insists that power is the only thing that counts — and the League is without power. His answer to the Judge's charge that there is no longer any freedom of speech in England is that it is all Russia's fault, since no sensible person would allow anyone freedom to utter Bolshevist ideas. Always acting and speaking humbly and modestly, he warns Bombardone and Battler to beware of what England will do if they take "any steps contrary to the interests of the British Empire"; but he admits that neither he nor they can guess what England will do — except muddle through. Thinking, he is sure, is "unEnglish." It leads one to lose his grip on facts and realities, and to substitute theories and visions for them. As a result of this speech Battler calls him a Machiavelli, but the more perspicacious Judge sees that there is no hypocrisy in it and calls it a "perfectly honest speech by a perfectly honest gentleman." On receiving the announcement of the approaching end of the world, Sir Orpheus insists that the story be publicly contradicted even if it is true, since he is sure that "People will throw off all decency, all prudence," if they are told that annihilation is so close upon them. Thus Sir Orpheus, as pleasant a specimen of a Conservative politician as Shaw can create, is well-meaning but futile; he stands on his platform of one hundred percent Anglophilism, but he does not trust the people themselves to know the truth and act sensibly on it.

### 3. The Liberal

Shaw's views on Liberalism are the conventional ones of any extreme leftist. For him, there is little to choose between the Conservative and the Liberal. The one may be a reactionary mossback, negative and blind to the needs of mankind; the other is magniloquent, but groping and wishywashy, unable to lay down a bold, judicious line of action and follow it. This is Shaw's picture of the Liberal, from Broadbent in *John Bull's Other Island,* through Burge and Lubin in *Methuselah,* to Glenmorison in *On the Rocks.*

Thus Thomas Broadbent, the English engineer who tries to become more Irish than the Irish, has his office walls decorated with "an impressive portrait of Gladstone, and several caricatures of Mr Balfour as a rabbit and Mr Chamberlain as a fox." Although he is "a lover of liberty," he is against the Jews. He is also against taxing the people's bread to support the Navy League. He is for Free Trade. He stopped going to see his father when the latter's mind gave way and he joined the Tariff Reform League. Now that "South Africa has been enslaved and destroyed," he remembers the Englishman's duty to Ireland — not to mention Finland and Macedonia. But he also seems to be a Little Englander, for he charges that "their confounded new empire" has ruined England by bringing in all kinds of "cosmopolitan riffraff." But his notion of the Englishman's burden is guiding Ireland under Home Rule. In fact, while campaigning to become the representative of Rosscullen in Parliament, he unconsciously characterizes himself and his type of Liberalism when he inveighs against "the windbags, the carpet-baggers, the charlatans, the — the — the fools and ignoramuses who corrupt the multitude by their wealth, or seduce them by spouting balderdash to them." When he and his partner Larry Doyle argue about the "great Liberal principle of Disestablishment," Larry reminds him: "I am not a Liberal: Heaven forbid!" But in the last speech of the play Shaw ironically has Broadbent say, with "sincere elevation," "I feel now as I never did before that I am right in devoting my life to the cause of Ireland." God pity Ireland when the Liberals take her under their wing!

Variations on this Liberal type are Joyce Burge and Henry Hopkins Lubin, both ex-Prime Ministers, one before and the other during the Coalition, who come to make a political call on the brothers Barnabas to persuade Franklyn to run for Commons. Both claim to be the real leader of the Liberal Party, which is now in Opposition, and each has the lowest possible private opinion of the other. In Lubin's view Burge is not fit to govern because he has "mere energy without intellect and without knowledge." His mind is untrained, since it "has not been stored with the best information, nor cultivated by intercourse with educated minds at any of our great seats of learning," whereas Lubin himself was once a classical scholar and a lawyer, who pretends to keep up with the latest artistic affairs and purrs with pleasure when Savvy tells him he must be the reincarnation of Horace. In Burge's opinion, Lubin is "that old dotard, that played-out old humbug" who sold his party to Coalition. To Franklyn, Burge is a distressing example of "the nauseous sham good fellowship our democratic public men get up for shop use." Lubin, on the other hand, is comfortable, easy-going, and self-assured, happy to flirt in a fatherly way with young Savvy and never at a loss to cover up a faux pas. Both want to be all things to all men. When Franklyn suggests that the Liberals may be superseded by the Labor Party, Burge quickly apprises him, "But I am in the truest sense myself a Labor leader." Lubin promptly counters with the statement that Burge has never really belonged to the people in spite of his claims to being a proletarian, since he really came only from the impecunious middle class; whereas he, Lubin, has carefully studied the Labor movement and its principles at the university, and discovered that "all this Trade Unionism and Socialism and so forth is founded on the ignorant delusion that wages and the production and distribution of wealth can be controlled by legislation or by any human action whatever." Although Savvy impudently contradicts his laissez-faire-ism with an "obsolete rot," he still displays a willingness to take Socialism and "steer it clear of Utopian absurdities."

Since the prime objective of both men is to get back into office and stay there at any cost, both are attracted by the new gospel of the Barnabas brothers from the political point of view. Burge misinterprets it, twisting it into the campaign cry, "Back to the Bible," and prophesies that it will put the Liberals into power for thirty years. Lubin, however, at first stands by Science and rejects Franklyn's interpretation of Genesis and the Fall, but when he is partially persuaded by Conrad all he can think of is: "Fancy my being the leader of the party for the next three hundred years." He is greatly startled, therefore, when he learns that according to the theory mere "citizens" as well as "statesmen" are to increase their life span to three centuries. Both men can think only in terms of some newly discovered physical elixir which will usher in the new era; mere "Will," of course, is not "practical." At the end of the scene, however, Burge plans to work the new slogan into his campaign; Lubin decides that his leg has been pulled — "very wittily."

This opinion is confirmed in the next play, in which Burge and Lubin have coalesced into Burge-Lubin, whom the voters of the twenty-second century have elected President of the British Isles five times and will probably re-elect five times more. This composite statesman is "good-looking and breezily genial," but Confucius, the Chinese Chief Secretary, calls him a "cheerful good-natured" barbarian, brave but stupid — a man who prefers the new game of marine golf to Chinese contemplation. Lusting in a respectable British fashion after the handsome Negress who is Minister of Health, he nevertheless rejects her announcement that she is disposed to be "approachable" at last, because, in spite of his vocal opposition to the new longlivers, he has secret hopes that he may turn out to be one of them himself, and fears that if he flies to meet her and is dropped into the bay by parachute he may get rheumatism for life. And rheumatism for another two and a half centuries is quite another matter from rheumatism for another twenty or so years. As Confucius comments: "Good. You have at last become prudent: you are no longer what you call a sportsman: you are a sensible coward, almost a grown-up man. I congratulate you." So even a politician can learn.

Thus young Glenmorison, the Scotch President of the Board of Trade in *On the Rocks,* is now ready to go along with Sir Arthur Chavender's new scheme for nationalized banks and loans because he knows that the policy will be approved by his Scotch followers, who are mostly small business men. He is therefore willing to accept Sir Arthur's other plans, dubious as he at first is about them, because "I represent the small man." Later, when he realizes that he must support the whole program to keep his seat in Parliament, he still insists that only constitutional means shall be followed even though "at the very least it will take fifty years to get it through." Sir Arthur, who has now gone beyond Liberalism to a modified Marxism, is sure that the world will not wait that long and that unless a shorter way can be found "the program will be fought out in the streets." Such drastic methods, however, will never be adopted by the Liberals.

### 4. The Democrat

Just as Shaw refuses to be taken in by any such pretty tag as "Liberal," so he also rejects the word "democrat" as a test and a shibboleth. Democracy has failed miserably to redeem its promises, rosy and reachable as they seemed only a few decades ago. Disguised as old Hipney in *On the Rocks,* Shaw lectures his audience regretfully on the outcome of those once-lovely visions: "But old Hipney can tell you something about Democracy at first hand. Democracy was a great thing when I was young and we had no votes . . . But that was when it was a dream and a vision, a hope and a faith and a promise. It lasted until they dragged it down to earth, as you might say, and made it a reality by giving everybody votes. The moment they gave the working men votes they found they'd stand anything. They gave votes to the women and found they were worse than the men; for the men would vote for men — the wrong men, but men all the same — but the women wouldn't even vote for women. Since then politics have been a laughing stock." And Hipney ends his indictment more in sorrow than in anger. For although, election after election, the people returned to office the corrupt, the hypocrite, the cruel imperialist and merciless militarist, instead of electing "men and women like me, that had spent their lives in the service of the people," it wasn't because they were consciously rewarding evil. They simply were children, swayed equally by cries that the Russians were coming or by promises to hang the Kaiser. "That was the end of democracy for me; though there was no man alive that had hoped as much from it, nor spoke deeper from his heart about all the good things that would happen when the people came to their own and had votes like the gentry."

No one can miss the heartfelt note of personal disillusionment in this long speech. Yet Shaw's faith in democracy and adult suffrage began to dissipate early. In *Captain Brassbound's Conversion* he makes good-natured fun of the way Brassbound's gang of brigands votes democratically on all matters of conduct and procedure. Drinkwater, when he sees that a vote is going against him, protests uselessly about "clawss feelin" and levels the accusation, "There's n'maw demmecrettick feelin eah than there is in the owl bloomin M division of Nootn Corswy coppers," but his protest avails nothing. Yet, as Drinkwater perceives, this democracy is hollow, and the men are actually lost without a strong leader. When threatened with mutiny, Captain Brassbound shrewdly promises, "I'll do my best with the rest under whatever leader you are willing to obey." But, as he surmises, nobody will take over the command.

To Shaw there is even a sexual aspect of democracy, for which he demands attention in the preface to *Man and Superman*. Admitting that the political implications of the sex question he is dealing with in his play are too big to be handled properly there, he nevertheless points out that the sex initiative of woman "is politically the most important of all the initiatives, because our political experiment of democracy, the last refuge of cheap misgovernment, will ruin us if our citizens are ill bred." England in 1903, he reminded his readers, was still in a period of transition, in which "aristocracy and plutocracy still furnish the figureheads of politics; but they are now dependent on the votes of the promiscuously bred masses." Just as in the theater, so in politics "We are all now under what Burke called 'the hoofs of the swinish multitude.'" Nor did Shaw see much cause for optimism as to the future, since this new mass electorate had failed almost without exception to vote for representatives of its own class. "The multitude thus pronounces judgment on its own units: it admits itself unfit to govern, and will vote only for a man morphologically and generically transfigured by palatial residence and equipage, by transcendent tailoring, by the glamor of aristocratic kinship." To Shaw in 1903 mankind had nothing to hope for politically from either democracy or aristocracy.

Nor had the situation improved by 1938, when he wrote *Geneva*. In this "political extravaganza" democracy in practice is depicted — unless caricatured is a more accurate word — in two characters, the Newcomer and the Widow. The Newcomer, "an obstinate-looking middle-aged man of respectable but not aristocratic appearance, speaking English like a shopkeeper from the provinces, or perhaps, by emigration, the dominions," becomes the focus of Shaw's ironic attack on the methods of politics versus the methods of business. The Newcomer invades the office of the International Committee for Intellectual Co-operation to demand its coöperation in putting his country back on the "rails." It seems that an election has recently been held in this nation of Jacksonsland (perhaps Australia) and that, although all the solid people thought the choice lay as usual between the National Party and the Labor Party, the winner was "an upstart kind of chap who called himself a Business Democrat." So when this fellow formed a government and became Prime Minister himself, he announced as his policy that, since the country had chosen by a democratic vote that his party should govern it on a business basis for the next five years, he must "get the nation's work done as quickly as possible." This meant that there should be no opposition to the party's operations. Since the defeated minority, however, refused to cease its obstructionism, he "organized a body of young men called the

Clean Shirts, to help the police." The Newcomer is forced by Begonia Brown to admit that this is what any businessman would have done in business, but he convinces her that business and politics are quite different matters. So Begonia fatuously agrees to apply for a warrant to the International Court at the Hague to arrest the Prime Minister on a variety of charges, running from "high treason and rebellion and breach of privilege" to "setting up a dictatorship and obstructing the lawful ingress of duly elected members to the legislative Chamber." Although the dictator of Jacksonsland is never actually brought to trial, Bombardone defends the same position with considerable Shavian cogency, and the Newcomer, with his continual plaints about "the principles of democracy," is thoroughly discomfited. At the same time, however, he expresses Shaw's diagnosis of the present international situation when he remarks, "Democracy is what I want . . . But now that everybody has a vote, women and all, where's democracy? Dictators all over the place." The Secretary sums him up by calling him "some sort of half-Americanized colonist. You are a lower middle-class politician. Your position is that of the rugged individualist, the isolationist, at bottom the Anarchist." Nevertheless, the Newcomer takes the announcement of the imminent end of the world in his stride. Nobody, he reminds the rest, is going to live forever anyhow, and he has had a pretty good time already. So he goes home to "cheer up the missus," in perfect faith that "Science cannot be wrong." This conviction alone, even without his trust in democracy, would be enough to brand him a perfect fool in Shaw's eyes.

The Widow, "a Creole lady of about forty, with the remains of a gorgeous and opulent southern beauty," is an even more egregious representative of a bastard type of democracy, which therefore presumably condemns all democracies. She comes, not from Jacksonsland, but from the Republic of the Earthly Paradise in Central America, where everybody carries a gun. The Republic is, according to her, "the most civilized country in the world" and "one of the leading States in the world in culture and purity of race." Before the last revolution its capital had more than 200,000 white inhabitants, of whom at least 15,000 are now left. Every president must swear to observe every particular of its constitution, which is "absolutely democratic." All these perfections, the Widow informs Begonia, were introduced by her late husband, who, immediately after he had been elected President and the first budget was passed, then prorogued the Parliament and "governed the country according to his own ideas whilst the people enjoyed themselves and made money in their own ways without any political disturbances or arguments."

Unfortunately the Widow's husband, the creator and quondam president of this utopia, had one democratic weakness. After easily putting down the revolutions which sometimes broke out (since he was a "military genius"), "instead of having his opponent shot in the proper and customary way, he pardoned him and challenged him to try again as often as he pleased." This quixotism proved his undoing. For when the Widow learned the reason for it — that he was carrying on an intrigue with her best friend, who happened to be his opponent's wife — she had to shoot her rival, as public opinion required her to do as a "self-respecting wife and mother." But although the unwritten law acquitted her, the scandal destroyed her husband's popularity so that he was defeated "at the next election by the man he had so foolishly spared." When, crushed by the loss of his love, he moped at home instead of going out and raising another army, he was finally shot by his enemies, who had really come to shoot the Widow, who was luckily out at the time.

The Widow has now come to Geneva to demand that the League bring the murderer of her husband to justice, so that her son will not be obliged to take up a blood feud. But her son becomes a Communist, and denounces blood feuds as a bourgeois tradition. The Widow, therefore, calling on "duty," "natural justice," "right and wrong," "conscience," "honor," and all the rest of the "ideals," vows to shoot her antagonist herself. In fact, she would shoot everybody in sight, including herself. Surprisingly enough, the wise and upright Judge succeeds in calming even this termagant, and she finally agrees not only not to kill herself but to dine with the Jew, whom she has insulted, and let "God execute his own judgment on us all" when the end of the world comes.

Though Shaw by this conversion somewhat blunts the edge of his attack, his Widow essentially personifies complete intolerance under the mask of democracy. Perhaps her very fickleness and emotional instability, too, support his contempt for the democratic principles that she travesties. Both the Jacksonian and the Paradisian types of democracy are located in their most characteristic forms, it would seem, in the non-European world.

## 5. *The Socialist*

Twice in his life Shaw devoted complete and lengthy non-dramatic works to the elucidation and defense of the Socialist thesis — not to mention his shorter Fabian tracts and innumerable other polemics. Yet, although *The Intelligent Woman's Guide to Socialism and Capitalism* and *Everybody's Political What's What?* (which re-uses great chunks from the former work without calling attention to the fact) sometimes wax humorous or ironic at the expense of the party's hangers-on or of the deviationists from the true party line, the contrast between the picture of Socialism in the expository and controversial prose and the picture of Socialists in the novels and plays is rather astonishing. Mere man, it would appear, is exceedingly fallible, and practically incapable of living up to the great ideas and theories which he has created through a combination of his imagination and his reason. Consequently, as time passes, Shaw's Socialist characters decrease considerably in vitality, pungency, dogmatism — and general interest. West, in his opinionated and dogmatic but always stimulating diagnosis of Shaw's intellectual development (or, rather, deterioration), finds the explanation of the disturbing phenomenon in his sub-title, a quotation from Lenin: "a good man fallen among Fabians."

The most minutely drawn of them all is of course Sidney Trefusis, the Unsocial Socialist — and he was created in 1883, just after Shaw had first read Marx. Sidney overflows with talk about landlords, gentility, the law of supply and demand, and such weighty social topics, but his approach to them is mixed. Sometimes he orates in a farcical vein, like a "low comedian," but at other times he preaches his new gospel with intense seriousness. It is no accident that Shaw makes Sidney the son of a poor Manchester "bagman," who became a rich cotton manufacturer and "a plutocrat and gentleman of landed estate" because he was shrewd and ruthless in his making of exchanges and his exploitation of labor. In view of Shaw's own hatred of the Manchester School of economics and the thorough basing of his own economic, social, and political philosophy, as Irvine sees it, on the Utilitarianism of Bentham and Mill, with Adam Smith, Ricardo, and Malthus in the background, very strongly colored, as West sees it, by the modifying influence of Jevons, the reader of *An Unsocial Socialist* is not surprised to learn that Sidney not only loathes the *laissez faire* capitalism represented by his father but also detests his mother's side of the family because they are country gentry. Temporarily reunited with his wife and reincarnated in his own character, he delivers long Fabian lectures to her, based on his plan "to liberate those Manchester laborers who were my father's slaves." When Henrietta, steeped in her adoration of him, offers to share his work, though she understands scarcely a word of what he has been saying, he is horribly dismayed and gets rid of her again, talking more Socialism to the bargeman who transports him. Taking his wife's death soon afterward very casually and callously as a natural and inevitable episode in life, he is surprised to find himself dropping a conventional tear in the presence of the corpse, and refuses to go to the funeral. This conduct so angers Jansenius that the bereaved father-in-law explodes, not very logically, "Nothing is sacred to you. This shows what Socialists are!" Nevertheless, Shaw himself seems to have been working to create this very impression, with his emphasis on Sidney's doctrine that one's duty to oneself is "the first and hardest of all duties" and on his sacrifice of the happiness of the individual to the presumed welfare of the group.

For more than half the novel the Socialism of Trefusis is a matter of extraneous talk rather than any real action. Eventually, however, he determines that he ought to run in the Birmingham election. As Gertrude Lindsay's father puts it, he "came out at the foot of the poll with thirty-two votes through calling himself a Social Democrat or some such foreign rubbish, instead of saying out like a man that he was a Radical." Sidney is more pleased than otherwise by his failure, since it confirms his low opinion of humanity, and he goes about offending almost everybody he meets by exposing the fallaciousness of their views and of society in general from the Socialist point of view. He is made still happier when he is twice mobbed and stoned by the very British workmen to whose cause he is devoting himself, simply because they can't bear to hear the truth about themselves. Though he also has a pretty poor opinion of women in general, just as he does of workmen and employers, he realizes the importance of instructing the female sex and converting them to Socialist principles. He still confidently assures Sir Charles Brandon that the end of it all will be "Socialism or Smash," and he is convinced that poverty must be abolished; but, maintaining that "A man cannot be a Christian in this country," he makes it clear that he will never consider dividing up his own considerable property, inherited from his father.

The impression left by Sidney, and by the novel in general, amusing as it is in many particulars, is then an equivocal and paradoxical one. This Shaw himself apparently realized, for when he finally got a publisher for the story he found it desirable to attach a sort of apology, which he entitled "Appendix. Letter to the Author from Mr. Sidney Trefusis." In this attempt at justification he had his protagonist lay the blame for many readers' misunderstanding of the truth on the shoulders of the author, who had misrepresented the real Sidney from beginning to end. "Hence some critics have been able plausibly to pretend to take the book as a satire on Socialism." The real Sidney, wrote Sidney Shaw, is not unsocial, unsympathetic, inhumane, or any of the other unpleasant things attributed to him by Bernard Shaw. In fact, he ends by stamping the whole story as "the wildest romance ever penned."

The Socialism of the Rev. James Morell is of a more temperate, friendly variety. He even goes so far as to praise the President of the Atheist League as "an excellent man," and recommend him to the Guild of St. Matthew as a substitute speaker — to the consternation of Lexy, who remonstrates, "But he always insists so powerfully on the divorce of Socialism from Christianity. He will undo all the good we have been doing." Conspicuous in Morell's library, it is true, are "a yellow backed Progress and Poverty, Fabian Essays, a Dream of John Ball, Marx's Capital, and half a dozen other literary landmarks in Socialism"; and he himself is an "active member" in the Christian Social Union as well as the Guild of St. Matthew. But, although he sincerely attempts to put his "foolish ideas" (as Burgess calls them to Eugene) into practice, it is obvious that Shaw does not expect that Morell will ever set the political world afire or do very much more than make inspirational speeches to women and clergymen.

The romantic and idealistic Gunner in *Misalliance,* with all his sentimentally revolutionary ideas about Russia, is still less a model for Socialistic imitation. When Gunner starts tossing epithets around, such as "morals of our pious capitalist class" and "rotten bourgeoisie," and Mrs. Tarleton protests against his language, Shaw allows her husband to quiet her with an "All right, Chickabiddy: it's not bad language: it's only Socialism." And even though Mrs. Tarleton asserts spiritedly, "Well, I won't have any Socialism in my house," when she learns more about poor Gunner as the son of her old friend Lucy Titmus she realizes that his ineffective presence can't really hurt her or anyone else. Lord Summerhays tells him off quite efficiently.

Conrad, Franklyn, and Savvy Barnabas, too, are all Socialists — though Franklyn insists that Savvy is only a Bohemian. The two men, however, were brought up in the "old bourgeois morality,"[33] and Franklyn, many years before, was even the chairman of the Liberal Association. In fact, Burge and Lubin both want him to return to politics, but Franklyn is too sensible to give their proposal any serious consideration. He now has more important things on his mind, such as living three hundred years.

Indeed, so far as the plays are concerned, Shaw's fullest portrayal of Socialists comes in *Man and Superman,* in the preface of which he proclaims: "In short, there is no future for men, however brimming with crude vitality, who are neither intelligent nor politically educated enough to be Socialists." Nevertheless, one of the most amusing of all the incidental scenes in the Shavian repertory is the introductory one of Mendoza's gang of brigands in the Sierra Nevada mountains. This comic opera band of ruffians is composed of one Anarchist, who has "reddish whiskers, weak eyes, and the anxious look of a small tradesman in difficulties" and is "pre-eminently the respectable man of the party"; three Social Democrats, who "are not on speaking terms," whose characters and views of Social Democracy are completely incompatible, and whose only common feature is that they wear red ties; some miscellaneous tramps who are neither Anarchists nor Socialists, but are described by their leader as "gentlemen and Christians"; and Mendoza himself, who freely confesses that he has long ago swallowed all the formulas, including Socialism ("though, in a sense, once a Socialist, always a Socialist"), but who is now engaged in putting Socialism into "common sense" practice by holding up motor cars in order to "secure a more equitable distribution of wealth" by restoring it to circulation among the working classes, who made it in the first place. The bickering and quarreling among the brigands afford a hilarious parody of many Socialist meetings Shaw had attended. The scene, in fact, is somewhat reminiscent of the democratic debates of Shaw's other band of robbers in *Captain Brassbound's Conversion.* Shaw later told Henderson that the "sulky Social-Democrat is the late Harry Quelch" and that the "anarchist is a little man with whom

I once worked in an office, not a bit an anarchist in real life, but that sort of man."

But there is also another Socialist in *Man and Superman*. When Mendoza tries to preserve his respectability by disclaiming John Tanner's suggestion that all his company are Socialists, Tanner reassures him: "I had no intention of suggesting anything discreditable. In fact, I am a bit of a Socialist myself." (And yet West, attacking the play in part as "a caricature of socialism," blindly remarks, "Tanner neither is, nor professes himself, a socialist.") Upon Straker's double comment that he has noticed that most rich men are becoming Socialists, and that Socialism must be looking up if even the brigands are taking to it, Mendoza agrees, and replies with a bit of Shavian political wisdom: "Until a movement shews itself capable of spreading among brigands, it can never hope for a political majority." The central figure in the discussion, Tanner, is generally regarded in his intellectual aspects as a reflection of Shaw himself, and in his external aspects as one of his main rivals and antagonists, Henry M. Hyndman, the founder of the Democratic Federation. Rider, for example, narrates gleefully a debate which once took place between Shaw and Hyndman on Marx's *Das Kapital*, and in which Shaw picked Hyndman vocally to pieces, since the latter's creed might have been summed up in "Marx is the only God, and Hyndman is his only prophet," whereas Shaw always had reservations about certain aspects of Marxism — and also had some prophetical aspirations himself. Irvine, whose analysis of Shaw's politics is the most penetrating and thorough that has yet been made, also sees in Tanner a reflection of Shaw himself and in Tanner's "feeble parlor socialism . . . a bitter comment on Fabian frustration," which is long on talk and short on action. Tanner, in other words, is a Sidney Trefusis brought up to date. The illusions of social progress are also satirized "in Tanner's endless verbal victories over Roebuck Ramsden, who is an advanced thinker of the sixties as Tanner is of the nineties. The implication is that the younger man will become as absurdly obsolete as the older — and the scientific workingman Straker will inherit the earth." This final interpretation, however, is probably debatable.

There is, though, nothing debatable about Shaw's over-all, dramatic portrayal of characters who call themselves Socialists. They are a grade or two above his Liberals, but not any higher.

## 6. *The Laborite*

As Shaw's just quoted remark indicates, the trend in the twenties was already away from Liberalism toward Labor, and Liberals who saw which side their bread was buttered on were turning it over to keep the butter off the tablecloth. It was not, however, a shift which Shaw could speak very well of, nor could he accept Labor as a satisfactory substitute for Marxism.

Certainly the Labor deputation from the Isle of Cats which comes to call on Sir Arthur Chavender in *On the Rocks* is as badly split as any democratic group could be. In fact, Aloysia Brollikins announces that what the Prime Minister is going to hear is "the voice of Labor," Alderman Blee calls it the "verdict of democracy," but the Communistic Viscount Barking damns it as the "bleating of a bloody lot of fools." When Sir Bemrose Hotspot growls that "These damned Liberals can't understand anything but virtuous indignation," Mayor Tom Humphries, the leader of the delegation, bristles up and demands, "Who are you calling a Liberal? I represent the Labor Party." He has already rudely denounced Sir Arthur, who has referred to the ill-sorted group as "the voice of the proletariat," by exclaiming, "Do you take us for Communists?" As a matter of fact, old Hipney, although reminding Sir Arthur that "the Labor movement is rotten with book learning," admits that neither he nor the Mayor has ever actually read Marx, but both of them have to pretend that they have. With these contradictions and deficiencies, Labor certainly contributes nothing toward solving the governmental crisis with which Chavender is confronted.

Just three years before Shaw wrote *On the Rocks* he had produced *The Apple Cart,* another prognosticating political extravaganza, in which the Cabinet contains at least one prime Labor representative, although all its members, from Proteus the Prime Minister down, belong to the same party, which has wiped out all the other parties at the last election. The most obvious Laborite, however, is the conceited, big-speaking Bill Boanerges, who has been appointed because he has just been made President of the Board of Trade. As King Magnus reminds him, his is a Trades Union seat, controlled by the Hydro-Electric Federation, but Boanerges is confident of the continued support of his own class, the workers, and reminds the King, "No king on earth is as safe in his job as a Trade Union official." Boanerges, in his vulgar equalitarianism, is another example of the results of our crude democratic system, and yet he himself is contemptuous of democracy. To him it is a useful device "for putting the right men in the right place." In arguing with the rest of the Cabinet about the value of the King's veto as "the only remaining defence of the people against corrupt legislation," he takes the King's part, and, echoing the remarks Magnus has recently made to him, sneers: "Democracy? Yah! We know what Democracy is worth. What we need is a Strong Man." He is, in fact, secretly ambitious to become the first British President himself, and therefore basks in Magnus's delicate flattery of him as a coming leader of the nation. He approves of the King's proposal to abdicate, and inquires of the rest, "Why not have done with this superstition of monarchy, and bring the British Commonwealth into line with all the other great powers today as a republic?" The mischievous Amanda calls him a "great boob," and twits him, "If you could see a joke, Bill, you wouldn't be the great popular orator you are."

And yet, contrary to the rest of the cast and to most of the spectators of the play, Shaw himself, with his customary perverseness, sees considerable promise for the future in Bill Boanerges, with all his naïveté. As he explains in the preface, there is in the King's Cabinet "only one friendly man who has courage, principle, and genuine good manners when he is courteously treated; and that man is an uncompromising republican, his rival for the dictatorship." Then, as if this were not enough, Shaw carefully adds that "with a little more experience in the art of handling effective men and women as distinguished from the art of handling mass meetings Mr. Bill Boanerges might surprise those who, because he makes them laugh, see nothing in him but a caricature."

### 7. *The Feminist*

In the same sentence Shaw refers to Lysistrata, the Powermistress General, as the "splendidly honest and devoted Die-Hard lady," who is, however, "too scornfully tactless to help much" in solving the King's political problem. But Lysistrata illustrates the heights to which woman has risen politically by the end of the twentieth century. She is "a grave lady in academic robes," whose sharp tongue and ability to put everybody in his place, combined with her costume, show that she has once been a schoolmistress. She makes a furious attack on the great corporation, Breakages, Ltd., and on its strangling effect on industrial life and efficiency. But although Proteus calls her the King's only supporter in the Cabinet, even she sorrowfully deserts him on the issue of the ultimatum and advises him to sign. Nevertheless, at the end Magnus addresses himself to her as the only one who has really understood what has been going on, and "tears come into her eyes" when she realizes that after all he is not going to have to come "into the House with us to keep old England in front and lead a new Party against Breakages."

Just as Lysistrata, known to her associates familiarly as Lizzie, represents the serious side of Shaw's attitude toward Feminism, so Amanda Postlethwaite, addressed by the rest as Mandy, represents his irrepressible comic side. These two women possess, on the whole, the most sense and practical understanding to be found in the Cabinet. The Postmistress General is "a merry lady in uniform like the men." She pets and soft soaps everybody, always with a laugh in her eye and a jest on her lips. Eventually she tells Magnus that she can't support him because there "isn't room for two monarchs in my realm. I am against you on principle because the talent of mimicry isn't hereditary." Her last speech to the sorrowing Lysistrata is, "Come home with me, dear. I will sing to you until you can't help laughing." Yet she too is resolved to keep up the fight against Breakages. She isn't afraid of the corporation because she knows that she can intimidate its directors by her speeches and her laughter.

Shaw's interest in Women's Rights goes back at least to the time of *John*

*Bull's Other Island,* where he has Aunt Judy remark acidly that she wouldn't give the vacant seat to either Doran or Broadbent. "Faith I wouldn't give it to a man at all," she explains. "It's a few women they want in parliament to stop their foolish blather." This incidental interest was brought to a focus a few years later in *Press Cuttings,* with its explanatory subtitle, "A Topical Sketch Compiled from the Editorial and Correspondence Columns of the Daily Papers during the Women's War in 1909." This was the time when Mrs. (or "General") Flora Drummond, the most militant of the early militant suffragets, was leading London demonstrations on a dazzling white charger, once chained herself in front of 10 Downing Street and threw away the key to the padlock, once tried to wrap up a couple of her disciples and mail them to the Prime Minister by parcel post, and led various hunger strikes when she and her friends were committed to Holloway Gaol. The clash between the suffragets and the anti-suffragets, which sometimes caught the mere male in the middle, furnished first-rate grist for Shaw's comic mill when he centered the opposition in Mrs. Carmina Banger and Lady Corinthia Fanshawe, with their demands that Prime Minister Balsquith and General Mitchener play more energetic roles in putting down Votes for Women. Yet Balsquith apparently speaks for Shaw even in 1909 when he remarks that he supposes that, after all, woman suffrage won't make much difference in England, for "It hasn't in other countries in which it has been tried."

Reflections of the Holloway Gaol episode also occur in Fanny O'Dowda's month's incarceration there with Lady Constance Lytton in *Fanny's First Play,* an experience which Fanny transfers to Margaret Knox in her inner play. Anastasia Vulliamy's retrospective history in *The Fascinating Foundling* also reflects the same well-publicized episode. As Anastasia explains her own character, she realized that she needed some serious interest in life to steady her. Being the possessor of an ungovernable appetite and also being naturally rather inclined to stoutness, she decided to try politics. "For me, a woman, politics meant Holloway Gaol and the hunger strike." Unfortunately, however, her plan was not a complete success since she came out with a tremendous appetite, after trying to devour the Governor of the prison, who was "a plump, chubby, tempting sort of man." Consequently, her whole experience in politics having proved a failure, she turns once more to love as her prime pursuit.

Begonia Brown as a specimen of woman in politics scarcely contributes anything more favorable to Shaw's picture of the situation in his own time. Perhaps the solution to the problem of developing more woman leaders like Lysistrata in the future lies in the preface to *In Good King Charles's Golden Days,* in which Shaw discusses "The Future of Woman in Politics." In spite of the completion of the establishment of representative government in England by the enfranchisement of women in 1928, he points out, the prophecy which he made during "the Suffragette revolt of 1913" and which gave such great offense to the agitators has come true. Although the electorate consists of approximately equal numbers of men and women, after seventeen years the nation "is misrepresented at Westminster by 24 women and 616 men." So in 1939 he returns to his old proposal, which he calls the Coupled Vote. What Britain needs, if representative and democratic government must continue (though he is by no means sure that it should), is "a constitutional amendment enacting that all representative bodies shall consist of women and men in equal numbers, whether elected or nominated or co-opted or registered or picked up on the street like a coroner's jury . . . In the case of elected bodies the only way of effecting this is by the Coupled Vote. The representative unit must not be a man *or* a woman but a man *and* a woman. Every vote, to be valid, must be for a human pair." But he somehow neglects to stipulate that, in the interests of the Life Force, the pair should be married, or at least engaged.

### 8. *The Communist*

In discussing *Little Eyolf* in the 1913 additions to *The Quintessence,* Shaw commented: "Thus we see that in Ibsen's mind, as in the actual history of the nineteenth century, the way to Communism lies through the most resolute and uncompromising Individualism." Citing the kind of education which James Mill gave his son John Stuart Mill, which made the latter a Socialist a "quarter of a century before the rest of his set moved in that direction," and reminding his readers that "Herbert Spencer lived to write despairing pamphlets against the Socialism of his ablest pupils," Shaw concludes that "There is no hope in Individualism for egotism." For when some brave Individualist brings a man face to face with himself, the latter realizes that "he finds himself face to face, not with an individual, but with a species, and knows that to save himself, he must save the race." As everyone knows, Shaw, like many others, found the Moses who was to lead the race out of bondage in Karl Marx, and the political theory that was to furnish the instrument in the Marxian Socialism which was to develop, with some modifications, into Communism.

Shaw's presentation of Communists as such, and not as First or Second International Socialists, is confined to three of his last plays — his "dotages," as he has agreed to let the general public call them: *On the Rocks, Geneva,* and *Buoyant Billions.* As a matter of fact, Blanche Patch is obviously right when she points out the paradox that "Whatever he may have thought of Communism, his enthusiasm for Communists was restrained." *On the Rocks* contains the most interesting series of portraits. There is Alderman Blee, "a thin, undersized lower middle class young man . . . , evidently with a good conceit of himself." Although he hasn't really studied Marx directly, his knowledge of what he thinks Marx said has made him cock-

sure and contemptuous of those who aren't Marxists. He perhaps still regards himself as more of a Socialist than a Communist, and insists that he
stands for Labor and democracy. He opposes Sir Arthur's plan to do away
with strikes, and distrusts the application of the principle of compulsory
labor. In the debate with the aristocrats over the merits of Chavender's
proposals, he distinguishes himself by a good deal of crude shouting and
bawling.

Viscount Barking, addressed by his fellow-members of the deputation
as "Toffy," is a "powerfully built loud voiced young man fresh from Oxford
University, defying convention in corduroys, pullover, and unshaven black
beard." To Sir Arthur's triumphant description of him as a "red Communist: what!" he glibly replies: "Red as blood. Same red as the people's."
As a matter of fact, he later reveals that his mother's father made his fortune
in pork pies, and bought his father's Norman title for her. Barking is prone
to explode in threats like "Break your bloody windows," and Sir Arthur is
driven to apologizing for him for "disgracing his class." Nevertheless,
Aloysia defends him by asserting, "He's rude but he's right." His radicalism,
however, turns out to be largely vocal, for, although he is finally the only
one of the delegation to accept all of Sir Arthur's new program, it is discovered that he wants to marry Flavia Chavender, and is willing to admit
that "liberty" is just a word.

It is Hipney and Chavender, however, between whom Shaw has divided
himself. Hipney, the real core of the delegation, is a "sunny comfortable
old chap," who is "aggressively modest, or pretends to be," and who is given
to admonitions like "Don't mind me . . . I don't matter." But when he
stays to talk to Sir Arthur after his associates have left the first meeting in
disgust, and clear-sightedly analyzes the present economic situation in comparison with the past, the audience perceives that it has a definite force to
deal with. He has been asked to run for Parliament, but he's too wise to
accept. "It would be the end of me, as it's been the end of all Labor men
that have done it. The Cabinet is full of Labor men that started as red-hot
Socialists; and what change has it made except that they're in and out of
Bucknam Palace like peers of the realm?" His cheerful cynicism has gone
so far as to convince him that "you can't teach people anything that they don't
want to know. Old Dr. Marx . . . thought that when he'd explained the
Capitalist System to the working classes they'd unite and overthrow it. Fifty
years after he founded his Red International the working classes of Europe
rose up and shot one another down . . . And they'd do it again tomorrow
if they were set on to do it." Although he hasn't studied Marx in the original
text himself, he knows that Marx "puts into every man and woman that does
read him a conceit that they know all about political economy and can look
down on the stuff you were taught at college as ignorant old-fashioned
trash." Of all the deputation, the Cabinet, and the rest, Basham properly

suspects Hipney of being the only one who is a true "revolutionary Socialist" and who, in spite of his pretended disillusion, really means business and will do something. Hipney's extremism, as a result of his experiences and observations, has now gone so far that he admits that he would be for "any Napoleon or Mussolini or Lenin or Chavender" who will kick the people in the way they should go. "You can't frighten me," he cries, "with a word like dictator." But what he really asks, echoing Shaw, is that the people be given a choice only between "qualified men"; then dictators will not be necessary. Basham pays him the compliment of concluding that Hipney is the one the police and the Conservatives should keep an eye on, not Chavender, and he informs Sir Arthur: "His heart is in the revolution: you have only your head in it." And the Duke of Domesday gives Hipney the final accolade: "He is absolutely unique . . . He is the only politician I ever met who had learnt anything from experience."

Though Irvine asserts dogmatically that Sir Arthur Chavender, a coalition Prime Minister, stands for Ramsay MacDonald after the latter's Cabinet crisis and failure, the identification should not be accepted too closely. For Chavender starts with ideas that MacDonald never held and develops others that MacDonald would have been shocked by. At first Sir Arthur's "enjoyment of his position leaves no doubt in his mind as to his own entire adequacy to it." He thanks Heaven that he is a Liberal, and talks about having seen visions and dreamed dreams, but tries to persuade himself that, although he has "striven towards ideals," he and the party "have found something in these realities that was missing in the ideals." But he is actually only making one of the speeches at which he is so good, for realities mean nothing to him. Faced with the problems of unemployment, he merely feels that the police should drive the unemployed away. To him, deputations like that from the Isle of Cats are "frightful nuisances even in the quietest times." In self-justification he claims that "this is a National Government, not a party one. I am up against my Conservative colleagues all the time." To please the Archbishop he is preparing a speech against Christian Communism and Socialism to be given at the Church House, since the prelate is worried because so many Anglo-Catholics are "going mad" on the subject and must be headed off; and in this speech he plans to stress the importance of the Family, which of course means the British Family. When faced with some of the conflicts in his own family, however, he wonders whether the prospects of Socialism's "destroying the family may not be altogether unattractive." In his discussion with Hipney he grants that he hasn't read Marx, but maintains that he has something better to do with his time than "to read the ravings of a half-educated German Communist." In fact, he truly sums himself up when he remarks with a flash of his famous genial humor, "What humbugs we Prime Ministers have to be, Mr. Hipney!"

But when the Lady Healer arrives she sees through him instantly, and calls him "a ghost from a very dead past," tells him frankly that he is "dying from an acute want of mental exercise . . . a bad case of frivolity." She laughs at him when he argues that his life has always been a "completely intellectual" one and when he praises the discipline of a classical training. But he finally yields to her invitation to come to her sanatorium in the Welsh mountains, because he thinks she knows how "to flirt intellectually with a tired thinker." So strong is her spell that he immediately wants to take Marx, Lenin, Trotsky, Stalin, and all the "lot" with him — although it is true that he miscalls Karl Marx Harry Marks.

On his return from the Welsh retreat Chavender has been transformed — to everyone's surprise and indignation — into a "Bolshy premier," and in his first speech gives the audience a "dose of boiling Socialism," proposing nationalization of everything except women. And he makes as brazen a plea for dictatorship as Shaw ever wrote. He has drawn up a new government program which contains at least one plank — Marxist though it may be — which will appeal to each different interest: Capitalist, Conservative, Liberal, Socialist, or Labor; and he almost gains their full support. Unfortunately, however, Sir Dexter Rightside quarrels with Sir Jafna Pandranath on racial grounds, and the whole coalition breaks up. Defeated, Sir Arthur decides not to stand for reëlection, realizing that "Until the men of action clear out the talkers we who have social consciences are at the mercy of those who have none." As to giving up his political career, he assures his solicitous wife that he is happy at having found himself out. He realizes now that he is not the man to lead the reform, much as he knows that reform is needed. Still, as the curtain goes down and the police are clubbing the unemployed outside, who are defiantly singing, "England, arise!" he ponders about the boys and girls of the future. "Suppose," he remarks to his wife, "England really did arise!"

So in *On the Rocks* there are no thorough and successful Communists after all. In fact, in all Shaw's plays there is only one such genuine specimen. *Buoyant Billions* starts out as if there were going to be another, for the hero, Junius Smith, is a fire-eating young Marxist to begin with, although he prefers to call himself simply a "world betterer" by profession, like Marx, Lenin, Stalin, Ruskin, Plato, Confucius, Gautama, Jesus, Mahomet, Luther, and William Morris. But by the end of the play he has married an eccentric heiress, Clementina Alexandra Buoyant, and adopted non-violence and vegetarianism as a mode of life. Only in Commissar Posky of *Geneva,* then, do we find a true-bred, double-distilled, up-to-date member of the Communist party — and of the Soviet breed too. In the trial at the Hague it is the Commissar only who knows all the answers and discomfits all the rest with the cogency of his questions and knowledge. His first speech after he has been introduced all round epitomizes Shaw's conception of the new state, for Posky admits that although the Soviets have shot a few Jews and other undesirables it has not shot them "as such: we civilize them. You see, a Communist state is only possible for a highly civilized people, trained to Communism from their childhood. The people we shoot are gangsters and speculators and exploiters and scoundrels of all sorts who are encouraged in other countries in the name of liberty and democracy." To judge from the plays, this kind of utopia has so far been able to take root only in Russia. No one else has been able to live consistently and successfully in such a rarefied atmosphere.*

## 9. *The Dictator*

At the top of Shaw's political scale, it would seem, is the dictator. Fascist, Nazi, Soviet; Italian, Russian, German, American, English, Spanish; emperor, colonial governor, Führer — it does not seem to matter much. The Strong Man is what the world needs today to keep it going right — or rather to get it going right.

The ideas of Lord Summerhays on colonial government and the treatment of natives incline strongly in this direction, as do those of Hipney and Chavender on governing the English. And the Inca of Perusalem, drawn during the First World War and obviously reflecting Kaiser Wilhelm II, has similar convictions. He admits to Ermyntrude that he "takes himself very seriously," for after all he "is in a position of half divine, half paternal responsibility toward sixty millions of people, whose duty it is to die for him at the word of command." Even though he is defeated and imprisoned now, he predicts that within ten years "every civilized country from the Carpathians to the Rocky Mountains will be a Republic," and then the Inca will have his real chance, for he will be "unanimously invited by those Republics to return from his exile and act as Superpresident of all the republics." But although he has diagnosed the outcome of the war and his own future so confidently, he still insists that he is not responsible for the fighting or for men dying. In the midst of some pretty silly farce, Shaw allows the Inca to indict mankind as guilty, for it has rejected the Inca's cultural contributions and called instead for destruction. But the Inca will yet rule men as he and they deserve.

The redirected authoritarianism of Annajanska, the Bolshevik Empress, is even more clearly established. Born the Grand Duchess, the favorite daughter of the Panjandrum of Beotia, upon the overthrow of the old aristocracy she has decided to join the Revolution, just as General Strammfest and Lieutenant Schneidekind have done. Strammfest, however, is an unconvinced convert; he still loves kings, and cannot understand the revolutionary ideas of the younger generation like Schneidekind and the members

* For a complete discussion of this important aspect of Shaw's political thought, the interested reader is referred to the unpublished doctoral dissertation of Paul Hummert, *Marxist Elements in the Works of Bernard Shaw,* in the Deering Library of Northwestern University.

of the new revolutionary parties like the Maximilianists, the Oppidoshavians, and the Moderate Red Revolutionaries. But Annajanska is wise beyond her years, birth, and education. Magnifying power and preaching the leadership of the able over the stupid, she transforms herself, Saint Joan-like, into a "man and a soldier" to rouse the army to enthusiasm, and the implications of the ending are that she will succeed. As in the cases of Magnus and the Inca, Shaw's doctrine is that even a reformed and intelligent aristocrat can take the Revolutionists themselves over, and lead them where they ought to go.

Boanerges, in *The Apple Cart,* is a potential dictator of the demagogue type. Indeed, the fact that he is "dressed in a Russian blouse and peaked cap," and is "heavily built and aggressively self-assertive," suggests that he is a sort of imitative combination of Mussolini and Stalin. But it is in *Geneva* that Shaw gives us his clearest pictures of the dictators of the thirties — a remarkable set of heroic caricatures in the play itself, which was produced just before the outbreak of the Second World War, but a seriously defended group of potentially great men in the preface, which was written at the end of the war, when their fates were either completed or predictable.

Bombardone, the Italian dictator, comes to the Hague, "dominant, brusque, every inch a man of destiny," proclaiming, "I am here because it is my will to be here. My will is part of the world's will." He considers himself both a nationalist and an internationalist, but primarily a potential "superleader." He admits that democracy now gives everybody an opportunity to rise according to his ability — witness himself as a "democratic institution," for whom ninety-five percent of the electorate would vote if given the chance. Bombardone has a comically exaggerated self-confidence, but he also has a kind of dignity of his own. Moreover, he is the prototype of all the dictators; the others have simply imitated him. As he points out, Ernest Battler, the German dictator, always has his example before him for encouragement. He is an idealist, and Begonia labels him a romantic. Nevertheless, he maintains that his business is government, not liberty and democracy; and he insists that he gives his people good government. He is convinced that he is doing God's work for Him, and is actuated by a sense of inspiration and divine mission. He indicates a sort of contempt for Battler and the Germans, partly because of their theories of "racial purity," which he does not believe in. Like Battler, however, he believes in the theory of some master race, and realizes that in a conflict of leaderships both he and his friend would rely on bayonets. His behavior on hearing the news of the coming end of the world is characteristic, for he immediately, with no personal fear, prepares to go home to keep things as much as possible in order and under discipline. Although Battler comments on him in ironic admiration, "What an actor!" he undeniably comes off the best of the lot in the test.

It is in the preface to the play, written in 1945, that Shaw renders his final verdict on Bombardone-Mussolini. He praises him for having made travel safe in Abyssinia by methods similar to those the British had used in subduing their colonies from India to Australia. And he continues: "It was not for us to throw stones at Musso, and childishly refuse to call his puppet king Emperor. But we did throw stones, and made no protest when his star was eclipsed and he was scandalously lynched in Milan." After all, he admits, the Italians themselves had now had enough of their dictator; and by this time he himself realizes that this ex-idol had had clay feet, for, when held up against the Shavian standards of authoritarian perfection, Mussolini "was neither a Caesar nor a Mahomet." And the final Shavian epitaph classifies Mussolini with Hitler — also defeated and dead after a career of "momentary grandeur" — as "these two poor devils."

Battler appears as an "unsmiling middle aged gentleman with slim figure, erect carriage, and resolutely dissatisfied expression." Although he has a highly exaggerated sense of his own importance and dignity, he confesses that he has always admired Bombardone tremendously; but he warns his fellow dictator that the other has a dangerous failing: "You think yourself the only great man in the world." Bombardone, however, contemptuously calls Battler an "understudy" to his face, and makes fun of the other's thinking himself "a blond beast." Battler calls himself "a man of peace; but it must be a voluntary peace, not an intimidated one. Not until I am armed to the teeth and ready to face all the world in arms is my Pacificism worth anything." Like Bombardone, he feels mystically that he is part of "a mighty movement in the history of the world" — which Ann Lindbergh would probably have called a "Wave of the Future." But he, unlike others, does not derive his mission from any "dead Jew"; in fact, the world must free itself from all Jewish influences, especially the Scriptures. Like the other dictators, he refuses to grant the authority of the Court to judge him; for might, not intellect, makes right. His surface self-confidence is so great that when he sends his troops into Ruritania (probably Belgium) and finds, to his anger, that the other nations will not support him, he promises to battle "alone: *contra mundum*" in spite of their "encirclement." Nevertheless, the news of the new ice age reveals his belligerence as so much bluff when he sees himself personally threatened, for he promptly "breaks down, sobbing convulsively," and crying, "My dog Blonda will be frozen to death. My doggie! My little doggie!" After this Teutonically sentimental and hysterical outburst, however, he recovers his old aplomb and announces dramatically: "we shall work to the last, and set an example to the new race of iceproof men who will follow us . . . We cannot work for ourselves to the last moment; but we can all work for honor."

Thus Shaw presents Hitler as a sort of *Ersatz* dictator, whose "whole stock-in-trade," as he puts it in his preface, "was a brazen voice and a doctrine made up of scraps of Socialism, mortal hatred of the Jews, and complete contempt for pseudo-democratic parliamentary mobocracy." In some of these matters, then, Shaw would obviously feel that Hitler was at least on the right track. But Hitler made two bad mistakes: he became "the creature and tool of the plutocracy," and he turned violently anti-Semitic. "Power and worship turned Hitler's head; and the national benefactor who began by banishing unemployment, tearing up the Treaty of Versailles, and restoring the selfrespect of sixty millions of his fellow countrymen, became the mad Messiah. . . ." So he, like Mussolini, ended as a "poor devil."

This stubbornly perverse sympathy for the Führer persisted into Shaw's last dramatic word, his posthumous *Farfetched Fables*. But when, at Newcastle-on-Tyne early in 1951, this ultimate testament achieved its tributary dedication to the memory of a once supreme genius, it was discovered that the animosity of the Lord Chamberlain had followed Shaw even to his grave, for one of the speeches, being made in a Genetic Institute far in the future, had been bowdlerized. It began: "They killed him because he made a riot in their temple and drove out the money-changers whom he took for thieves, being too young and not enough of a financier to know how useful and necessary they were to pilgrims." But the censor banned the next anticlimactic sentence, reminiscent of the confused racial memories in *Back to Methuselah:* "His name was Hitler, poor chap."

A somewhat mixed showing is made by General Flanco de Fortinbras, "a middle aged officer, very smart, and quite conventional." He is as contemptuous of the other two dictators as they are of him. Bombardone stresses the fact that Flanco has not yet been elected "Leader," and so is "a mere soldier." The Commissar remarks in addition that "Half Europe describes him as your valet." Sensing the hostility of the rest, Flanco asserts insolently, "A man of action always is out of place among talkers." He is, in fact, inordinately conceited about himself as a military leader, even when using the troops of others, such as Bombardone. The three dictators, however, can agree on one thing: their hatred of Communism; and Battler and Bombardone both commend Flanco for the way he is saving his country from its horrors. He regards himself as a practical leader, not a Marxian idealist; and he prides himself on being "a Catholic officer and gentleman, with the beliefs, traditions, and duties of my class and faith." To him there are only two classes, gentlemen and cads; and two faiths, Catholics and heretics; but in order not to hurt the feelings of the others he creates a new category for them of "freaks" — which the Judge, to their pleasure, defines as "an organism so extraordinary as to defy classification." Unlike the others, Flanco is not interested in any world state; all he wants is to keep his own country in order and under the dominion of the Roman Catholic Church. Supported by his religion and by his skepticism of science, he behaves calmly and bravely when faced with the threat of the end of the world, and thinks only of saving as many souls as he can.

In the preface to the play Shaw does not even deign to mention Francisco Franco by name, although he discusses the problems of dictators and totalitarianism, "great men" and "genuine democracy," at considerable length, and illustrates his conclusions with his usual picturesque profuseness from the pages of history. Summing it all up, he argued: "Upstart dictators and legitimate monarchs have not all been personal failures. From Pisistratus to Porfirio, Ataturk, and Stalin, able despots have made good by doing things better and more promptly than parliaments." The trouble with the failures was that they did not keep their heads and recognize their limitations.

The careful reader will have noticed, however, that in the play itself Shaw does not summon the greatest and most successful dictator of them all, Joseph Stalin, to the public hearing before the International Court of Justice. The interests of Communism are expounded and defended, when necessary, by Commissar Posky; but the contributions of the Marshal himself to civilization are never given an opportunity to be challenged.

# X

## THE SUPERMAN

FOR SOME TIME it must have been evident to the reader that Shaw's Dictators and Strong Men are, to a greater or less degree, incipient Supermen — that is, they possess in varying measure, according to how far he can approve of their objects and attainments, certain of the qualities which mankind must develop unless it wants to extinguish itself. In the third act of *Man and Superman,* for instance, he had had Juan, like Thomas Hardy before him in *Jude the Obscure,* predict that one day soon many people, convinced of the futility of man and the hopelessness of his future, would begin to "oppose to the Force of Life the device of sterility." (In fact, man's genius has always been consecrated more to destruction than to creation.) But, he went on, this condition of voluntary extinction of the human race would never actually be reached, because before then the Life Force would reveal itself in a fresh way. A new, and to us a superhuman, sort of being would be bred and would suddenly appear. And, at last, Progress — which, since the days of Adam and Eve, metaphorically speaking, has never really occurred in anything but material ways (which are not important) — would begin.

Anyone who has tried seriously to understand the Shavian conception of the Superman soon discovers that Shaw uses the term with various meanings and applications, and that one must be on his guard as to whether it concerns the Superman Past, the Superman Present, or the Superman Future. In *The Revolutionist's Handbook,* however, Shaw starts one of his most important sections dogmatically with the statement, "The need for the Superman is, in its most imperative aspect, a political one," and goes on to another of his chronic attacks on "Proletarian Democracy," to which, he explains, we have been driven "by the failure of all the alternative systems; for these depended on the existence of Supermen acting as despots or oligarchs," nor, when such persons sometimes providentially appeared, were they able for very long to "impose superhumanity on those whom they governed." The usual politician or demagogue is too small a man to be able to cope with large masses of people or great political movements, so that "when social aggregation arrives at a point demanding international organization before the demagogues and electorates have learnt how to manage even a country parish properly . . . , the whole political business goes to smash." Consequently, concludes Shaw, "unless we can have a Democracy of Supermen," we shall certainly be coming again soon to "that recurrent catastrophe." (It should be noted, incidentally, that this desire for a "Democracy of Supermen" is not so much a typically Fabian doctrine as it was the faith of Shaw's favorite poet of his youth, Shelley.)

Since this prophecy was made at the very beginning of the twentieth century, Shaw must have been simultaneously pleased and dismayed by the advent of two world wars — though, it should be suggested, proletarian democracy was by no means fully responsible for their outbreak. But he was even more pleased by the emergence of a new type of leader and a new type of social organization which, although scarcely producing or promising to produce "a Democracy of Supermen," still apparently offered him a very satisfactory sort of substitute until the really new and original model of Superman Future should put in an appearance. As Irvine amusingly describes the Shavian evolution: "The eighties made him a socialist. The nineties made him a 'mystic' — a rather Benthamite mystic in the cult of the superman. His superman was somewhat inferior as an *objet d'art,* but he had admirable mechanical works inside, and many years later Shaw discovered that the blueprints fitted Joseph Stalin remarkably well."

Perhaps, however, it is not quite fair to imply that the ultimate goal of perfection has been reached in Stalin. In the preface to *Misalliance* in 1910, Shaw confessed: "The precise formula for the Superman, *ci-devant* The Just Man Made Perfect, has not yet been discovered. Until it is, every birth is an experiment in the Great Research which is being conducted by the Life Force to discover that formula." As the naively ebullient Tarleton had stated in the play itself: "Still, you know, the superman may come. The superman's an idea. I believe in ideas. Read Whatshisname." Ideas — even some of Shaw's ideas — are fluid, and can develop, and even improve.

*The Revolutionist's Handbook,* once more, affords a useful starting point. Here Shaw, repeating his insistence that he did not steal his conception of the Superman from Friedrich Nietzsche, commences, "The cry for the Superman did not begin with Nietzsche, nor will it end with his vogue." And then he raises the question which, he says, has always previously silenced this cry: "what kind of person is this Superman to be?" Though he banters with the picture of "Some sort of goodlooking philosopher-athlete, with a handsome healthy woman for his mate," he admits that, "Vague as this is, it is a great advance on the popular demand for a perfect gentleman and a perfect lady." No, he maintains, "The proof of the Superman will be in the living; and we shall find out how to produce him by the old method of trial and error, and not by waiting for a completely convincing prescription of his ingredients." It is true that everyone agrees that a "superior mind" is essential, but it would be "football club folly" to assume that this would necessarily be the product of a superior body. Consequently, he concludes, if there is to be a Superman, "he must be born of Woman by Man's intentional and well-considered contrivance," and "we shall still have to trust to the guidance of fancy (*alias* Voice of Nature), both in the breeders and the parents, for that superiority in the unconscious self which will be the true characteristic of the Superman." From this point, a long and provocative discussion of mating and eugenics ensues.

As the argument continues, however, it becomes evident that some other traits of the Superman can be specified after all. For, because "Man does desire an ideal Superman with such energy as he can spare from his nutrition, and has in every age magnified the best living substitute for it he can find," he "is never without an array of human idols who are nothing but sham Supermen." Contemporary man, however, does not foresee that "the real Superman will snap his fingers at all Man's present trumpery ideals of right, duty, justice, religion, even decency." Thus the true Superman will be a Shavian anti-idealist — in other words, a realist. With a rather strange optimism, however, Shaw goes on to prophesy that the average man (the Philistine?) will not object to the production of what he calls "Great Men or Heroes" on this basis, because he himself — the average man — flouts these same ideals daily without knowing it, and will therefore imagine these Great Men, "not as true Supermen, but as himself endowed with infinite brains, infinite courage, and infinite money." This optimism about the future had apparently developed since Shaw wrote *The Sanity of Art* in 1895, although his views on the iconoclasm of the Superman remained fixed. In debating how much selfishness and dishonesty we ought to stand for from a gifted person because of his gifts, Shaw decided, "The Superman will certainly come like a thief in the night, and be shot accordingly, but we cannot leave our property wholly undefended on that account. On the other hand, we cannot ask the Superman simply to add a higher set of values to current respectable morals; for he is undoubtedly going to empty a good deal of respectable morality out like so much dirty water, and replace it by new and strange customs." Conventional people, Shaw predicted, will be horrified by every step in his progress. This early view, as a matter of fact, is more typical than that in the *Handbook*.

Although in his earlier writings Shaw had implied that the Super Man was to be essentially only a very Superior Man, with qualities which have always been found in isolated men, but with these qualities distilled and concentrated, after a time he came to wonder whether this new genus would be sufficient. Even when he wrote his preface to *The Dark Lady of the Sonnets* in 1910 he had decided that man's past attempts to deal with the problems of civilization "were and still are so stupid that we call for The

Superman, virtually a new species, to rescue the world from mismanagement." This vision of a new species, rather than a genus, was to be supported when he wrote *Heartbreak House* during the First World War and had Hector prophesy that either "some new creature" would have to come "to supplant us . . . or the heavens will fall in thunder to destroy us." Nevertheless, even here Shaw's prevalent doctrine of the exciting unexpectedness, the unpredictability, and therefore the miraculous potentialities of life must be recalled as a slight corrective. As he complains in a postscript to the preface for a new edition of *Man and Superman,* "Worst of all, I have been accused of preaching a Final Ethical Superman: no other, in fact, than our old friend the Just Man Made Perfect! This misunderstanding is so galling that I lay down my pen without another word." And in the preface to *On the Rocks,* as well as in *Everybody's Political What's What?,* he reminds his followers that he is not presenting his creed of Creative Evolution, with its picture of future life, "as anything more than another provisional hypothesis."

Whatever the details of Shaw's visions of the Superman, nothing can be plainer than that the conception forms the backbone of his philosophy.* Henderson, in his first book on Shaw, records a conversation that he once had with his friend on the subject of art, and especially on the paintings of Michael Angelo. One of the reasons for Michael Angelo's greatness as both artist and man, Shaw decided after a close and intensive examination of the Delphic Sybil in company with Anatole France, was that "his every subject is a person of genius. He never had a commonplace subject. His models are extraordinary people. They are Supermen and Superwomen." And the lesson that Shaw gained from this experience, he said, was that he should always put people of genius into his works. His method has always been to set "a genius over against a commonplace person." The genius of today, then, may well lead to the Superman of tomorrow.

## 1. *Superman Past*

In *The Revolutionist's Handbook,* in discussing "The Perfectionist Experiment at Oneida Creek," with its communistic principles and organization, Shaw refers to its leader, John Humphrey Noyes, as "one of those chance attempts at the Superman which occur from time to time in spite of the interference of Man's blundering institutions." Though he goes on, in examining the history of the famous Oneida community and its ultimate failure, to conclude that "the voluntary relapse of the communists into marriage, capitalism, and customary private life" proved that "the real solution was not what a casual Superman could persuade a picked company to do

* For a further background for this statement, see my article, "Bernard Shaw, Philosopher," *PMLA,* LXIX (March 1954).

for him, but what a whole community of Supermen would do sponta-
neously," the passage affords a key to Shaw's view of what little the Life
Force has been able to accomplish with the Superman in the past.

To judge from various allusions, in Shaw's opinion the first specimen of
the tentative Superman in history — or, to be more exact, mythology — was
Prometheus. Or perhaps there might be a rivalry for priority between him
and Siegfried — Wagner's Siegfried in particular. For both these heroes, as
Shaw cites them in the preface to *Three Plays for Puritans,* were diabolonians. "From Prometheus to the Wagnerian Siegfried, some enemy of the
gods, unterrified champion of those oppressed by them, has always towered
among the heroes of the loftiest poetry. Our newest idol, the Superman,
celebrating the death of godhead, may be younger than the hills; but he is
as old as the shepherds." But Siegfried is Shaw's favorite. As he describes
this hero in *The Perfect Wagnerite,* he "knows no law but his own humor . . . , is, in short, a totally unmoral person, a born anarchist, . . . an
anticipation of the overman of Nietzsche." Naturally, the creators of such
heroes, Nietzsche and Wagner, take on certain supermanly qualities themselves, especially Shaw's musical idol, Wagner, whom, together with Mozart,
he would place at the top of the musical ladder. Interestingly enough, Shaw
also read into his interpretation of Wagner's Siegfried something of the
character of the Russian anarchist, M. A. Bakunin, who had been associated
with Wagner as a leader in the Saxon revolt in 1848. Irvine, in tracing the
genealogy of Shaw's Superman, after he has decided that the dramatist's
Life Force theory owes more to Ibsen, Schopenhauer, and Samuel Butler
than it does to Nietzsche, also finds little of Nietzsche in this Shavian Superman, which he thinks owes "more to Wagner — and most of all, one is
tempted to say, to Jeremy Bentham." And he adds that in Shaw's writings
critics sometimes also mistake Marx for Nietzsche.

So far as the religious and the mythological precursors of the Superman
are concerned, Shaw once announced, in an address on "The Religion of
the Future" in 1911, that Christ himself was one of the attempts of the Life
Force at evolving a greater man; but that Christ was a failure. Nevertheless,
in the preface to *Androcles* Shaw attributes to Christ many of the ideas on
society, Socialism, and the family which he himself holds.

In the realm of more authentic history he also has certain favorites whom
he mentions with some frequency. A passage in his "First Aid to Critics"
in *Major Barbara* discusses the prime importance of environment in bringing out character, and the ability of the "master-minds of the world" to
perceive the possibility of eliminating caste barriers in choosing their officers,
governors, and councilors. Here the "master-minds" that he selects to illustrate his theory are Napoleon, Julius Caesar, and Louis XI. And, in *The
Revolutionist's Handbook* again, he alludes to "our few accidental supermen,
our Shakespears, Goethes, Shelleys, and their like," after having recurred

earlier to his principle of a "Democracy of Supermen" when he maintains that "Until there is an England in which every man is a Cromwell, a France in which every man is a Napoleon, a Rome in which every man is a Caesar, a Germany in which every man is a Luther plus a Goethe, the world will be no more improved by its heroes than a Brighton villa is improved by the pyramid of Cheops."

Only two, or perhaps three, of these Supermen of the historical past has Shaw written plays about directly — Napoleon in *The Man of Destiny,* Caesar in *Caesar and Cleopatra,* and Shakespeare in *The Dark Lady of the Sonnets* and *Shakes vs. Shav.* But in the two last-named playlets Shakespeare is scarcely a Superman, and so these little pieces can properly be overlooked. First, then, we are once more posed with the problem of what Shaw really thought about Napoleon, since his name turns up over and over again in widely varying contexts. As the hero in *The Man of Destiny* Napoleon is both Shaw's first historical character and his first preliminary sketch of the incipient Superman from the past. (According to Henderson, Shaw once wrote to Mansfield, "I studied the character from you, and then read up on Napoleon and found that I had got him exactly right.") The General is of course a realist in most things, but he also has strange streaks of unconscious idealism in his character. As an "original observer" ("originality" is one of the prime "supermanly" qualities) he has rebelled against the old-fashioned "art of war," and discovered the value of artillery. In addition to his "prodigious powers of work," he has developed "a clear, realistic knowledge of human nature in public affairs." Compact of imagination without being hampered by illusions, he is able to be "creative without religion, loyalty, patriotism or any of the common ideals." Somewhat paradoxically, his power springs largely from the fact that he himself swallowed all these ideals in his boyhood, and now, therefore, "having a keen dramatic faculty, is extremely clever at playing upon them by the arts of the actor and stage manager." Thus he has been able to use the very lack of food, clothes, pay, etc., for his army — a lack which "would have embarrassed an idealist soldier" — as a means of inciting the men to greater efforts than ever for the sake of the loot awaiting them. The craving of the world for "miracles and heroes" is being satisfied in him, even though it has actually been unnecessary for him to perform any true "heroic miracles" to overcome his rather feeble opposition. Therefore Shaw predicts, with all the certitude of hindsight, that it will be "difficult for the romanticists of a hundred years later to credit the little scene" which he is going to present (in a central point of which, as a matter of fact, Shaw admits that his arch-enemy, that prolific purveyor of the well-made play, Victorien Sardou, had anticipated him by using it in *Dora*).

In the action of *The Man of Destiny* it is the Strange Lady who often sees more penetratingly into Napoleon's real motives than he himself does.

Yet it is he who, in spite of his obvious pleasure in her flattery, insists to her
that "there's no such thing as a real hero." Caught momentarily off his
guard, he agrees with her that he has really wanted to win his battles for
himself — though he quickly corrects himself by substituting "for humanity
— for my country." When he announces pretentiously that "self-sacrifice is
the foundation of all true nobility of character," she is not taken in, and
reminds him that only "womanish heroes" act "through love, through pity,
through the instinct to save and protect someone else." When she enthusiastically preaches to him the duty to oneself, he instinctively responds, and
makes it clear that, in his pursuit of self-realization, he has always regarded
himself as above both honor and the desire for mere happiness. Though at
first angered by her remark that she adores a man "who is not afraid to be
mean and selfish," he finally admits tacitly that he has neither principles,
conscience, nor scruples, and in his climactic speech about the three sorts
of people in the world concludes: "The low people and the high people are
alike in one thing: they have no scruples, no morality. The low are beneath
morality, the high above it. I am not afraid of either of them: for the low
are unscrupulous without knowledge, so that they make an idol of me;
whilst the high are unscrupulous without purpose, so that they go down
before my will." And as for the middle people, who are dangerous because
they have both knowledge and purpose, he is confident that he can overcome
them too because they are "chained hand and foot by their morality and
respectability."

This essentially complimentary picture of Napoleon, from the Shavian
point of view, did not, however, continue to characterize Shaw's attitude.
By the time of *The Revolutionist's Handbook* Tanner-Shaw had looked at
the later career of the Emperor and concluded: "Napoleon seems to have
ended by regarding mankind as a troublesome pack of hounds only worth
keeping for the sport of hunting them." A few years later, in the preface to
*Misalliance,* in which Shaw discusses Napoleon as an illustration of the
realistic imagination as against the romantic, he nevertheless calls Wellington a greater realist than Napoleon, and labels Napoleon at the Battle of
Waterloo "an academic soldier" anyhow — a complete reversal of his earlier
estimate. (He later made the same comparison to Pearson in naming the
"two kinds of generals: those who followed the rules and those who broke
them, the professional and the amateur, Napoleon and Wellington.") After
the revulsions of the First World War Shaw was ready to go even further
and in the preface to *Heartbreak House* is discovered crying that in the war
some young men "found themselves actually becoming artists in war, with
a growing relish for it, like Napoleon and all the other scourges of mankind." In *Tragedy of an Elderly Gentleman* he burlesqued Napoleon by
reincarnating him as Cain Adamson Charles Napoleon, the strutting Emperor of Turania. Just before the outbreak of the Second World War, in

the preface to *The Millionairess*, Napoleon has become "a very ordinary snob in his eighteenth-century social outlook," "a routine soldier," and "fundamentally a commonplace human fool." And yet "this shabby-genteel Corsican subaltern (and a very unsatisfactory subaltern at that) dominated Europe for years." Toward the end of the Second World War, in *Everybody's Political What's What?*, Shaw's disillusionment is complete, and the "upstart" Napoleon is bracketed with the "upstart" Hitler, both of whom have been worshiped by their "fellowcountrymen not as the villains of historical melodrama, but as its heroes." The genius who started out to be a first-rate specimen of Superman Past has turned into a sham and a counterfeit after all.

No such deterioration took place, however, in the case of Julius Caesar — a role which Shaw told Henderson he had written for Forbes-Robertson. Yet Caesar, whom Apollodorus describes as not "merely the conquering soldier, but the creative poet-artist," was also a superior kind of "man of destiny." In fact, he so characterizes himself in his soliloquy before the Sphinx: "My way hither was the way of destiny; for I am he of whose genius you are the symbol: part brute, part woman, and part God — nothing of man in me at all." This supreme Caesarean egoism, which continues to mark Shaw's portrayal, is not repugnant, since it is mixed with a steady stream of seemingly honest self-criticism, stripped of illusions. This General is a consistent realist. Cleopatra is penetrating: "Caesar loves no one. . . . He has no hatred in him: he makes friends with everyone as he does with dogs and children. His kindness to me is a wonder . . . His kindness is not for anything in me: it is his own nature." This is the secret of Caesar's greatness, as Shaw stresses it in his notes following the play — his inner "nature," his "originality," his "selfishness." "I have been careful to attribute nothing but originality to him," Shaw explains. "Originality gives a man an air of frankness, generosity, and magnanimity by enabling him to estimate the value of truth, money, or success in any particular instance quite independently of convention and moral generalization." For this reason, such a man's "lies are not found out: they pass for candors." He knows how to give away money generously — when he can get the most in return for it. He recognizes the really crucial moments in determining success. "Hence, in order to produce an impression of complete disinterestedness and magnanimity, he has only to act with entire selfishness; and this is perhaps the only sense in which a man can be said to be *naturally* great. It is in this sense that I have represented Caesar as great."

This devastating candor on Shaw's part, of course, the ordinary spectator or reader rejects or fails to understand. Shaw's further statement that, since Caesar has "virtue, he has no need of goodness," the average man would dismiss as mere perverse and meaningless paradox, for he would not accept Shaw's definition of virtue as living according to "nature," with none of the restraints of convention. And the additional assertion that Caesar "is neither forgiving, frank, nor generous" because he is too great to need to be any of these things would seem to be pure subversiveness.

Yet this is the light in which Caesar's actions and words in the play are to be viewed — though to most people the character becomes much less admirable in the process. This is how we are to evaluate his seeming kind-heartedness and understanding toward little Ptolemy and his fatherly advice to Cleopatra; his own moments of boyishness and the quickness with which his "dignity collapses" under Rufio's bluntness; his apparently magnanimous refusal to read the letters showing who are his enemies in Rome, and his lack of resentment at treachery, which he calls "natural"; his development of a new wisdom and mercy since his days in Gaul; his sentimentality, which Cleopatra evaluates as part of his cleverness; his failure to be disturbed by the burning of the library at Alexandria, because the fire has distracted the enemy, so that he and his party can escape to the lighthouse; his presumably mendacious statement that "Caesar is no Caesarean. Were Rome a true republic, then were Caesar the first of Republicans"; and especially his atti-tude toward revenge, which is focused in the murder of Pothinus by Ftata-teeta, at the behest of Cleopatra. For, contrary to the opinion of Rufio, Lucius, Apollodorus, and Britannus that Pothinus deserved death, Caesar bitterly accuses Cleopatra of having "renounced" him through her deed. For revenge defeats its own ends. "And so," he cries, "to the end of history, murder shall breed murder, always in the name of right and honor and peace, until the gods are tired of blood and create a race that can under-stand." Nevertheless, in spite of these humanitarian and eminently sensible views, Caesar approves of Rufio's slaying of Ftatateeta, which he says was done "without malice." It was a "natural slaying," not performed with all the mummery of so-called civilized justice. And yet one wonders about the logic of Shaw's reasoning in these distinctions. Has there really been no "judgment" on Rufio's part when he decides that the blood-drunk nurse must be put out of the way as a potential menace to society? Hasn't Rufio already admitted that he kills "by instinct," just as Cleopatra yielded to her instinct in ridding herself of Pothinus? And will the continuation of the process of revenge be any the less dangerous, no matter what the motivation for the act of death may be?

In the *Self Sketches,* in correcting what Shaw calls one of Duffin's "blun-ders," he reiterates the full statement that he once gave to Cecil Chesterton to the effect that he has "no hatred of 'physical violence of any sort.'" On the other hand, "Physical violence is the weapon by which stupidity and villainy can always defeat mind and virtue . . . One of the first points of honor in civilized society should be that mental combats must not be fought out with fists nor crime by torture." But Shaw's praising of John Paul Jones's "sound instinct" in being prepared "to kill a mutineer if necessary, but not to flog him" would scarcely prevent the dead man's relatives or friends from desiring or even trying to obtain revenge for the punishment inflicted, no matter what its motive. Although the several methods of eliminating or exterminating the unfit in Shaw's various "Judgment Day" plays like *Heartbreak House, The Inca of Perusalem, The Simpleton of the Unexpected Isles, Back to Methuselah,* and *Geneva,* or in prefaces like those to *Androcles and the Lion* and *Getting Married,* are relatively painless, the fact remains that in some of them violent means are used to accomplish what is essentially an intellectual end, which itself has been established by the author's rendering a judgment on what is good and what is bad for society.

Nevertheless, Shaw's own estimate of the greatness of Caesar emerges again at the end of the play when Cleopatra, angered and insulted as she realizes that her mentor has forgotten her in the rush of preparations for departure, still reminds him of his own principles of government: "Without punishment. Without revenge. Without judgment." Only a Superman could consistently live up to such a standard. None of Shaw's other historical supermanly predecessors, such as the Kaiser Wilhelm adumbrated in the Inca of Perusalem, could do so. And all Nature's trial experiments in *Geneva* turn out to be failures. Bombardone, who is "every inch a man of destiny," prophesies that when "the empires of the world federate, its leaders will govern the world; and these leaders will have a superleader who will be the ablest man in the world: that is my vision." But what happened to Mussolini, practically under Shaw's eyes? Although Ernest Battler swears that "we shall work to the last, and set an example to the new race of iceproof men who will follow us," Shaw in his preface admits that Hitler turned out to be only a "pseudo Messiah and Madman." Even of the Commissar the Judge decides that, though the other is undoubtedly a man of ability, with no fears for the future, "there is no evidence that he is a superman. Twenty years ago he would have been talking as great nonsense as any of you . . . Perhaps I should have said folly." So the Judge sums up his verdict: "Man is a failure as a political animal. The creative forces which produce him must produce something better." This verdict Shaw confirms in his own person in his section on "Great Men" in his preface: "The geniuses themselves are steeped in vulgar superstitions and prejudices . . . The apparent freaks of nature called Great Men mark not human attainment but human possibility and hope." And this hope resides in the belief that it has not been proved that death itself is "natural." No, "it is life that is natural and infinite." The future of life is unpredictable, for "new faculties . . . come suddenly and miraculously." Nature has always moved by jumps, never betrayed or announced in advance. Cheerless as the prospect looks at present, perhaps the genesis of the coming race is no further away than tomorrow.

## 2. *Superman Present*

Examples of the non-historical type of Superman Present in Shaw's plays — that is, of fictitious characters of today with supermanly qualities but without any prototypes in world affairs — also indicate that it is important to distinguish the pretender from the real thing, and that satisfactory specimens of the real thing are very rare birds themselves. One must be on his guard, for instance, against the pseudo-Superman like the artist Louis Dubedat, whose very denials suggest that he has privately thought of himself in the Superman category. For when Louis announces to the doctors his disbelief in morality, because he is a disciple of Bernard Shaw, who is "the most advanced man now living," and who doesn't believe in anything, he apologizes coyly as follows: "Of course I havn't the ridiculous vanity to set up to be exactly a Superman; but still, it's an ideal that I strive towards just as any other man strives towards his ideal." Dubedat's deficiency as a Superman is implicit in that last statement. No real Superman — and no genuine Shavian — would confess to following an ideal blindly, even the ideal of a Superman. And yet, as a matter of fact, isn't this actually what Shaw himself has done in offering his Superman for the world to look toward? Can it be that the Superman is only a mask which Shaw has invented for himself to hide unpalatable truth about the future of mankind?

Just as Shaw has projected himself to some degree into the pseudo-Superman artist of *The Doctor's Dilemma*, so he has partially disguised himself under the walrus whiskers and rubber hat of Alf Doolittle, the serio-comic dustman of *Pygmalion*, and the most "original" character in the play. Doolittle, a tremendous take-off on the Shavian philosophic man, is at first haunted by the specter of middle-class morality, and then is abruptly metamorphosed into a "gentleman." In a totally unexpected transformation, which plunges the audience into a tornado of laughter much as did Captain Brassbound's sudden appearance in a frock coat and top hat, Alf Doolittle emerges in the fifth act "resplendently dressed as for a fashionable wedding," with a "flower in his buttonhole, a dazzling silk hat, and patent leather shoes," and accuses Higgins of having ruined him, destroyed his happiness, and delivered him "into the hands of middle class morality." For Higgins thoughtlessly wrote a letter to old Ezra D. Wannafeller, "an old blighter in America that was giving five millions to found Moral Reform Societies all over the world," and described Doolittle to him as "the most original moralist at present in England." Consequently, when Wannafeller died, his will was found to leave Alfred "a share in his Predigested Cheese Trust worth three thousand a year on condition that I lecture for his Wannafeller Moral Reform League as often as they ask me up to six times a year." So, with the responsibilities of respectability, his life is wrecked. As he says, "I have to live for others and not for myself: that's middle class morality."

He's so "intimidated" that he's going to get married in "the middle class way," which, he laments, "ain't the natural way." Shaw, however, generously provides a relatively happy ending for Alf Doolittle, for in the epilogue the reader is told how Alf becomes "extremely popular in the smartest society by a social talent which triumphed over every prejudice and every disadvantage. Rejected by the middle class which he loathed, he had shot up at once into the highest circle by his wit, his dustmanship (which he carried like a banner), and his Nietzschean transcendence of good and evil." Even a Nietzschean Superman is better than none.

Bentley Summerhays in *Misalliance* is also only an embryo, but in some ways also probably reflected the young Bernard Shaw (note the initials). An "afterthought" of a child to parents in their forties, Bentley is all brains with as little body as is necessary to carry these brains. He "has a hard and penetrating intellect and a remarkable power of looking facts in the face; but unfortunately, being very young, he has no idea how very little of that sort of thing most of us can stand." The play ends with the breaking of Bentley's engagement to Hypatia when she decides that Joey Percival is the lad for her. Much upset at his friend Johnny's betrayal, Bentley resolves never to marry, and consents to fly away with the manly woman Lina in her aeroplane, in spite of his fear of height and such mechanical contraptions. Perhaps, Shaw implies, this experience will make a man of him, so that he will be able to control his behavior in the way his brains deserve.

Two of Shaw's previously discussed diabolonian realists have pronounced supermanly qualities. In his preface to *Three Plays for Puritans* Shaw discusses Dick Dudgeon's diabolonianism along with that of Siegfried, William Blake, and Nietzsche. And Andrew Undershaft, with his self-confidence, massive strength, and cynical realism, mixed with a mystical trust in the operations of the Life Force, is as complete and admirable a representative of Superman Present as Shaw has portrayed.

Into all these fragmentary, incipient supermen it is almost self-apparent that Shaw has written something of himself. Hesketh Pearson, at the very end of his gossipy but richly informative biography of his Irish idol, says that he once asked Shaw, "Is there a conscious portrait of yourself in any of your plays?"

"No," was Shaw's reply, "except the character of 'G.B.S.' in all of them."

When he made this dogmatic denial, however, Mr. Shaw must have been either in a state of complete amnesia or at least in a fit of absent-mindedness. Or perhaps it was merely another case of his favorite prank of mystification or obfuscation. Though truly the character of G.B.S. permeates all his novels and plays, the personal identity of Bernard Shaw also peers around the slipped mask in a dozen or more of them, and winks with confidential jocoseness at any alert reader who is willing to respond. As certain movie directors have been known to place their living signatures on their

work by sliding themselves into the picture in the minor flesh, or as Fra
Lippo Lippi in his painting for the nuns at Sant' Ambrogio's sneaked himself unobtrusively into the luminous concourse of God Himself with the
Madonna, the Babe, the angels, and several selected saints, so Mr. Shaw
has stamped himself into novel after novel, play after play, and has created
such alter egos as Sidney Trefusis, his own Charteris (who may be compared with Cabell's Charteris to the illumination of both), his Valentine, his
Tanner, his Blanco Posnet, his Joey Percival, and his Bishop Bridgenorth, to
be followed by his Captain Shotover, his King Magnus, his Sir Arthur
Chavender, his King Charles, and — most notably — his Elderly Gentleman
in *Back to Methuselah*.

Like Henry IV, who is purported to have sent counterfeits dressed in
his armor into the Battle of Shrewsbury to mislead, baffle, or overawe the
enemy, so Shaw has many times given to certain characters who are in other
ways not at all like himself particular idiosyncrasies, tastes, or notions peculiarly his own. Sometimes, in his typically topsy-turvy fashion, he attributes
certain of his pet concepts to people whose absurdities he is otherwise exposing. Thus Dr. Paramore in *The Philanderer*, the devoted vivisectionist
and therefore Shaw's natural abhorrence, turns on poor, stupid Colonel
Craven with an exposé of the inhumanity of machine-guns and the cruelty
of fox-hunting. Craven himself, the victim of the non-existent "Paramore's
Disease," has been transformed into "an object of public scorn — a miserable
vegetarian and teetotaler" by the treatment of the doctor. Somewhat more
gently handled is the case of the well-meaning, overgrown baby, the Rev.
James Mavor Morell, who owes much of his following among women and
liberals to the fact that he likes to think that he is an advanced Socialist,
whereas he really does not understand Socialism any better than Roebuck
Ramsden understands evolution.

Another aspect of this sort of self-revelation in reverse is perhaps Shaw's
waggish habit of putting his name into the mouths of certain of his characters who claim, or have been assigned, discipleship under him without really
knowing what Shavianism means. In *Fanny's First Play* Shaw gets a bit
of good-humored revenge on his highbrow fellow-critic Walkley, under the
name of Trotter, by having him driven to such distraction by the Cambridge
Fabian, Fanny, that he bursts out: "And now I'm told that I'm a centre
of Immoralism! of modern Minxism! a trifler with the most sacred subjects!
a Nietzschean!! perhaps a Shavian!!!" Louis Dubedat, the bohemian artist,
sets all the doctors back on their heels when, on his deathbed, he blandly
proclaims, "All your moralizings have no value for me. I don't believe in
morality. I'm a disciple of Bernard Shaw." In response to Sir Patrick's puz-
zlement and B.B.'s nonchalance he adds: "Of course I havn't the ridiculous
vanity to set up to be exactly a Superman; but still, it's an ideal I strive
towards just as any other man strives towards his ideal." B.B., now aroused

to intolerance, stops him coldly with, "When a man pretends to discuss science, morals, and religion, and then avows himself a follower of a notorious and avowed antivaccinationist, there is nothing more to be said . . . But there are things that place a man socially; and antivaccination is one of them." Poor Sir Patrick, completely out of his depth, bleats, "Bernard Shaw? I never heard of him. He's a Methodist preacher, I suppose." Whereupon Louis, outraged, bursts forth: "No, no. He's the most advanced man now living: he isn't anything." Against such superlatives the discussion in *Annajanska, the Bolshevik Empress,* between Strammfest and Schneidekind as to the relative strengths of the Maximilianists, the Moderate Red Revolutionaries, and the Oppidoshavians shines tame and pale.

Another instance of Shaw laughing at himself or at his own work occurs in *How He Lied to Her Husband,* the ironical echo of *Candida,* in which the poet is not only an addict of Shaw's favorite sport, boxing, but is actually an amateur boxing champion — while Cashel Byron in *The Admirable Bashville* and *Cashel Byron's Profession* becomes a professional. To ex-Lieutenant Hotchkiss of *Getting Married,* the "Celebrated Coward" according to his own calling-cards, Shaw not only attributes many of his own favorite philandering propensities but also makes him spout some of his own great admiration for Mahomet.

Not always, however, does Shaw attribute his private views only to the butts of his satire. Robert Smith, hero of *Immaturity,* is a successful but discontented bookkeeper, interested in poetry and music halls, and critical of everyone around him, just like the young G.B.S. Owen Jack's flaming personality in *Love among the Artists,* with his devotion to truth at any cost, his connoisseurship in music, and his adeptness in phonetics and dramatic elocution, also comes straight from the author. In *Major Barbara* it is impossible to decide which mask Shaw himself is lurking behind, so quickly does he pass his spokesmanship around among munitions tycoon Undershaft, Greek professor Cusins, and Salvationist Barbara herself, who is marked with Shaw's own antipathy to intoxicants. In *John Bull's Other Island* he has split himself between the expatriate Irishman, Larry Doyle, who has an "instinct against going back to Ireland," but who nevertheless does so (as Shaw did), and the whimsical, unfrocked priest, Father Keegan, both of whom voice Shaw's own criticizing of the dreaming, unreal, romantic mysticism of so many people in his native land. And in *Mrs. Warren's Profession* his quondam collaborator and stern critic William Archer even accused him of hiding behind the woman's skirts of Vivie Warren.

Many times the presence of G.B.S. speaking through his puppets is betrayed by the irresistible temptation of some character to sit down or jump up on whatever happens to be handy and start preaching. In this province, for instance, during the somewhat mysterious swapping of roles at the end of *The Devil's Disciple,* ex-minister Anderson announces to the assembled crowd: "So I am starting life at fifty as Captain Anthony Anderson of the Springtown militia; and the Devil's Disciple here will start presently as the Reverend Richard Dudgeon, and wag his pow in my old pulpit . . ." So Blanco Posnet, another diabolonian "pioneer of civilization in a territory of the United States of America," ends Shaw's "Sermon in Crude Melodrama" by "rushing from the bar to the table and jumping up on it" with the exclamation: "Boys, I'm going to preach you a sermon on the moral of this day's proceedings." But the English share the sermonizing impulse, in an even more extreme form — as witness Aubrey the clergyman-burglar in *Too True To Be Good.*

The personal element also insinuates itself many times into portrayals of the private and domestic relations between certain types of characters. Take, for instance, Julia Craven and Grace Tranfield in *The Philanderer.* Here, fortunately, Shaw's own admission, made to Pearson, is available. The original of the jealous and predatory Julia was Mrs. Jennie Patterson, a young widow who was a music pupil of his mother's. Grace was Florence Farr, an attractive and "advanced" young actress who played leading roles in two of Shaw's early plays. Charteris was, of course, Shaw.

The philandering Valentine in *You Never Can Tell* was also Shaw, and Gloria was, in some degree, Charlotte Payne-Townshend, whom Shaw was courting while writing the play. In *The Apple Cart* he introduced not only himself and Mrs. Shaw but also the latest in his series of actress sweethearts, Mrs. Pat Campbell. Here, in the completely extraneous "Interlude" in the boudoir of Orinthia, the official but purely — and very — decorative mistress of the clever King Magnus, Shaw manages to insert a sort of public apology to Mrs. Shaw for any worries he might once have caused her, for he takes great pains to make Magnus assert: "I defy you to make me more happy than our strangely innocent relations have already made me."

In his respect and admiration for his wife Shaw was always consistent so far as his public portrayal of her in his plays was concerned. He mirrors her again in the tidy housewife, Catherine of Braganza, the spouse of the philandering Charles II, in *In Good King Charles's Golden Days.* There seems to be little reason to doubt that Mrs. Shaw is again reflected in the perfect wife of a public man, Lady Chavender in *On the Rocks,* and that the conversation between her and Sir Arthur Chavender, the Prime Minister, at the end of the play on his political career represents the gist of many conversations between Bernard and Charlotte Shaw.

Another case of admitted self-identification by Shaw appears in Joey Percival, whom he calls "the leading young man" of *Misalliance.* In view of Mrs. Campbell's favorite alias for her inamorato, perhaps the name "Joey" alone would be almost enough of a clue. But Joey Percival is early described by his college friend Bentley as the "man with three fathers": "the regulation natural chap," "a tame philosopher" whom the first one kept in the house, and an Italian priest his mother always had about. When Frank Harris got Shaw to go over his manuscript, he elicited the confession that such a conception would never have occurred "if I had not had three fathers myself: my official father, the musician, and my maternal uncle." The musician, or "Italian priest," was of course George John Vandeleur Lee, the eccentric music master of Shaw's mother, who for some time boarded at the Shaw home in Dublin and whom she finally followed to London, always preserving the "strangely innocent relations" of Magnus and Orinthia. The maternal uncle was his Uncle Walter. These identifications Shaw confirms in his *Self Sketches*. In such ways are characters in fiction created.

Sometimes, however, the Shavian mask may match the face even in certain of its physical features, as in the already-cited case of Charteris, with his velvet jacket and cashmere trousers, and especially "the arrangement of his tawny hair, and of his moustaches and short beard." Many times when Shaw seems to be especially attracted to one of his male characters he will, if possible, give him the special property of hairness,[34] usually of some particular variety of red — in fact, his own face, with its contrast of pale skin and orange whiskers, was once described as resembling "an unskilfully poached egg." So Sidney Trefusis, the unsocial Socialist, not only is a vegetarian and a teetotaler, with all Shaw's ideas, philandering propensities, and a satanic grin, but also sports a conspicuous reddish-brown beard. So also Bluntschli, the Swiss soldier of fortune, is given a set of "short crisp bronze curls" and "clear quick blue eyes" to redeem his otherwise "undistinguished appearance" and to go along with his sense of humor, his quick wittedness, and his lack of illusions. Blanco Posnet, too, along with his previously cited Shavian ideas, is given "an upturned, red moustache" and an "arrangement of his hair in a crest on his brow."

Bishop Bridgenorth is even more easily recognized. "He is still a slim active man, spare of flesh . . . He has a delicate skin, fine hands, a salient nose with chin to match, a short beard which accentuates his sharp chin by bristling forward, clever humorous eyes, not without a glint of mischief in them, ready bright speech, and the ways of a successful man who is always interested in himself and generally rather well pleased with himself." When it is discovered that this ingratiating clergyman — the "preacher" again — is the raisonneur of the play, expressing Shaw's own liberal views on such themes as marriage and divorce, and his interest in Mahomet, one is not surprised to hear him admit that he is very much fonder of his wife than he is even of his salvation.

In *Heartbreak House* there is the whimsical but tragic Captain Shotover, "an ancient but still hardy man with an immense white beard." When he tells Ellie that he has "a wife somewhere in Jamaica: a black one . . . Unless she's dead," one immediately thinks of the "redhaired Irishman" with the pointed beard in *The Adventures of the Black Girl in Her Search for God,* who, after he has been taught nicer habits and a more refined language in which to express his ideas about Socialism and Creative Evolution, is finally married off to the Black Girl by Voltaire and helps her to bear some "charmingly coffee-colored" children. Shaw in *Heartbreak House,* then, has apparently made an amalgamation of himself and a sea-captain-turned-clergyman, who was the father of Lena Ashwell (Lady Simpson) and who, as Rattray tells us, was by Shaw's own admission the partial inspiration for his character. But the play as a whole, in West's opinion, betrays Shaw's pessimistic view of the inherent meaninglessness of life and the helplessness of trying to stand up against the capitalist and the efficient imperialist.

But perhaps John Tanner, with his alter ego, Don Juan Tenorio, is a fairer specimen of Shaw's Superman Present, particularly since the play which gives them being is the one in which Shaw first offered his full-fledged philosophy to a somewhat dubious world. Shaw pictures Tanner as "too young to be described simply as a big man with a beard . . . He has still some of the slimness of youth; but youthfulness is not the effect he aims at . . . and a certain high chested carriage of the shoulders, a lofty pose of the head, and the Olympian majesty with which a mane, or rather a huge wisp, of hazel colored hair is thrown back from an imposing brow, suggest Jupiter rather than Apollo. He is prodigiously fluent of speech, restless, excitable (mark the snorting nostril and the restless blue eye, just the thirty-secondth of an inch too wide open), possibly a little mad . . . A sensitive, susceptible, exaggerative, earnest man: a megalomaniac, who would be lost without a sense of humor." When Shaw's young protégé, Granville Barker, created the role of Tanner in 1905, he made up to be as like Shaw in the nineties as possible, but when Robert Loraine, another protégé, gave an even more successful production in New York later in the same year he refused to follow Barker's example. Shaw himself is authority for the statement that, externally at least, he had in mind as the model for Tanner his Socialist rival, Henry M. Hyndman, a down-the-line Marxist and the leader of the Democratic Federation. Consequently, in spite of Tanner's exemplification of most of Shaw's ideas on the Life Force, Socialism, Heaven and Hell, art, happiness, and so on, and his authorship of the notorious *Revolutionist's Handbook,* it is not safe to identify him in every detail with his skittish author. Still, Shaw's confession in the biographical sketch that he wrote for Harris in 1919 and reprinted in his *Self Sketches* makes the main identification conclusive. For in the final act in which the hero struggles in vain against marriage, there is, writes Shaw, "a poignantly sincere utterance which must have come from personal experience . . . Tanner, with all his extravagances, is first hand: Shaw would probably not deny it and would not be believed if he did."

It is essential, however, to discriminate rather carefully between Tanner and Don Juan, since the former presents only a broken mundane image of the advanced man, whereas the latter offers an other-world sublimation progressing in the direction of what may yet be. But neither Tanner nor Don Juan is a Superman. If people had only recognized this patent fact immediately, a good deal of confusion would have been avoided. Duffin, in his endeavor to interpret the title, *Man and Superman,* is perhaps the best example of this mix-up. Relatively early in his book he first grapples with the problem as follows: "Of several possible interpretations that may be thrust upon the title of the play, one is connected with Ann, who, as the huntress-Everywoman, is herself the Superman. The title means, 'Man and — Woman.' Or if Tanner is the Superman, Ann is then the super-Superman." This explication, however, apparently did not quite satisfy even its author, for seventy or so pages later he again attacks the problem thus: "in a less profound, a merely political sense, Tanner himself stands for the Superman, his chief claim to political distinction lying in his violently revolutionary instincts . . . Yet a third interpretation of the title points to 'Enery Straker — the superman of the future; a forecast more probable than pleasing, like the England of Mr Wells's book, *The Sleeper Awakes."*

Note that all these explanations are made without reference to the central scene in the play, the dream in hell. One might easily conclude that most of the critics have never read *Man and Superman;* they have merely seen it performed — and therefore, unless they were extraordinarily lucky, they saw it performed as it has been almost invariably performed: without the third act, and therefore mutilated, emasculated. And without the third act the title has no meaning.[35] It is not until the very end of Tanner's and Mendoza's mutual dream that the word Superman is mentioned; and it is used nowhere else in the play. The person who uses it, and explains it, rather inadequately, to the Statue, after Don Juan has left the scene, is the Devil. Though the conception makes some impression on the pliable Statue, it is Ana who really takes it to herself. To her demand, "Tell me: where can I find the Superman?" the Devil replies, "He is not yet created, Señora." The Statue's skeptical comment, "And never will be, probably," does not satisfy Ana, who exclaims, "Not yet created! Then my work is not yet done." She crosses herself devoutly and declares, "I believe in the Life to Come." And then she cries "to the universe," "A father — a father for the Superman!" The possible implications of this scene, together with Shaw's own generally overlooked explanation, have already been discussed in the analysis of Ann Whitefield as a pursuing woman. But, no matter whether Ana pursues Don Juan to heaven, there to make him the father of her Superchild, or whether, on a more terrestrial plane, Ann and Tanner are to become a couple of Supermanly parents, or whether, as Shaw himself suggested, Ana, as the Immortal

Woman, may yet bear the Superman to the Eternal Father, nothing can be clearer than that there is no Superman in the play itself. The Superman is still to come.

These conclusions are borne out by Shaw's prefatory comments on his play, even though his remarks on Tanner are not completely consistent. Treating the problem of sex in its relationship to the genius and to the ordinary person, Shaw writes, "what is true of the great man who incarnates the philosophic consciousness of life and the woman who incarnates its fecundity, is true in some degree of all geniuses and all women." The great works of art are accomplished "by people who are free of the otherwise universal dominion of the tyranny of sex." Thus, "When it comes to sex relations, the man of genius does not share the common man's danger of capture, nor the woman of genius the common woman's overwhelming specialization." According to this theory, Tanner can scarcely be a "man of genius," since he is too definitely and even happily captured by the end of the play, though he continues to insist that he is not a happy man. On the other hand, a few pages later, Shaw asserts that, contrary to the practice of most "romancers," who simply state that their heroes are men of extraordinary genius without producing any evidence to prove the claim, he himself has actually provided the proofs for his hero, since he has printed the latter's *Revolutionist's Handbook* as an appendix. Perhaps Tanner is to be regarded as a great man politically, but an ordinary man domestically.

At any rate, Tanner's political and moral radicalism and sharp-sightedness conflict throughout with his blindness as to Ann's real objective. He is also taken in like the rest in assuming that Violet Robinson is not married, though he praises her for her independence. Perhaps, however, he unconsciously foresees his fate from the outset, since on his first appearance he ironically remarks, apropos of his guardianship of Ann, "I might as well be her husband." For a man with such advanced ideas about the Life Force and the creative urge in woman, he is of course comically obtuse as to the real state of affairs. Yet, as he reviews his youthful biography to Ann, it is clear that he was once a romancer himself, with the usual conceptions of duties and ideals, which her conduct helped him to get rid of as he grew up into the present reformer and iconoclast. By the time of the play he has become a sort of reincarnation of Sidney Trefusis, pursued by a devouring woman, wealthy but radically Socialistic, realistic in most matters, and, like Andrew Undershaft, "unashamed" — as he himself boasts. At the final curtain, however, subordinating the power of the individual will, which Shaw has always exalted so high, to the "world's will," which is more powerful than our own, Tanner is prepared to dwindle into a husband. Nevertheless, one would give a great deal to be able to look in on the household ten years later to see what has come of such a mating.

Don Juan is — philosophically if not comically — more interesting. Shaw's intentions as to the relationship between his duo of heroes come out much more clearly in his stage directions describing Juan than any actor could bring them out in his impersonation. For Juan has a "more critical, fastidious, handsome face, paler and colder, without Tanner's impetuous credulity and enthusiasm, and without a touch of his modern plutocratic vulgarity." Since Juan does not consider himself one of the wicked, he is bored with hell, in which the wicked are quite comfortable, since it was made for them. In fact, he cannot understand why he is there at all, since in life he "repudiated all duty, trampled honor underfoot, and laughed at justice." Heaven or hell, he concludes, is really only an accident, since if the Statue's foot had not slipped he would have killed Juan instead of the other way round, and their positions would now be reversed. The Devil soon becomes greatly disappointed in Juan, of whom he had expected so much, for the new recruit turns out to be a "cold selfish egoist" and a social failure, a man with too much intellect and too little heart. Juan's decision to leave hell, "the home of the unreal and of the seekers for happiness," for heaven, "the home of the masters of reality" (earth being "the home of the slaves of reality"), confirms the Devil's estimate. Juan's ambition to spend the rest of his life in contemplation — particularly in the contemplation of life, which would result in life contemplating itself — is too metaphysical for the Devil to understand.

So the characters are plunged into the gigantic central "discussion" of what Shaw himself labels his "drama of ideas." What the Life Force needs, finding itself enmeshed in the struggle between the body and the mind, is a brain to use as its instrument. Though there is an element of contradiction between Shaw's own theory of idealism and Juan's eloquent exposition of the power of an idea, Shaw tries to resolve it by having Juan assert, "But I am not now defending the illusory forms the great ideas take," and then comes to another of his fundamental precepts: that man "can only be enslaved whilst he is spiritually weak enough to listen to reason." As Shaw had preached in *The Quintessence,* the Will, the instinct, the intuition, the imagination are as far beyond reason as reason is beyond faith. Although the specialization of the sexes, says Juan, has let man's "superfluous energy" go to "his brain and his muscle," the true goal of the Life Force is brains, not beauty or physical perfection. The objective is "the philosophic man." Man has attempted to "make himself something more than the mere instrument of Woman's purpose." Though the Life Force itself is stupid and blundering, it will eventually win over death. That "raw force" will be built up "into higher and higher individuals, the ideal individual being omnipotent, omniscient, infallible, and withal completely, unilludedly self-conscious: in short, a god." Yes, Juan rhapsodizes, "The great central purpose of breeding the race, ay, breeding it to heights now deemed superhuman: that purpose which is now hidden in a mephitic cloud of love and romance and prudery and fastidiousness, will break through into clear sunlight as a purpose no longer to be confused with the gratification of personal fancies, the impossible realization of boys' and girls' dreams of bliss, or the need of older people for companionship or money." Nature has no morality, and Nature is a manifestation of the Life Force. Thus, although there seems to have been no essential progress up to the present, the philosopher's brain is working toward it, seeking a means of guiding Nature more quickly to the goal.

Then and only then, after Juan has expounded his creed of the Life Force to the last detail and answered — to Shaw's satisfaction, at least — all of the audience's questions about it, is Juan apotheosized to heaven, and the Devil left to lament gloomily: "His going is a political defeat. I cannot keep these Life Worshippers: they all go." And here is the point — the sole point — where the idea of the Superman is introduced, an idea, as the Devil says, "as old as Prometheus," recently raked up again by a "confirmed Life Force worshipper," a German Polish madman named Nietzsche, and also illustrated by a musician named Wagner, who "once drifted into Life Force worship, and invented a Superman called Siegfried." But, as the Devil points out, Wagner was sensible enough to repent afterwards. Nietzsche, however, went to heaven.

However, as the Devil and the Statue take their places on the grave trap in the stage and begin to descend slowly on it into the abyss, lighted up by red fire, Ana remains behind, crying to the universe for a father of the Superman who is to come.

## 3. Superman Future

Shaw's prophetic plays in which he has been concerned with the future of life and not merely with the future of politics, as in *The Apple Cart,* are three in number — *Back to Methuselah, The Simpleton of the Unexpected Isles,* and *Farfetched Fables.* But whereas the first, as Shaw himself proclaimed, was written in order to clarify and extend the philosophy of *Man and Superman,* there is some question as to whether *The Simpleton* should be taken simply as a postscript to *Methuselah,* as *Farfetched Fables* is, or as a partial retraction of it. For, except for a generalized optimism in the face of present failure in the middle play, there is no similarity in the pictures of the new Superrace in the two larger works. In *Man and Superman* Shaw had expressed his opinion that the millennium might be hastened by using the mind of man as a tool in the service of the Life Force. So, in *The Thing Happens,* Mrs. Lutestring and Archbishop Haslam, the first-discovered of the longlivers, although they have attained their longevity unconsciously (apparently as a result of the subterranean activities of the Will), decide consciously that it is their duty to the race to marry, particularly since their children conceived in matings with ordinary shortlivers have all died. Presumably, then, longlivers produce longlivers, who are essential in the development of a perfect Superman. It might be noted, incidentally, that even in this momentous match it is the woman — or Superwoman — who takes the initiative in making the proposal.

But in *The Simpleton* the conscious experimentation in the direction of a Superrace proves to be an utter failure. Mrs. Lutestring in the earlier play had referred to the new taste of women and story writers in the twenty-second century for "men with golden complexions," and even Burge-Lubin was familiar with "a very interesting book by the librarian of the Biological Society suggesting that the future of the world lies with the Mulatto." In *The Simpleton* the six leading adult characters — four Englishmen, Mr. and Mrs. Hyering, Sir Charles and Lady Farwaters; and the oriental priest and priestess, Pra and Prola — decide to get together for a little eugenic experiment in miscegenation. As Sir Charles explains it to the amazed and startled Iddy Hammingtap, "Its object was to try out the result of a biological blend of the flesh and spirit of the west with the flesh and spirit of the east. We formed a family of six parents." Sir Charles is forced to admit, however, that the "result has been a little disappointing from the point of view of numbers; but we have produced four children, two of each sex, and educated them in the most enlightened manner we were capable of." These four Superchildren, aged between seventeen and twenty, are beautiful physical specimens, with varying colors of hair and complexion, but, confesses Pra, "I am convinced that there is something lacking in the constitution of the children." Though they have been very carefully fed on the most scientific of diets, and "though they have artistic consciences, and would rather die than do anything ugly or vulgar or common, they have not between the whole four of them a scrap of moral conscience." Lady Farwaters continues the exposition, explaining that from their babyhood these children with "the east in their brains and the west in their blood" and "at the same time the east in their blood and the west in their brains," loved to invent fairy tales, "until a fairyland was built up, with laws and religious rituals, and finally a great institution which they called the Superfamily." And now Iddy, the simple-minded, baby-faced young English clergyman, is offered the chance to join this Superfamily as a mate not only to Vashti and Maya but, as Pra frankly informs him, to "all the ladies here." Iddy, though a little shocked, thinks, "Oh, how nice and comfortable that would be! They would be mothers to me," and accepts.

But, again, eugenics betrays the amateur geneticist. Several years later Pra sums up the results as follows: "Our dream of founding a millennial world culture: the dream which united Pra and Prola as you first knew them, and then united us all six, has ended in a single little household with four children, wonderful and beautiful, but sterile. When we had to find a husband for the blossoming girls, only one man was found capable of merging himself in the unity of the family: a man fed on air from his childhood.

And how has this paragon turned out? An impotent simpleton." Waiving the point of how he knows whether it is the girls who are sterile or Iddy who is impotent, or both, it is nevertheless true that the whole British empire has been brought to the brink of civil war by the leaking out of the news of the experiment. Only the arrival of the Angel of Judgment Day intervenes, after the children have expressed their various jingoistic and totalitarian ideas, admit that they have no minds or imaginations of their own, only wish to worship Prola and put all their burdens on her, and then, with their usual capriciousness, decide to rebel against her. So the four pseudo-Superchildren — who, as Mrs. Hyering says, "wern't born fools: we made fools of them" — are the first to vanish when heaven delivers its verdict. Only the memory of the love of Maya remains. They were, as Shaw explains in his preface, only "four lovely phantasms who embody all the artistic, romantic, and military ideals of our cultural suburbs."

Still Shaw will not let his public despair because of the fiasco of this fantastic eugenic experiment, for he leaves Pra and Prola alone on the stage to talk the situation over. To Pra's prophecy that "The coming race will not be like them," Prola replies with the assurance that she and he have not been total failures: "Women will never let go their hold on life . . . this is a world of miracles." If they continue to strive, there will always be unexpected changes, for the "Unexpected Isles are the whole world." They agree that the "fountain of life" is within the Woman, but that she has given the key of it to the Man. They need one another, and Life needs them both. "All hail, then," cries Pra, "the life to come!" And Prola echoes, "All Hail. Let it come."

Presumably it has come in the last two parts of *Methuselah,* and *The Simpleton* can be written off simply as the record of one of the abortive efforts of the Life Force between the twentieth and the twenty-second centuries, when the first longliver appears. There have, of course, been similar miscarriages before, even if they were not quite so spectacular. In *In the Beginning* Cain has supermanly aspirations. But when, "twirling his mustache," he reminds his mother, "There is something higher than man. There is hero and superman," Eve scornfully deflates him with, "You are no superman: you are Anti-Man." And she adds that when he dies, men will say, "He was a great warrior; but it would have been better for the world if he had never been born." What Cain really is, of course, is a sort of primitive Darwinian, preaching the survival of the fittest through war. He is therefore the natural object of Shaw's evolutionary antipathy.

Conrad in *The Gospel of the Brothers Barnabas* has a vision of what we might call the "Meta-Man." In reply to Lubin's question about a "scientific opposition" to his theory of Creative Evolution, Conrad admits: "Well, some authorities hold that the human race is a failure, and that a new form of life, better adapted to high civilization, will supersede us as we have superseded the ape and the elephant." When Burge queries wisely, "The superman, eh?" Conrad brings him up short with, "No. Some being quite different from us . . . The force behind evolution, call it what you will, is determined to solve the problem of civilization; and if it cannot do it through us, it will produce more capable agents."

To judge from the rest of the play and its voluminous preface, however, Shaw himself seems to have decided in favor of an evolutionary development of Man into Superiorman rather than the spontaneous manifestation of a completely new type of being. At least, as Lilith promises at the end of the cycle, "I will not supersede them until they have forded this last stream that lies between flesh and spirit, and disentangled their life from the matter that has always mocked it." Thus, in *The Thing Happens,* the chief feature that differentiates Mrs. Lutestring and Archbishop Haslam from their more mortal associates is the air of utter self-possession and awful gravity that invests them. In *Tragedy of an Elderly Gentleman,* the longlivers are unyouthful, severe, and determined. They have no sense of humor, and no romance. They cannot understand figurative speech or sentimental feelings. Only the "primaries" (that is, those still in their first century) ever sleep. And they all have their electrical emanations in varying degrees. But they are all still recognizably human.

Finally, in *As Far As Thought Can Reach,* the young people are handsome and graceful, though they "neither romp nor hug in our manner." The He-Ancient and the She-Ancient, too, have changed in no basic respects, though both are marked with the stigmata of intense and profound thought. Clothed only in a kind of linen kilt, the man "seems to be in the prime of life; and his eyes and mouth shew no signs of age." But his face is inscribed with "a network of lines, varying from furrows to hairbreadth reticulations, as if Time had worked over every inch of it incessantly through whole geologic periods." He is, moreover, bald — completely hairless except for his eyelashes. And his power of concentration on what is within is so tremendous that he walks into other people without knowing they are there. Most of the Ancients, indeed, have forgotten how to speak. Thinking is all they care about. The She-Ancient is his proper counterpart, wearing only a perfunctory ceremonial robe and being "equally bald, and equally without sexual charm, but intensely interesting and rather terrifying." Only her voice betrays her sex, for "her breasts are manly, and her figure otherwise not very different." Austerity, not comfort, marks the life of these sublimated Struldbrugs. As the He-Ancient blasts the disrespectful youth, Strephon: "Infant, one moment of the ecstasy of life as we live it would strike you dead." As Duffin reminds us, too, the Ancients (though not the young people) have in a most un-Shavian fashion lost all sense of humor, "which was invented in the Garden of Eden, and which Conrad Barnabas admitted might lubricate the wheels of Creative Evolution." In this respect the She-Ancient is especially deficient, and thus marks a rather surprising change in the female sex, since "It is noteworthy that while Eve in Part I was Adam's superior in nearly every way (and she remains so in the Dream-Epilogue), in the latest age this order is reversed. The youths are generally better stuff than the maidens, and while the He-Ancient is entirely admirable, the She-Ancient is made positively unpleasant." In the concentrated sobriety of the He-Ancient, in fact, Blanche Patch goes even further than Duffin, for she sees in the character a reflection of the aged G.B.S. himself, who, she believes, never "had a thoroughly frivolous afternoon" and even in his humanitarianism displayed no real humanity.

In only one way does Shaw suggest that these citizens of the thirty-second millennium differ essentially and externally from mankind as we know it (though "citizens" is probably not the appropriate word, since, according to Marxian prophecy, in this utopia the state seems to have withered away, all luxuries have been eliminated, only elementary necessities are produced, and life has become simple and idyllic). Acis, one of the young folks, informs the Newly Born that the Ancients eventually get tired of life (which they cannot lose unless they meet an unavoidable accident); or, at least, they weary of living the same life. Consequently, by the mere exercise of their powerful wills, they change themselves physically in wonderful ways. Though the audience has to take this surprisingly frivolous picture on faith, the Ancients sometimes grow extra heads, or arms, or legs, or anything that may appeal to them. The power of mind over matter is infinite.

Shaw's whole conception of evolution, as he makes abundantly clear in his preface, is Lamarckian, and anti-Darwinian. Mutations occur because of an inner, though perhaps unconscious, desire on the part of the multitudinous forms of life to change from what they are. And these purposeful changes in the individual are conveyed in the form of tendencies and inclinations to his descendants. In other words, Shaw aligns himself solidly with the Vitalists. To him there is no question but that acquired characteristics are inherited. Here is another reason why he is convinced that Soviet Russia is a more advanced country than the West. For Soviet Russia has advanced and exalted Professor Trofim Lysenko, Director of the Institute of Selection and Genetics, with his theories of vernalization and environmentalism as opposed to Mendelian inheritance, until he stands at the head of the Communist scientific hierarchy.[36] As Shaw has pointed out in a recent article, debating with such American biologists as Nobel Prize winner, Professor H. J. Muller, Lysenko has merely applied and activated the theories that Shaw and other Creative Evolutionists have been preaching all along. In these matters, as even Professor C. E. M. Joad in *G.B.S. 90* admits, Shaw's "thought is remarkably coherent and the doctrine of Creative Evolution informs and unifies his doctrines on every other topic." Shaw has been influenced, it is true, by Samuel Butler, Henri Bergson, and S. Alexander (in

*Space, Time, and Deity*), as well as Lamarck (not to mention Darwin himself, whom Shaw does not regard as actually a complete "Darwinian"), but he has evolved a consistent scientific, social, and political system from all these elements.

The last word is given to Lilith — a person who, as Shaw confessed to Pearson, "wasn't anybody, and there was no character to express," delivering a speech which was "ground out as pure argument." And Lilith, the apparent personification of the Life Force, is herself uncertain as to the future. "Is this enough; or must I labor again?" she soliloquizes. "Shall I bring forth something that will sweep them away and make an end of them as they have swept away the beasts of the garden, and made an end of the crawling things and the flying things and of all them that refuse to live forever?"[37] She does not know. But she does know, "Of Life there is no end." Perhaps, eons away, Life will produce a real Superman. But never, in *Tragedy of an Elderly Gentleman* and *As Far As Thought Can Reach,* does Shaw call any of his characters Supermen.

There are no real Supermen in any of Shaw's plays, with one possible, but dubious, exception.

Shortly before his death, as the fifty-second of his published plays, Shaw perpetrated the last of his farces-of-ideas, the heavily beprefaced *Farfetched Fables,* a sort of perverted extension of *Back to Methuselah* and a final reiteration of most of his earlier leading ideas on almost every subject. Here, in the "Sixth and Last Fable," he at last achieved the goal which he and Creative Evolution had been seeking all his life.

The scene is on the Isle of Wight, in a Sixth Form school building, which in the previous fables has been metamorphosed from an Anthropometric Laboratory, through an office of the Diet Commissioners, into a Genetic Institute. And at last the ambition which has, consciously or unconsciously, according to Shaw, actuated life for all its life has been realized: some men have got rid of their bodies and have evolved into pure thought. This state has been reached by the preliminary adoption of a new diet of air and water, following the discovery that, after all, vegetarianism itself (remember that G.B.S. was himself a vegetarian) was producing nothing but a restless, pugnacious race of supergorillas rather than supermen. Nevertheless, because the old hunger and thirst for bread, beer, and onions became transformed into a thirst for knowledge of nature and pure power over it, the "supergorilla became the soldier and servant of Creative Evolution." The will and the desire of the Hermaphrodite in the Genetic Institute, expressed in his intense and unceasing prayer for deliverance from his body, eventuates in the evolution of a race of supermen whom Shaw calls "the disembodied."

Reincarnated as the female Teacher in the Sixth Form school room, lecturing to a group of five obstreperous but inquisitive youths and maidens, who receive numbers but no names in the expressionist fashion, G.B.S. distils his theory that these "Disembodied Bodies still exist as Thought Vortexes, and are penetrating our thick skulls in their continual pursuit of knowledge and power, since they need our hands and brains still as tools in that pursuit." "What," the Teacher asks, "is an immortal soul but a disembodied thought?"

In *As Far As Thought Can Reach* Shaw had apparently been stumped by the problem of representing a disembodied thought on stage. At the age of ninety-three he solved the problem, which after all was ridiculously simple. "A youth, clothed in feathers like a bird, appears suddenly," read the stage directions, and announces that he is the word made flesh. His name is Raphael, although the cheeky Youth 3 prefers to call him a Cockyolly Bird. When even the Teacher is somewhat skeptical of Raphael's explanation of his manifestation, the bird-man inquires blandly, "Why not? Evolution can go backwards as well as forwards. If the body can become a vortex, the vortex can also become a body." Therefore, explains Raphael, restraining his magnetic field so that it will not harm these soft earth-dwellers, he has incarnated himself. He is seeking experience. Curiosity motivates the disembodied even more than it does the embodied. The physical passions of man have been replaced by "intellectual passion, mathematical passion, passion for discovery and exploration: the mightiest of all the passions."

And with this short-lived, tantalizing glimpse into the brave new world which he inhabits, Shaw's only stage specimen of the perfected though somewhat caricatured superman vanishes, in spite of the protesting yells of the students. The Teacher, taking advantage of the pedagogical opening afforded by the whole unorthodox manifestation, thereupon assigns the Book of Job for the next lesson as an example of how even the old god who was once supposed to have made the universe "crushed Job by shewing that he could put ten times as many unanswerable questions to Job as Job could put to him."

One of the questions that a twentieth-century Job might like to pose G.B.S. with might well run like this: Why, if an immortal soul is but a disembodied thought, and since, by implication, men do possess immortal souls (yet Blanche Patch states that Shaw actually regarded the idea of personal immortality as an "unimaginable horror" and believed that the Life Force abandons our bodies at the moment of death), does not mankind already achieve Supermanhood simply through the operation of death, which can liberate the soul from the body for its eternity of contemplation much more expeditiously than all the groping best intentions of the Life Force?

The culminating instance of Shaw's writing himself concretely into his work occurs in *Back to Methuselah*. Part IV, entitled *Tragedy of an Elderly Gentleman,* is all about Joseph Popham Bolge Bluebin Barlow, O.M., an elderly gentleman who has come back from Baghdad, the new capital of the British empire, "on a pious pilgrimage to one of the numerous lands of my fathers," that is, to Ireland, where the longlivers have withdrawn from the rest of the world to set up their new civilization.

First, there is nothing particularly suspicious about the man, in spite of his white beard and the reminiscence of Joey in his name. But when the Elderly Gentleman suddenly begins to utter ideas which seem to be foreign to his originally bourgeois and conformist character, the alert listener begins to prick up his ears. He hears the Elderly Gentleman insist that he is not an Agnostic, that he is not "the dust of the ground," but that he is "a living soul." As he grows bolder under the influence of his second nurse, Zoo, but still remains rather pompously conceited in the expression of his opinions, we learn that he "is not interested in the chemicals and the microbes," but rather in the "divine spark," "the breath of life itself." He has learnt to "fear the discoveries we owe to science" when these discoveries discard the truths of religion and reject the belief in a soul. When she even laughs at some of his most "advanced" ideas, he becomes more and more disturbed. On her pointing out that so far during all the time he has been in Galway he has been asked questions, but has asked none, he acknowledges that this questioning has almost driven him mad, and continues: "Do you see my white hair? It was hardly grey when I landed: there were patches of its original auburn still distinctly discernible." As the curtain goes down on the first act of the play, the Elderly Gentleman follows Zoo in despair, his re-education well under way.

The pathetic fix of the Elderly Gentleman increases as his education continues and he receives jolt after jolt of disillusionment as to the society in which he has been living and which he has regarded as the apex of civilization. He finally implores the Oracle, who has carefully remained veiled, to allow him to stay in her land. She tries to dissuade him by reminding him that if he does he will die of discouragement. With clear vision and great dignity he replies, "If I go back I shall die of disgust and despair. I take the nobler risk." Again she warns him that he is not prepared to live there, but he insists that he knows the risk: "It is the meaning of life, not of death, that makes banishment so terrible to me."

And so, with the pity of a Superiorwoman of one hundred and seventy years of age on a shortliver who only has ambitions to become a Superman, she "offers him her hands. He grasps them and raises himself a little by clinging to her. She looks steadily into his face. He stiffens; a little convulsion shakes him; his grasp relaxes; and he falls dead." The electrical emanation from her powerful mental field has been more than he can bear. The pythoness comments, looking down at the body, "Poor shortlived thing! What else could I do for you?" It has, indeed, been a worthy, almost a majestic, death that the Elderly Gentleman has at last attained.

But does it imply that George Bernard Shaw admits that even he could not sustain life in the intense, rarefied atmosphere of purified thought that he has foreseen as culminating the immeasurable processes of Creative Evolution and the self-realization of the Life Force? If so, it is still a generous death suffered in the greatest of causes — the emancipation of man from the purely material bonds which in the past have prevented the spiritual progress of which he is, we hope, capable.[38]

# APPENDIX: WHAT'S IN A NAME [39]

Shaw was always fond of insisting that he was a "classical" playwright and that his plays belonged in the "classical" tradition — to the confusion of the critics who accused him of being not only an iconoclast and a destroyer of all conventions, but also — even worse — an inept and bungling dramatist who could not write real "plays" at all. The latter school of criticism, however, is by this time fighting only a sporadic rear-guard action, since by the mid-twentieth century the theater itself has rendered the verdict by the way in which it has kept at least a dozen of Shaw's plays alive and kicking on the active stage after most of the works of his contemporaries and predecessors — with the exception of Shakespeare — have been consigned to the private study and the public library shelf.

The accuracy with which Shaw selected his term can be attested in several ways. Obviously his plays are now "classic" in the sense that so many of them have become part of the standard repertory, and that he himself is acknowledged as the leading English playwright of his generation — and one of the very few who will be remembered non-academically by future generations. He has also adhered to the ancient and "classical" theory of comedy, which holds that the object of the genre is to reform society's manners, morals, and institutions, and that this reform is to be accomplished — not, as the sentimentalists of the eighteenth century believed, by setting up models and patterns of refined and virtuous behavior for the imitation of the playgoer — but by the use of laughter and satire as reformatory instruments.

Even more specifically, however, it can be maintained that, from several viewpoints, Shaw's plays can be appropriately described as "comedies of humors," and that therefore they can take their position naturally in a tradition that is not only three or four centuries old in its modern European form but also in some ways goes straight back to the theater of the Greeks and Romans. The "humors" technique of characterization (which of course differs from, but does not exclude, the use of "humor" as a means of comic entertainment) extends all the way from Menander and Aristophanes, through Plautus and Terence, to Ben Jonson, Molière, Sheridan, the farcical Adelphi "screamers" of the early nineteenth century, and *Of Thee I Sing*. The tracing in of character by broad and unmistakable strokes, the use of dominating traits and motives, the dependence on types and categories, even the application or invention of ludicrously appropriate — even if highly artificial — names to act as short cuts to the essence of the characters, all announce themselves conspicuously and unabashedly in the plays of Bernard Shaw.

The story of what's in a name — especially a Shavian name — is a titillating and often a riddlesome one. Probably no serious modern author — at least since the times of Dickens and Thackeray — has gone to such extremes in placing the initial burden of his characterization on "humors" names as has Shaw. Sometimes these names are so outrageously farcical and grotesque that one is almost as much ashamed of oneself for laughing at them as was Shaw when, in a subtitle, he apologetically described his one-acter, *The Fascinating Foundling,* as "A Disgrace to the Author." Sometimes they have subtler overtones, which may be missed by the tone-deaf listener. At other times they demand a knowledge of certain kinds of literary or historical information before the proper association can be established. Guffawing, punning, alluding, or delicately hinting, however, these names are an essential part of the Shavian technique of characterization.

A parallel to the most obvious and self-explanatory of these slapstick names may perhaps be found in the farces, the pantomimes, the music hall revues, and even the Gilbert and Sullivan operas which Shaw, like other Britons, was in the custom of attending since his youth. It is noteworthy, indeed, that the habit of using such designations does not begin to set in until he begins to write plays of his own. It is scarcely noticeable at all in the novels. Consequently, when in the last of these, *An Unsocial Socialist,* Sidney (after Sidney Webb?) Trefusis in his rustic disguise takes the name of Jeff Smilash, which he ultimately explains as "a compound of the words smile and eyelash. A smile suggests good humour; eyelashes soften the expression and are the only features that never blemish a face," the reader is struck by the introduction of a new type of nomenclature, which is followed up in Shaw's first play, *Widowers' Houses,* with such names as Lickcheese, the miserable, servile rent-collector, whose humility turns to cheap arrogance and self-assertion when by a little sharp practice he finds a way to make some money of his own. On a subtler plane the name of his employer, Sartorius, suggests to those who are familiar with Carlyle that its owner is well-tailored, imposing, and important-looking, as indeed he is. And Cokane, Trench's indigent relative, companion, and secretary, though not personally addicted to cocaine, is fidgety, touchy, and essentially dull-minded, feeling that it is really beneath the dignity of a "gentleman" like himself to work, and behaving generally as if the idleness and luxury of the fabulous land of Cockaigne were his natural perquisites.

Onomatopoeic and pictorial names have a considerable appeal to Shaw. When the Orderly in *Press Cuttings* announces Mrs. Banger, the secretary to the Anti-Suffraget League, to Balsquith, the latter comments, "Curious that quiet people always seem to have violent names," whereupon the Orderly impudently corrects him, "Not much quiet about her, sir." Strega Thundridge, "the female Paderewski" of *The Music-Cure,* pounds away deafeningly at Liszt's transcription of Schubert's "Erl König," Chopin's "Polonaise in A Flat," and the bass of the final wedding march; in view of her successful pursuit of the pretty young Lord Reginald Fitzambey, it is particularly appropriate that she be named Strega, since *striga* is the Latin word for a witch who specializes in attacking children. Viscount Barking in *On the Rocks,* with his powerful build and loud voice, suits his words and his actions to his name. The mere mention of the name of Lady Gushing, president of the Titled Ladies' League of Social Service in *The Simpleton,* is sure to bring a laugh. Lady Utterword is described in *Heartbreak House* as "precipitate in speech and action," just as her husband's hasty disposition is echoed in his Christian name, Hastings. The "illustrious predecessor" of the Envoy in *Tragedy of an Elderly Gentleman* and former leader of the Potterbill party against the Rotterjacks, through his name, Sir Fuller Eastwind, gives the Oracle a classic opportunity to utter a prophecy which his flatulence twists to his own political purposes. Sir Broadfoot Basham is Chief Commissioner of Police in *On the Rocks;* and as for Sir Dexter Rightside in the same play — well, "you know what a regular old Diehard he is." And Admiral Hotspot is a back-slapper and fire-eater, much like General Sandstone ("Old Red") in *Press Cuttings.* As for Adolf Hitler, Shaw could not possibly have resisted a chance to dub such a person Ernest Battler.

Sir Ruthless Bonehead, Egregious Professor of Mechanistic Biology to the Rockefeller Foundation, is merely mentioned on Judgment Day in *The Simpleton,* but Sir Ralph

Bloomfield Bonington, a highly respected doctor of similar proclivities and a head "like a tall and slender egg," plays a role of some importance in *The Doctor's Dilemma*. Sir Cardonius Boshington is the Lord Chancellor in *The Fascinating Foundling,* and President Bossfield of the U.S.A. in *The Apple Cart* is described as "that booby bull-roarer." Lord Augustus Highcastle, who does his bit in World War I, is described as "a distinguished member of the governing class," who never forgets his august birth and high position. In *Too True To Be Good,* Colonel Tallboys, "every inch a commanding officer," who "won his cross as a company-officer, and has never looked back since," is measured against Private Napoleon Alexander Trotsky Meek, whose antithetical Christian names and surname help to characterize him as Shaw's own favorite friend and admiration, Lawrence of Arabia, who later actually changed his name to Shaw — because, according to Patch, a clergyman caller once took him for Shaw's nephew. Almost every detail of this loving caricature of Lawrence is authentic — from his insignificant, unsoldierly appearance, his modest omniscience and quick-wittedness, his hiding of his identity and his voluntary shifting of rank from colonel to private, and his expertness in blowing up trains and railroad bridges with mines, down to the motorcycle, a gift from the Shaws, which ironically brought him to his death.

Alf Doolittle, until his appointment to the philosophical lectureship, has always got away with as little work as possible. England, symbolized by Captain Shotover and his Heartbreak House, has been the scene of many previous battles as well as the air raid which ends the play. The Russophile young man in *Misalliance* who finally reveals his real name to be Julius Baker is first called Gunner by Tarleton because he is found carrying a revolver; and the romantic Lord Summerhays who rebukes him might perhaps better have spelled his name Summerhaze. Hector Hushabye has lulled himself and many others to sleep with his tales of derring-do. Sir Charles and Lady Farwaters find themselves in waters far away from Old England in *The Simpleton,* and Hugo Hyering becomes the political secretary to the Unexpected Isles. The Rev. Phosphor Hammingtap (i.e., Iddy, short for Idiot), who has been fed on a special diet of nitrates, explains both that his first name came from Phosphorus, the name of the Morning Star, and that the original family name had been Hummingtop, which was changed by his grandfather when the later was at Oxford. Certainly Iddy's general behavior is dizzy enough to deserve the older form of the name. In *Overruled* Sibthorpe Juno's name sounds "like something to drink," Gregory Lunn's "sounds like a powder," and Mrs. Seraphita Lunn is known as Sally at home. Not only does the title of the Duke of Domesday go back to the Domesday Book, but he and Domesday Towers are now on the brink of financial doom. The letters of Patricia Smith to Alastair Fitzfassenden in *The Millionairess* are all signed "Polly Seedystockings," presumably as a hint "that she wants him to buy her another dozen." Old Tim Goodenough is the lorry driver in the same play, and Mr. Superflew, the middleman, is specifically attacked by Epifania as "superfluous." The American millionaire in *Pygmalion,* Ezra D. Wannafeller, is obviously a composite of Rockefeller and Wanamaker. Aurora Bompas in *How He Lied to Her Husband* is the (somewhat dimming) light of Henry Apjohn's life; and both of these unromantic surnames contribute to the theme of disillusionment in the play. Valentine is the philandering dentist who gets captured in *You Never Can Tell.* And there are all the Buoyants in *Buoyant Billions.*

The point of most of these names depends largely on a pun or a play on words of some sort. Such concealed hints of character are also tucked away, for example, in at least three of the names in *Candida*. Candida herself (a name, according to Patch, "borrowed from an Italian lady who became a Marchioness") is — superficially at least — frank, open, honest, immaculate; as her husband says, "I thought of your goodness — your purity. That is what I confide in." Candida's Philistine father, Burgess, is, to his own mind at any rate, a prime representative of the British freeman, a bourgeois citizen of the most valuable type. As for Morell, there is some reason, in view of his speeches, for thinking that his name might well be pronounced "moral." Similarly, the name of Count O'Dowda in *Fanny's First Play* should perhaps be pronounced "O'Dowdy" since he dresses in an "obsolete costume" which, though it possesses a "studied elegance," is a hundred years out of date.

Old Crampton in *You Never Can Tell* is cramped and sour in nature. Dr. Paramore in *The Philanderer* is distinguished by his self-love, and so Sylvia remarks, "I should like papa to live for ever just to take the conceit out of Paramore." Lop off the suffix from the name Bluntschli in *Arms and the Man,* and the bluff, realistic character of the captain emerges. In *The Devil's Disciple* Dick Dudgeon has been living his life in a high state of what the dictionary describes as "a feeling of offence, indignation, or anger"; and there is certainly a touch of swinishness in the character of Major Swindon. Until Captain Brassbound meets Lady Cicely, his soul has obviously been choked in fettering bonds. Cutler Walpole in *The Doctor's Dilemma* is described by Sir Patrick as "a clever operator, . . . though he's only one of your chloroform surgeons"; and his great prosperity is due to the skilful knife with which he cuts and snips away at the useless organs of the human body. Dr. Blenkinsop's excessive humility and apologeticalness, on the other hand, make him something of a milksop. Nor would I put it beyond Shaw to have had thoughts of a hot kiss in mind when he named his dedicated philanderer in *Getting Married* Hotchkiss.

The robust, energetic Broadbent, who becomes an expatriate John Bull, introduces himself to Tim Haffigan by saying, "My name is Broadbent. If my name were Breitstein, and I had a hooked nose and a house in Park Lane, I should carry a Union Jack handkerchief and a penny trumpet, . . . and clamor for the destruction of the last remnants of national liberty — " and goes on to describe himself as a sound and thorough English Liberal. The generic name of the Newcomer in *Geneva* — like the Widow, the Commissar, etc. — is self-explanatory.

Sometimes Shaw in his philosophy of nomenclature proceeds by a system of comic reversal or transferral. Thus Sally Lunn should really be Mrs. Juno, since she is tall, imposing, and handsome — in fine, as she herself complacently admits, "rather a fine figure of a woman." Lady Cicely thinks that Felix Drinkwater is such a nice, respectable name, but Brassbound informs her that his mate is better known as "Brandyfaced Jack." Violet Robinson is anything but a violet born to blush unseen, and Leo Bridgenorth, a woman of the restless, fragile, but predatory type, is given the name of a male lion. And either the names or the roles of Boss Mangan and Mazzini Dunn should — strictly speaking — be reversed, since Mangan, the entrepreneur, has the name of the nineteenth century Irish romantic and patriotic poet, and Mazzini, his managing and operating agent, named after the Italian revolutionary leader, should never, according to his daughter, have been in business, since both his parents were poets who, as friends of Mazzini, gave their son not only the latter's name but also only "the noblest ideas."

A considerable number of Shaw's names, like the preceding pair, require special annotation or elucidation. As Shaw himself, commenting on the rapid disappearance from public memory of such once-famous names as Balfour, Walkley, and Cannan, informed Winsten, "I've been asked to write a key to my plays because I introduce so many people who were household names in my time, when the play was written, and they are now completely forgotten." Unfortunately this key was never provided, so speculation is still in order.

Thus the insipidity of Mrs. Warren's artist-architect friend Praed may have been intended to suggest a contrast with the light, pointed occasional verse of W. M. Praed. The Christian name of Dr. Colenso Ridgeon, who is otherwise modeled on Shaw's famous doctor friend, Sir Almroth Wright, is certainly due to the author's admiration for the celebrated liberal Anglican bishop of Natal, John William Colenso, whose views on polygamy, eternal punishment, and the traditional interpretation of the Pentateuch so fluttered the orthodox dovecotes in the third quarter of the nineteenth century. Shaw ascribes the lines in Sir Colenso's face to "overwork and restless skepticism, perhaps partly of curiosity and appetite, rather than that of age." Similarly, Bentley Summerhays, the big-headed young intellectual of *Misalliance,* is obviously supposed to be a spiritual descendant of the great but stubbornly perverse classical scholar, Richard Bentley, master of Trinity College, Oxford, in the early eighteenth century. Since Julius Sagamore, Epifania's lawyer and the nephew of Pontifex Sagamore, has just returned from Australia to take over as much of his uncle's practice as possible, some reference to Samuel Butler and the Pontifexes in *The Way of All Flesh* is probably intended. As for Epifania Ognisanti di Parerga herself, not only does Shaw confess that he modeled her on his friend Lady Nancy Astor, but her Christian names seem to mean "Revelation All-Holy" — a more or less appropriate and prophetic selection by her parents in view of her own evaluation of herself. Lady Britomart, a matron of similarly pronounced character, has perhaps a double ancestry, for Britomart was Spenser's female knight of chastity, and Britomartis was a Cretan deity, presiding over hunting, fishing, and the fruits of the earth. Even the shop of the draper was invaded by the inquisitory G.B.S. For it is not unlikely that in naming his underwear manufacturer Tarleton in *Misalliance* he wickedly had in mind the cotton fabric called *tarlatan* — such stiff, scratchy undergarments being perhaps calculated to direct the attention of their purchasers away from their mere physical comfort to the intellectual diversions provided free by Tarleton's lending libraries.[40] Similarly, the name of Mrs. Lutestring in *The Thing Happens* is likely to puzzle people who do not know that lutestring, or lustring, is a plain, stout silk, once widely used for the dresses of upper servants. In this light Mrs. Lutestring's identification of herself to Burge-Lubin and Archbishop Haslam in the twenty-second century as an ex-parlor-maid, a "woman in a black dress and white apron, who opened the house door when people knock or rang, and was either your tyrant or your slave," has considerably more pertinency. Zoo, in the next play of the series, is "a girl of fifty, and rather childish at that." Since "zoo" comes from the Greek, meaning "animal," and Zoo is apparently a sort of reincarnation of young Savvy (short for "Savage") Barnabas, Shaw obviously wants us to think of her as a young animal.[41]

In the Bridgenorth family circle the unorthodox Bishop is known as "The Barmecide," obviously in allusion to the tale about the vizier in *The Arabian Nights* who spread the imaginary feast before his guest, the clever and coöperative beggar; the Bishop, therefore, is good-naturedly teased by his relatives such as Lesbia for being a dispenser of largely illusory benefits. Father Anthony, the Bishop's ascetic ex-solicitor of a chaplain, was christened Oliver Cromwell Soames by his father, "an eminent Nonconformist divine," but hastened to surrender the Puritan and perhaps Galsworthian name (since Soames Forsyte was also a lawyer whose imagination was tormented by women) when he was ordained. Shaw's appropriation of the name of the sorely beset early Christian monk, Anthony of the "Temptations," for his celibate priest is emphasized by the Bishop's playfully serious request, "*Saint* Anthony! Tempt him, Mrs. Collins: tempt him."

Bombardone in *Geneva* suggests the bass stop of that name on the organ or the deep, brass, tuba-like wind instrument of the orchestra; moreover, to the few (probably not including Shaw himself) who are familiar with Abraham Cowley's Latin school play, *Naufragium Joculare,* it recalls Bombardomachides, Cowley's version of the stock type of the braggart soldier. Nor is Shaw averse to punning in foreign languages. General Aufsteig, the Elderly Gentleman's traveling companion, who has risen up to his position, is "really the Emperor of Turania in disguise." The actual name of General

Aufsteig, we learn later, is Cain Adamson Charles Napoleon — an "upstart's" name if there ever was one! And in *Annajanska* General Strammfest is at heart still a stern, solid disciplinarian of the old school, while Lieutenant Schneidekind is a smart young officer, who might also literally slice children in his zeal for the revolutionary cause.

One of the most elaborate uses of all these types of name-play occurs in *Fanny's First Play*, in both the play-within-a-play and the play-without-a-play. In the outer play the four dramatic critics are collected for Count O'Dowda (or O'Dowdy) by the impresario Cecil Savoyard, whose crassness and vulgarity should perhaps not be attributed so much to the Savoy Theatre and its productions, notably the D'Oyly Carte Gilbert and Sullivan operas and the repertory plays (including Shaw) recently given there by Vedrenne and Barker, as to the general association of the term with hurdygurdy musicians and monkeys. The representative critics whom Savoyard has induced by various kinds of bribery and wheedling to attend the private performance are named Flawner Bannal, the voice of the British playgoer; Vaughan, who "does music as well as the drama"; his close friend Trotter, with his French and Aristotelian leanings; and Gilbert Gunn, one of "the chaps that go for the newest things and swear they're old-fashioned." Although Henderson explicitly denies that Hannen Swaffer, the popular, common man's critic for *The Daily Mail, The Daily Mirror, The Daily Express, The Daily Herald*, etc., etc., was the model for Bannal, whom he describes as a "sort of composite critic — who writes for *The Daily Telegraph* on weekdays and *The Referee* on Sundays," it is hard to believe that there was not at least a very strong dash of Swaffer and his banalities in the characterization. But there is no doubt about the identification of the other three, since their names as well as their qualities fit so closely into the reality. Vaughan is E. A. Baughan of *The Daily News*. Gilbert Gunn is Gilbert Cannan of *The Star*, journalist, novelist, dramatist, and lawyer. And Trotter is none other than Arthur Bingham Walkley of *The Times*, the dedicatee of *Man and Superman*, whom Shaw had at that time linked with himself as a twin pioneer of the New Jornalism,[42] who helped make "an epoch in the criticism of the theatre and the opera house by making it a pretext for a propaganda of our own views of life." Nevertheless, as Henderson points out, Walkley's aid in the fight had been far less vigorous and wholehearted than that of William Archer. In fact, "Walkley, the classical scholar and Gallic wit, taunted Shaw, under the name of Euthrypo, with being an impossibilist" — the name, incidentally, which Lady Cicely applied to Captain Brassbound.

In the inner play Shaw illustrates another propensity — that of taking famous names from past history or contemporary life, and applying them, as in the cases of Mangan and Mazzini Dunn, to his own imaginary characters. Thus the name Knox applies partly to the heroine's father, who is a man always troubled by a worrying conscience, but even more to Mrs. Knox, who talks a great deal about sin, grace, and redemption. Mr. Gilbey, on the other hand, reacting against his Uncle Phil, chairman of the Blue Ribbon Committee, admits frankly, "I do like spirits; and I make a merit of it, and I'm the King Cockatoo of the Convivial Cockatoos." Shaw does not specify, however, that Gilbey and his club specialize in Gilbey's Distilled London Dry Gin. Nor does Nurse Guinness in *Heartbreak House* indulge herself in the ale which made her name famous; but she does have the duty of keeping Captain Shotover supplied with the rum necessary to maintain him in the seventh degree of concentration, and her husband, the burglar, Billie Dunn, was obviously one of the drinking Dunns.

Most of the reapplied and distorted names used by Shaw are those of politicians, nor are they twisted so far out of shape as to be difficult of recognition by the average citizen. In fact, when he finally printed *Press Cuttings* in 1926, with its two leading characters, Mitchener and Balsquith, he was forced to introduce it with the following note: "By direction of the Lord Chamberlain the General and the Prime Minister in this play must in all public performances of it be addressed as General Bones and Mr.

Johnson, and by no means as General Mitchener and Mr. Balsquith . . . General Mitchener, by the way, is not the late Lord Kitchener, but an earlier and more highly connected commander. Balsquith (Balfour-Asquith) is obviously neither of these statesmen, and cannot in the course of nature be both." Shaw's explanation, however, is more acceptable in the first case than in the second, since Asquith was Prime Minister at the time of the action (1909), and Balfour had held the office up to 1905. Kitchener, on the other hand, had just left India, had been made field marshal, and had become commander-in-chief in the Mediterranean. In 1909, too, Alfred, Viscount Milner, the imperialist colonial administrator, who had been associated with Kitchener in the Boer War and the peace negotiations, had returned to public prominence by opposing the Finance Bill and Lloyd George's budget. Thus perhaps Mitchener equals Milner-Kitchener. The "earlier and more highly connected commander" whom Shaw admits to was, as Henderson suggests, probably George William Frederick Charles, Duke of Cumberland and uncle of Queen Victoria. When Robert Loraine acted the role, he made up unmistakably like the Duke, who had died in 1904. The Secretary for War at this time was Viscount Haldane, who was pressing in Parliament for the adoption of universal compulsory military service just as "Old Red" Sandstone[43] (a name which echoes that of the famous military college at Sandhurst) had recently done in the play. Finally, the allusions to the two suffraget leaders are to Mrs. Flora Drummond and Christabel Pankhurst. The person who chained "herself" to the doorscraper and turns out to be Balsquith in disguise reflects "General" Drummond, who led demonstrations on a dazzling white horse, once chained herself to the railings in front of 10 Downing Street and threw away the key to the padlock, and even tried to wrap up two of her colleagues and despatch them by parcel post to the Prime Minister. Bellachristina, who shakes the disguised Balsquith's hand and advises him to say that he is a vegetarian, because the diet in Holloway Gaol is better for vegetarians, is obviously Christabel, the eldest daughter of Mrs. Emmeline Pankhurst, the direct actionist suffraget.

The interest of present-day readers in *The Gospel of the Brothers Barnabas* bogs down badly because of the interminable political arguments of Joyce Burge and H. H. Lubin. The eternally smiling, overly genial, spell-binding Burge, "a well-fed man turned fifty, with broad forehead, and grey hair which, his neck being short, falls almost to his collar," is of course the Welsh Liberal ex-Prime Minister, Lloyd George. The charming, aristocratic Henry Hopkins Lubin, Savvy's "sweet old thing" and Burge's rival for party leadership, as well as being another ex-Prime Minister, is obviously Herbert Henry Asquith; but why he is named Lubin I have not been able to discover.[44] Similarly, that "bitterest old Tory left alive," Lord Dunreen, is perhaps Lord Curzon, who expected to become Prime Minister; but the point of the name-play escapes me.[45]

Possessing a radiant political personality and a musical voice much like a composite of Burge's and Lubin's is Sir Orpheus Midlander, the Foreign Secretary in *Geneva*. Although Irvine identifies him dogmatically as "a Sir Edward Grey straight out of 'Common Sense about the War,'" Sir Austen Chamberlain is a much more plausible candidate, in spite of Patch's implication that something of Neville also went into the character. Not only was Sir Austen, a Conservative, Foreign Secretary from 1924 until his death in 1937, but his family had for generations been associated with Birmingham, which is of course in the Midlands; and he himself always boasted proudly of his origin there. As Sir Orpheus says, the family money was made by his grandfather, as was the case with the Chamberlains. Sir Austen was much interested in the League, and attended all its meetings. Viscount Grey of Falloden, on the other hand, although also devoted to the cause of the League, not only resigned as Foreign Secretary late in 1916, but — unlike Midlander — was a Liberal. There is, however, no question about the identity of General Flanco de Fortinbras in the same play. Described, as the Commissar remarks, by half Europe as Bombardone's valet, the gentlemanly, clericalistic, Fascistic Flanco is Caudillo Franco, from strong arms ("fort en bras") to weak head.

Roebuck Ramsden, the somewhat atrophied progressive in *Man and Superman,* of course represents nobody but himself. Yet Shaw, acting *in loco parentis,* may well have named him Roebuck after the Independent M.P., John Arthur Roebuck, who — as Henry Adams puts it — "had been a tribune of the people, and, like tribunes of most other peoples, in growing old, had grown fatuous." As for the name Ramsden, to a man with Shaw's eccentric sense of humor the possible combination of "roe," "buck," and "ram" might well have proved irresistible. Certainly anyone who can transform Dean Inge into the "Chinese sage Dee Ning," quoted by Zoo in *Methuselah,* would not boggle at such a simple corruption. The Gloomy Dean of St. Paul's, Shaw's good friend, is of course reintroduced as the gaunt and dejected Elder in the third act of *Too True.*

The Oriental streak in Shaw's nomenclature is also represented by Burge-Lubin's secretary, Confucius, but most elaborately by the eugenically experimental family in *The Simpleton,* written not long after Shaw had visited India on a round-the-world tour. Here, on one of the Unexpected Isles, which has rather recently come up out of the Pacific, we find Pra and Prola, who seem to be the parents most closely related to the Superchildren, Maya, Vashti, Kanchin, and Janga. Although the names Pra and Prola sound vaguely Oriental, an exact source is not easily assignable. As Prola informs the Young Man about Pra, "He has many names; but he answers to Pra when you call him." Perhaps, since Prola is a priestess of "the goddess who is beyond naming, the eternal mother, the seed and the sun, the resurrection and the life," her name may be related to the Latin "proles," or "offspring," in which case Pra, the male element, may come from "prae," that is, "before." But the linguistic ground is much firmer in the case of the children. Vashti at once suggests the famous queen of Ahasuerus (or Xerxes I), "which," according to the Book of Esther, "reigned from India even unto Ethiopia." When she proudly refused to display her beauty to the court on the command of the drunken king of the Medes and Persians, he "put her away" and finally married Esther. Since the symbolical meaning that Shaw attaches to Vashti through Iddy's valedictory explanation is Pride, the association seems accurate. Maya, to Iddy, is the great symbol of Love; but in the Indian philosophy of the Vedanta and the Upanishads Maya is also the doctrine that the variegated universe springs from the development of form and name out of a single Brahman, but that every worldly object tends to change its form from what it is into something different. Still, in this philosophy of earthly imperfection and relativity, all remains united as part of the central Brahman or spirit. Thus in the play Vashti is also Maya, and Maya Vashti, for they become one in "the Kingdom of Love." Moreover, the two beautiful but stupid boys, who represent Heroism and Empire, are also part of this mystical Brahman, and all four children disappear together, just as when alive they have to some extent parroted and overlapped one another. This complex and rather obscure allegory, however, is further complicated by the fact that the boys' names, Kanchin and Janga, come from Shaw's splitting in two the name of the famous peak in the Himalayas called Kanchinjanga,[46] one of the highest mountains in the world, the attaining of which Shaw perhaps regarded as typifying both Heroism and Empire.

Bentley, in calling attention to Shaw's very simple and meager explanation of his allegorical abstractions in *The Simpleton,* also reminds the reader that in *Heartbreak House* the same quartet has appeared, Hesione standing for Love, Ariadne for Empire, Randall for Pride, and Hector for Heroism. These names, too, which in general illustrate Shaw's classical phase, demand further exploration. The prototype of Hector (who calls himself Marcus Darnley in his private junkets with worshiping women — Darnley from the unhappy but romantic husband of Mary, Queen of Scots, and

Marcus, obviously, from Mark Antony, whose identification is clinched when Captain Shotover, echoing Dryden, reminds Hector that men think the "world well lost" for vampire women) is too clearly Homeric to need comment. Randall, with his love for his sister-in-law Ariadne and her flouting of him, may have been suggested vaguely by the tragic popular ballad, "Lord Randal" — but of course this is not classical. The two Shotover sisters, however, definitely have their somewhat muddied roots in Greek mythology. Ariadne Utterword, who in the play, at the age of nineteen, has married Sir Hastings, a perennial colonial governor,[47] in order to escape from her disordered home and family, and has now returned to renew acquaintance, is in the legend the daughter of Minos, King of Crete, and Pasiphae, daughter of Helios and mother of the Minotaur. When Theseus comes to slay the Minotaur, Ariadne falls in love with him, helps him to overcome the monster, and runs away from home with him. When he later deserts her, she is discovered and married by Dionysus, thus becoming a goddess personifying spring and representing the regeneration of the earth from the clutch of winter. Though only the first part of this tale seems clearly to fit Ariadne, in spite of her later flirtations with Randall and Hector, the myth of Hesione, daughter of Laomedon, King of Troy, is more closely tied in with Shaw's character. When the Trojan maiden was chained by her father to a rock to be devoured by the sea-monster in order to appease the wrath of Apollo and Poseidon, Hercules appeared and killed the monster; but, because Laomedon broke certain promises to him, he killed the king and married Hesione to his Greek friend Telamon. In this way she became one of the contributing causes of the Trojan War. That Shaw has some distorted version of this myth in mind is suggested by the fact that in Hector's long talk with the Captain about aspiration and materialism, when the latter remarks that often the materialists, "when we are tempted to seek their destruction . . . bring forth demons to delude us, disguised as pretty daughters, and singers and poets and the like, for whose sake we spare them," Hector inquires, "May not Hesione be such a demon, brought forth by you lest I should slay you?" The modern situation, however, although containing similar elements, does not work out quite like the legendary one.

In many miscellaneous ways Shaw steals his names from classical sources. Lesbia Grantham in *Getting Married* is a "Lesbian" in the sense that she would like to have children, but detests husbands. Hypatia, of *Misalliance,* reflects the famous Alexandrian beauty and bluestocking of the fifth century, who fascinated men, but would not let herself be dominated by them. Nestor is "a juryman with a long white beard, drunk, the oldest man present" in *Blanco Posnet.* Sir Orpheus Midlander, like the musical husband of Eurydice, can cast a spell through the beauty and persuasiveness of his voice strong enough to move the hearts of Pluto and Proserpine, or Parliament; but he knows better than to look back. And Morell's secretary-typist, Proserpine Garnett, is slyly named after the Queen of the Underworld.

Since the setting of *Androcles and the Lion* is Rome in the early Christian era, the names of the characters are naturally Roman or Greek, running from Spintho, the reformed rake, to Megaera, Androcles's spouse appropriately named after one of the Furies. Lavinia probably has no particular significance, though Lavinia was the wife of Aeneas. But the patronymic Lentulus, of a famous Roman family, meant "rather slow"; and Metellus, the name of another great family, originally meant "hired." Of these minor names perhaps that of Ferrovius is the most fitting, since the giant primitive Christian is obviously a man of iron.

A lengthier attempt to establish a sort of parallel between classical myth and history and modern life is found in *The Apple Cart.* Here Proteus, the clever Prime Minister of King Magnus (i.e., "the Great"), is, like the prophetic old man of the sea in the Greek myth, constantly changing his form and slipping away from those who try to grasp or stop him, and thus suggests Ramsay MacDonald, the smooth and clever Labor leader and politician, whose joining the Coalition government eventually weaned him away from his party. The King's secretaries have Roman or Greek names, Pamphilius and Sempronius — Pamphilus (*sic*) appearing in two of Terence's comedies and one of Aristophanes', and Sempronius being the Roman senator who was a traitor to Cato the Younger. These names, however, seem to have no special application. But most of the names of the Cabinet do. Crassus, Colonial Secretary, the opulent and wealthy "jobber," the tool of the industrialists and capitalists, is the reincarnation of the Roman triumvir and financier, Marcus Licinius Crassus (the very name means "fat" or "crass"). Nicobar, Foreign Secretary, is his friend and partner, who at the end also decides to give up politics as "a mug's game." Pliny, Chancellor of the Exchequer, is good-natured, scholarly, and credulous, like the author of the *Natural History*. Balbus, Home Secretary, "rude and thoughtless," and called the "bully" by Proteus, suggests the Roman general and consul, a favorite of Caesar, who, when brought to trial for assuming the rights of a Roman citizen when born an alien, was defended by Cicero, Pompey, and Crassus. Lysistrata, Powermistress General, of course suggests Aristophanes' feminist who led the Athenian ladies in their sex strike against war. The name of the Postmistress General, Amanda, means that she "ought to be loved" — a condition that she achieves by her cheerful and humorous disposition, her jests, and her mimicries.

Though the nomenclature in the play is predominantly classical, it is also hybrid. The American ambassador is named Vanhattan — obviously a telescoping of Van Manhattan. The name of the Princess Royal is Alice — quite properly at the time Shaw was writing the play. Magnus's "mistress" is romantically named Orinthia, with no particular significance that I can discover. The Queen, however, is domestically called Jemima, which means "a dove" in Hebrew. The Biblical influence is carried further through Shaw's styling the loud and garrulous new President of the Board of Trade Boanerges — the name given by Christ to James and John because he thought that by their kind of preaching they deserved to be called "Sons of Thunder." According to Patch, it was also the name which T. E. Lawrence gave to his motorcycle — that anonymous gift from the Shaws, which brought him to his death. Bill Boanerges was a Shavian distortion of his old associate John Burns, who in his youthful days as a fomenter of "Bloody Sunday in Trafalgar Square" had been known as "the man with the red flag" and who, after a political career as an Independent Radical had brought him into the Liberal Cabinet of Sir Henry Campbell-Bannerman, became President of the Board of Trade just before the outbreak of the First World War.

In *Major Barbara* Christ's parable of Lazarus and Dives, the poor man and the rich man, is used to give a name to Undershaft's partner, by a sort of reverse association, for Lazarus, the rich man, although popularly honored and feared as a munitions maker, much prefers symphony concerts and art exhibits. In the preface, discussing the deserving and the undeserving poor, Shaw perversely explains: "Peter Shirley is what we call the honest poor man. Undershaft is what we call the wicked rich one: Shirley is Lazarus, Undershaft Dives."[48] The brothers who first propound the new gospel of long living in *Methuselah,* however, are named Barnabas with more clarity, since Barnabas means "Son of Consolation."[49]

In *Methuselah,* too, Shaw tries to wear his erudition lightly. Cain's pampered wife, to whom he loved to return after having slain a few score beasts or human enemies, is named Lua — and Lua was a Roman goddess, associated with Saturn, to whom captured arms were devoted. Though the other characters in the first play of the series and in the epilogue are all Biblical or Talmudic (note Lilith), by A.D. 31,920 society has turned purely classical again. Since in the new civilization the Marxian ideal of a non-urban life has at long last been attained, the young people are given pastoral names like Strephon, Chloe, Acis, Ecrasia, and Amaryllis (which Shaw has the other young folks expl___ ___ ___ "love," "mother," and "lilies"). The bearded sculptor is called ___, ___ ___ one Martellus. And the young scientist who has fashioned the living human auto___ ' Ozymandias and Semiramis-Cleopatra, is, inevitably, named Pygmalion, perhaps in honor of Professor Higgins. Ozymandias, the proud and mighty, of course quotes Shelley; and his consort boasts of her queenly power and beauty. After they have displayed the baseness of their human emotions, however, they are unemotionally put out of the way by the Ancients, in accordance with Shaw's theory that the person dangerous to society should be destroyed without anger or revenge.

In *Methuselah,* in fact, Shaw brings to a climax his persistent fascination by names. In *In the Beginning* he gives the audience an elementary lesson in language origins and vocabulary building, when Adam and Eve, prompted by the Serpent, begin to invent words like "dead," "birth," "miracles," and "procrastinate," to fit their new experiences. By the thirty-first century A.D., however, the language has begun to shrink, and such words as "decent," "landlord," and "married" are no longer understood. A process of corruption has also set in. As Zoo remarks, "Well, thoughts die sooner than languages." The Elderly Gentleman explains part of his full name, Joseph Popham Bolge Bluebin Barlow, O.M., to her by telling her that its historical section, Bolge Bluebin, derives from the time, a thousand years ago, when two of his ancestors, "Joyce Bolge and Hengist Horsa Bluebin, wrestled with one another for the prime ministership of the British empire, and occupied that position successively with a glory of which we can in these degenerate days form but a faint conception." There is now also a tradition of "an ancient writer whose name has come down to us in several forms, such as Shakespear, Shelly, Sheridan, and Shoddy" (Shaw modestly omits "Shaw"); and a monument has been erected to "an ancient and very fat sage called Sir John Falstaff," who was the first preacher of the civilized doctrine "that cowardice was a great patriotic virtue." The same process that has transformed Dean Inge into Dee Ning has affected the historians and philosophers. The "father of history" is now known as Thucyderodotus Macollybuckle (i.e., Thucydides Herodotus Macaulay Buckle), an attempt to reproduce whose "Perfect City of God" was made in "the northern part of these islands by Jonhobsnoxius, called the Leviathan." Here Thomas Hobbes and John Knox seem to have effected some kind of union with St. Augustine. And by A.D. 31,920 a legend is still told of "a supernatural being called the Archangel Michael," who was "a mighty sculptor and painter," and founded "in the centre of the world a temple erected to the goddess of the centre, called Mediterranea." (A few minutes later, however, Shaw slips and lets the She-Ancient refer to the "fable of Michael Angelo.") Pygmalion, the biologist, however, is more interested in the tradition from the "primitive ages" about the "remarkable early experimenter" who first "breathed the breath of life" into inert matter, a being whose name has descended in several forms, such as Jove and Voltaire.

The comicalness as well as the appropriateness of names has, then, frequently tempted Shaw into ludicrous flights of pure exuberance. He cannot resist giving characters names like Alastair Fitzfassenden, Aloysia Brollikins, and Susan Simpkins, which seem to have no particular significance, but tickle the elementary risibilities. *Passion, Poison, and Petrifaction* yields Lady Magnesia Fitztollemache and Adolphus Bastable. *The Fascinating Foundling* offers Horace Brabazon and Anastasia Vulliamy — whom Mercer announces as "Miss Anaesthesia." The Secretary in *Geneva* epitomizes the average reader's reaction when, on first hearing the name of Begonia Brown, he understands it as "Ammonia," and then sums up his verdict as "Farcical."

Low, broad, and fantastic as much of this nomenclature is, it is still an essential and characteristic part of Shaw's philosophy of characterization as a means of conveying his ideas in his role of "classic" dramatist. Indeed, he loudly calls attention to this fact in the preface to, if not apology for, his own most arrant collection of this sort, *Trifles and Tomfooleries:* "Besides, tomfoolery is as classic as tragedy. High comedy seldom achieves a whole act without revealing traces of its origin in the altercations and topical discussions of the circus clown with the ringmaster." Then, after a corroborative allusion to Molière's M. Jourdain, he adds, "I could cite many examples from plays of my own which pretend to be highly serious." This admission is not surprising, since at the end of the preface to *Back to Methuselah* he had already asserted, after listing the serious subjects he had previously treated in his plays, that these were "all worked into a series of comedies of manners in the classic fashion, which was then very much out of fashion." And not long afterward, in explaining what he had done in *Saint Joan,* he was to reiterate, "I write in the classical manner for those who pay for admission to a theatre because they like classical comedy or tragedy for its own sake."

It is no cause for wonder, therefore, to discover that the older playwrights and novelists whom Shaw alludes to most frequently and most admiringly in his discussions of his own dramaturgy are those of the various classical or anti-romantic schools of the past. He has clearly made a considerable study of the drama from the historical point of view, for he refers to many forgotten minor figures with almost as much familiarity as he does to the major. In fact, one of the most amazing dramatic evaluations that I can recall anywhere in dramatic history occurs in one of the earliest prefaces that he wrote for his plays, that for the "unpleasant" volume in 1898. In this preface, entitled "Mainly about Myself," he dogmatically chose, as "the greatest dramatist, with the single exception of Shakespear, produced by England between the Middle Ages and the nineteenth century," none other than Henry Fielding, who began his writing career by devoting "his genius to the task of exposing and destroying parliamentary corruption, then at its height." Though without mentioning titles, but obviously with political satires like *Pasquin* and *The Historical Register for 1736* in mind, Shaw then goes on to compare his own current encounters with "the Queen's Reader of Plays" and Fielding's losing battle with Robert Walpole, as a result of which "Fielding, driven out of the trade of Molière and Aristophanes, took to that of Cervantes." That the praise of Fielding was genuinely meant and was not merely part of Shaw's early, spirited campaign against the great literature which maintained its place by tradition alone is shown by continued references in the same vein. In his very first dramatic preface, that to *Widowers' Houses* in 1893, in defending himself for having altered his erstwhile collaborator, William Archer's, original plans for the play as being too artificial, he had wondered how "any man in his senses can deliberately take as his model the sterile artifice of Wilkie Collins or Scribe, and repudiate the natural artistic activity of Fielding, Goldsmith, Defoe and Dickens, not to mention Aeschylus and Shakespear." The combination is a bit heterogeneous, but its intent is as clear as Shaw's recommendation in the preface to *The Admirable Bashville* in 1909 that the repertory theaters should "amuse themselves and their congregations with occasional performances of Carey's Chronohotonthologos, Fielding's Tom Thumb, and even Bombastes Furioso" (by W. B. Rhodes in 1810). The heavily burlesque element in these earlier plays does not, for Shaw, at all vitiate their value as works of art and criticism. Thus he placed himself in similar company in the preface to *Overruled* in 1912, reminding his readers that the charm of the theater lies in make-believe, not in illusive reality: "I have seen performances of my own plays which were to me far wilder burlesques than Sheridan's Critic and Buckingham's Rehearsal; yet they have produced sincere laughter and tears such as the most polished metropolitan productions have failed to elicit." And he goes on to praise Fielding for his wisdom in representing Partridge as enjoying so intensely the performance of the King in *Hamlet* because anyone could see that the King was an actor, whereas Partridge failed to admire Garrick as Hamlet himself because Garrick's Hamlet might have been a real man. "Theatrical art," concludes Shaw, "begins as the holding up to Nature of a distorting mirror."

Shaw's fondness for the seventeenth and eighteenth centuries is significant, because, as he explains at the end of the preface to *Methuselah,* comedy, from the time of Molière to that of Oscar Wilde, although "a destructive, derisory, critical, negative art, kept the theatre open when sublime tragedy perished." Nevertheless, because of their lack of positive religion, most playwrights since Shakespeare — and especially those from Congreve to Sheridan — "were so sterile in spite of their wit that they did not achieve between them the output of Molière's single life time." And the only "saved soul in that pandemonium," he finds, is Oliver Goldsmith.

Only two writers of prose fiction occur with any frequency in these discussions of the technique of playwriting. They are Charles Dickens and John Bunyan; for both were propagandists, moralists, and social reformers, and both used an exaggerative, representative type of characterization. In the preface to *Immaturity* Shaw relates that one of his earliest recollections was reading *The Pilgrim's Progress* aloud to his father; and in the preface to *Three Plays for Puritans,* appropriately, Bunyan becomes "our greatest English dramatizer of life." Over and over again Shaw mentions his youthful and his mature fondness for Dickens, and admits that he has modeled certain of his own characters, like Mrs. Dudgeon, on Dickens originals. The introduction to *Methuselah* again admits that in the nineties he was finding that "the surest way to produce an effect of daring innovation and originality" was threefold: one aspect was to revive "the ancient attraction of long rhetorical speeches"; another was "to lift characters bodily out of the pages of Charles Dickens"; and the third was "to stick closely to the methods of Molière."

Augustin Hamon claims to have been the first to call attention to the influence of Molière on Shaw, but this discovery, after all, did not demand much perspicacity, since Shaw had been cheerfully confessing his indebtedness and admiration for a long time. For his first play, *Widowers' Houses,* for instance, he requested of his readers: "you will please judge it, not as a pamphlet in dialogue, but in intention a work of art as much as any comedy of Molière's is a work of art." Though Henderson insists that "The inevitable comparison with Molière must be made very cautiously," he himself calls attention to an address in which Shaw unequivocally pronounced Molière "the greatest dramatist who ever lived." Later, Henderson groups Shaw with "the greatest comedic figures of world-literature — with Aristophanes and Euripides, with Molière and Swift, with Cervantes and Mark Twain — who see comedy as irresistibly tragic, tragedy as germinally comic." Hamon sees the similarity to Molière not only in Shaw's anti-romanticism, his handling of exposition through each character's self-introduction, his meliorism, his repetition of characters, passages, and phrases, his general technique, and, especially, his use of character types, but even notes the frequent shakiness of Shaw's grammar as similar to the Frenchman's neglect of the same rules. The judicious critic, however, remembering the pitfalls of deciding whether one writer has been influenced by another writer simply because he likes him and is like him, will probably be content with the general conclusion that Shaw and Molière belong to the same comic school.

The absence of the names of any Elizabethan playwrights, except Shakespeare, from the preceding list of great authors with whom Shaw could apparently feel some personal affinity is no cause for wonder — except in one case: Ben Jonson. In reviewing a revival of Marlowe's *Doctor Faustus* in 1896 Shaw splenetically relieved himself of his antipathy toward Shakespeare's contemporaries as follows: though Marlowe's famous blank verse has "charm of color and movement," and the play acts unexpectedly well, "the fellow was a fool for all that," since "the moment the exhaustion of the imaginative fit deprives him of the power of raving," he "becomes childish in thought, vulgar and wooden in humor, and stupid in his attempts at invention." Webster could find in Nature no murderer cruel enough to satisfy him; nor could Chapman discover any hero who was bully enough for him. Though Greene was sometimes "really amusing," Marston was "spirited and silly-clever," Tourneur was often able to string two good lines together, and Beaumont and Fletcher were sometimes capable of writing as well as Bulwer, "the whole obscene crew of these blank-verse rhetoricians" were bloodthirsty, lewd, ostentatious, and ranting. They were successful only because "their public was ignorant and Philistine." As for Jonson, though his verses and criticism sometimes showed some heart and affection, he was to Shaw in 1896 merely a "brutish pedant." As Shaw grew older, however, he must have read and reflected more on Jonson, as he did on Shakespeare, for when he came to write *The Millionairess* he opened up his discussion of the play by declaring that it "does not pretend to be anything more than the comedy of humorous and curious contemporary characters such as Ben Jonson might write were he alive now." So, after a lapse of forty years, Shaw at long last comes round to perceiving the link between himself and rocky old Ben, the caustic critic of the minds and manners of his day, and the essential founder of the English "humors" school of which Shaw himself is, so far, the last illustrious member. And by 1946, in a lengthy verbal dispute which Pearson titles "A Bardic Battle," we find Shaw defending even Chapman, whom Pearson now damned as "dull and pedantic," and Shaw now regarded as "really a great literary figure." Shakespeare's passage on Ajax in *Troilus and Cressida,* Shaw now insisted, is no caricature of Jonson, but "a gorgeous tribute from a friend."

The habit of simplifying the complexities of actual life by classifying mankind, with its infinity of variety, contradiction, and inconsistency, into a number of major genera, each with its sub-species, is a leading characteristic of the comedy of humors. It is also, of course, found just as conspicuously in the medieval morality play and the modern expressionistic drama. Shaw has invented nothing here, but he has given new evidence of the practical validity of the old theories. At the same time it would be a mistake to minimize the fact that many of his characters come directly from life. He once observed to Henderson that in his plays, as in all fiction, there is "an element due altogether to the purely accidental experiences of the author, which defies exegesis," and when Henderson suggested that Shaw probably frequently created characters who were composites of his acquaintances, the other remarked "pithily": "I probably never do anything else." Yet when Shaw went on to add, "But I have never done it consciously," he was merely being hastily flippant, as other Shavian confessions on the same point prove. His statement in the *Self Sketches,* for instance, to the effect that "Some of my characters are close portraits: for others I have used a model just as a painter does," is simply a condensation of the longer explanation of his method in the preface to *Immaturity,* wherein he expands the same comparison and adds: "I have copied nature with many degrees of fidelity, combining studies from life in the same book or play with those types and composites and traditional figures of the novel and the stage which are called pure fictions."

In further extension of this general idea Shaw even calls attention to the fact that he has often made his characters more articulate and self-analytical than normal human beings in their position would be. "But my sort of play," he remarks in the *Self Sketches,* "would be impossible unless I endowed my characters with powers of self-consciousness and self-expression which they would not possess in real life. You could not have Esop's fables unless the animals talked." Here he is bringing together such remarks as he had previously made in passages like the prefaces to *Saint Joan* and *Man and Superman.* In the former he had carefully explained that his dramatic treatment of such historical figures as Cauchon, Lemaître, and Warwick had to make them and the Middle Ages intelligible not only in themselves but to a twentieth-century audience in a way that the actual persons could not have done, since they were themselves part of the Middle Ages; in the latter he accepted full responsibility for the opinions of Tanner and all his other characters, "pleasant and unpleasant," and assured his readers that all of them "are right from their several points of view; and their points of view are, for the dramatic moment, mine also." This is a kind of reciprocal ventriloquism, perhaps, in which at one moment the manipulator is speaking through the dummy and at another moment the dummy is using the vocal apparatus of the manipulator. As Shaw put it in a conversation with his neighbor Winsten about 1946, "Anyhow, it doesn't really matter what age one is born in: the description of a great man in Greek days would apply equally to a great man of today. That is why my historical plays are so absorbing: they are easy to write because the facts are a gift: all that has to be done is to supply the ideas and the people personifying the ideas."

Shaw's procedure by the use of character categories has of course been recognized by previous critics, such as Hamon, whose discussion, however, is neither adequate nor logically analyzed. And Shaw himself has admitted it, at least tacitly, in many passages in which he presents various kinds of lists in which mankind is grouped according to different types and classifications. The concept has certainly been contributed to, also, by his views on human progress, or lack of it, and his application of the doctrine that climatology, and environment in general, have a determining effect on the development of types of character.

For clearly, if people have not changed essentially since the days of Adam and Eve, metaphorically speaking, then an author is justified in portraying Cleopatra as if she were a flapper of the early twentieth century and drawing Caesar as if he were a present-day Bernard Shaw. Similarly, Saint Joan might naturally become the militant, devoted, nationalistic, and manly girl leader of a modern Russian war epic. Thus Shaw, in describing the comrades and playfellows of Androcles and his lion, asserts, "Therefore my martyrs are the martyrs of all time, and my persecutors the persecutors of all time," and goes on to classify his persecuted Christians into four types, illustrated by Androcles, the "humanitarian naturalist," Lavinia, the "clever and fearless freethinker," Ferrovius, the "comparatively stupid and conscience ridden" Pauline convert, and Spintho, the repentant "blackguardly debauchee." In the notes to *Caesar and Cleopatra,* too, Shaw, in defending his thesis that there is no basis for "the common assumption that the civilized contemporaries of the Hittites were unlike their civilized descendants of today," advises his readers: "Go back to the first syllable of recorded time, and there you will find your Christian and your pagan, your yokel and your poet, helot and hero, Don Quixote and Sancho, Tamino and Papageno, Newton and bushman unable to count eleven, all alive and contemporaneous, and all convinced that they are the heirs of the ages and the privileged recipients of THE truth (all others damnable heresies), just as you have them to-day."

Most pertinent of all, however, are the two sections in *The Revolutionist's Handbook* entitled "Progress an Illusion" and "The Conceit of Civilization." In the first Shaw enumerates certain types of reformers and "earnest people who get drawn off the track of evolution by the illusion of progress": the Anarchist, the Fabian, the Salvationist, the Vegetarian, the doctor, the lawyer, the parson, the professor of ethics, the gymnast, the soldier, the sportsman, the inventor, and the political program-maker. In the second section this method of cataloguing is used even more effectively to indicate that time has wrought no improvement or even change in the kinds of men: "The democratic politician remains exactly as Plato described him; the physician is still the credulous impostor and petulant scientific coxcomb whom Molière ridiculed; the schoolmaster remains at best a pedantic child farmer and at worst a flagellomaniac; arbitrations are more dreaded by honest men than lawsuits; the philanthropist is still a parasite on misery as the doctor is on disease; the miracles of priestcraft are none the less fraudulent and mischievous because they are now called scientific experiments and conducted by professors . . ." And so the anathematized list goes on through landowner, modern gentleman, newspaperman, city magnate, vivisector — in fact, most of the categories discussed in the preceding chapters of this book are cited by Shaw himself as typical of the divisions and characters of man.\*

As for the determination of type by environment even more than by heredity, Shaw, as might be expected from his biological credo, aligns himself explicitly with the environmentalists. In his lengthy essay, "Imprisonment," for instance, he declares that no one who has ever visited a prison can doubt that there is a very marked prison type, and affirms that, contrary to most theorists, "the types that were said to take a million years to produce can be produced in five." Using as his authority a pamphlet entitled "The Influence Which Our Surroundings Exert on Us," by Sir William Arbuthnot Lane, "one of our most distinguished surgeons" (for the skeptic can quote medical research when it is to his purpose), Shaw relates how it has been proved that "by keeping a man at work as a deal porter, a çoal trimmer, a shoemaker or what not, you can, within a period no longer than that spent in prison by typical criminals, produce a typical deal porter, coal trimmer, and so on, the changes involved being grotesque skeletal changes for which Huxley or Owen would have demanded a whole evolutionary epoch." Not only, he concludes, does a confining prison environment produce an artificial criminal type, but other confining environments have similar results — as witness the effect of the girlhood of Queen Victoria on her later character!

There are ethnic types too, as well as social types. In attempting to diagnose the dangerous and eccentric racial theories of Adolf Hitler in the preface to *The Millionairess,* Shaw hazards the guess that the Führer in his youth was fascinated by Houston S. Chamberlain's *Foundations of the 19th Century,* originally written in German, and there found an ethnology which fitted his needs. Although by 1935 Shaw himself is beginning to renege a bit on the reliability of Chamberlain, whom he confesses he had advised everybody to read at the time of the appearance of the book, he still admits: "All these types with which writers like Chamberlain play: the Teutons and Latins, the Apollonians and Dionysians, the Nordics and Southics, the Dominants and Recessives, have existed and keep cropping up as individuals, and exciting antipathies or affinities quite often enough to give substance to theories about them." Though Shaw denies that these types can any longer be separated as races or species, he nevertheless agrees that we "still have nations with national characteristics (rapidly fading, by the way), national languages, and national customs." And from here he goes on to a discussion of the effect of climate on human physiology, asserting that even in Africa, "where pink emigrants struggle with brown and black natives for possession of the land," the sun sterilizes the pinks so quickly that "Cabinet ministers call for more emigration to maintain the pink population."

---

\* And yet, with the frequent forgetfulness and self-contradiction that Pearson illustrates richly in his *G.B.S.: A Postcript,*[50] we later find Shaw dogmatizing as follows to his biographer in a criticism of some of the latter's remarks in his original biography: "You are still a bit in the nineteenth century in respect of arranging religion, politics, science, and art in braintight compartments, mostly incompatible and exclusive. They don't exist that way at all. There is no such thing as the religious man, the political man, the scientific man, the artistic man; in human nature they are all mixed up in different proportions, and that is how they are mixed up in my plays." Pearson might have supported his vigorous refusal to agree with the aging dramatist by reminding Shaw that, after all, the roots of all the latter's own ideas and conceptions were themselves more than "a bit in the nineteenth century."

These climatological doctrines had marked Shaw's thinking from the beginning. As I have already pointed out, in the notes to *Caesar and Cleopatra,* in presenting Britannus as "the unadulterated Briton," he had remarked that later on "the Roman and Norman conquests must have for a time disturbed the normal British type produced by the climate." While admitting that he has been told that it is not scientific "to treat national character as a product of climate," he dismissed the objection contemptuously by adding, "This only shews the wide difference between common knowledge and the intellectual game called science." In *Captain Brassbound's Conversion* his description of the physiognomy of Captain Kearney, the American, had stressed his belief that this "curious ethnological specimen" was developing "climatically in the direction of the indigenous North American" — that is, the Indian. In the preface to *John Bull's Other Island* he had expatiated on Larry Doyle's speech on the subject of the so-called Irish race by stating: "There is no Irish race any more than there is an English race or a Yankee race. There *is* an Irish climate, which will stamp an immigrant more deeply and durably in two years, apparently, than the English climate will in two hundred." Thus the "secondary" Woman in *Methuselah* remarks to the Elderly Gentleman: "Perhaps you do not know that you are on the west coast of Ireland, and that it is the practice among the natives of the Eastern Island to spend some years here to acquire mental flexibility. The climate has that effect." And Zozim later informs the bewildered Gentleman and the Envoy that the political party of Colonizers and Exterminators are thinking of trying North America as the location for their experiments, since the Red Men of that country used to be white, but "passed through a period of sallow complexions, followed by a period of no complexions at all, into the red characteristic of their climate." Although in his preface Shaw concedes that "Perhaps nobody is at heart fool enough to believe that life is at the mercy of temperature," he nevertheless discusses at considerable length the controversy between George Henry Lewes and Robert Owen as to the effect of environment on character, and ends by siding against Owen and his fellow Socialists because most of them had adopted Darwinism. Juno in *Overruled* states Shaw's whole case succinctly when he exclaims ardently to Mrs. Lunn, "It is climate and not race that determines the temperament." The passage in the play may be comic, but the intent of the remark, as so often in Shaw, is perfectly serious.

Thus there should be no question as to the validity of the approach in this book to the ideas and methods of Bernard Shaw in his novels and plays. His ideas are transformed into the types of human beings who hold them; these types are epitomized in skilfully drawn and usually quite credible and human individuals; and these individuals in turn become the mouthpieces for the ventriloquism of their author. But, though the author plays his own role with the greatest zest and frequency, he also, like any other good performer, enacts various other roles to highlight and emphasize his own part. Sometimes these other parts are personally repugnant to him. As he has Lydia say in *Cashel Byron's Profession,* "Now, Lucian, in the course of my reading I have come upon denunciations of every race and pursuit under the sun. Very respectable and well-informed men have held that Jews, Irishmen, Christians, atheists, lawyers, doctors, politicians, actors, artists, flesh-eaters, and spirit-drinkers are all of necessity degraded beings. Such statements can be easily proved by taking a black sheep from each flock, and holding him up as a type." Shaw is obviously not always above this technique himself, but at least he recognizes its dangers and potential unfairnesses.

In introducing an English translation of several plays by Brieux Shaw pointed out that Brieux had taken a larger task than had Molière, who "unmasked the doctor, the philosopher, the fencing master, the priest. He ridiculed their dupes: the hypochondriac, the academician, the devotee, the gentleman in search of accomplishments. He exposed the snob." Shaw's range is of course broader than that of either the seventeenth- or the twentieth-century Frenchman; but all three are primarily concerned with the exposure of the hypocrite or "idealist." Shaw might have started off, perhaps, with a somewhat different classification from his tripartite one of Philistines, idealists, and realists, and their many ramifications. In *The Perfect Wagnerite,* for example, in talking about the denizens of Wagner's *Ring* country, he explained: "Really, of course, the dwarfs, giants, and gods are dramatizations of the three main orders of men: to wit, the instinctive, predatory, lustful, greedy people; the patient, toiling, stupid, respectful, money-worshipping people; and the intellectual, moral, talented people who devise and administer States and Churches. History shows us only one order higher than the highest of these: namely, the order of Heroes." Yet even here he seems to be adumbrating two of his three main types of human beings—one the Philistine and two varieties of idealists—under slightly different guises, and to be setting them opposite to his third main type, the realist, who verges on the Hero or Superman. From these all the rest descend.

*The Sanity of Art* contains another of Shaw's many personal confessions and credos. "I deal," he admonishes his audience, "with all periods; but I never study any period but the present. . . ; and as a dramatist I have no clue to any historical or other personage save that part of him which is also myself." Here, then, is no claim to godliness or universality, except insofar as the macrocosm is reflected in the microcosm of the individual man. If this individual, however, happens to be a certain red-headed Irishman, born in Dublin in 1856 and destined to become the most useful gadfly of the twentieth century, one may expect to find in that microcosm all the energy, sometimes practically uncontrollable, of the fissionable atom. And anyone who elects to write a book about this red-headed Irishman should also remember his warning, issued in the preface to *Widowers' Houses* in 1893, that if a critic "wishes to be specially ingenious, he will say of a character — a red-headed one, for instance — that it is not a human being at all, but a type of the red-haired variety of mankind."

# *Addenda*

1.  For a complete account of Shaw's relationship with Annie Besant, see my two-volume biography, *The First Five Lives of Annie Besant* (Chicago, 1960; London, 1961) and *The Last Four Lives of Annie Besant* (London and Chicago, 1963). [N.B. Later references to these volumes in my previous addenda will therefore have to be simplified.]

2.  Read *their* for *thir*.

3.  Read *H. C. Duffin* for *H.S. Duffin*.

4.  *A Casebook on Candida*, edited by Stephen S. Stanton (New York, 1962), provides rich material for a thorough study of the background and interpretations of the play. Especially interesting articles on the subject since the original publication of my book are as follows: Irving McKee, "Bernard Shaw's Beginnings on the London Stage," PMLA, LXXIV (Sept. 1959), 474-8, and Walter N. King, "The Rhetoric of *Candida*," *Modern Drama*, II (Sept. 1959), 71ff.

5.  For more information on Canon H.C. Shuttleworth and his liberal activities, see index to my biography, *The First Five Lives of Annie Besant* (Chicago and London, 1960, 1961).

6.  It is true that in *Arms and the Man* Raina has turned from an idealist into a realist by the end of the play, but we do not follow her into her new function as a wife and probable mother.

7.  Brassbound's Oedipus complex is undeniable, even though later, when Shaw became acquainted with Freud, he had a generally low opinion of the other's theories.

8.  Just as Sartorius in *Widowers' Houses* had kept his daughter Blanche in ignorance of hers.

9.  Their relationship was much like that between Dr. Edward B. Aveling and his common-law wife, Eleanor Marx, daughter of Karl. See p. 151 of this book and the indexes to *The First Five Lives of Annie Besant* and *The Last Four Lives of Annie Besant* (Chicago and London, 1963).

10. For Captain Frederick J. Wilson, see H. M. Geduld, "The Comprehensionist," *Shavian*, Oct. 1963.

11. For *Charles Shaw* read *H.C. Duffin*. Shaw's description of Vivie Warren would also classify her as a Manly Woman.

12. But Shaw himself told Felix Barker about a Miss Orme who actually lived at Honoria Fraser's address (see *New Yorker*, Nov. 27, 1954, p. 175).

13. McKee, *op. cit.*, pp. 470-4, discusses Shaw's original title for the play, *Alps and Balkans*, the reactions of the first reviewers, and especially the distortion of Shaw's intentions by both actors and audiences by making Bluntschli the central character rather than Sergius.

14. In his preface to *Three Plays for Puritans* Shaw remarks: "Let those who have praised my originality in conceiving Dick Dudgeon's strange religion read Blake's Marriage of Heaven and Hell; and I shall be fortunate if they do not rail at me for a plagiarist."

15. A very similar situation is to be found in chapter 87 of Tobias Smollett's *Peregrine Pickle*.

16. Archibald Henderson, in *George Bernard Shaw: Man of the Century* (New York, 1956), p. 29, tells a story which may have some bearing on the subject of the "dark-eyed" Rachel. At the romantic age of fifteen he became so infatuated with a young brunette that the affair eventually developed into youthful engagement. But "one day he went for a walk with this 'dark lady' . . . ; and after walking some distance he suggested that they turn back as he was tired!" This unflattering reaction, which resulted in their disengagement, corresponds roughly with the story in *Man and Superman* of the walk of Tanner and Rachel in the garden with their arms uncomfortably around one another—a walk which resulted in Rachael's "cutting" him when she learned that he had told Ann about it. A further echo of this affair turns up in a letter of Shaw to the brunette Stella Campbell on Aug. 19, 1912: "Once, in my catfish teens, I fell wildly in love with a lady of your complexion; and she, good woman, having a sister to provide for, set to work to marry me to the sister. Whereupon I shot back into the skies from which I had descended, and never saw her again. Nor have I, until this day, ever mentioned that adventure to any mortal; for though dark ladies still fascinated me they half laughed at me, half didn't understand me, and wholly thought me cracked."

17. For somewhat contradictory accounts of the "happiness" of the Shaws together, see Janet Dunbar, *Mrs. G.B.S.* (New York, 1963), and Lawrence Langner, *G.B.S. and the Lunatic* (New York, 1963).

18. Note, too, that the Serpent has been in existence not only before Adam and Eve but also before Lilith.

19. In spite of this clearly indicated line of descent, with its obvious doubling of roles, Shaw wrote to Lawrence Langner on July 29, 1921, that in order to avoid extravagance in casting he would suggest that the

actress for Eve double as Mrs. Lutestring, the Oracle, and the She-Ancient and the actress for Savvy as Zoo and the Newly Born. (See Langner, *op. cit.*, p. 42)

20. . . . .with no question of self. In the dream-epilogue after her rehabilitation and . . .

21. based somewhat on Beethoven.

22. Shaw himself said that Irving Fiske's article, "Bernard Shaw's Debt to William Blake" (*Shavian Tract No. 2*) published by the Shaw Society in England), is perhaps the best essay about himself ever written—though he corrects the word *Debt* by saying that he reached his own ideas independently. For Shaw's full attitude toward Bunyan, see Norbert F. O'Donnell, "Shaw, Bunyan, and Puritanism," PMLA, (1957).

23. Henderson, *op. cit.*, p. xxix, adds Aubrey Beardsley on Shaw's own authority.

24. Note that the Capeks' *R.U.R.*, or Rossum's Universal Robots, had been produced in 1921, the year Shaw's play was first printed.

25. For further light on Shaw's views on Ireland, see David H. Greene and Dan H. Laurence (eds.) *The Matter with Ireland* (London, 1963).

26. As seen in *The Matter with Ireland,* Shaw was for Home Rule, but always within the Commonwealth.

27. Louisa is the name of the unwilling Spanish girl whom the Portuguese Jew, Isaac Mendoza, is engaged to marry in Sheridan's *The Duenna.*

28. For a further discussion of the subject, see my article, "What Shaw Really Thought of Americans," *Shaw Review,* May 1960.

29. For a fuller discussion of this subject, see my article, "Bernard Shaw, Ladies and Gentlemen," *Modern Drama,* Sept. 1959.

30. Change *Vandaleur* to *Vandeleur*

30A. John O'Donovan, in "The Seventeenth Self Sketch," *The Shavian,* Oct. 1963, says that this is the proper spelling of this often misspelled name, and gives a short biographical sketch carrying Mrs. Shaw's association with Lee back ten years before G.B.S. says it began. O'Donovan also states that Mrs. Shaw followed Lee to London "within a fortnight" and maintains that for some time G.B.S. seriously considered that he was illegitimate.

31. For (*whatever that is*) substitute (*apparently irrigation*).

32. For a full account of their relationship, see Stanley Weintraub, *Public Shaw and Private Shaw* (New York, 1963).

33. In 1960, however, Lloyd George's son confirmed Lubin's quickly withdrawn remark that Burge "has a reputation as a profligate" by publishing a biography of his father in which he charged that the latter had had innumerable mistresses and several illegitimate children.

34. Read *hairiness*.

35. For an expansion of this idea and an analysis of the whole play from this point of view, see Frederick P.W. McDowell, "Heaven, Hell and turn-of-the-century London: Reflections upon Shaw's *Man and Superman*," *Drama Survey*, Winter 1963.

36. Lysenko, from 1955 to 1961 severely criticized and downgraded because of the failure of Soviet crops grown according to his theories, has recently been reactivated and restored as "arbiter of the Communist party line in agricultural sciences," according to an article by James Sullivan in the Chicago *Tribune*, Dec. 22, 1963.

37. Shaw, however, slipped into a slight Homeric nod when, earlier in the same play, he had Pygmalion admit that in the first stage of his experiments with the Life Force the earliest form of eyes and ears that he had been able to create turned into maggots!

38. I still believe in this identification in spite of the anecdote told by Langner, *op. cit.*, pp. 49-50, concerning Langner's attempt to break down Shaw's usually inflexible determination never to let any of his plays be cut after he had finished writing them. When Langner called on Shaw in 1922 with the hope (this time realized) of cutting *Tragedy of an Elderly Gentleman* to get a longer New York run, he and the Shaws looked over some photographs of the New York production. Shaw spotted some of Albert Bruning as the Elderly Gentleman and exclaimed, "Look, Charlotte . . . they've given the actor a make-up so that he looks like me! Why, the Elderly Gentleman was an old duffer. Why on earth did you suggest me?" "Because he talked on and on," replied Langner. "Besides, he said he could not live in a world without truth, by which of course we assumed you had written yourself into the character." Mrs. Shaw later chimed in, "After all . . . . you did intend him to be an old duffer and it is hard to listen to an old duffer going on and on."

   Since, however, Shaw did allow the role to be cut and never insisted on changing Bruning's appearance, it seems likely that he and Mrs. Shaw were only having a little fun at Langner's and Shaw's own expense, especially at the latter's approaching septuagenarianism.

39. For a brief supplement to this appendix, see Stanley Weintraub, "'Humors' Names in Shaw's Prentice Novels," *Names*, Dec. 1957.

40. As Bentley remarks early in the play, "I'd as soon have dressed myself in a nutmeg grater."

41. Savvy's real name is of course Cynthia, the name of the moon goddess, also known as Artemis or Diana, who was a virgin and a huntress. This identification would properly fit Shaw's description of Savvy as a "Simple-Lifer" and lightly clothed outdoor girl.

42. For *Jornalism* read *Journalism*.

43. The name *Sandstone* may also represent a combination of Sanderson and Gladstone.

44. It is possible, however, that he had in mind an archaic masculine name meaning "beloved friend."

45. At the end of the nineteenth century, however, a Lord Dunraven was active in Tory politics.

46. The attempt of an international expedition to scale this peak had failed in 1930 and had been written up in the newspapers not long before the Shaws' trip to the Orient.

47. This Christian name has definite overtones of Sir Warren Hastings, first governor-general of India in the late eighteenth century, and his conduct of his administration. Shaw probably intended no allusion to the defeat of the Saxons by William the Conqueror at the Battle of Hastings in 1066.

48. Andrew Undershaft derived his name from the Church of St. Andrew Undershaft, London. Chaucer mentions "the great shaft of Cornhill" from which the church got its name; it was originally a maypole or fertility symbol. Nor should the original St. Andrew of the Twelve Apostles be overlooked. By an amusing transfer of association, Shaw named Undershaft's daughter Barbara after the saint who was the patroness of gunners and artillerymen. According to the legend she became a martyr through being killed by her father for refusing to sacrifice to the pagan gods. He was thereupon struck by lightning and burned to death.

49. It is amusing to note that several times Shaw carefully works the word "consolation" into the dialogue of the play. In *The Gospel of the Brothers Barnabas* he has Conrad ask Burge and Lubin, "What consolation will it be for us then that you two are able to tell off one another's defects so cleverly in your afternoon chat?" and Burge replies, "If you come to that, what consolation will it be that you two can sit there and tell both of us off? you, who have no responsibility. . . ." Similarly, in *The Thing Happens,* the new Barnabas tells Burge-Lubin, "Thank you: I need no consolation," and later, after Burge-Lubin has remarked, "Devilish poor consolation, that," Mrs. Lutestring adds, "There were other consolations in those days for people like me."

50. Read *Postscript.*

51. Substitute *Lemaitre* for *D'Estivet.*

52. *Quelch, Harry, 248.*

53. For Wilson, Captain Arthur, read Wilson, Captain Frederick J.

# Index

The following combined index and bibliography of persons and works referred to in this book is divided into three parts: I. Works about Shaw; II. Works by Shaw; and III. Characters in Shaw's works or people connected with his life and thought.

In the parentheses after the titles of Shaw's works in II, an asterisk indicates the date of completion of these works, figures in ordinary type indicate the date of publication, and figures in italics indicate the date of first production of each play.

The figures in parentheses after the names of characters in III refer to the works in which they appear as indicated by the Arabic number preceding each title in II.

All other figures indicate the pages in this book where the above-mentioned kinds of material are referred to. Italicized figures indicate passages of particular importance concerning the characters in III.

II. WORKS BY SHAW

## III. PEOPLE IN SHAW'S LIFE AND WORKS

Trefusis, Sidney (78), 54, 57, 60, 79, 84,
  *133–134*, 139, 142, 149, 212, *246–247*,
  249, 274, 277, 280, 292
Tremouille, Monseigneur de la (63), 230
Trench, Dr. Harry (80), *29–30*, 55, 56, 79,
  84, 86, 174, 192, 237, 292
Trotsky, Leon, 73, 182, 183, 256
Trotter (23), 110, *221*, 274, 296
Turner, J. M. W., 143
Tyndall, John, 107
Twain, Mark, 303

Undershaft, Andrew (43), 31–32, 36, 49,
  *63–65*, 73, 75–76, 101, 174, 179, 184, 188,
  190, 216, 218, 273, 275, 280, 300
Undershaft, Barbara (43), *75–76*, 94, 110,
  217, 275
Undershaft, Lady Britomart (43), 36, 63,
  75, *100–101*, 119, 123, 216, 295
Undershaft, Stephen (43), 63, 101, *119*, 179,
  218
Ussher, Archbishop James, 148
Utterword, Lady Ariadne (31), *22–23*, 34,
  71, 109, 136, 138, 236, 292, 298–299
Utterword, Sir Hastings (31), 23, 292, 299
Utterword, Randall (31), 23, 298

Valentine, Dr. (81), 22, 69, 86, 108, 117,
  135, *195–196*, 200, 274, 276, 293
Vanhattan, Ambassador (5), *177–178*, 180,
  184, 300
Varinka (30), 164
Vashti (68), 225, 283, *298*
Vaughan (23), ix, *221*, 296
Vedrenne, Charles, 296
Velasquez, 151, 152
Verdi, Giuseppe, 58
Vesey, Jim (33), *26*, 138
Vesey, Mrs. (33), 27
Victoria, Queen, 306
Villiers, Barbara (36), *83*, 147
Voltaire, François M. A. de, 130, 164, 184,
  185, 188, 278, 301
Vulliamy, Anastasia (25), 235, 252, 301

Wagner, Richard, 15, 26, 122, 144, 146, 266,
  282, 308
Waiter, The (35), 195
Waiter, The (81). *See* Boon

Walker, Bill (43), 64, 75
Walkley, Arthur B., 105, 143, 166, 274, 294,
  296
Wallas, Graham, 57
Walpole, Cutler (20), 152, *197*, 218, 294
Walpole, Robert, 302
Wannafeller, Ezra D. (59), 272, 293
Warren, Mrs. Kitty (48), *38–39*, 40, 56, 64,
  80, 110, 294
Warren, Vivie (48), 38–39, *56–57*, 64, 80,
  106, *121–122*, 146, 223, 275
Warwick, Earl of (63), 21, 66, 160, 174,
  186, *207–208*, 229, 305
Watts, G. F., 7
Waynflete, Lady Cicely (14), 37–38, *94–97*,
  176, 200–201, 294, 296
Webb, Beatrice, 14, 123
Webb, Sidney, 32, 58, 292
Webber, Lucian (1), 54, 160; (15), 307
Webster, John, 304
Wellington, Duke of, 268
Wells, H. G., 36, 111, 131, 279
Westermarck, E. A., 135
Whistler, James M., 3
Whitefield, Ann (44), 17, 63, 81, *90–94*,
  116, 128, 136, 149–150, 279, 280
Whitefield, Mrs. (44), 91–92, 116, 177
Whitefield, Rhoda (44), 91, 116
Widow, The (26), 73, 113, 172, 173, 186,
  201, 243, *244–245*, 294
Wilde, Oscar, 26, 38, 151, 303
Wilhelm II, 179, 257, 271
Wilks (68), 173
Williams, Fleming, 14
Wilson, Captain Arthur, 47
Wilson, Maria (78), *212*
Wilson, Mr. (15), 212
Wright, Sir Almroth, 196, 294
Wylie, Agatha (78), 84, *133–134*

Young Woman, The (68). *See* Mrs. Hyering
Youth 3 (24), 288
Yeats, W. B., 168

Z (79), *87*
Zola, Emile, 3, 6
Zoo Ennistymon (75), 104, 289, 295, 298,
  301
Zozim (75), 307